Hebrew Myths
begins with a comparative study of the Biblical creation. The myths of Lucifer, the birth of Adam and Eve and the Fall are analyzed. Then the study proceeds chronologically through the Book of Genesis exploring the accounts of Cain and Abel, Noah, the Tower of Babel, the life of Abraham, Esau and Jacob, and concludes with the death of Joseph. Maps show "the world of Genesis," of Abraham, and Palestine under the Judges.

The author of more than ninety books, Robert Graves is world-renowned as a poet, novelist, essayist, translator, critic, and classicist. His concentration has been in poetry, and his latest **Collected Poems** received both the gold medal of the National Poetry Society of America and the Foyle Award in England. In 1961 Mr. Graves was elected to the Chair of Poetry at Oxford. His home for the past three decades has been on Majorca.

Raphael Patai, an outstanding anthropologist, folklorist and Biblical scholar, author of more than two dozen books and editor of a number of important serial and periodic publications, is Director of Research of the Theodor Herzl Institute in New York. Dr. Patai has lived for fifteen years in Jerusalem where he was Director of the Palestine Institute of Folklore and Ethnology and has, since 1948, taught anthropology at several major American universities.

HEBREW MYTHS

THE BOOK OF GENESIS

Hebrew Myths: The Book of Genesis

Robert Graves and Raphael Patai

McGraw-Hill Book Company
New York

First McGraw-Hill Paperback edition, 1966
Reprinted by arrangement with Doubleday and Co., Inc.
Library of Congress Catalog Card Number 63-19845

345678910 MUMU 765432

ISBN 07-024125-2

CONTENTS

MAPS

HEBREW MYTHS

THE BOOK OF GENESIS

INTRODUCTION

Myths are dramatic stories that form a sacred charter either authorizing the continuance of ancient institutions, customs, rites and beliefs in the area where they are current, or approving alterations. The word 'myth' is Greek, mythology is a Greek concept, and the study of mythology is based on Greek examples. Literalists who deny that the Bible contains any myths at all are, in a sense, justified. Most other myths deal with gods and goddesses who take sides in human affairs, each favouring rival heroes; whereas the Bible acknowledges only a single universal God.

All pre-Biblical sacred documents in Hebrew have been either lost or purposely suppressed. They included *The Book of the Wars of Yahweh* and the *Book of Yashar*, epic accounts of the Israelites' desert wanderings and their invasion of Canaan. That these books were written in the early poetic Hebrew style, can be seen from the brief fragments quoted from them in *Numbers* XXI. 14; *Joshua* X. 13 and 2 *Samuel* I. 18. A third book, reputedly compiled in seven parts at Joshua's orders, described Canaan and its cities (*Joshua* XVIII. 9). The *Book of the Story of Adam* (*Genesis* V. 1) suggests a detailed account of the first ten generations from Adam to Noah. *The Book of Yahweh* (*Isaiah* XXXIV. 16) seems to have been a mythological bestiary. Several other lost books mentioned in the Bible, such as the *Acts of Solomon*, the *Book of Genealogy*, the *Chronicles of the Kings of Judah, Of the Kings of Israel, Of the Sons of Levi*, must have contained many mythic references.

Post-Biblical sacred documents are abundant. In the thousand years after the Bible was first canonised, the Jews of Europe, Asia and Africa wrote prolifically. Theirs were either attempts to clarify the Mosaic Law; or historical, moralistic, anecdotal and homiletic comments on Biblical passages. In both cases the authors included much mythic material, because myth has always served as a succinct validation of puzzling laws, rites and social customs.

Now, although the canonical books were regarded as written by divine inspiration and the least taint of polytheism had therefore to be exorcized from them, the apocryphal books were treated more leniently. Many suppressed myths were also allowed to re-emerge in the unquestionably orthodox context of the post-Biblical midrashim. For example in *Exodus* we read that Pharaoh's horses, chariots and horsemen pursued the Children of Israel into the midst of the sea (*Exodus* XIV. 23). According to one midrash (Mekhilta diR. Shimon 51, 54; Mid. Wayosha 52) God assumed the shape of a mare and decoyed the ruttish Egyptian stallions into the water. If the mare-headed Goddess Demeter had been described as drowning King Pelops's chariotry in the River Alpheus by such a ruse, this would have been acceptable Greek myth; but to the pious reader of the midrash it was no more than a fanciful metaphor of the lengths to which God could go in protecting His Chosen People.

The Bible itself allows us only brief hints of its lost mythological riches. Often the reference is so terse that it passes unnoticed. Few, for instance, who read: 'And after him was Shamgar ben Anath who smote of the Philistines six hundred men with an ox-goad, and he also saved Israel' (*Judges* III. 31), connect Shamgar's mother with the bloodthirsty Ugaritic Love-goddess, the maiden Anath, in whose honour Jeremiah's priestly town of Anathot was named. The myth of Shamgar is irrecoverable, yet he must have inherited his virgin mother's warlike prowess; and the ox-goad with which he smote the Philistines was doubtless a gift from her father, the Bull-god El.

Genesis nevertheless still harbours vestigial accounts of ancient gods and goddesses—disguised as men, women, angels, monsters, or demons. Eve, described in *Genesis* as Adam's wife, is identified by historians with the Goddess Heba, wife of a Hittite Storm-god, who rode naked on a lion's back and, among the Greeks, became the Goddess Hebe, Heracles's bride (see 10. 10). A prince of Jerusalem in the Tell Amarna period (fourteenth century B.C.) styled himself Abdu-Heba—'servant of Eve' (see 27. 6). Lilith, Eve's predecessor, has been wholly exorcized from Scripture, though she is remembered by Isaiah as inhabiting desolate ruins (see 10. 6). She seems, from midrashic accounts of her sexual promiscuity, to have been a fertility-goddess, and appears as Lillake in a Sumerian religious text, *Gilgamesh and the Willow Tree* (see 10. 3–6).

There are pre-Biblical references to the angel Samael, *alias* 'Satan'. He first appears in history as the patron god of Samal, a small Hittite-Aramaic kingdom lying to the east of Harran (see 13. 1). Another faded god of Hebrew myth is Rahab, the Prince of the Sea, who unsuccessfully defied Jehovah ('Yahweh'), the God of Israel—much as the Greek God Poseidon defied his brother, Almighty Zeus. Jehovah, according to Isaiah, killed Rahab with a sword (see 6. *a*). A Ugaritic deity worshipped as Baal-Zebub, or Zebul, at Ekron was insulted by King Ahaziah (2 *Kings* I. 2 ff) and centuries later the Galileans accused Jesus of traffic with this 'Prince of the Demons'.

Seven planetary deities, borrowed from Babylon and Egypt, are commemorated in the seven branches of the Menorah, or sacred candlestick (see 1. 6). They were combined into a single transcendental deity at Jerusalem—as among the Heliopolitans, the Byblians, the Gallic Druids and the Iberians of Tortosa. Scornful references to gods of enemy tribes humiliated by Jehovah occur throughout the historical books of the Bible: such as the Philistine Dagon, Chemosh of Moab, and Milcom of Ammon. Dagon, we know from Philo Byblius to have been a planetary power. But the God of *Genesis*, in the earliest passages, is still indistinguishable from any other small tribal godling (see 28. *1*).

Greek gods and goddesses could play amusing or dramatic parts while intriguing on behalf of favoured heroes, because the myths arose in different city-states which wavered between friendship and enmity. Yet among the Hebrews, once the Northern Kingdom had been destroyed by the Assyrians, myths became monolithic, and centred almost exclusively on Jerusalem.

In Biblical myth, the heroes sometimes represent kings, sometimes dynasties, sometimes tribes. Jacob's twelve 'sons', for instance, seem to have been once independent tribes which banded together to form the Israelite amphictyony or federation. Their local gods and populations were not necessarily of Aramaean race, though ruled by an Aramaean priesthood. Only Joseph can be identified, in part, with a historical character. That each of these 'sons', except Joseph, is said to have married a twin-sister (see 45. *f*), suggests land-inheritance through the mother even under patriarchal government. Dinah, Jacob's only daughter born without a twin, is best understood as a semi-matriarchal tribe included in the Israel confederacy. The *Genesis* account of her rape by Shechem and the midrash about her subsequent marriage to Simeon should be read in a political, not a personal, sense (see 29. *1–3*).

Other hints of an ancient matriarchal culture occur in *Genesis:* such as the right of a mother to name her sons, still exercised among the Arabs, and matrilocal marriage: 'Therefore shall a man leave his father and mother and cleave unto his wife' (*Genesis* II. 24). This Palestinian custom is proved by the account in *Judges* of Samson's marriage to Delilah; and explains why Abraham, the Aramaean patriarch who entered Palestine with the Hyksos hordes early in the second millennium B.C., ordered his servant Eliezer to buy Isaac a bride from his own patrilocal kinsmen of Harran—rather than let him marry a Canaanite woman, and be adopted into her clan (see 36. *1*). Abraham had already sent away the sons borne to him by his concubines, lest they should inherit jointly with Isaac (see 35. *b*). Matrilocal marriage is the rule in early Greek myth, too: one mythographer records that the first to defy this tradition was Odysseus, who carried Penelope away from Sparta to Ithaca; and that she returned to Sparta after their divorce.

Just how powerful goddesses were under the Jewish monarchy can be seen from Jeremiah's denunciation of his co-religionists who attributed Judaea's downfall to their breach of faith with Anath and cried: 'Let us once more worship the Queen of Heaven, as our fathers did before us!'

Every ruler who reforms national institutions or, like King Josiah, has reforms pressed upon him, must either write a codicil to the old religious charter, or produce a new one; and this involves the manipulation or complete re-writing of myths. It became clear that if Judaea—a small buffer state between Egypt and Assyria—was to keep its political independence, a stronger religious discipline must be inculcated, and the people trained in handling arms. Hitherto most Israelites had embraced the easy-going Canaanite cult in which goddesses played the leading rôle, with kings as their consorts. This, though all very well in peaceful times, could not steel the Jews to resist the invading armies of Egypt and Assyria. A small, tough Israelite minority was led by the Guild of Prophets who made a point of dressing as shepherds or herdsmen in honour of their pastoral God. These prophets saw that Israel's sole hope of national independence lay in an authoritarian monotheism, and ceaselessly declaimed against goddess-worship in the Canaanite sacred groves. The Book of *Deuteronomy*, published under Josiah, bans numerous Canaanite rites, among them ritual prostitution, ritual sodomy, and all forms of idolatry. The subsequent demise of the Davidic crown converted all the Babylonian exiles to this view. When Zerubbabel rebuilt Jehovah's temple, He no longer had any competitors. The Baals, Astartes, Anaths and all the other old Canaanite deities were dead so far as the Judaeans returning from captivity were concerned. *Genesis*, which is far more closely linked with Greek, Phoenician, Hittite, Ugaritic, Sumerian and other bodies of myth than most pious Jews and Christians care to admit, was thereafter edited and re-edited from perhaps the sixth century B.C. onwards, for moralistic ends. The Ham myth was once identical with that of the conspiracy against the shameless god Cronus by his sons Zeus, Poseidon and Hades: Zeus, the youngest, alone dared castrate him, and as a result became King of Heaven. But Ham's (or Canaan's) castration of Noah has been excised from *Genesis* just before the line: 'Noah awoke from his wine, and knew what his little son had done unto him.' The revised version, a moral lesson in filial respect, sentences Ham to perpetual servitude under his elder brothers for no worse a crime than accidentally seeing his father's nakedness (see 21. 1–4).

Yet the Biblical editors had been careless about excising all favourable mention even of human sacrifice (see 47. 11) and the idolatrous worship of teraphim (see 46. 2). Tabernacles, a Canaanite vintage feast, could not be suppressed but only purged of sexual abandon, and converted to the joyful worship of a Supreme God by being associated with the Israelite use of tents in the Wilderness; even so, the light-headedness of women devotees continued to trouble Pharisee sages. The Canaanite feast of unleavened bread was similarly converted into a commemoration of Israel's Exodus from Egypt.

A main theme of Greek myth is the gradual reduction of women from sacred beings to chattels. Similarly, Jehovah punishes Eve for causing the Fall of Man. Further to disguise Eve's original godhead—her title 'Mother of All Living' survives in *Genesis*—the mythographers represented her as formed from Adam's rib, an anecdote based apparently on the word *tsela,* meaning both 'rib' and 'a stumbling'. Still later mythographers insisted that she was formed from Adam's barbed tail . . . (see 10. 9). The Greeks, too, made woman responsible for man's unhappy lot by adopting Hesiod's fable of Pandora's jar, from which a Titan's foolish wife let loose the combined spites of sickness, old age and vice. 'Pandora'—'all gifts'—it should be observed, was once a title of the Creatrix.

Greek myths account for curses and taboos still in force after a thousand years; and the Greek Hell contained warning instances of criminals punished, like Tantalus, for eating forbidden food; like the Danaids, for husband murder; like Peirithous, for the attempted seduction of a goddess. Yet the Greeks never glossed their myths with pietistic comment: such as that Abraham's attempted sacrifice of Isaac took place on the first of Tishri, when all Israel blows a ram's horn to remind God of Abraham's piety and implore forgiveness of their sins. Or that the Feast of Atonement scapegoat commemorates Jacob's deception by the Patriarchs when they sprinkled Joseph's long-sleeved tunic (or 'coat of many colours') with blood of a kid (see

53. 3). Although the Isaac myth is paralleled in the Greek account of Athamas's attempted sacrifice to Zeus of his son Phrixus—a sacrifice interrupted by Heracles's arrival and the divine appearance of a ram—this occasion was remembered only because the ram supplied the Golden Fleece for which Jason's Argonauts eventually sailed in quest. *Genesis* presents it as the crucial episode in Hebrew history (see 34. 9).

Nor were the Greek myths used as texts for political sermonizing. The account of Esau's ill-treatment at Jacob's hands was later rounded off by a prophecy that he would one day break Jacob's yoke from off his neck—an addition clearly intended to justify an Edomite revolt against Judaea in King Joram's reign (see 40. 3). This text was given a new meaning when the Roman invaders crowned Herod the Wicked, an Edomite, King of the Jews: Edom then became a synonym for 'Rome', and the Pharisees counselled the Jews to make no armed rebellion but to expiate their ancestor's ill-treatment of Esau with patience and forbearance (see 40. 4). A full historical prescience was attributed to Israelite heroes, including a fore-knowledge of the Mosaic Law; and whoever in the Scriptures performs any solemn act is understood to be thereby determining the fate of his descendants for all eternity. Thus when Jacob, on his way to meet Esau, divides his household and cattle into three groups, sending gifts with each at intervals, he is warning his descendants that they should always prudently guard against the worst. According to the midrash, Jacob prayed: 'Lord, when afflictions descend upon my children, pray leave an interval between them, as I have done!' (see 47. 2). And the apocryphal *Testaments of the Twelve Patriarchs* credits these patriarchs with a precise knowledge of later history.

The Jacob myth illustrates another difference between Greek and Hebrew religious attitudes. He steals flocks and herds from his kinsman by altering their colour; the Greek hero Autolycus does likewise; and these two myths apparently have the same Palestinian source. Autolycus is a clever thief, and no more; but since Jacob, re-named Israel, was to become the saintly ancestor of all Jews, his deceit has been justified on the ground that Laban had twice cheated him. And, instead of using vulgar magic, as Autolycus did, on animals already the property of others, Jacob conditions their colour and establishes his ownership of them by studied use of pre-natal influences—the lesson being that Jews may defend themselves against oppressors by legitimate means only (see 46. 1).

No moral conclusions were drawn from the deeds of Greek heroes, unless it were a warning against fortune's fickleness. Whereas the destruction of Troy brought nothing but ill-luck on every important Greek leader, and famous warriors of an earlier generation, such as Theseus and Bellerophon, had been destined to end miserably, victims of divine nemesis, yet Abraham, Isaac, Jacob and Joseph died in peaceful old age and were honourably gathered to their fathers. This contrast is sharpened when we recall that the story of Joseph and Potiphar's wife Zuleika is identical with that of Bellerophon and his step-mother Anteia (see 54. 1). Major Hebrew prophets were likewise blessed: Enoch and Elijah rose straight to Heaven; but the Greek seer Teiresias foresaw the doom of Thebes and died in ignoble flight. And although Moses, who rescued his people from the Egyptian Sphinx—namely, the power of Pharaoh—had to expiate a particular fault on Mount Pisgah, he was honourably mourned by all Israel and buried by God Himself; whereas Oedipus, who saved his people from the Theban Sphinx, and had much the same nativity as Moses, died in miserable exile hounded by the Furies of Mother-right.

The main difference between Greek and Hebrew myths—apart from this glaring contrast in the rewards of virtue—is that the Greek were royal and aristocratic: accounting for certain religious institutions in particular city-states, presided over by priests who claimed descent from the gods or heroes concerned. Only the hero, or his descendants, could hope for a pleasant after-existence in the Fortunate Isles or the Elysian Fields. The souls of slaves and foreigners, despite exemplary lives, were sentenced to a dismal Tartarus where they flew blindly about, twittering like bats. Among the synagogue Jews, on the contrary, all who obeyed the Mosaic Law, whatever their birth or station, were made free of a Heavenly Kingdom which would arise from the ashes of our present world. The Greeks never took so democratic a step: though excluding from the Mysteries (which gave initiates an assurance of Paradise) all persons with criminal records, they still confined admission to the free-born.

Greek myths are charters for certain clans—descendants of Perseus, Pelops, Cadmus or whoever it may have been—to rule certain territories so long as they placated the local gods with sacrifices, dances and processions. Annual performance of such rites enhanced their authority. Hebrew myths are mainly national charters: the myth of Abraham for the possession of Canaan, and for patrilocal marriage; the myth of Jacob for Israel's status as a chosen people; the myth of Ham for the owning of Canaanite slaves. Other myths uphold the supreme sanctity of Mount Zion against the rival shrines of Hebron and Shechem (see 27. 6 and 43. 2). A few later ones are written to solve serious theological problems: such as the origin of evil in man, whose ancestor Adam was made by God in His own image and animated by His own spirit. Adam erred through ignorance, Cain sinned deliberately, and a late myth therefore makes him a bastard begotten by Satan on Eve (see 14. *a*).

In Greek myths the time element is occasionally disregarded. Thus Queen Helen who retained her beauty throughout the ten years' siege of Troy, and for ten years afterwards, was said by some to have borne King Theseus a daughter one generation before this siege began. Yet the two stories are not reported by the same author, and Greek scholars could assume either that there were two Queen Helens or that one of the mythographers had erred. In Biblical myths, however, Sarah remains irresistibly beautiful after she has passed her ninetieth birthday, conceives, bears Isaac, and suckles all her neighbours' children as well as him. Patriarchs, heroes and early kings live to nearly a thousand years. The giant Og survives Noah's deluge, outlives Abraham, and is finally destroyed by Moses. Time is telescoped. Adam sees all the future generations of mankind hanging from his gigantic body; Isaac studies the Mosaic Law (revealed ten generations later) in the Academy of Shem, who lived ten generations before him. Indeed, the hero of Hebrew myth is not only profoundly influenced by the deeds, words and thoughts of his forebears, and aware of his own profound influence on the fate of his descendants; he is equally influenced by the behaviour of his descendants and influences that of his ancestors. Thus King Jeroboam set up a golden calf in Dan, and this sinful act sapped the strength of Abraham when he pursued his enemies into the same district a thousand years previously.

Fanciful rabbinic expansions of the *Genesis* stories were still being made in the Middle Ages: answers to such questions by intelligent students as—'How was the Ark lighted? How were the animals fed? Was there a Phoenix on board?' (see 20. *i–j*)

Greek myths show no sense of national destiny, nor do Roman myths until it was supplied by gifted Augustan propagandists—Virgil, Livy and the rest. Professor Hadas of Columbia University has pointed out close correspondences between the *Aeneid* and *Exodus* —the divinely led exodus of refugees to a Promised Land—and concludes that Virgil borrowed from the Jews. It is possible, too, that Livy's moral anecdotes of Ancient Rome, which are quite unmythical in tone, were influenced by the synagogue. Of course, Roman morals differed altogether from the Jewish: Livy rated courageous self-sacrifice above truth and mercy, and the dishonourable Olympians remained Rome's official gods. Not until the Hebrew myths, borrowed by the Christians, gave subject people an equal right to salvation, were the Olympians finally banished. It is true that some of these came back to power disguised as saints, and perpetuated their rites in the form of Church festivals; yet the aristocratic principle had been overthrown. It is also true that Greek myths were still studied, because the Church took over schools and universities which made the Classics required reading; and the names of Constellations illustrating these myths were too well established to be altered. Nevertheless, patriarchal and monotheistic Hebrew myth had firmly established the ethical principles of Western life.

Our collaboration has been a happy one. Though the elder of us two had been brought up as a strict Protestant, and the younger as a strict Jew, we never disagreed on any question of fact or historical assessment; and each deferred to the other's knowledge in different fields. A main problem was how much scholarly reference could be included without boring the intelligent general reader. This book could easily have run to twice its present length by the inclusion of late pseudo-mythic material rivalling in dullness even the *Wars of the Children of Light and the Children of Darkness*, which was found among the Dead Sea Scrolls; and by the citation of learned commentaries on small disputed points. Our gratitude is due to Abraham Berger and Francis Paar of the New York Public Library for bibliographic advice, and to Kenneth Gay for help in preparing the book for the press. Although of dual authorship, *Hebrew Myths* serves as a companion volume to *The Greek Myths* (Graves), its material being similarly organized.

R.G.

R.P.

1

THE CREATION ACCORDING TO *GENESIS*

(*a*) When God set out to create Heaven and Earth, He found nothing around Him but Tohu and Bohu, namely Chaos and Emptiness. The face of the Deep, over which His Spirit hovered, was clothed in darkness.

On the first day of Creation, therefore, He said: 'Let there be light!', and light appeared.

On the second day, He made a firmament to divide the Upper Waters from the Lower Waters, and named it 'Heaven'.

On the third day, He assembled the Lower Waters in one place and let dry land emerge. After naming the dry land 'Earth', and the assembled waters 'Sea', He told Earth to bring forth grass and herbs and trees.

On the fourth day, He created the sun, moon and stars.

On the fifth day, the sea-beasts, fish and birds.

On the sixth day, the land-beasts, creeping things and mankind.

On the seventh day, satisfied with His work, He rested.[1]

(*b*) But some say that after creating Earth and Heaven, God caused a mist to moisten the dry land so that grasses and herbs could spring up. Next, He made a garden in Eden, also a man named Adam to be its overseer, and planted it with trees. He then created all beasts, birds, creeping things; and lastly woman.[2]

1. *Genesis* I–II. 3.
2. *Genesis* II. 4–23.

*

1. For many centuries, Jewish and Christian theologians agreed that the accounts of the world's origin given in *Genesis* were not only inspired by God, but owed nothing to any other scriptures. This extreme view has now been abandoned by all but fundamentalists. Since 1876, several versions of Akkadian (that is, Babylonian and Assyrian) Creation Epics have been excavated and published. The longest of these, known as *Enuma Elish* from its initial two words—which mean 'when on high'—is assumed to have been written in the early part of the second millennium B.C. It has survived almost complete on seven cuneiform tablets containing an average

of 156 lines apiece. The discovery did not altogether astonish scholars familiar with Berossus's summary of Creation myths, quoted by Bishop Eusebius of Caesarea; for Berossus, born in the fourth century B.C., had been a priest of Bel at Babylon.

2. Another version of the same Epic, written both in Babylonian and Sumerian as a prologue to an incantation for purifying a temple, was discovered at Sippar on a tablet dated from the sixth century B.C. It runs in part as follows:

The holy house, the house of the gods, in a holy place had not yet been made;
No reed had sprung up, no tree had been created;
No brick had been laid, no building had been erected;
No house had been constructed, no city had been built;
No city had been made, no creature had been brought into being;
Nippur had not been made, Ekur had not been built;
Erech had not been made, Eana had not been built;
The Deep had not been made, Eridu had not been built;
Of the holy house, the house of the gods, the habitation had not been made;
All lands were sea.

Then there was a movement in the midst of the sea;
At that time Eridu was made, and Essagil was built,
Essagil, where in the midst of the deep the god Lugal-du-kuda dwells;
The city of Babylon was built, and Essagil was finished.

The gods, the spirits of the earth, Marduk made at the same time,
The holy city, the dwelling of their hearts' desire, they proclaimed supreme.

Marduk laid a reed on the face of the waters,
He formed dust and poured it out beside the reed;
That he might cause the gods to dwell in the dwelling of their hearts' desire,
He formed mankind.

With him the goddess Aruru created the seed of mankind.
The beasts of the field and living things in the field he formed.
The Tigris and Euphrates he created and established them in their place;
Their name he proclaimed in goodly manner.
The grass, the rush of the marsh, the reed and the forest he created,
The green herb of the field he created,

The lands, the marshes and the swamps;
The wild cow and her young, the wild calf, the ewe and her young,
the lamb of the fold.
Orchards and forests;
The he-goat and the mountain goat . . .

The Lord Marduk built a dam beside the sea.

. . . .

Reeds he formed, trees he created;
Bricks he laid, buildings he erected;
Houses he made, cities he built;
Cities he made, creatures he brought into being.
Nippur he made, Ekur he built;
Erech he made, Eana he built.

3. The longer Creation Epic begins by telling how 'when on high the heavens had not been named', Apsu the Begetter and Mother Tiamat mingled chaotically and produced a brood of dragon-like monsters. Several ages passed before a younger generation of gods arose. One of these, Ea god of Wisdom, challenged and killed Apsu. Tiamat thereupon married her own son Kingu, bred monsters from him, and prepared to take vengeance on Ea.

The only god who now dared oppose Tiamat was Ea's son Marduk. Tiamat's allies were her eleven monsters. Marduk relied upon the seven winds, his bow and arrow and storm-chariot, and a terrible coat of mail. He had smeared his lips with prophylactic red paste, and tied on his wrist a herb that made him proof against poison; flames crowned his head. Before their combat, Tiamat and Marduk exchanged taunts, curses and incantations. When they came to grips, Marduk soon caught Tiamat in his net, sent one of his winds into her belly to tear out the guts, then brained and shot her full of arrows. He bound the corpse with chains and stood victoriously upon it. Having chained the eleven monsters and cast them into prison—where they became gods of the underworld—he snatched the 'Tablets of Fate' from Kingu's breast and, fastening them upon his own, split Tiamat into halves like a shell-fish. One of these he used as firmament, to impede the upper waters from flooding the earth; and the other as a rocky foundation for earth and sea. He also created the sun, the moon, the five lesser planets and the constellations, giving his kinsmen charge over them; and finally created man from the blood of Kingu, whom he had condemned to death as the instigator of Tiamat's rebellion.

4. Much the same account appears in the Berossian summary though Bel, not Marduk, is its divine hero. In the corresponding Greek myth, perhaps of Hittite provenience, Mother Earth created the giant Typhon, at whose advent the gods all fled to Egypt, until Zeus boldly killed him and his monstrous sister Delphyne with a thunderbolt.

5. The first account of Creation (*Genesis* I. 1–II. 3) was composed at Jerusalem soon after the return from Babylonian Exile. God is here named 'Elohim'. The second account (*Genesis* II. 4–22) is also Judaean, possibly of Edomite origin, and pre-Exilic. Here God was originally named 'Yahweh', but the priestly editor has changed this to 'Yahweh Elohim' (usually translated as 'the Lord God'), thus identifying the God of *Genesis* I with that of *Genesis* II, and giving the versions an appearance of uniformity. He did not, however, eliminate certain contradictory details in the order of creation, as will be seen from the following tables:

Genesis I	*Genesis* II
Heaven	Earth
Earth	Heaven
Light	Mist
Firmament	Man
Dry Land	Trees
Grasses and Trees	Rivers
Luminaries	Beasts and Cattle
Sea-beasts	Birds
Birds	Woman
Cattle, Creeping things, Beasts	
Man and Woman	

Jews and Christians have always been puzzled by these contradictions, and tried to explain them away. The seven-day scheme in the first account provides the mythical charter for man's observance of the Sabbath; since God, who rested on the seventh day, blessed and hallowed it. This point is expressly made in one version of the Ten Commandments (*Exodus* xx. 8–11). Some early rabbinic commentators observe that the main elements were created in the first three days; and embellished in the second three; and that a close symmetry can be discerned between the first and fourth days, the second and fifth, the third and sixth.

First Day Creation of the heavens its separation from darkness.	*Fourth Day* Creation of the luminaries—sun, moon and stars—to separate day from night and season from season.
Second Day Creation of the heavens and separation of the upper waters from the lower.	*Fifth Day* Creation of birds that fly through the heavens, and of fish that swim through the lower waters.

Third Day	*Sixth Day*
Creation of dry land and establishment of its immobile woods and herbs.	Creation of beasts, men and creeping things that walk on dry land.

6. This scheme, and others like it, prove the rabbis' desire to credit God with systematic thought. Their labours would not have been needed, however, had it occurred to them that the order of Creation was tied to the order of the planetary gods in the Babylonian week, and therefore to the seven branches of the Menorah, or Sacred Candelabrum—both Zechariah in his vision (IV. 10), and Josephus (*Wars* V. 5. 5), make this identification of the Menorah with the Seven Planets—and that God claimed all these planetary powers for Himself. Since Nergal, a pastoral god, came third in the week, whereas Nabu, god of astronomy, came fourth, pasture was given precedence to the stars in the order of Creation. The *Enuma Elish* has the following order: separation of heaven from earth and sea; creation of planets and stars; creation of trees and herbs; creation of animals and fish (but the fifth and sixth tablets are fragmentary); Marduk's forming of man from Kingu's blood.

7. The second Creation account is vaguer than the first, divulges less about the pre-Creation Universe, and has no structure comparable to that of *Genesis* I. In fact, it implies that the work of Creation occupied a single day. The opening statement recalls several Near Eastern cosmogonies, by describing the pre-Creation Universe in terms of the various things which had not hitherto existed. Trees and shrubs were not yet in the earth, grasses and herbs had not yet sprung up because God had not yet sent rain, and there was still no man to till the soil (*Genesis* II. 5). Then came the great day in which God created the generations of heaven and earth (*Genesis* II. 4a): a mist rose from the soil (presumably at His command), and watered it. The soil (*adama*) was now in condition for man (*adam*) to be formed from it. God duly breathed life into man's nostrils and gave him a living soul. Then He planted a garden, eastward of Eden, and ordered man to dress and keep it (*Genesis* II. 6–9, 15).

8. *Genesis* I resembles Babylonian cosmogonies, which begin with the emergence of earth from a primeval watery chaos, and are all metaphorical of how dry land emerges annually from the winter floods of Tigris and Euphrates. Creation is thus represented as the world's first flowering after the primeval watery chaos: a Spring season, when birds and beasts mate. *Genesis* II, however, mirrors Canaanite geographic and climatic conditions. The pre-Creation Universe is sun-scorched, parched and barren, as if after a long summer. When finally autumn approaches, the first sign of rain is morning mist risen dense and white from the valleys. Creation as pictured in *Genesis* II. 4 ff took place on just such an autumn day. The Babylonian version, which made Spring the creative season, was borrowed during the Captivity, and the first of Nissan became a Jewish New Year's day. The

earlier autumnal version, however, required the first of Tishri to be observed as the true New Year's day.

9. Irreconcilable views as to the season of Creation were held by rival Jewish schools from the first century A.D. onward. Philo of Alexandria maintained, with the Greek Stoics, that the Universe had been created in the Spring, and was followed by Rabbi Jehoshua and others. But Rabbi Eliezer preferred the autumnal Creation, and his view gained the upper hand among the Orthodox; it was decided that the first of Tishri had been God's New Year's day. Others, while agreeing on an autumnal Creation, held that God's New Year fell on the twenty-fifth of Elul, and that the first of Tishri, five days later, celebrated Adam's birth.

10. Creation being originally understood in terms of procreation, not fabrication, its central figure was a matriarch. Thus in the Greek myth, Eurynome, Goddess of All Things, rose naked from Chaos, divided sea from sky, danced upon the waves, stirred up the wind, was impregnated by it in the shape of a great serpent named Ophion or Ophioneus, and laid the World Egg. A similar story is told in *Orphic Fragments* 60, 61, 70 and 89: Night, the Creatrix, lays a silver egg from which Love is hatched to set the Universe in motion. Night lives in a cave, displaying herself in triad as Night, Order and Justice.

11. Most Near Eastern myths, however, derive from a time when part, at least, of the matriarch's divine prerogatives had been delegated to her male warrior-escort. This stage is reflected in the *Enuma Elish*'s account of how the Universe proceeds from a union between Apsu the Begetter and Mother Tiamat; and in Berossus's account of the Creation—summarized by Alexander Polyhistor—where after El's victory over Tiamat, the Goddess Aruru formed man from El's own blood kneaded with clay.

12. The Syrian philosopher Damascius (early sixth century A.D.) summarizes a primitive version of the *Enuma Elish* myth, paralleled by the Egyptian Sky-goddess Nut's union with the Earth-god Geb; and by the Greek Sky-god Uranus's union with the Earth-goddess Gaia. Damascius names Tiamat before Apsu, and accords similar precedence to the female of each divine couple he mentions.

13. Were it not for the Tehom-Tiamat parallel, we should never guess that Tehom represents the formidable Babylonian Mother-goddess who bore the gods, was rebelled against by them, and finally surrendered her own body to serve as building material for the Universe. Not even the female gender of the Hebrew name 'Tehom' can be read as significant in this connection, since in Hebrew every noun must either be male or female, and many cosmic terms are female even when lacking the female suffix *ah*, or of ambivalent gender.

14. Yet goddesses were well known to the Hebrews of Biblical times who worshipped in the groves of the Goddess Asherah (*Judges* III. 7; VI. 25–26, 30; 1 *Kings* XVI. 33; XVIII. 19), and bowed down to her images (2

Kings xxi. 7; 2 *Chronicles* xvii. 6, etc.). They also honoured Astarte, the goddess of the Phoenicians and Philistines (*Judges* ii. 13; x. 6; 1 *Samuel* xxxi. 10; 1 *Kings* xi. 5, 33; 2 *Kings* xxiii. 13, etc.). Not long before Nebuchadrezzar's destruction of the Judaean Kingdom (586 B.C.), Jewish women were offering cakes to her as the 'Queen of Heaven' (*Jeremiah* vii. 18): *alias* Anath, whose name survives in the Bible as that of Shamgar's mother (*Judges* iii. 31; v. 6) and of the priestly village Anathot, Jeremiah's home, now Anatha, north of Jerusalem. She had become so dear to Jews of both sexes, that those who escaped to Egypt vowed to serve her with libations and cakes made in her image (*Jeremiah* xliv. 15–19).

15. Though Astarte and Asherah were worshipped by all classes to the very end of the Judaean monarchy, nowhere in the Bible is any hint found of their connexion with El or Elohim—unless God's repudiation in *Ezekiel* xxiii of the lecherous Aholah and Aholibah is directed against these goddesses rather than against Jerusalem and Samaria, the main seats of their worship. Nor does any Hebrew tradition assign to either goddess the rôle of Creatrix. Yet Astarte's dove suggests that she had once been so regarded.

16. The monotheistic editor of the cosmogony in *Genesis* i and ii could assign no part in Creation to anyone but God, and therefore omitted all pre-existing elements or beings which might be held divine. Such abstractions as Chaos (*tohu wa-bohu*), Darkness (*hoshekh*), and the Deep (*tehom*) would, however, tempt no worshippers: so these took the place of the ancient matriarchal deities.

17. Though the revolutionary concept of an eternal, absolute, omnipotent and only God was first proposed by Pharaoh Akhenaten (see 56. 1. 4.), and either adopted by the Hebrews, whom he seems to have protected, or re-invented by them, yet the name 'Elohim' (usually translated as 'God'), found in *Genesis* i, is the Hebrew variant of an ancient Semitic name for one god of many—Ilu among the Assyrians and Babylonians; El among the Hittites and in the Ugaritic texts; Il, or Ilum, among the South Arabians. El headed the Phoenician pantheon and is often mentioned in Ugaritic poems (dating from the fourteenth century B.C.) as 'Bull El', which recalls the golden bull-calves made by Aaron (*Exodus* xxxii. 1–6, 24, 35) and Jeroboam (1 *Kings* xii. 28–29) as emblems of God; and Zedekiah's impersonation of God as an iron-horned bull (1 *Kings* xxii. 11).

18. In *Genesis* ii, the name 'Elohim' is combined with a second divine name pronounced *Yahweh* (usually transcribed as *Jehovah,* and translated as 'Lord') and regarded as an abbreviation of the full name *Yahweh asher yihweh,* 'He causes to be what is' (*Exodus* iii. 14). In personal names, this was further shortened into *Yeho* (e.g., *Yehonathan,* or 'Jonathan'), or *Yo* (e.g., *Yonathan* or 'Jonathan'); or *Yahu* (e.g., *Yirm'yahu* or 'Jeremiah'); or *Yah* (e.g., *Ahiyah*). That *Yahweh* in *Genesis* is given the divine sur-

name *Elohim*, shows him to have become a transcendental God, credited with all the great feats of Creation.

The titles and attributes of many other Near Eastern deities were successively awarded to Yahweh Elohim. For instance, in the Ugaritic poems, a standing epithet of the God Baal, son of Dagon, is 'Rider of Clouds'; *Psalm* LXV. 5 awards it to this Hebrew God, who also, like Baal 'The God of Saphon', has a palace in the 'farthest north' (*yark'the ṣaphon*), imagined as a lofty mountain (*Isaiah* XIV. 13; *Psalm* XLVIII. 3).

19. Moreover, many of the acts attributed in Ugaritic mythology to the bloodthirsty Goddess Anath are attributed in the Bible to Yahweh Elohim. The Ugaritic description of how Anath massacres her enemies:

She plunged knee-deep in the blood of soldiers,
Neck-high in the gore of their companies.
Until she is sated
She fights in the house . . .

recalls the second Isaiah's vision of God's vengeance upon Israel's enemies (*Isaiah* LXIII. 3):

Yes, I trod them in Mine anger,
And trampled them in My fury;
And their lifeblood sprinkled upon My garments,
And I have stained all My raiment . . .

Prophets and psalmists were as careless about the pagan origins of the religious imagery they borrowed, as priests were about the adaptation of heathen sacrificial rites to God's service. The crucial question was: in whose honour these prophecies and hymns should now be sung, or these rites enacted. If in honour of Yahweh Elohim, not Anath, Baal or Tammuz, all was proper and pious.

2

THE CREATION ACCORDING TO OTHER BIBLICAL TEXTS

(*a*) According to others, God created Heavens, complete with Sun, Moon and stars, by a single word of command. Then, clad in a glorious garment of light, He stretched out the Heavens like a round tent-cloth, exactly cut to cover the Deep. Having confined the Upper Waters in a fold of His garment, He established His secret Pavilion above the Heavens, walling it with a thick darkness like sackcloth, carpeting it with the same, and resting its beams upon the Upper Waters. There He set up His divine Throne.[1]

(*b*) While performing the work of Creation, God would ride across the Deep upon clouds, or cherubs, or the wings of the storm; or catch at passing winds and make them His messengers. He set Earth on immovable foundations: by carefully weighing the mountains, sinking some as pillars in the waters of the Deep, arching the Earth over them and locking the arch with a keystone of other mountains.[2]

(*c*) The roaring waters of the Deep arose and Tehom, their Queen, threatened to flood God's handiwork. But, in His fiery chariot, He rode the waves and flung at her great volleys of hail, lightning and thunderbolts. He despatched her monstrous ally Leviathan with a blow on its skull; and the monster Rahab with a sword thrust through its heart. Awed by His voice, Tehom's waters subsided. The rivers fled backwards up the hills and down into the valleys beyond. Tehom, trembling, acknowledged defeat. God uttered a shout of victory, and dried the floods until Earth's foundations could be seen. Then He measured in the hollow of His hand what water was left, poured it into the Sea Bed, and set sand dunes as its perpetual boundary; at the same time making a decree which Tehom could never break, however violently her salt waves might rage—she being, as it were, locked behind gates across which a bolt has been shot.[3]

(*d*) God then measured out dry earth, fixing its limits. He allowed Tehom's fresh waters to rise as valley springs, and rain to fall gently on the mountain tops from His upper chambers. Thus He made grass grow as fodder for cattle; also corn and grapes for the nourishment of man; and the great cedars of Lebanon for shade. He ordered the Moon to mark the seasons; and the Sun to divide day from night and summer from winter; and the stars to limit the blackness of night. He filled the earth with beasts, birds and creeping things; and the sea with fishes, sea-beasts and monsters. He let wild beasts roam about after dark; but once the Sun arose they must return to their lairs.[4]

The Morning Stars, as they watched, burst into a song of praise; and all the sons of God shouted for joy.[5]

(*e*) Having thus completed the work of Creation, God withdrew to a sanctuary on Mount Paran in the Land of Teman. Whenever He leaves this dwelling place, Earth trembles and mountains smoke.[6]

1. *Psalm* XXXIII. 6; CIV. 2; *Isaiah* XL. 22 and XLIV. 24; *Psalm* CIV. 6; *Isaiah* L. 3; *Psalm* XVIII. 10–12; 1 *Kings* VIII. 12; *Psalms* CIV. 3; XCIII. 1–2.
2. *Psalm* XVIII. 10 and *Nahum* I. 4; *Proverbs* XXX. 4; *Psalm* CIV. 3–5; *Isaiah* XL. 12; *Psalm* LXV. 7.
3. *Psalm* XCIII. 3; *Jeremiah* XXXI. 35; *Job* IX. 13; *Psalm* LXXXIX. 11; *Job* XXVI. 12–13; *Isaiah* LI. 9; *Psalm* CIV. 6–8; LXXIV. 13–14; *Nahum* I. 4; *Psalm* XVIII. 15–16; *Isaiah* XL. 12; *Psalm* XXXIII. 7; *Jeremiah* V. 22; *Job* XXXVIII. 8–11.
4. *Psalm* LXXIV. 17; *Job* XXXVIII. 5; *Psalm* CIV. 10–26; *Jeremiah* XXXI. 35.
5. *Job* XXXVIII. 7.
6. *Habakkuk* III. 3; *Psalm* CIV. 32.

*

1. This third account of the Creation, built up from Biblical references elsewhere than in *Genesis*, recalls not only Babylonian, but Ugaritic and Canaanite, cosmogonies; and notably expands the brief reference to Tohu, Bohu and the Deep. Such a Creator as El, Marduk, Baal, or Jehovah, must first struggle against water—personified by the Prophets as Leviathan, Rahab, or the Great Dragon, not only because the Creatrix whom he displaces is a goddess of Fertility, and therefore of water, but because the matriarchate can be portrayed in myth as a chaotic commingling of the two sexes which delays the establishment of patriarchal social order—like rain pouring down into the sea, which delays the appearance of dry land. Thus male and female principles must first be decently separated, as when the Egyptian cosmocrator Shu lifted the Sky-goddess Nut from her embrace of the Earth-god Geb; or when Yahweh Elohim tore the Upper Male Waters from their embrace of the Lower Female Waters (see 4. *e*). The Babylonian Marduk, when slicing Tiamat in two, was really parting her from Apsu, God of the Upper Waters.

2. In Ugaritic mythology, Baal fixes the sea bed as the abode of the defeated water, which is treated as both a deity and an element:

O fisherman . . .
Take a large seine in thy two hands,
Cast it into El's beloved Yamm,
Into the Sea of El, the Benign,
Into the Deep of El . . .

3. What 'Tohu' and 'Bohu' originally meant is disputed. But add the suffix *m* to Tohu (*thw*) and it becomes Tehom (*thwm*), the Biblical name for a primitive sea-monster. Tehom, in the plural, becomes Tehomot (*thwmwt*). With the same suffixes, Bohu becomes Behom and Behomot (*bhwmwt*), a variant form of Job's Behemoth, the dry-land counterpart of the sea-monster Leviathan. Leviathan cannot be easily distinguished from Rahab, Tannin, Nahash or any other mythical creatures that personify water. The story underlying *Genesis* I. 2 may therefore be that the world in its primeval state consisted of a sea-monster Tohu and a land-monster Bohu. If so, Tohu's identity with Tehomot, and Bohu's with Behemoth (see 6. *n–q*), has been suppressed for doctrinal reasons (see 1. 13, 16)—Tohu and Bohu being now read as unpersonified states of emptiness or chaos; and God being made responsible for the subsequent creation of Tehomot (or Leviathan) and Behemoth.

4. The Babylonian sea-monster corresponding with the Hebrew Tehomot appears as Tiamat, Tamtu, Tamdu and Taawatu; and in Damascius's *First Principles* as Tauthe. Thus the root is *taw*, which stands in the same relation to Tiamat as Tohu does to Tehom and Tehomot. Moreover, that *tehom* never takes the definite article in Hebrew proves it to have once been a proper name, like *Tiamat*. Tehomot, then, is the Hebrew equivalent of Mother Tiamat, beloved by the God Apsu, whose name developed from the older Sumerian Abzu; and Abzu was the imaginary sweet-water abyss from which Enki, God of Wisdom, emerged. Rahab ('haughtiness') is a synonym of Tehomot; in *Job* XXVI. 12 occur the parallel lines:

By His power He threatened the Sea,
And by His skill He shattered Rahab.

5. The hovering of the Spirit of God over the waste of waters in *Genesis* I. 2 suggests a bird, and in an early Biblical poem God is compared to an 'eagle hovering over her young' (*Deuteronomy* XXXII. 11). But the word *ruah*, usually translated as 'spirit', originally means 'wind', which recalls the Phoenician creation myth quoted by Philo of Byblus: the prime chaos was acted upon by Wind which became enamoured of its own elements. Another Byblian cosmogonist makes Baou, the female principle, impregnated by this wind. The Goddess Baou, wife to the Wind-god Colpia, was also identified with the Greek Goddess Nyx ('Night'), whom Hesiod

makes the Mother of All Things. In Greece she was Eurynome, who took the Serpent Ophioneus for a lover (see 1. 10).

6. The heretical Ophites of the first century A.D. believed that the world had been generated by a serpent. The Brazen Serpent made, according to Hebrew tradition, by Moses at God's command (*Numbers* XXI. 8–9) and revered in the Temple Sanctuary until the reforming King Hezekiah destroyed it (2 *Kings* XVIII. 4), suggests that Yahweh had at one time been identified with a Serpent-god—as Zeus was in Orphic art. Memory of Yahweh as a serpent survived in a late midrash according to which, when God attacked Moses (*Exodus* IV. 24 ff) in a desert lodging place in the dead of night, He assumed the shape of a huge serpent and swallowed Moses as far as his loins. The custom at Jerusalem of killing the sacrificial victims on the north side of the altar (*Leviticus* I. 11; M. Zebahim V. 1–5) points to an early North-Wind cult, like that at Athens. In the original myth, presumably, the Great Mother rose from Chaos; the wind of her advent became a serpent and impregnated her; she thereupon became a bird (dove or eagle) and laid the world-egg—which the serpent coiled about and hatched.

7. According to a Galilean psalm (LXXXIX), God created Heaven and Earth, north and south, Tabor and Hermon, only after subduing Rahab and scattering His other enemies. And according to *Job* IX. 8–13, when He stretched out the Heavens and trod upon the sea-waves, the 'helpers of Rahab' stooped beneath Him. These helpers suggest Tiamat's allies in her struggle against Marduk, when he 'subdued' her with a sacred imprecation.

8. Biblical allusions to Leviathan as a many-headed sea-monster, or as a 'fleeing' serpent (*nahash bariah*), or 'crooked' serpent (*nahash aqalaton*), recall the Ugaritic texts: 'If you smite Lotan . . . the crooked serpent, the mighty one with seven heads . . .' and: 'Baal will run through with his spear, even as he struck Lotan, the crooked serpent with seven heads.' The language approximates Biblical Hebrew: Leviathan (*lwytn*) appears as *lotan; nḥsh brḥ* as *bthn* (= Hebrew *pthn*, 'serpent') *brḥ*; and *nḥsh 'qltwn*, as *bthn 'qltn* in Ugaritic (*ANET* 138b).

9. Tiamat's mate Apsu, a personification of the Upper Waters, has been correlated (by Gunkel and others) with the Hebrew term *ephes*, meaning 'extremity, nothingness'. The word usually appears in dual form: *aphsayim* or *aphse ereṣ*, 'the ends of the earth' (*Deuteronomy* XXXIII. 17; *Micah* V. 3; *Psalm* II. 8; etc.). Its watery connotation survives in a Biblical prophecy (*Zechariah* IX. 10): 'His dominion shall be from sea to sea and from the river to the ends of the earth,' where poetic convention requires that 'the ends of the earth' should also mean 'river', presumably the Ocean Stream. Similarly, in *Proverbs* XXX. 4, *aphsayim* corresponds with 'waters':

> *Who hath bound the waters in His garment?*
> *Who hath established all the* aphsayim *of the earth?*

That the Creator holds the cosmic elements in his fist, or hands, is a favourite theme of Near Eastern myth. God's victory over *ephes* or *aphsayim* has been recorded in *Psalm* LXVII. 8 and 1 *Samuel* II. 10. Isaiah (XLV. 22), after declaring that God alone created the earth, addresses the *aphsayim* in His name: 'Look unto me and be saved, all ye *aphsayim* of the earth!'

10. Though the Hebrew prophets disguised the names of Apsu, Tiamat and Baou as empty abstractions, yet *Isaiah* XL. 17:

> *All the nations are as nothing before Him,*
> *They are accounted by Him as* Ephes *and* Tohu . . .

immediately follows a passage recalling God's feats in the days of Creation. And in *Isaiah* XXXIV. 11–12, Tohu, Bohu and Ephes are used with plain reference to their mythological meaning, when the prophet predicts Edom's destruction:

> *He* [God] *shall stretch over it*
> *The line of* Tohu
> *And the stones of* Bohu . . .
> *And all her princes*
> *Shall be* Ephes . . .

11. 'He confined Tehom with a bolt and two doors,' refers to a double door and the bolt shot across its wings. The same image occurs in the *Enuma Elish:* after Marduk had killed Tiamat and formed the Heavens from one half of her body, he 'shot a bolt across, and placed watchers over it to prevent Tiamat from letting out her waters.' The text of the *Enuma Elish* suggests that *nahash bariah*, the phrase in *Isaiah* XXVII. 1 and *Job* XXVI. 13 describing Leviathan, could also mean 'the bolted-in serpent'. *Bariah*, without any change in vocalization, means 'bolted, shut in', as well as 'fleeing'.

12. Paran, on which God took up His abode according to *Habakkuk* III. 3, is one of several mountains in Teman ('the South-land') which He is said to have thus honoured; the others being Horeb, Sinai and Seir (*Exodus* III. 1; *Deuteronomy* XXXIII. 2). From Paran He would ride out vengefully on the wings of the storm (*Zechariah* IX. 14). The mountainous wilderness of Paran, Zin and Kadesh, where the Israelites wandered for forty years, and where God appeared to them in fire (*Exodus* XIX. 1–3 and 16–20), had associations not only with Moses, but with Elijah (1 *Kings* XIX. 8), and Abraham (see 29. *g*).

3
MYTHICAL COSMOLOGY

(*a*) So great was the work accomplished at the Creation that a walk from east to west across the Earth would take a man five hundred years — if he lived to finish it; and a walk from north to south would take him another five hundred years. These distances correspond with those from Earth to the First Heaven, and from the First Heaven to its summit. As for Earth itself — one-third of its surface is desert, one-third sea, and the remaining third habitable land.[1]

Some reckon the width of Earth as 6000 parasangs, namely 18,000 miles, in all directions; and the height of the sky as 1000 parasangs, or 3000 miles.[2] Others believe Earth to be even larger: Egypt, they say, measures 400 by 400 parasangs, or 1200 by 1200 miles; yet Egypt is one-sixtieth the size of Ethiopia, Ethiopia one-sixtieth of the Earth's surface, Earth one-sixtieth of Eden, and Eden one-sixtieth of Gehenna. Thus Earth is to Gehenna as a small lid to an immense pot.[3]

Eastward of the habitable world lies the Garden of Eden, abode of the righteous. Westward lie the Ocean and its islands; and behind them the Desert, a parched land where only snakes and scorpions crawl. Northward stretch Babylonia and Chaldaea, and behind them are storehouses of Hell-fire and storehouses of snow, hailstones, fog, frost, darkness and gales. Here live demons, harmful spirits, the host of Samael; here also is Gehenna, where the wicked are confined. Southward lie the Chambers of Teman, storehouses of fire, and the Cave of Smoke, whence rises the hot whirlwind.[4]

(*b*) According to others, the East is the quarter from which light and heat spread across the world; the West contains the storehouses of snow and hailstones from which cold winds blow; dews and rains of blessing come from the south; the north breeds darkness.[5]

God fastened down the firmament to the rim of Earth on the east, south and west, but left the northern part loose, announcing: 'Should anyone say "I am God!", let him fasten down this side too, in proof of his godhead.'[6]

(*c*) The seven Earths, separated from one another by intervals of whirlwind, are named in ascending order: *Ereṣ, Adama, Ḥarabha, Ṣiyya, Yabbasha, Arqa, Tebhel* and *Ḥeled.*[7]

(*d*) *Arqa,* the Fifth Earth, contains Gehenna and its seven layers, each with its storehouses of darkness. The highest of these is *Sheol,* and beneath lie others named Perdition, The Lowest Pit, The Bilge, Silence, The Gates of Death and The Gates of the Shadow of Death. The fire of each layer is sixty times fiercer than that immediately below. Here the wicked are punished, and angels torture them.[8]

Tebhel, the Sixth Earth, contains hills, mountains, valleys and plains, inhabited by no fewer than three hundred and sixty-five kinds of creatures. Some have the heads and bodies of oxen, but are endowed with human speech; others have twin heads, four ears and four eyes, twin noses and mouths, four hands and four legs, yet only one trunk. When seated they look like two people; but when they walk, like one. As they eat and drink, the twin heads quarrel and accuse each other of taking more than a fair share; nevertheless, they pass for righteous beings.[9]

Ḥeled, our own Earth, the seventh, needs no description.[10]

(*e*) Opinions vary as to whether there are two, three, seven or ten Heavens;[11] but doubtless their number agrees with that of the seven Earths.[12] The Firmament covers Earth like a dome-shaped lid;[13] its edges touch the surrounding Ocean. The hooks of Heaven are sunk in these waters.[14]

An Arab once led Rabba bar Bar-Hana to the very edge of Earth, where the Firmament is fastened down. Rabba had brought a basketful of bread and, since this was the hour of prayer, set it on the heavenly window-ledge. Later he looked in vain for the basket, and asked: 'Who has stolen my bread?' The Arab answered: 'No man, but the wheel of the Firmament has turned while you prayed. Wait until tomorrow, and you will eat bread again.'[15]

Some describe Earth as a hall open only to the north; because once the Sun, moving from east to west, has reached the north-western corner, it turns and goes upwards and backwards, this time behind the dome of the Firmament. Thus, since the Firmament is opaque, the Sun's return journey causes night upon Earth. After reaching the east, however, it passes once more below the dome of the Firmament, and shines for all mankind.[16]

(*f*) Rabbi Shimon ben Laqish names the seven Heavens as follows: *Wilon, Raqi'a, Sheḥaqim, Zebhul, Ma'on, Makhon,* and *'Arabhoth.*[17] They are all fixed and vaulted over Earth, one above the other, like the skins of an onion; except only *Wilon,* the lowest, which shades the uppermost earth from the heat. At daybreak, therefore, *Wilon* stretches across the sky; but at sundown is rolled away to enable the Moon and stars to shine from *Raqi'a,* the Second Heaven.[18]

(*g*) In *Sheḥaqim,* a pair of millstones grind manna for the righteous; in *Zebhul* are found the Heavenly Jerusalem, the Temple, and the altar upon which the Archangel Michael offers sacrifices; in *Ma'on,* hosts of ministering angels hymn God's mercy all night long, but fall silent at dawn, thus allowing Him to hear His praises sung by Israel below; *Makhon* contains storehouses of snow and hailstones, lofts of dews and rains, chambers of storms, and caves of fog; in *'Arabhoth* abide Justice, Law and Charity, the treasures of Life, Peace and Blessing, the souls of the righteous, the souls of the yet unborn, the dew with which God will revive the dead, the chariot seen by Ezekiel in a vision, the ministering angels, and the Divine Throne.[19]

(*h*) According to a very different view, the lowest Heaven contains clouds, winds, air, the Upper Waters, the two hundred angels appointed to watch the stars, and storehouses of snow, ice and dews with their guardian angels.

In the Second Heaven complete darkness reigns over the sinners chained there in expectation of Judgement.

In the Third Heaven lies the Garden of Eden, full of marvellous fruit trees, including the Tree of Life under which God rests whenever He comes on a visit. Two rivers issue from Eden: one flowing with milk and honey, the other with wine and oil; they branch out into four heads, descend, and surround the Earth. Three hundred Angels of Light, who unceasingly sing God's praises, watch over the Garden, which is the Heaven to which righteous souls are admitted after death. Northward of Eden stretches Gehenna, where dark fires perpetually smoulder, and a river of flame flows through a land of biting cold and ice; here the wicked suffer tortures.

In the Fourth Heaven are chariots ridden by the Sun and Moon; also great stars, each with a thousand lesser stars as followers, that accompany the Sun on its circuit: four to the right, another four to the left. Of the two winds that draw these chariots, one is shaped like a phoenix, the other like a brazen serpent; though, indeed, their faces resemble those of a lion, and their lower parts those of Leviathan. Each wind has twelve wings. To east and west of this Heaven stand gates through which the chariots pass at their appointed hours.

The Fifth Heaven houses the gigantic Fallen Angels, who crouch there in silent and everlasting despair.

In the Sixth Heaven live seven Phoenixes, seven Cherubim singing God's praises without cease, and hosts of radiant angels engrossed in astrological study; besides other angels who guard the hours, years, rivers, seas, crops, pastures, and mankind, recording for God's attention whatever unusual sights they observe.

The Seventh Heaven, one of ineffable light, holds the Archangels, Cherubim, Seraphim, and divine wheels; here God Himself occupies His Divine Throne, and all sing His praises.[20]

These seven Heavens and seven Earths are prevented from falling apart and dropping into the Void beneath by immense hooks attached to the rim of each Heaven and linking it with the rim of a corresponding earth. The uppermost Earth has, however, been hooked to the rim of the Second Heaven (not the First, which is no more than a huge folding veil); the Second Earth is hooked to the Third Heaven, and so forth. In addition, each Heaven is similarly fastened to its neighbouring Heaven. The entire structure thus resembles a fourteen-storeyed tower the top storey of which, *'Arabhoth*, hangs on God's arm—though some say that God holds up the Heavens with His right hand, and the Earths with His left.

Every day God mounts a cherub and visits all these worlds, where He receives homage and adoration. On His return journey, He rides on the wings of the Wind.[21]

1. Mid. Konen, 27.
2. B. Pesahim 94a.
3. B. Pesahim 94a.
4. Mid. Konen, 27–31.
5. Num. Rab. 2.10; 3.12; Mid. Konen, 38; Pesiqta Hadta, 49.
6. PRE, ch. 3.
7. Mid. Konen, 32–33. In other sources somewhat different names are given, cf. Zohar Hadash, 20b.
8. Mid. Konen, 30, 35–36.
9. Mid. Konen, 36.
10. Mid. Konen, 36.
11. Gen. Rab. 176–77; B. Hagiga 12b.
12. Cf. Ginzberg, LJ, V. 10.
13. Mid. Konen, 33.
14. PRE, ch. 3.
15. B. Baba Bathra 74a.
16. B. Baba Bathra 25b.
17. B. Hagiga 12b.
18. Mid. Konen, 37.
19. B. Hagiga 12b.
20. 2 *Enoch* III–IX, and parallel rabbinic sources, Ginzberg, LJ, V. 158 ff.
21. Mid. Konen, 33–34.

*

1. These rabbinical doctrines, mostly borrowed at haphazard from Greek, Persian and Babylonian sources, were meant to impress hearers with the amazing range and complexity of God's works; and the very irreconcilability of any two theories supported this impression. The sages accepted the Biblical concept of a flat earth, and were all baffled by the Sun's reappearance in the East each morning. One small fragment of mathematical science has slipped in: the measure of the earth's dimensions comes reasonably close to that offered by the Ptolemaic physicist, Eratosthenes of Cyrene, in the third century B.C.

The placing of Gehenna not only in the Underworld, but on earth, and in one of the heavens, is perhaps deliberate: an echo of *Amos* IX. 2—'though they dig into hell, there shall Mine hand take them; though they climb up into heaven, thence will I bring them down.'

2. *Teman* means both 'south' and 'southland'. Esau had a grandson of that name, his father being Eliphaz. A 'chief of Teman' is twice mentioned in a passage that also names Husham of the Southland (*temani*) as a King of Edom. 'Eliphaz the Temanite' (*temani*) was one of Job's comforters; elsewhere the distant 'Southland' appears as a region of mysterious 'chambers' and 'southern whirlwinds'. The late midrash (see *b.*) on these chambers refers either to Yemen in South Arabia, or to Tayma, a settlement in North Arabia, about 250 miles east of the entrance to the Gulf of Aqaba.

3. *Hashmal* is a divine substance which, according to the first chapter of *Ezekiel*, provides the fiery splendour of God's Throne and Countenance. The Septuagint translates *electron*, which in Greek is connected with *Elector*, a name for the sun, and thus means 'shining with a golden light'; hence either amber, or amber-coloured *electrum*, an alloy of gold and silver. *Hashmal* is modern Hebrew for 'electricity', because the rubbing of amber to attract particles of dust was, it seems, the earliest experimental use of electricity. But the association of lightning with the power of God being ancient, Ezekiel may have regarded this divine *hashmal* as the source of lightning.

4. In Talmudic times, speculations on the structure of the Universe were called *ma'asse merkabhah*, 'matters of the chariot', because of the divine chariot described by Ezekiel. The Pharisees regarded the study of these matters as dangerous, and several stories are told about learned men who failed to take proper precautions: Ben Azzay died suddenly, Ben Zoma lost his mind, Elisha ben Abuya became a heretic; Rabbi Akiba alone escaped harm by humility and circumspection (*B. Hagiga* 14b–16a).

5. That the entire Universe hangs from God's arms is first quoted in the Babylonian Talmud (*B. Hagiga* 12b): 'Rabbi Yose said: "The earth rests on columns, the columns on water, the water on mountains, the mountains on wind, the wind on the whirlwind, and the whirlwind hangs from God's arm."' But it can hardly be reconciled with His daily visits to each Heaven and Earth.

6. *Ereṣ* means 'earth'; so do *adama* and *arqa* (an Aramaic loan-word); *ṣiyya*, 'dryness'; *yabbasha*, 'dry land'; *ḥarabha*, 'parched land'; *tebhel* and *ḥeled*, 'world'.

Wilon means 'curtain'; *raqi'a*, 'firmament'; *sheḥaqim*, 'clouds' or 'grindstones'; *zebhul*, 'dwelling'; *ma'on*, 'residence'; *makhon*, 'emplacement'; and '*arabhoth*, 'plains'.

4

GLOSSES ON THE CREATION STORY

(*a*) God created the Heavens from the light of His garment. When He spread them out like a cloth, they began to stretch farther and farther of their own accord, until He cried 'Enough!' He created Earth from the snow beneath His Divine Throne: throwing some of this on the waters, which froze and turned to dust. Earth and Sea also stretched farther and farther, until He cried 'Enough!'[1]

(*b*) Some, however, say that God wove together two skeins, one of fire and one of snow, for His creation of the world; and two more, of fire and water, for the creation of the Heavens. Others hold that the Heavens were made of snow alone.[2]

(*c*) Under the ancient rule of Water such disorder and chaos prevailed that wise men avoid all mention of it. 'Likening God to a king who has built his palace above a vast privy,' they say, 'would be apt but irreverent.'[3]

(*d*) God therefore banished Tohu and Bohu from Earth, though retaining them as two of five layers that separate the seven Earths. Tohu may be readily discerned as the horizon's thin green line from which, every evening, Darkness rises across the world. 'Bohu' is also the name given to certain glittering stones sunk in the abyss where Leviathan lurks.[4]

(*e*) God found the male Upper Waters and the female Lower Waters locked in a passionate embrace. 'Let one of you rise,' He ordered, 'and the other fall!' But they rose up together, whereupon God asked: 'Why did you both rise?' 'We are inseparable,' they answered with one voice. 'Leave us to our love!' God now stretched out His little finger and tore them apart; the Upper He lifted high, the Lower He cast down. To punish their defiance, God would have singed them with fire, had they not sued for mercy. He pardoned them on two conditions: that, at the Exodus, they would allow the Children of Israel to pass through dry-shod; and that they would prevent Jonah from fleeing by ship to Tarshish.[5]

(*f*) The divided Waters then voiced their agony of loss by blindly rushing towards each other, and flooding the mountain tops. But when the Lower Waters lapped at the very foot of God's throne, He shouted in anger and trampled them under His feet.[6]

(*g*) Others say that the Lower Waters, heart-broken at being no longer so close to God, shrieked: 'We have not been found worthy of our Maker's presence,' and tried to reach His throne as suppliants.[7]

(*h*) On the third day, when God set Himself to gather the Salt Waters in one place—thus letting dry land emerge—they protested: 'We cover the entire world, and even so lack elbow room; would you confine us still further?' Whereupon God kicked their leader Oceanus to death.[8]

(*i*) These difficulties past, God allotted a separate place to each body of Waters. Yet at the horizon they are parted by no more than the breadth of three narrow fingers.[9]

(*j*) At times, the Sea still menaces her barrier of sand. A seasoned mariner once told Rabbah of Babylon: 'The distance between one wave and its fellow may be three hundred leagues; and each may rise to a height of three hundred leagues also. Not long ago, a wave lifted our ship so close to a small star that it spread to the size of a field on which forty measures of mustard seed might grow. Had we risen higher yet, the star's breath would have scorched us. And we heard one wave call to its fellow: "Sister, is anything left in the world that you have not already swept away? If so, let me destroy it." But the wave answered: "Respect the power of our Lord, sister; we may not cross the barrier of sand by even the width of a thread . . ."'[10]

(*k*) God also forbade Tehom, the sweet Underground Waters, to rise up—except little by little; and enforced obedience by placing a sherd above her, on which He had engraved His Ineffable Name. This seal was removed once only: when mankind sinned in Noah's day. Thereupon Tehom united with the Upper Waters and together they flooded the earth.[11]

(*l*) Since then, Tehom has always crouched submissively in her deep abode like a huge beast, sending up springs to those who deserve them, and nourishing the tree roots. Though she thus influences man's fate, none may visit her recesses.[12]

(*m*) Tehom delivers three times more water to Earth than the rain. At the Feast of Tabernacles, Temple priests pour libations of wine and water on God's altar. Then Ridya, an angel shaped like a three-year-old heifer with cleft lips, commands Tehom: 'Let your springs rise!', and commands the Upper Waters: 'Let rain fall!'[13]

(*n*) Some say that a gem bearing the Messiah's name—which floated with the wind until the Altar of Sacrifice had been built on

Mount Zion, and then came to rest there—was the first solid thing God created. Others, that it was the Foundation Rock supporting His altar; and that, when God restrained Tehom's waters, He engraved His forty-two-letter Name on its face, rather than on a sherd. Still others say that He cast the Rock into deep water and built land around, much as a child before birth grows from the navel outward; it remains the world's navel to this day.[14]

(*o*) Later, when Adam wondered how Light had been created, God gave him two stones—of Darkness and of the Shadow of Death—which he struck together. Fire issued from them. 'Thus it was done,' said God.[15]

1. PRE, ch. 3; cf. Gen. Rab. 3–4, 20; B. Hagiga 12a.
2. Tanhuma Buber Gen. 8; Gen. Rab. 31 and 75, and parallel sources.
3. Yer. Hagiga 77c mid.
4. Gen. Rab. 75; cf. Pesiqta Hadta, 59; Mid. Konen, 35–36; B. Hagiga 12a; based on *Isa.* XXXIV. 11; XLV. 19 and *Job* XXVI. 7.
5. Mid. Konen, 25.
6. Gen. Rab. 34–35; Seder Rabba diBereshit, 314; Mid. Aseret Hadibrot, 63; Mid. Tehillim, 414; PRE, ch. 5.
7. *Sefer Raziel*, 315.
8. PRE, ch. 5; Mid. Tehillim, 415; Ex. Rab. 15, 22; Num. Rab. 18.22; Tanhuma Hayye Sara 3, p. 32b.
9. Gen. Rab. 17.
10. B. Baba Bathra 73a.
11. Yer. Sanh. 29a bot.; Mid. Shemuel, ch. 26; Yalqut Reubeni i:4 f.; ii: 109; cf. *Enoch* LIX. 7–10; PRE, ch. 23; all based on *Gen.* VII. 11.
12. *Genesis* XLIX. 25; *Ezekiel* XXXI. 4; XXVI. 19; XXXI. 15; *Job* XXXVIII. 16.
13. Gen. Rab. 122, 294; B. Taanit 25b.
14. Yalqut Reubeni, i:4 ff., 22; ii: 109; Mid. Adonay Behokhmah, 63; Seder Arqim, 70a; B. Yoma 54b; PRE, ch. 35; Mid. Tehillim, 91; Zohar iii. 322; cf. Patai, *Man and Temple*, 85.
15. Mid. Tehillim, 404; Num. Rab. 15.7.

*

1. In Ugaritic mythology, as in Hebrew, water always takes a dual form: thus there are two Floods, two Oceans, and two Deeps. Allusion is also made to the desire of the male waters for the female: when Kothar wa-Khasis built the Rain-god Baal's house, he was forbidden to open any windows through which the amorous Yamm ('the Sea') might catch sight of the god's two wives—Padriya ('Flashing One') daughter of Ar ('Light'), and Talliya ('Dewy') daughter of Rabb ('Distillation'). The house-walls were clouds, as in God's Celestial Pavilion (see 2. *a*). When about to attack Yamm, Baal 'opens a window within the house, makes rifts in the clouds, and gives forth his holy voice, which convulses the earth . . . so that the mountains quake . . .'

2. The metaphor of the king who built his palace above a privy may

refer to male and female prostitution, and other Canaanite 'abominations' practised on Mount Zion in honour of Baal and Asherah, before the monotheistic reform of the Temple rites (2 *Kings* XXXIII. 4 ff).

3. Three-year-old heifers are widely associated with Moon-worship because their horns resemble a new moon and because the Moon has three phases. In Babylonian astrology (see 1. 14), the Moon held the planetary power of water; and, under Mosaic Law, perfect ritual cleanliness could be conveyed by a 'water of separation' (*Numbers* XIX. 2 ff) mixed with the ashes of a red heifer. Ridya's appearance as a heifer at Tabernacles, which introduces the rainy season, is therefore mythically apt.

4. The waters' plea for pardon when God threatened to singe them, is reminiscent of the *Iliad* where Hephaestus kindles a brush fire on Xanthus's banks and makes his waters boil until he surrenders. Yet a common source is possible: Homer's debt to Near Eastern myths has become yearly more apparent.

5. God's use of snow and fire for Creation may be derived from *Psalm* CXLVIII. 4–8:

> *Praise Him ye heavens of the firmament, and ye waters that be above the firmament.*
> *Let them praise the name of the Lord, for He commanded and they were created.*
> *He has established them for ever and for ever; He has made a decree which shall not pass.*
> *Praise the Lord from the earth, ye dragons and all deeps,*
> *Fire and hail, snow and vapours and a stormy wind fulfilling His word.*

6. There are parallels in Egypt to the Jewish Temple legend that a rock on which the Sanctuary stood was the first solid thing created. The Pythoness's stone seat at Delphi also became known as 'the world's navel'.

7. Rabbah, a Babylonian Jew of the third century A.D., had travelled far. An apocryphal collection of his adventures recalls Lucian's early-second-century *True History;* but has a moralistic, rather than a satiric, intention.

8. The name of the God of Israel came to be regarded as too holy to be pronounced, except by the High Priest in the Holy of Holies on the Day of Atonement. In Talmudic times the sages entrusted their disciples once every seven years with the secret pronunciation of the Tetragrammaton YHWH (B. Kiddushin 71a), which otherwise was always spoken as *Adonai.* At the same time, twelve-letter, forty-two-letter and seventy-two-letter names of Yahweh, perhaps connected with Calendar Mysteries (Graves, *White Goddess,* ch. xvi) were also known to the initiated; when, however, these names were abused by sorcerers, they were suppressed,

and only the more pious priests continued to use them when giving their benediction; but even so purposely sang them indistinctly, 'swallowing' some phonemes and expanding others into sustained melodious lines (B. Kiddushin, *ibid.*). This is reminiscent of the Egyptian ritual in which, according to Demetrius of Alexandria, the gods were celebrated with seven vowels sung in succession.

9. The allegory of the two stones from which Adam struck fire is based on *Job* XXVIII. 3:

> *Man setteth an end to darkness and searcheth*
> *out the furthest bound, the stones of thick darkness*
> *and of the shadow of death.*

The midrash about the stone, rock or potsherd which God placed upon Tehom, thereby preventing her from rising up and flooding the earth, has a Sumerian prototype. An Enki-Ninhursag myth relates that the primeval waters of the Kur, or Nether World, rose violently to the surface, thus preventing any fresh waters from reaching fields and gardens. Thereupon Ninurta, god of the stormy South Wind and son of Enlil set a pile of stones over the Kur and restrained the flood.

5

EARLIER CREATIONS

(*a*) In the beginning God created numerous worlds, destroying one after the other as they failed to satisfy Him. All were inhabited by man, a thousand generations of whom He cut off, leaving no record of them.[1]

(*b*) After these first essays in creation, God was left alone with His great Name, and recognized at last that no world would satisfy Him unless it offered man a means of repentance. Hence, before making a new start, He created seven things: the Law, Gehenna, the Garden of Eden, the Divine Throne, the Celestial Pavilion, the Messiah's Name, and Repentance.[2]

(*c*) When two Divine Days—namely two thousand terrestrial years—had passed, God asked the Law, who had become His counsellor: 'What if I should create yet another world?' 'Lord of the Universe,' she asked in return, 'if a king has neither army nor camp, over what does he rule? And if there is no one to praise him, what honour has he?' God listened and approved.[3]

(*d*) Yet some say that the Law pleaded against God's creation of mankind with: 'Do not leave me at the mercy of sinners who drink evil like water!' God answered: 'I created Repentance as a remedy for such; the Divine Throne as my Seat of Judgement; the Pavilion, to witness sacrifices of atonement; the Garden of Eden, to reward the righteous; Gehenna, to punish the unrepentant; yourself, to occupy the minds of men; and the Messiah, to gather in the exiles.'[4]

1. Gen. Rab. 23, 68, 262–63.
2. Mid. Tehillim, 391; PRE, ch. 3.
3. PRE, ch. 3; cf. Gen. Rab. 20.
4. Yalqut Reubeni, i:22, quoting Sode Raza.

*

1. It is not known whether the discovery of fossils far older than the four thousand years which had elapsed since Adam's day troubled the rabbis. If so, their account of previous experimental creations was more plausible than the theory held by such Victorian zoologists as Philip Gosse: God, he said, had inserted fossils in the rocks to try the Christian's faith.

2. It became an article of belief that the Law was eternal (cf. *Matthew* v. 18), and had existed before Creation. Hebrew myth, a charter confirming successive historical changes in religion, becomes allegorical at this late stage and defines the doctrine of individual salvation (see 61. 5).

3. Gehenna was the Jewish Hell. Its name is borrowed from the Valley of Hinnom at Jerusalem, which included Tophet (2 *Kings* XXIII. 10): a site originally used for human sacrifices to the God Moloch (2 *Chronicles* XXXIII. 8), afterwards for burning the city's rubbish.

4. The equivalence of one divine day with a thousand terrestrial years is derived from *Psalm* XC. 4: 'A thousand years in Thy sight are but as yesterday.'

6

THE PRIMEVAL MONSTERS DESCRIBED

(*a*) In the days before Creation, Rahab, Prince of the Sea, rebelled against God. When commanded: 'Open your mouth, Prince of the Sea, and swallow all the world's waters,' he cried: 'Lord of the Universe, leave me in peace!' Whereupon God kicked him to death and sank his carcase below the waves, since no land-beast could endure its stench.[1]

(*b*) Others hold that God spared Rahab's life, and that afterwards, when envious angels stole and threw into the sea 'The Book of Raziel', a compendium of divine wisdom which God had given Adam, He ordered Rahab to dive down and recover it. The Prince of the Sea obeyed without demur, yet later comforted God's enemies by supporting the Egyptians in their quarrel with the Children of Israel, and pleading for Pharaoh's army which God was about to drown in the Red Sea. 'Spare the Egyptians,' he cried, 'be content with the rescue of Israel!' But God, lifting His hand, destroyed Rahab and all his helpers. Some style Rahab 'the Celestial Prince of Egypt'. Others do not distinguish him either from Leviathan or Oceanus; or from the boastful Great Dragon who claimed to have created all seas and rivers, but whom God hauled ashore in a net, with his progeny, afterwards shattering their skulls and piercing their sides. When they still would not die, He set guardians to watch over the Great Dragon, who will finally be despatched on the Day of Reckoning.[2]

(*c*) Leviathan's monstrous tusks spread terror, from his mouth issued fire and flame, from his nostrils smoke, from his eyes a fierce beam of light; his heart was without pity. He roamed at will on the surface of the sea, leaving a resplendent wake; or through its lowest abyss, making it boil like a pot. No weapon in the armoury of mankind could dint his scales. Heaven's inhabitants themselves feared him. Yet God caught Leviathan with a hook, hauled him up from the Deep, tied down his tongue with a rope, thrust a reed through his nostrils, and pierced his jaws with a thorn—as though he had been a river fish. Then He threw the carcase in the bottom of a boat and took it off, as if to market.[3]

(*d*) When God created fishes and sea-beasts from light and water, He allowed Leviathan, who was larger than all his fellows put together, to rule them from a throne raised on a colossal underwater rock. Some say that he had many heads, or that there were two Leviathans—the Fleeing Serpent and the Crooked Serpent—both of whom God destroyed. Others, that He spared Leviathan as being one of His creatures, but wholly tamed him (or ordered the archangel Jahoel to do so), and still deigns to sport with him on the wide seas for three full hours a day. Great sea-dragons serve as Leviathan's food. He drinks from a tributary of the Jordan, as it flows into the ocean through a secret channel. When hungry, he puffs out a smoky vapour which troubles an immense extent of waters; when thirsty, he causes such an upheaval that seventy years must elapse before calm returns to the Deep, and even Behemoth on the Thousand Mountains shows signs of terror. But Leviathan fears one single creature only: a little fish called Chalkis, created by God for the sole purpose of keeping him in check.[4]

(*e*) Others hold that Leviathan has been confined by God to an ocean cave, where the world's whole weight rests upon him. His huge recumbent body presses down on Tehom, which prevents her from flooding the earth. Yet, since sea water is too salt for Leviathan's taste, thirst often compels him to raise one fin; the sweet waters of Tehom surge up and he drinks awhile, then drops the fin again.[5]

(*f*) Some say that Leviathan has as many eyes as the year has days, and radiant scales that obscure the very sun; that he grips his tail between his teeth and forms a ring around the Ocean. The firmament's lower band, which carries the signs of the Zodiac, is therefore also called 'Leviathan'.[6]

(*g*) Few men have ever been granted even an inkling of Leviathan's bulk; but once Rabh Saphra, as he sailed in a ship, saw a two-horned beast lifting its head from the waters. Engraved upon the horns he read: 'This tiny sea-creature, measuring hardly three hundred leagues, is on his way to serve as Leviathan's food.'[7]

(*h*) Some sages reconcile the rival traditions that God killed, and did not kill Leviathan, by believing Him to have created both a male and a female. According to these, God butchered the female and gelded the male, to prevent them from mating and thereby destroying the world—they say it would have been unseemly for Him to kill the male and sport with the female . . . When this lonely survivor sees God approach, he lays aside his grief; the righteous, watching the play, are likewise cheered by anticipation of what awaits them—

knowing that on Judgement Day they shall banquet off its flesh. From the female's hide, God made bright garments to clothe Adam and Eve; and preserved her flesh in brine for the same banquet.[8]

(*i*) Leviathan, like Rahab, exudes a fearful stench. Were it not that from time to time the monster purifies himself by sniffing the sweet flowers of Eden, all God's creatures would surely stifle.[9]

(*j*) Those who hold that Leviathan's life was spared, foresee a great angelic hunt in which he is the quarry. Yet even the boldest angels must flee from him as he stands at bay; and, if they rally to the attack, can only blunt their weapons on his scales. When, at length, Gabriel tries to haul him out of the Deep to which he has returned, Leviathan will swallow hook, line and fisherman. Then God in person must net and slaughter him.[10]

(*k*) God will not only prepare a magnificent banquet from Leviathan's flesh, distributing for sale in the streets of Jerusalem what the righteous cannot eat, but make them tents from his hide, and adorn the city walls with what is left—until they shine to the ends of the world.[11]

(*l*) Others predict a duel between Leviathan and Behemoth. After an earth-shaking struggle on the sea-shore, Behemoth's curved horns will rip Leviathan open, while Leviathan's sharp fins mortally stab Behemoth.[12]

(*m*) Yet others hold that Leviathan was to have been Behemoth's mate; but that God parted them, keeping Behemoth on dry land and sending Leviathan into the sea, lest their combined weight might crack Earth's arches.[13]

(*n*) Behemoth, the first land-beast created, resembles a prodigious hippopotamus: with a tail bigger than the trunk of a cedar, and bones like pipes of brass. He rules the land-creatures, as Leviathan those of the sea. They gambol around him, where he takes his ease among lotus, reed, fern and willows, or grazes on the Thousand Mountains. It is disputed whether Behemoth was fashioned from water, dust and light, or simply told to arise from Earth; also, whether he was born solitary, or once had a mate, as have all living creatures.[14] Some say that if Behemoth did possess a mate, he cannot have coupled with her: since their offspring would surely have overwhelmed the world. Others, that God prudently gelded the male and cooled the female's ardour; but spared her until the Last Days, when her flesh will delight the righteous.[15]

(*o*) God lets Behemoth graze on the Thousand Mountains, and though he crops these bare in a single day, yet each night the grass grows again and, by morning, stands as high and rank as before. Behemoth is said to be a flesh-eater also: the Thousand Mountains supporting with their pasture many beasts that serve as his food. Summer heat makes him so thirsty that all the waters flowing down Jordan in six months, or even a year, barely suffice for a single gulp. He therefore drinks at a huge river issuing from Eden, Jubal by name.[16]

(*p*) Behemoth is called 'the Ox of the Pit.' Every year, at the summer solstice, he rises on his hind legs, as God has taught him, and lets out a fearful echoing roar that restrains all wild beasts from preying on man's flocks and herds for the next twelve months. He will often raise his great bushy tail and let the birds of the air take shelter there; then lower it gently and let the beasts of the field do likewise. Behemoth, despite his enormous strength, is as merciful as a good king should be: solicitous that none of the birds shall be harmed by their fellow-subjects, the beasts.[17]

(*q*) Although some believe that Leviathan and Behemoth will murder each other, it is predicted by others that God will send Michael and Gabriel against both creatures and that, when they fail to despatch either, He will shoulder the task Himself.[18]

1. B. Baba Bathra 74b; Num. Rab. 18.22; Mid. Wayosha, 46.
2. Mid. Wayosha, 47; Mid. Sekhel Tobh, 182; Ginzberg, LJ, I. 156; V. 26; *Isaiah* LI. 9; *Psalm* LXXIV. 13; *Isaiah* XXVII. 1; *Job* VII. 12; *Ezekiel* XXIX. 3–4 and XXXII. 2–6; cf. *Psalm* CXLVIII. 7; *Psalms of Solomon* II. 25–32; Gunkel, *Schöpfung und Chaos*, 78 ff.
3. *Isaiah* XXVII. 1; *Psalm* LXXIV. 14; *Job* XL. 25–32; XLI. 2–26.
4. *Psalm* LXXIV. 14; *Isaiah* XXVII. 1; *Psalm* CIV. 24–26; *Job* XL. 29; B. Baba Bathra 74b–75a; Gen. Rab. 52; Mid. Konen, 26; Alpha Beta diBen Sira B, 27a–28b, 36a; PRE, ch. 9; Targ. Yer. Gen. I. 20; Mekhilta Bahodesh 7, 69b; Mekhilta diR. Shimon 109; Mid. Yonah, 98; Pesiqta diR. Kahana 188a; *Apoc. Baruch* XXIX. 4; B. Shabbat 77b; Pirke Rabbenu Haqadosh, 512a; Iggeret Baale Hayyim 3, 12.
5. *Apoc. Baruch* XXIX. 4; Seder Rabba diBereshit, 9; Baraita diMaase Bereshit, 47; Pesiqta Rabbati, 194b.
6. Kalir, in the piyyut Weyikkon Olam, following the Lamentations in the Roman Mahzor, ed. Mantova, 1712, p. 115; Pesiqta diR. Kahana, 188a; B. Baba Bathra 74b; Ginzberg, LJ, V. 45.
7. B. Baba Bathra 74a.
8. B. Baba Bathra 74b; B. Aboda Zara 3b; PRE, ch. 9; Mid. Yonah, 98; Sepher Hassidim, 476; cf. Zohar 2, 216.
9. B. Baba Bathra 75a.
10. B. Baba Bathra 75a; Mid. Alphabetot 438.
11. *Apoc. Baruch* XXIX. 4; B. Baba Bathra 75a–b; Targum *ad Ps.* CIV. 26; cf. Pesiqta diR. Kahana 29, 188a–b; Mid. Alphabetot 438; Pirqe Mashiah 76.
12. Lev. Rab. 13.3.
13. 4 *Ezra* VI. 47–52; *Enoch* LX. 7–8.
14. *Job* XL. 15–24; *Psalms* I. 10; Mid. Konen, 26; PRE, ch. 11; Gen. Rab. 52.
15. B. Baba Bathra 74b.
16. Mid. Konen, 26; Pesiqta Rabbati, 80b–81a; Lev. Rab. 13.3; 22.10; Num. Rab. 21.18; PRE, ch. 11.

17. Mid. Konen, 37; Mid. Adonay Behokhma, 64; Pesiqta Hadta, 48; Kalir, in the piyyut Weyikkon Olam, following the Lamentations in Roman Mahzor, ed. Mantova, 1712, p. 114b.
18. Pesiqta diR. Kahana, 29, 188a–b; Mid. Alphabetot 98; Ginzberg, LJ, V. 43.

*

1. God's watch over the Great Dragon even after its death, and His restraint of Tehom by use of a magical sherd (see 4. *k*), recall the *Enuma Elish,* where Marduk sets watchers over Tiamat's carcase to prevent an escape of water.

2. Leviathan, in some aspects, resembles a whale; in others, a crocodile. Why he is called 'the Celestial Spirit of Egypt', and why Ezekiel (xxix. 3) calls Pharaoh 'the great dragon that lies among his rivers', can be seen from a victory song in honour of Thotmes III: 'I let [the vanquished peoples] behold your Majesty in the likeness of a crocodile feared in the waters, which no man dares approach.'

3. Crocodiles were worshipped at Crocodilopolis, Ombos, Coptos, Athribis and Thebes. Their mummies have been found in several Egyptian cemeteries. According to Plutarch, crocodiles were believed to lay their eggs exactly above the level of the next Nile flood—a great assistance to farmers who came across them. Crocodiles were also native to Palestine, and survived in the River Zerka until the beginning of this century. A small Gnostic stele from Caesarea shows them being hunted; according to Diodorus Siculus, they were caught on baited hooks, and killed with iron forks, though seldom, because of their sanctity. He wrote that the crocodile feared only the ichneumon, a creature no bigger than a little dog, which ran up and down the banks of the Nile breaking their eggs for the benefit of mankind.

The chalkis, a substitute for the ichneumon in Jewish tradition, is a gregarious fish. Some commentators make it a sardine, others a herring: which seems an apter choice, because in Northern European folklore the herring is preferred to the whale as King of the Sea.

4. Leviathan perhaps borrowed his stench from Tehom-Tiamat, whose name seems to have been connected by early popular etymology with the Arabic *tahama* ('stinking'), and *Tihama,* a name for the low-lying southwest Arabian shore. This etymology would have been strengthened by the phenomenon of a stranded whale: no dead animal smells stronger.

5. Behemoth resembles a wild ox in so far as he roved on the Thousand Mountains—doubtless at the sources of the Nile—and would one day rip Leviathan open with his curved horns. For the most part, however, he is a hippopotamus. Herodotus, Diodorus and Pliny, in writing of the Nile, all pair the hippopotamus and crocodile. That the hippopotamus has enormous strength, frequents the reedy parts of rivers, can stay under water for as long as ten minutes, but is herbivorous and therefore inoffensive to other beasts, agrees with the account of Behemoth in *Job* xl. 15–24. According to Herodotus, the female hippopotamus was worshipped at Pamprenis as Set's wife. She was called Taurt ('the great one'), and made patroness of pregnancy, but never humanized like other animal deities. Diodorus notes that it would be disastrous to mankind if hippopotami were to breed unmolested, and that some Egyptians therefore harpoon them. Possibly this comment and Diodorus's praise of the ichneumon's concern for the future of mankind has suggested the inevitable castastrophe if Leviathan and Behemoth were to mate. The mild hippopotamus caused such damage to Nile crops that by Roman times it had been practically exterminated.

6. Both crocodile and hippopotamus were sacred to Set, and supernatural pictures of them in the Egyptian *Book of the Dead*, which honours Osiris, Set's enemy, may have prompted Jewish mythologists to identify them with the Babylonian monsters.

7. Crocodiles and hippopotami are, according to Diodorus, all but inedible, but Herodotus says that they were sometimes eaten, presumably at an annual totem feast: hence the flesh of Leviathan and Behemoth reserved for the righteous on the Last Day. The poor of the Middle East have always hungered for flesh feasts to supplement their predominantly cereal diet.

8. Oceanus, whom Hesiod makes the eldest of the Titans and father of three thousand rivers, and whom Homer calls a god inferior only to Zeus, was supposed to girdle the earth like a serpent, just as the Zodiac girdles the sky. He was thus readily identified with Leviathan, the Great Dragon and Rahab; Scandinavian myths also make him a dragon. His appearance on the coins of Tyre, a city against which Isaiah (XXIII. 1–18), Amos (I. 10) and Joel (IV. 4) prophesied destruction, may account for the brutal kick which God dealt him (see 4. *h*).

9. The many-headed Leviathan of *Psalm* LXXIV. 14, is the seven-headed monster on Hittite cylinder seals, and mentioned in Ugaritic mythology. It also occurs on a Sumerian mace-head, and on a Babylonian seal from the third millennium B.C.

10. Mythical water-monsters in relief decorate six small panels at the base of the Menorah candelabrum shown on Titus's triumphal arch at Rome. This arch commemorates his sack of Jerusalem in 70 A.D. King Solomon had placed five such golden candelabra on either side of the Great Altar, besides supplying silver ones. When Nebuchadrezzar destroyed the Temple in 586 B.C., he took them all away. Some decades later, another golden Menorah stood in the Second Temple, built by Zerubbabel. This, in turn, was carried off by Antiochus Epiphanes, King of Syria (175–163 B.C.), but replaced by Judas Maccabeus. Close correspondences between the candelabrum shown on Titus's Arch and the account in *Exodus* of the pre-Exilic Menorah suggest that, though the author of *Exodus* has described no more than stem and branches, yet the monsters of the Maccabean Menorah also occurred on the Solomonic one.

11. The Menorah's cosmic significance was first mentioned by Zechariah (IV. 10), who had learned in a vision that its seven lamps were 'the eyes of Yahweh that run to and fro through the universe', namely the seven planets (see 1. 6). This view was endorsed by Josephus and Philo, contemporaries of Titus, and by midrashic writers of two or three centuries later. The annual lighting of the Temple candelabra at the autumn festival will have commemorated God's creation of stars on the fourth day: because the Menorah's central stem rises into the fourth branch, and because Babylonian priests held the fourth planet sacred to Nabu who invented astronomy. Probably, then, the Menorah monsters represent those which God overcame before He began His work of Creation.

On the lower left panel, a pair of dragons face each other in similar positions, though their wings and tails differ. These may be read as two Leviathans: the Fleeing Serpent and the Crooked Serpent. The symmetrical and identical fish-tailed creatures with somewhat feline heads shown in the top left and right panels are, perhaps, the 'great dragons' of *Genesis* I. 21. The dragon on the lower central panel, with its head twisted haughtily up and backward, suggests Rahab ('haughtiness'). An indistinct monster on the lower right may be Tehom or Ephes. A relief on the top central panel vaguely resembles the familiar pair of Phoenician winged creatures always shown facing each other: possibly they are cherubim, God's messengers, whose effigies surmounted the Ark of the Covenant. It may have been in memory of these reliefs that a second-century Tannaitic rule explicitly forbids representations of dragons with spikes protruding from their necks as being emblems of idolatry, though smooth-necked dragons, such as those shown on the base of the Menorah, are permitted (Tos. Avodah Zarah, v.2).

12. Solomon is said to have won much of his wisdom from the 'Book of Raziel,' a collection of astrological secrets cut on sapphire, which the angel Raziel kept. The idea of a divine book containing cosmic secrets appears first in the Slavonic *Book of Enoch* (xxxiii), which states that God had written books of wisdom (or, according to another version, dictated them to Enoch), that He then appointed the two angels Samuil and Raguil (or Semil and Rasuil) to accompany Enoch back from heaven to earth, and commanded him to give these books to his children and children's children. This may well be the origin of the 'Book of Raziel' which, according to Jewish tradition, was given by the Angel Raziel to Adam, from whom it descended through Noah, Abraham, Jacob, Levi, Moses and Joshua until it reached Solomon. According to the Targum on *Ecclesiastes* x. 20: 'Each day the angel Raziel standing upon Mount Horeb proclaims the secrets of men to all mankind, and his voice reverberates around the world.' A so-called *Book of Raziel*, dating from about the twelfth century, was probably written by the Kabbalist Eleazar ben Judah of Worms, but contains far older mystical beliefs.

7

THE REEM AND THE ZIZ

(*a*) So strong and fierce is the enormous wild-ox called Reem that any attempt at teaching it to draw a plough or harrow would be extreme folly. God alone can save mankind from those terrible horns.[1]

(*b*) Only a single pair of reems ever exists at the same time. The bull lives at one end of Earth, the cow at the other. Every seventy years they meet and copulate, whereupon the cow bites the bull to death. She conceives twin-calves, a male and a female; but, in the eleventh and last year of her pregnancy, becoming too gravid to move, lies down and rolls from side to side. There she would starve, were it not for her copious spittle which waters the fields all around and makes them grow sufficient grass to sustain life. At last her belly bursts open, the twins leap out, and she expires. Immediately, the young reems separate—the male calf going east, the female west—to meet again after seventy years.[2]

(*c*) King David, as a boy, led his father's sheep up what he mistook for a mountain but was, in fact, a sleeping reem. Suddenly it awoke and rose to its feet. David clasped the reem's right horn, which reached to Heaven, praying: 'Lord of the Universe, lead me to safety, and I will build You a temple one hundred cubits in span, like the horns of this reem.' God mercifully sent a lion, the King of Beasts, before whom the reem crouched in obeisance. Since, however, David was himself afraid of the lion, God sent a deer for it to pursue. David then slid down from the reem's shoulder and escaped.[3]

(*d*) Many generations later, Rabba bar Bar-Hana, the famous traveller, saw a day-old reem-calf bigger than Mount Tabor, with a neck measuring three leagues around. The dung it dropped into the river-bed of Jordan caused the stream to overflow.[4]

(*e*) Yet the reem would have perished in the Flood, had not Noah saved two of its young. He found no room for them in the Ark, but bound their horns to the stern and let their nose-tips rest on deck. Thus they swam behind, leaving a furrow-like wake which spread as far as the distance between Tiberias and Susita on the opposite shore of Lake Gennesaret.[5]

(*f*) In Rabbi Hiyya bar Rabha's day, a newly born reem-calf came to Israel and uprooted every tree in the land. A fast being proclaimed, Rabbi Hiyya prayed God for deliverance; whereupon its dying mother lowed from the desert, and it went back to her.[6]

(*g*) The Ziz is so named because his flesh has many different flavours: tasting like this (*zeh*) and like this (*zeh*). He is a clean bird, fit for food, and capable of teaching mankind the greatness of God.[7]

(*h*) All birds, including the Ziz, their King, were created on the Fifth Day from marsh, and thus rank between land and sea-beasts.[8] But if God had not given the weaker birds a merciful dispensation, they could never have held their own against eagle, hawk and other birds of prey; for in the month of Tishri, He commands the Ziz to lift his head, flap his wings, crow aloud, and fill birds of prey with such terror that they spare the lesser breeds.[9]

(*i*) God set one of the newly created Ziz's feet upon a fin of Leviathan, and found that his head reached the Divine Throne. His outspread wings can darken the sun, and restrain the fiery South Wind from parching all Earth.[10]

(*j*) The same Bar-Hana reports that, on a sea voyage, he and his shipmates saw the Ziz standing in mid-Ocean; yet the waves wetted only his ankles. 'We judged that the sea must be shallow,' writes Bar-Hana, 'and thought to disembark and cool ourselves. But a heavenly voice warned us: "Seven years ago, a ship's carpenter dropped his axe at this spot and it has not yet touched bottom!"'[11]

(*k*) There is also a hen-Ziz. Though taking good care of her single huge egg, and hatching it on some far mountain, she once accidentally let fall one that was addled. The stinking contents drowned sixty cities and swept away three hundred cedar-trees.[12]

(*l*) Eventually, the Ziz will share the fate of Leviathan and Behemoth: to be slaughtered and served as food for the righteous.[13]

1. *Psalms* xxii. 22; xcii. 11; *Job* xxxix. 9–10.
2. Agudat Agadot 39; Ginzberg, LJ, I. 30–31.
3. Mid. Tehillim 195, 395, 408.
4. B. Baba Bathra 73b.
5. Gen. Rab. 287; B. Zebahim 113b.
6. See preceding note.
7. Lev. Rab. 22.10; Mid. Tehillim 363; B. Gittin 31b; B. Baba Bathra 25a; Targ. *Job* iii. 6; xxxviii. 36; xxxix. 13; B. Bekhorot 57b; B. Menahot 66b, B. Sukka 5a; B. Yoma 80a; Sifra 1.14; Gen. Rab. 173.
8. B. Hullin 27b; Pesiqta diR. Kahana 35a; Tanhuma Buber Num. 122; Tanhuma Huqqat 6; Num. Rab. 19.3; Eccl. Rab. 7.23; Mid. Konen, 26; Philo, *De Mundi Opif.* 20; PRE, ch. 9; Targ. Yer. *ad Gen.* i. 20.

9. Mid. Konen, 37–38; Mid. Adonay Behokhma, 65–66; Pesiqta Hadta, 48.
10. Mid. Konen, 26; Lev. Rab. 22.10; Gen. Rab. 173; B. Gittin 31a; B. Baba Bathra 25a.
11. B. Baba Bathra 73b.
12. B. Bekhorot 57b; B. Menahot 66b; B. Yoma 80a.
13. Mid. Tehillim 153.

*

1. Balaam, in his blessing, compared God's matchless strength to that of a reem (*Numbers* XXIII. 22; XXIV. 8); and Moses used the same metaphor in his blessing of Joseph (*Deuteronomy* XXXIII. 17). According to Doughty's *Arabia Deserta*, the *reem* of Northern Arabia, though called a 'wild-ox', is a large, very fleet antelope (*beatrix*), whose venison is esteemed above all other by the Bedouin. Because its long, sharp, straight horns can transfix a man, Arab hunters keep at a respectful distance until their shots have wounded it mortally. Leather from a buck's tough hide makes the best sandals; its horns serve as tent-pegs or picks.

Since the Palestinian reem had become extinct by late Biblical times, and single horns from Arabia were imported to Alexandria as rarities, the third century B.C. Septuagint translators rendered 'reem' as *monokerōs*, or 'unicorn'; thus confusing it with the one-horned rhinoceros. Balaam's comparison of God's strength to that of a reem explains later exaggerated accounts of its size. The Noah's Ark story answers a disciple's question: 'Why did the reem, if it were so huge, not drown in the Deluge?'

2. The original meaning of *ziz* (in the phrase *ziz sadai*, or 'ziz of the field'—*Psalms* I. 11 and LXXX. 14) seems to have been 'insects', or possibly 'locusts', from the Akkadian word *zizanu*, or *sisanu*. But when the Septuagint appeared, this had been forgotten, and it was translated in the First Psalm as 'fruit of the field', though in the Eightieth Psalm as 'wild ass'. St. Jerome's Latin Vulgate (completed A.D. 405) altered the Septuagint's 'fruit of the field' to 'beauty of the field'; and 'wild ass' to 'peculiar beast'. The Aramaic Targum and the Talmud, on the other hand, explain *ziz* as *tarnegol bar* ('wild cock'), or *ben netz* ('son of the hawk'), or *sekhwi* ('cock'), or *renanim* ('jubilations') or *bar yokhni* ('son of the nest'); thus connecting it with elaborate Iranian myths about the sacred cock of Avesta, and with the *roc* or *rukh* also called *saēna* or *simurgh*, of the *Arabian Nights* and Persian folklore, which could carry off elephants and rhinoceroses as food for its young. Rashi of Troyes, the eleventh-century scholar, comes closer to the original sense with 'a creeping thing, named *ziz*, because it moves on, *zaz*, from one place to another.'

8

THE FALL OF LUCIFER

(*a*) On the Third Day of Creation God's chief archangel, a cherub by name Lucifer, son of the Dawn ('Helel ben Shahar'), walked in Eden amid blazing jewels, his body a-fire with carnelian, topaz, emerald, diamond, beryl, onyx, jasper, sapphire and carbuncle, all set in purest gold. For awhile Lucifer, whom God had made Guardian of All Nations, behaved discreetly; but soon pride turned his wits. 'I will ascend above the clouds and stars,' he said, 'and enthrone myself on Saphon, the Mount of Assembly, thus becoming God's equal.' God, observing Lucifer's ambitions, cast him down from Eden to Earth, and from Earth to Sheol. Lucifer shone like lightning as he fell, but was reduced to ashes; and now his spirit flutters blindly without cease through profound gloom in the Bottomless Pit.[1]

1. *Isaiah* XIV. 12–15; 2 *Enoch* XXIX. 4–5; *Luke* X. 18; 2 *Cor.* XI. 14; Septuagint and Vulgate to *Isaiah* XIV. 12–17; Targum *Job* XXVIII. 7.

*

1. In *Isaiah* XIV. 12–15, the King of Babylon's pre-ordained fall is compared to that of Helel ben Shahar:

How art thou fallen from heaven,
O Lucifer son of the Dawn!
How art thou cast down to the ground,
Despoiler of nations!

And thou saidst in thy heart:
'I will ascend to heaven,
Above the stars of El
Will I lift my throne;
I will sit on the Mount of Meeting,
In the utmost North.

'I will ascend above the hills of cloud;
I will be like unto the Most High!'

Yet thou art brought down to Sheol,
To the bottomless abyss.

This short reference suggests that the myth was familiar enough not to need telling in full: for Isaiah omits all details of the archangel's punishment by God (here named *Elyon*, 'the Most High'), who resented rivals in glory. Ezekiel (XXVIII. 11–19) is more explicit when he makes a similar prophecy against the King of Tyre, though omitting Lucifer's name:

Moreover the word of the Lord came unto me, saying:
'Son of man, take up a lamentation upon the King of Tyrus, and say unto him: "Thus saith the Lord God: Thou sealest up the sum full of wisdom, and perfect in beauty.
'"Thou hast been in Eden, the garden of God; every precious stone was thy covering, the sardius, the topaz, and the diamond, the beryl, the onyx, and the jasper, the sapphire, the emerald, and the carbuncle, and gold: the workmanship of thy tabrets and of thy pipes was prepared for thee in the day that thou wast created.
'"Thou art the anointed cherub that covereth; and I have set thee so: thou wast upon the holy mountain of God; thou hast walked up and down in the midst of the stones of fire.
'"Thou wast perfect in thy ways from the day that thou wast created, till iniquity was found in thee.
'"By the multitude of thy merchandise they have filled the midst of thee with violence, and thou hast sinned: therefore I will cast thee as profane out of the mountain of God: and I will destroy thee, O covering cherub, from the midst of the stones of fire.
'"Thine heart was lifted up because of thy beauty, thou hast corrupted thy wisdom by reason of thy brightness: I will cast thee to the ground, I will lay thee before kings, that they may behold thee.
'"Thou hast defiled thy sanctuaries by the multitude of thine iniquities, by the iniquity of thy traffic; therefore will I bring forth a fire from the midst of thee, it shall devour thee, and I will bring thee to ashes upon the earth in the sight of all them that behold thee.
'"All they that know thee among the people shall be astonished at thee: thou shalt be a terror, and never shalt thou be any more."'

2. Helel ben Shahar was originally the planet Venus, the last proud star to defy sunrise: a simple Hebrew allegory which has, however, been combined with the myth of Phaethon's fall—burned to death when he presumptuously drove his father Helius's sun-chariot. This myth, though Greek, seems to have originated in Babylon where, every year, a masterless sun-chariot symbolizing the demise of the Crown—during which a boy-

surrogate occupied the royal throne for a single day—careered through the city streets. The surrogate, a favourite of the Goddess Ishtar (who controlled the planet Venus) was afterwards sacrificed. Isaiah seems, therefore, to be prophesying that the king must suffer the same death as his surrogate. In Greek myth, Phaethon son of Apollo became identified with a namesake, Phaethon son of Eos ('Dawn'); according to Hesiod, the Goddess Aphrodite (Ishtar) carried him off to guard her temple. Ezekiel's King of Tyre worshipped Ishtar and watched boys being burned alive as surrogates of the God Melkarth ('Ruler of the City').

3. Although *Job* XXXVIII. 7 describes the 'morning stars' singing together, the name 'Helel' occurs nowhere else in Scripture; but Helel's father, Shahar ('Dawn'), appears in *Psalm* CXXXIX. 9 as a winged deity. Ugaritic mythology makes Shahar, or Baal son of El, a twin-brother to Shalem ('Perfect'). The Mountain of the North ('Saphon') which Helel aspired to ascend, can be identified with Saphon, Mount of God, upon which, according to Ugaritic myth, stood Baal's Throne. When Baal was killed by Mot, his sister Anath buried him there. Saphon, or Zaphon, the 5800-foot mountain—now called Jebel Akra—on which the North-Semitic Bull-god El also ruled 'in the midst of his divine assembly', rises near the mouth of the Orontes. The Hittites named it Mount Hazzi, and held it to be the place from where Teshub, the Storm-god, his brother Tashmishu, and his sister Ishtar sighted the terrible stone-giant (the 'diorite man' as some scholars translate it) Ullikummi who planned their destruction; launched their attack against him, and finally defeated him. The Greeks named it Mount Casius, home of the monster Typhon and the she-monster Delphyne who together disarmed Zeus, King of Heaven, and kept him prisoner there in the Corycian Cave until the god Pan subdued Typhon with a great shout and Hermes, god of Cunning, rescued Zeus. The Orontes had been known as 'Typhon'. Saphon was famous for the destructive North winds that whirled from it over Syria and Palestine. All these myths refer to conspiracies against a powerful deity; in the Hebrew alone no mention is made of God's initial discomfiture.

4. Lucifer is identified in the New Testament with Satan (*Luke* X. 18; 2 *Corinthians* XI. 14), and in the Targum with Samael (Targ. ad *Job* XXVIII. 7).

9

THE BIRTH OF ADAM

(*a*) On the Sixth Day, at God's command, Earth was delivered of Adam. And as a woman remains unclean for thirty-three days after the birth of a male child, so likewise did Earth for thirty-three generations—until the reign of King Solomon, before which time God's Sanctuary could not be built at Jerusalem.[1] The elements of fire, water, air and darkness combined in Earth's womb to produce living creatures;[2] yet, though all her offspring were conceived on the First Day, herbs and trees made their appearance on the Third, sea-beasts and birds on the Fifth, land-beasts, creeping things and Man on the Sixth.[3]

(*b*) God did not use earth at random, but chose pure dust, so that Man might become the crown of Creation.[4] He acted, indeed, like a woman who mixes flour with water and sets aside some of the dough as a *halla* offering: for He let a mist moisten the earth, then used a handful of it to create Man, who became the world's first *halla* offering. Being the son of *Adama* ('Earth'), Man called himself 'Adam' in acknowledgement of his origin; or perhaps Earth was called Adama in honour of her son; yet some derive his name from *adom* ('red'), recording that he was formed from red clay found at Hebron in the Damascene Field near the Cave of Machpelah.[5]

(*c*) It is improbable, however, that God used earth from Hebron, this being a less holy site than the summit of Mount Moriah, Earth's very navel, where the Sanctuary now stands: for there Abraham was blessed because of his readiness to sacrifice Isaac. Hence some relate that God commanded the Archangel Michael: 'Bring Me dust from the site of My Sanctuary!' This He gathered into the hollow of His hand and formed Adam, thus binding mankind by natural ties to the mountain on which Abraham would expiate his forefathers' sins.[6]

Some say that God used two kinds of dust for Adam's creation: one gathered from Mount Moriah; the other a mixture culled at the world's four corners and moistened with water drawn from every river and sea in existence. That, to ensure Adam's health, He used male dust and female soil. That Adam's name reveals the formative elements of his creation: its three Hebrew letters being their initials—

epher ('dust'), *dam* ('blood') and *marah* ('gall')—since, unless these are present in equal measure, man sickens and dies.[7]

(*d*) God disdained to fetch Adam's dust Himself, and sent an angel instead—either Michael to Mount Moriah, or Gabriel to the world's four corners. Nevertheless, when Earth gainsaid the angel, knowing that she would be cursed on Adam's account, God stretched forth His own hand.[8]

Some insist that dust for Adam's trunk was brought from Babylonia, for his head from Israel, for his buttocks from the Babylonian fortress of Agma, and for his limbs from certain other lands.[9]

The various colours found in man are a reminder of these different kinds of dust: the red formed Adam's flesh and blood; the black, his bowels; the white, his bones and sinews; the olive-green, his skin.[10]

By using dust from every corner of the world, God has ensured that in whatever land Adam's descendants die, Earth will always receive them back. Otherwise, if an Easterner should travel to the West, or a Westerner to the East, and the hour of his death came upon him, the soil of that region might cry: 'This dust is not mine, nor will I accept it; return, sir, to your place of origin!' But whereas Adam's body was fashioned from terrestrial elements, his soul was fashioned from celestial ones; though some believe that this also proceeded from Earth.[11]

(*e*) The hour at which God created Adam's soul has been much disputed: whether at dawn on the Sixth Day (his body being made a little later), or whether on the Fifth Day before the appearance of sea-beasts; or whether this precious thing was the very first of God's handiworks. Some hold that the creation of Adam's inert clod preceded not only his soul, but even Light itself. They say that God, when about to breathe His spirit into it, paused and reminded Himself: 'If I let Man live and stand up at once, it may later be claimed that he shared My task . . . He must stay as a clod until I have done!' At dusk on the Sixth Day, therefore, the ministering angels asked: 'Lord of the Universe, why have You not yet created Man?' He made answer: 'Man is already created, and lacks only life.' Then God breathed life into the clod, Adam rose to his feet, and the work of Creation ended.[12]

(*f*) God had given Adam so huge a frame that when he lay down it stretched from one end of Earth to the other; and when he stood up, his head was level with the Divine Throne. Moreover, he was of such indescribable beauty that though, later, the fairest of women seemed like apes when compared with Abraham's wife Sarah, and though Sarah would have seemed like an ape when compared with

Eve, yet Eve herself seemed like an ape when compared with Adam, whose heels—let alone his countenance—outshone the sun! Nevertheless, though Adam was made in God's image, yet he too seemed like an ape when compared with God.[13]

(*g*) All living things approached the radiant Adam in awe, mistaking him for their Creator. But as they prostrated themselves at his feet, he rebuked them saying: 'Let us come before God's presence with thanksgiving; let us worship and bow down, kneeling before the Lord our Maker . . .' God was gratified, and sent angels to pay Adam homage in Eden. They bowed submissively, roasted his meat and poured his wine. The envious Serpent alone disobeyed; whereupon God expelled him from His presence.[14]

Some say that all the ministering angels conceived a hatred for Adam, lest he might become God's rival, and tried to scorch him with fire; God, however, spread His hand over Adam and made peace between him and them.[15]

Elsewhere it is told that Adam's huge frame and radiant countenance so amazed the angels that they called him 'Holy One', and flew trembling back to Heaven. They asked God: 'Can there be two divine Powers: one here, the other on Earth?' To calm them, God placed His hand on Adam and reduced his height to a thousand cubits. Later, when Adam disobediently ate from the Tree of Knowledge, God further reduced his stature to a mere hundred cubits.[16]

(*h*) It has been said that God did not shrink Adam's body, but trimmed innumerable flakes off his flesh. Adam complained: 'Why do You diminish me?' God replied: 'I take only to give again. Gather these trimmings, scatter them far and wide: wherever you cast them, there they shall return to dust, so that your seed may fill the whole Earth.'[17]

(*i*) While Adam lay a prostrate clod, stretched immobile across the world, he could nevertheless watch the work of Creation. God also showed him the Righteous Ones who should descend from him—not in vision, but by pre-creating them for his instruction. These Righteous Ones were dwarfed by Adam's frame and, as they thronged about him, some clung to his hair, others to his eyes, ears, mouth and nostrils.[18]

1. Agudat Agadot 77.
2. Gen. Rab. 100; Mid. Agada Gen. 4; cf. Aptowitzer, HUCA VI. 212; Zohar, Gen. 92; Philo, *De Mundi Opif.* 13.
3. *Genesis* I. 9–13, 20–27.
4. *Genesis* II. 6–7; Philo, *De Mundi Opif.* 47; Yer. Shabbat 5b mid.; cf. Tanhuma Buber Gen. 23; Tanh. Noah 1, Wayiqra 53, Metzora 9; Gen. Rab. 126, 160;

Yalqut Makhiri Prov. 20:25; Metzora 69; Baraita diMass. Nidda in Tosephta Atiqta; Abot diR. Nathan 117; Otzar Midrashim 10.

5. Gen. Rab. 156; Num. Rab. 19:63; Mid. Tehillim 74; Pesiqta Rabb. 61b; Pesiqta diR. Kahana 34a, 36b; Mid. Qoheleth 7:27; Mid. Abkir, ed. Marmorstein, 131; Sepher Yuhasin 232; Otzar Midrashim 317; cf. Abot diR. Nathan 119; Josephus Flavius *Ant.* i.1.2; Siegfried, Philo von Alex. 391; Theodoret., Quaest. 60 in Gen.; Dillmann, *Gen.* 53; G. Rosen, ZDMG, 1858:500; Grünbaum, ZDMG, 1877: 299.
6. Gen. Rab. 132; Yer. Nazir 56b top; Mid. Hagadol, Gen. 73; Num. Rab. 4:8; Mid. Tehillim 92; Seder Eliyahu Zuta, 173; PRE, ch. 11 and 20: Apoc. Mos. ed. Tischendorf, 21; Mid. Konen, 27.
7. Targum Yer. *ad Gen.* II. 7; Gen. Rab. 130–31; cf Mid. Abkir, 131; Philo, *De Mundi Opif.* 51; *De Decalogo* 8; *De Somn.* 1:3; Num. Rab. 14:12; Mid. Hagadol Gen. 73, 101; B. Sota 5a; cf. PRE, ch. 12; Otzar Midrashim 164.
8. Mid. Konen, 27; Yerahme'el 15; Ginzberg, LJ, I. 54; V. 71, 72.
9. B. Sanh. 38a–b.
10. Targum Yer. *ad Gen.* II. 7; PRE, ch. 11.
11. PRE, ch. 11; Rashi *ad Gen.* II. 7; Tanhuma Pequde 3; Tanhuma Buber Lev. 33; Gen. Rab. 54, 128; Mid. Tehillim 529.
12. Gen. Rab. 54–56, 199, 230f; Mid. Tehillim 529; Lev. Rab. 14.1: Tanhuma Buber Lev. 32; Yalqut, 34; Liqqutim 2; cf. Ginzberg, LJ, V. 64; Patai, *Adam* I:187.
13. B. Baba Bathra 58a; Lev. Rab. 20.2.
14. PRE, ch. 11; cf. Zohar Gen. 442; Lev. 214; Ephr. Syr. Gen. main part 1; *Schatzhöhle* 4; Hagoren, 40; Vita Adae, 12; B. Sanh. 59b; Abot diR. Nathan 5; Bereshit Rabbati 24; Eldad Hadani, 77 f.
15. Abot diR. Nathan 23.
16. Otzar Midrashim 70f., 428b; BHM iii. 59; Eldad Hadani 66; Hagoren, 40; Sepher Hassidim, 200; B. Hagiga 12a; Gen. Rab. 102, 178; PRE, ch. 11; cf. Lev. Rab. 14.1; 18.2; Pesiqta Rabbati 115b; Tanhuma Buber Lev. 37, etc.
17. Sepher Hassidim, 290.
18. Ex. Rab. 40.3.

*

1. It is doubtful whether the masculine word *Adam* ('man') and the feminine *adama* ('earth') are etymologically related. However, such a relation is implicit in *Genesis* II, and accepted by Midrashic and Talmudic commentators. A less tenuous connexion, first suggested by Quintilian (i. v. 34), exists between the Latin *homo* ('man') and *humus* ('earth'): modern linguists trace both to the ancient Indo-European root which, in Greek, produced *chthon* ('earth'), *chamai* ('on the earth') and *epichthonios* ('human').

2. The myth of Man's creation from earth, clay or dust is widely current. In Egypt, either the God Khnum or the God Ptah created man on a potter's wheel; in Babylonia, either the Goddess Aruru or the God Ea kneaded man from clay. According to a Phocian Greek myth, Prometheus used a certain red clay at Panopeus; what was left there continued for centuries to exude an odour of human flesh.

3. A *halla* was the priest's share in 'the first of your dough' (*Numbers* xv. 17–21); but the rabbis ruled that dough should be subject to the Law only if it amounted to an *omer*, and that the priest's share should be one-twelfth of the whole, or one-twenty-fourth if mixed at a bakery rather than a private dwelling (M. Eduyot i. 2; M. Halla ii. 17).

4. The ancient Hebrews regarded what we call olive-green as the ideal complexion. Thus it is said of Esther, in praise of her beauty, that 'her skin was greenish like the skin of a myrtle.' (B. Megilla 13a).

5. Speculations about Adam's origin vexed Christians and Moslems who knew no Hebrew. According to the Slavonic *Enoch*, based on a Greek original, 'Adam's name comes from the initials of the four principal winds: Anatole, Dysis, Arctos and Mesembria,' because his body was made of dust gathered at the cardinal points of the compass. According to the Syriac *Cave of Treasures*, God's angels saw His right hand stretched across the world, and watched while He took dust, as little as a grain, from the whole earth, and a drop of water from all the waters of the universe, and a little wind from all the air, and a little warmth from all the fire, and placed these four weak elements together into the hollow of His hand, and thus created Adam. The Moslems relate that the angels Gabriel, Michael, Israfil and Azrail brought dust from the four corners of the world, and with it Allah created the body of Adam; to form his head and heart, however, Allah chose dust from a site at Mecca, where the Holy Ka'aba later rose. Mecca is the navel of the earth for Moslems; as Mount Moriah was for the Hebrews; and Delphi for the Greeks.

6. An Arab tradition of Jewish origin agrees that Earth had rebelled against Adam's creation. When Allah sent first Gabriel and then Michael to fetch the necessary dust, she protested on each occasion: 'I invoke Allah against you!' Thereupon he sent the Angel of Death, who swore not to return until he had accomplished the divine will. Earth, fearing his power, let him gather white, black and copper-red dust—hence the different-coloured races of mankind.

7. That God made Adam perfect, although liable to be misled by a wrong exercise of free will, is the main moral of these myths and glosses. It deprives man of an excuse to sin, and justifies God's command to Abraham: 'I am Almighty God, walk before Me and be perfect!' Nevertheless, the origin of evil continued to puzzle the sages. They invented a myth of Eve's seduction by Samael, who begot Cain the murderer on her (see 14. *a*), though *Genesis* specifically makes Adam father Cain as well as Abel.

8. Adam's rebuke to the angels is borrowed from the Ninety-Fifth Psalm.

10

ADAM'S HELPMEETS

(*a*) Having decided to give Adam a helpmeet lest he should be alone of his kind, God put him into a deep sleep, removed one of his ribs, formed it into a woman, and closed up the wound. Adam awoke and said: 'This being shall be named "Woman", because she has been taken *out of man*. A man and a woman shall be one flesh.' The title he gave her was Eve, 'the Mother of All Living'.[1]

(*b*) Some say that God created man and woman in His own image on the Sixth Day, giving them charge over the world;[2] but that Eve did not yet exist. Now, God had set Adam to name every beast, bird and other living thing. When they passed before him in pairs, male and female, Adam—being already like a twenty-year-old man—felt jealous of their loves, and though he tried coupling with each female in turn, found no satisfaction in the act. He therefore cried: 'Every creature but I has a proper mate!', and prayed God would remedy this injustice.[3]

(*c*) God then formed Lilith, the first woman, just as He had formed Adam, except that He used filth and sediment instead of pure dust. From Adam's union with this demoness, and with another like her named Naamah, Tubal Cain's sister, sprang Asmodeus and innumerable demons that still plague mankind. Many generations later, Lilith and Naamah came to Solomon's judgement seat, disguised as harlots of Jerusalem.[4]

(*d*) Adam and Lilith never found peace together; for when he wished to lie with her, she took offence at the recumbent posture he demanded. 'Why must I lie beneath you?' she asked. 'I also was made from dust, and am therefore your equal.' Because Adam tried to compel her obedience by force, Lilith, in a rage, uttered the magic name of God, rose into the air and left him.

Adam complained to God: 'I have been deserted by my helpmeet.' God at once sent the angels Senoy, Sansenoy and Semangelof to fetch Lilith back. They found her beside the Red Sea, a region abounding in lascivious demons, to whom she bore *lilim* at the rate of more than one hundred a day. 'Return to Adam without delay,' the angels said, 'or we will drown you!' Lilith asked: 'How can I return to Adam and live like an honest housewife, after my stay beside the Red Sea?' 'It will be death to refuse!' they answered. 'How can I die,' Lilith asked again, 'when God has ordered me to take charge of all newborn children: boys up to the eighth day of life, that of circumcision; girls up to the twentieth day. None the less, if ever I see your three names or likenesses displayed in an amulet above a newborn child, I promise to spare it.' To this they agreed; but God punished Lilith by making one hundred of her demon children perish daily;[5] and if she could not destroy a human infant, because of the angelic amulet, she would spitefully turn against her own.[6]

(*e*) Some say that Lilith ruled as queen in Zmargad, and again in Sheba; and was the demoness who destroyed Job's sons.[7] Yet she escaped the curse of death which overtook Adam, since they had parted long before the Fall. Lilith and Naamah not only strangle infants but also seduce dreaming men, any one of whom, sleeping alone, may become their victim.[8]

(*f*) Undismayed by His failure to give Adam a suitable helpmeet, God tried again, and let him watch while he built up a woman's anatomy: using bones, tissues, muscles, blood and glandular secretions, then covering the whole with skin and adding tufts of hair in places. The sight caused Adam such disgust that even when this woman, the First Eve, stood there in her full beauty, he felt an invincible repugnance. God knew that He had failed once more, and took the First Eve away. Where she went, nobody knows for certain.[9]

(*g*) God tried a third time, and acted more circumspectly. Having taken a rib from Adam's side in his sleep, He formed it into a woman; then plaited her hair and adorned her, like a bride, with twenty-four pieces of jewellery, before waking him. Adam was entranced.[10]

(*h*) Some say that God created Eve not from Adam's rib, but from a tail ending in a sting which had been part of his body. God cut this off, and the stump—now a useless coccyx—is still carried by Adam's descendants.[11]

(*i*) Others say that God's original thought had been to create two human beings, male and female; but instead He designed a single one with a male face looking forward, and a female face looking back. Again He changed His mind, removed Adam's backward-looking face, and built a woman's body for it.[12]

(*j*) Still others hold that Adam was originally created as an androgyne of male and female bodies joined back to back. Since this posture made locomotion difficult, and conversation awkward, God divided the androgyne and gave each half a new rear. These separate beings He placed in Eden, forbidding them to couple.[13]

1. *Genesis* II. 18–25; III. 20.
2. *Genesis* I. 26–28.
3. Gen. Rab. 17.4; B. Yebamot 63a.
4. Yalqut Reubeni *ad. Gen.* II. 21; IV. 8.
5. Alpha Beta diBen Sira, 47; Gaster, MGWJ, 29 (1880), 553 ff.
6. Num. Rab. 16.25.
7. Targum *ad Job* I. 15.
8. B. Shabbat 151b; Ginzberg, LJ, V. 147–48.
9. Gen. Rab. 158, 163–64; Mid. Abkir 133, 135; Abot diR. Nathan 24; B. Sanhedrin 39a.
10. *Gen.* II. 21–22; Gen. Rab. 161.
11. Gen. Rab. 134; B. Erubin 18a.
12. B. Erubin 18a.
13. Gen. Rab. 55; Lev. Rab. 14.1: Abot diR. Nathan 1.8; B. Berakhot 61a; B. Erubin 18a; Tanhuma Tazri'a 1; Yalqut Gen. 20; Tanh. Buber iii.33; Mid. Tehillim 139, 529.

*

1. The tradition that man's first sexual intercourse was with animals, not women, may be due to the widely spread practice of bestiality among herdsmen of the Middle East, which is still condoned by custom, although figuring three times in the Pentateuch as a capital crime. In the Akkadian *Gilgamesh Epic*, Enkidu is said to have lived with gazelles and jostled other wild beasts at the watering place, until civilized by Aruru's priestess. Having enjoyed her embraces for six days and seven nights, he wished to rejoin the wild beasts but, to his surprise, they fled from him. Enkidu then knew that he had gained understanding, and the priestess said: 'Thou art wise, Enkidu, like unto a god!'

2. Primeval man was held by the Babylonians to have been androgynous. Thus the *Gilgamesh Epic* gives Enkidu androgynous features: 'the hair of his head like a woman's, with locks that sprout like those of Nisaba, the Grain-goddess.' The Hebrew tradition evidently derives from Greek sources, because both terms used in a Tannaitic midrash to describe the bisexual Adam are Greek: *androgynos*, 'man-woman', and *diprosopon*, 'two-faced'. Philo of Alexandria, the Hellenistic philosopher and commentator on the Bible, contemporary with Jesus, held that man was at first bisexual; so did the Gnostics. This belief is clearly borrowed from Plato. Yet the myth of two bodies placed back to back may well have been founded on observation of Siamese twins, which are sometimes joined in this awkward manner. The two-faced Adam appears to be a fancy derived from coins or statues of Janus, the Roman New Year god.

3. Divergences between the Creation myths of *Genesis* I and II, which allow Lilith to be presumed as Adam's first mate, result from a careless weaving together of an early Judaean and a late priestly tradition. The older version contains the rib incident. Lilith typifies the Anath-worship-

ping Canaanite women, who were permitted pre-nuptial promiscuity. Time after time the prophets denounced Israelite women for following Canaanite practices; at first, apparently, with the priests' approval—since their habit of dedicating to God the fees thus earned is expressly forbidden in *Deuteronomy* xxiii. 18. Lilith's flight to the Red Sea recalls the ancient Hebrew view that water attracts demons. 'Tortured and rebellious demons' also found safe harbourage in Egypt. Thus Asmodeus, who had strangled Sarah's first six husbands, fled 'to the uttermost parts of Egypt' (*Tobit* viii. 3), when Tobias burned the heart and liver of a fish on their wedding night.

4. Lilith's bargain with the angels has its ritual counterpart in an apotropaic rite once performed in many Jewish communities. To protect the newborn child against Lilith—and especially a male, until he could be permanently safeguarded by circumcision—a ring was drawn with natron, or charcoal, on the wall of the birthroom, and inside it were written the words: 'Adam and Eve. Out, Lilith!' Also the names Senoy, Sansenoy and Semangelof (meanings uncertain) were inscribed on the door. If Lilith nevertheless succeeded in approaching the child and fondling him, he would laugh in his sleep. To avert danger, it was held wise to strike the sleeping child's lips with one finger—whereupon Lilith would vanish.

5. 'Lilith' is usually derived from the Babylonian-Assyrian word *lilitu*, 'a female demon, or wind-spirit'—one of a triad mentioned in Babylonian spells. But she appears earlier as 'Lillake' on a 2000 B.C. Sumerian tablet from Ur containing the tale of *Gilgamesh and the Willow Tree*. There she is a demoness dwelling in the trunk of a willow-tree tended by the Goddess Inanna (Anath) on the banks of the Euphrates. Popular Hebrew etymology seems to have derived 'Lilith' from *layil*, 'night'; and she therefore often appears as a hairy night-monster, as she also does in Arabian folklore. Solomon suspected the Queen of Sheba of being Lilith, because she had hairy legs. His judgement on the two harlots is recorded in 1 *Kings* iii. 16 ff. According to *Isaiah* xxxiv. 14–15, Lilith dwells among the desolate ruins in the Edomite Desert where satyrs (*se'ir*), reems, pelicans, owls, jackals, ostriches, arrow-snakes and kites keep her company.

6. Lilith's children are called *lilim*. In the *Targum Yerushalmi*, the priestly blessing of *Numbers* vi. 26 becomes: 'The Lord bless thee in all thy doings, and preserve thee from the Lilim!' The fourth-century A.D. commentator Hieronymus identified Lilith with the Greek Lamia, a Libyan queen deserted by Zeus, whom his wife Hera robbed of her children. She took revenge by robbing other women of theirs.

7. The Lamiae, who seduced sleeping men, sucked their blood and ate their flesh, as Lilith and her fellow-demonesses did, were also known as *Empusae*, 'forcers-in'; or *Mormolyceia*, 'frightening wolves'; and described as 'Children of Hecate'. A Hellenistic relief shows a naked Lamia straddling a traveller asleep on his back. It is characteristic of civilizations where

women are treated as chattels that they must adopt the recumbent posture during intercourse, which Lilith refused. That Greek witches who worshipped Hecate favoured the superior posture, we know from Apuleius; and it occurs in early Sumerian representations of the sexual act, though not in the Hittite. Malinowski writes that Melanesian girls ridicule what they call 'the missionary position', which demands that they should lie passive and recumbent.

8. *Naamah*, 'pleasant', is explained as meaning that 'the demoness sang pleasant songs to idols'. *Zmargad* suggest *smaragdos*, the semi-precious aquamarine; and may therefore be her submarine dwelling. A demon named Smaragos occurs in the *Homeric Epigrams*.

9. Eve's creation by God from Adam's rib—a myth establishing male supremacy and disguising Eve's divinity—lacks parallels in Mediterranean or early Middle-Eastern myth. The story perhaps derives iconotropically from an ancient relief, or painting, which showed the naked Goddess Anath poised in the air, watching her lover Mot murder his twin Aliyan; Mot (mistaken by the mythographer for Yahweh) was driving a curved dagger under Aliyan's fifth rib, not removing a sixth one. The familiar story is helped by a hidden pun on *tsela*, the Hebrew for 'rib': Eve, though designed to be Adam's helpmeet, proved to be a *tsela*, a 'stumbling', or 'misfortune'. Eve's formation from Adam's tail is an even more damaging myth; perhaps suggested by the birth of a child with a vestigial tail instead of a coccyx—a not infrequent occurrence.

10. The story of Lilith's escape to the East and of Adam's subsequent marriage to Eve may, however, record an early historical incident: nomad herdsmen, admitted into Lilith's Canaanite queendom as guests (see 16. 1), suddenly seize power and, when the royal household thereupon flees, occupy a second queendom which owes allegiance to the Hittite Goddess Heba.

The meaning of 'Eve' is disputed. *Hawwah* is explained in *Genesis* III. 20 as 'mother of all living'; but this may well be a Hebraicized form of the divine name Heba, Hebat, Khebat or Khiba. This goddess, wife of the Hittite Storm-god, is shown riding a lion in a rock-sculpture at Hattusas—which equates her with Anath—and appears as a form of Ishtar in Hurrian texts. She was worshipped at Jerusalem (see 27. 6). Her Greek name was Hebe, Heracles's goddess-wife.

11

PARADISE

(*a*) Having formed Man from dust, God planted a paradisal garden eastward of Eden and stocked it with trees, whose fruit were blazing jewels, among them the Tree of the Knowledge of Good and Evil. The river that flowed through Eden afterwards divided into four streams. Pishon waters the Land of Havilah where gold, carbuncle and onyx are found; Gihon waters Cush; Tigris runs beyond Assyria; and Euphrates is the fourth. God set Adam here, and permitted him to attend the Divine Assembly.[1]

(*b*) After Adam's expulsion, God appointed the Cherubim, also called 'the Flame of Whirling Swords', to guard Eden.[2]

(*c*) It is disputed where this terrestrial Paradise lies: whether in a desert,[3] or on the Mountain of God;[4] and whether westward or northward, rather than eastward, of Israel. A certain king of Judah once set himself to discover it. He ascended Mount Lebiah, from the summit of which could be heard the sound of whirling swords on the far bank of a river. Having lowered a number of his courtiers into the valley, he told them: 'Follow the sound!' But none came back.[5]

(*d*) Eden has seven gates,[6] and the outermost opens from the Cave of Machpelah at Hebron. Adam came upon it while burying Eve's body there. As he dug, a divine fragrance greeted his nostrils. He dug deeper, hoping to regain his lost abode, but a deafening voice cried 'Halt!'[7] Adam lies buried in the same cave; his spirit still guards the gate of Eden,[8] through which shines a celestial light.[9] The fragrance of Eden once so pervaded the neighbouring field, that Isaac chose it as a place of prayer.[10] For some twenty generations, it also clung to the garments of skin which God gave Adam, and which were handed down to his male descendants in the elder line.

Others claim that the outermost gate of Eden opens from Mount Zion.[11]

(*e*) The first man after Adam who entered Paradise alive was Enoch. He saw the Tree of Life, under whose shade God often rests. Its beauty of gold and crimson transcends all other things created; its crown covers the entire garden; and four streams—of milk, honey, wine and oil—issue from its roots. A choir of three hundred angels tends this Paradise—which some, however, say is situated not on Earth but in the Third Heaven. Isaac, the next man to visit it, studied there three years; and later his son Jacob gained admittance. Yet neither of these recorded what he saw.[12]

(*f*) Moses was taken to Eden by Shamshiel, its guardian angel, who among other wonders showed him seventy jewelled thrones made for the righteous and standing on legs of fine gold, ablaze with sapphires and diamonds. On the largest and costliest sat Father Abraham.[13]

(*g*) After Moses, no mortal was found worthy of Paradise except Rabbi Jehoshua ben Levi, a teacher of exceptional piety,[14] who entered by means of the following ruse. When he grew very old, God commanded the Angel of Death to grant him a dying wish; Jehoshua thereupon asked for a view of his appointed place in Paradise, but before they set out, side by side, demanded the Angel's sword—'lest, by some mischance, you may frighten me to death.' The Angel handed him the sword and, when they reached Paradise, set Jehoshua astride the boundary wall, saying: 'Look down! Yonder is your appointed place.'

Jehoshua then leaped from the wall, and though the Angel seized hold of his cloak, trying to haul him back, vowed that he would stay. When God's ministering angels complained to Him: 'This man has taken Paradise by storm,' He answered: 'Go and enquire whether Jehoshua ever broke a vow while in the world; if not, let him likewise be true to this one.' They went, enquired, and reported: 'He has kept every vow.' 'Then he shall stay,' God pronounced.

The Angel of Death, seeing that he had been outwitted, asked for his stolen sword. This Jehoshua withheld, well aware that the Angel could not enter Paradise. A divine voice then cried: 'Restore the sword for his needs!' Jehoshua answered: 'Lord, I will do so, if he swears never to draw it when You take a man's soul. Hitherto he has slaughtered his victims like beasts, even children in their mothers' bosoms.' The Angel renounced this savage practice, and Jehoshua gave him back the sword.

Thereupon Elijah commanded the righteous: 'Make room! Make room!' and Jehoshua, going farther into Paradise, saw God seated among thirteen companies of the righteous. God asked: 'Jehoshua ben Levi, have you ever beheld the rainbow?' He answered: 'Lord of the Universe, what person of my age has been refused this great sight?' God smiled and said: 'Are you not Jehoshua ben Levi?' For while a single truly pious man is alive on earth, the Rainbow no longer needs to remind God of His promise, made in Noah's day, that he would never again flood the whole world as a punishment of its wickedness. God knew that Jehoshua, not having seen a rainbow in all his life, had evaded this question to avoid the sin of presumption.

The Angel of Death then lodged a complaint against Jehoshua with the sage Gamaliel. Gamaliel said: 'Jehoshua did well! Now go back and tell him to survey Eden and its treasure houses, and make a report for me. Especially I wish to know whether there are Gentiles in Paradise, and whether there are Children of Israel in Hell.'

This mission the Angel of Death carried out; and Jehoshua reported to Gamaliel as follows: 'Paradise has seven gates, each leading to the next. The First House, facing the entrance, holds converts who came to God of their own free will. Its walls are crystal, its beams cedar, and Obadiah the righteous prophet rules over it.

'The Second House is similarly built, and holds the penitents of Israel. Manasseh ben Hizkiyahu rules over it.

'The Third House is of silver and gold. There grows the Tree of Life, under whose shade sit Abraham, Isaac and Jacob, the patriarchs of the twelve tribes, all those Israelites who went out of Egypt, and the whole generation of the Wilderness; also King David, his son Solomon as all the kings of Judah—except Manasseh, who lies in Hell. Moses and Aaron guard this house, which contains fine silver vessels, costly oils, couches, stools, canopies, and candelabra of gold, pearls and precious stones.

'When I asked: "For whom are these preserved?", King David answered: "For the righteous of Israel, dwelling in the world whence you came." And when I asked again: "Are any of Esau's descendants here?", he answered: "No, for if one such performs a good deed, God rewards him while he yet lives, but at the end he inherits Hell; whereas among the Children of Israel, every man receives his punishment while he yet lives, but afterwards wins a place in Paradise—unless he causes Israel to sin, as did King Manasseh."

'The Fourth House is built of gold, its beams are olive wood, and holds the righteous whose lives were bitter as the unripe olive.

'The Fifth House, through which Gihon flows, is built of silver, crystal, pure gold and glass. Its beams are gold and silver, and the fragrance of Lebanon pervades every hall. Here I saw silver and golden couches, sweet spices, with red and purple cloths woven by Eve; also scarlet yarn, and goat's hair braided by angels; and here dwell the Messiah son of David, and Elijah. When the Messiah asked me: "How do the Children of Israel spend their time in the world whence you come?", I replied: "In hourly preparation for your coming." At this he wept.

'The Sixth House holds those who have died while performing their duty to God.

'The Seventh House holds those who have died of grief for Israel's sins.'[15]

(*h*) Some say that the inhabitants of Paradise stand on their heads and walk on their hands; as do all the dead. If a sorcerer summons a dead spirit by conjuration, it always appears upside-down; unless summoned by order of a king—as the witch of En-Dor summoned Samuel at Saul's demand—whereupon it stands on its feet to show respect for royalty.[16]

(*i*) When Adam was expelled from Eden, God let him take away certain spices, namely saffron, nard, sweet calamus and cinnamon; also a few Paradisal seeds and cuttings of fruit trees, for his own use.[17]

Moses built the Tabernacle with wood fetched by Adam out of Paradise.[18]

1. *Genesis* II. 8–14; *Ezekiel* XXVIII. 13.
2. Philo, *De Mundi Opif.* 60.
3. *Isaiah* LI. 3; *Joel* II. 3.
4. *Ezekiel* XXVIII. 16.
5. Shet b. Yefet, *Hem'at ha-Hemda* 14a.
6. BHM, ii. 52; Yalqut, Gen. 20; Zohar Hadash, p. 41.
7. Zohar Hadash, Midrash Ruth, p. 158 (beginning "weamar R. Rahumai").
8. Zohar Hadash, p. 41.
9. Zohar Genesis 250b.
10. Zohar Exodus 39b.
11. Gen. Rab. 744; PRE, ch. 20; Targum Yer. *Genesis* III. 23.
12. Perek Shirah; Midrash Shir 42a; Seder Gan Eden 132–33, 194; cf. Slavonic Enoch (2 *Enoch*) VIII; *Apoc. Mosis* XXXVII; Yalqut Shir 982.
13. Wertheimer, Bate Midrashot i. 284–85.
14. B. Ketubot 77b.
15. BHM, ii.28–30, 48–50.
16. *Genesis* XXIV. 65; Tanhuma Buber Lev. 82; Lev. Rab. 26.7; and medieval sources cited by Ginzberg LJ, V. 263.
17. *Apoc. Mosis* XXIX; *Adamschriften* 16; Mid. Tehillim 445, note 66.
18. Joshua b. Shu'aib, Derashot al haTorah, Constantinople, 1523, end of Terumah; referring to *Exodus* XXVI. 15 ff.

*

1. For the origin of the Paradise concept common to Europe, the Orient, Central and North America, and Polynesia—see Chapter 12.

2. Adam's terrestrial Paradise, the Garden of Eden, was speculatively located first on the 'Mountain of God', Mount Saphon in Syria; next at Hebron, once the most fertile valley of Southern Palestine and famous for its oracular shrine; then at Jerusalem, after King David had moved his capital there from Hebron; and during the Babylonian captivity, at the

head of the Persian Gulf—a delta watered by four main streams: Tigris, Euphrates, Choaspes, and the Pallakopas Canal. The wording of *Genesis* II. 8, 'God planted a garden eastward *in* Eden,' and 10, 'a river went out of Eden to water the garden,' made for geographical confusion. Some understood 'Eden' as the central part of the garden; others, as the region enclosing the garden. Further confusion persuaded some Babylonian Jews to identify Eden with Beth Eden (*Amos* I. 5; *Ezekiel* XXVII. 23), the Bit Adini of Assyrian inscriptions, which flourished in the tenth and ninth centuries B.C. Beth Eden lay in Armenia, the presumed source not only of the Tigris and Euphrates, but of the Nile—Alexander the Great held this view—and of the Orontes (Pishon?), which is the main river of Havilah (Northern Syria?), as the Nile is of Egypt (Cush). Josephus and the Septuagint (*Jeremiah* II. 18) equate the Gihor with the Nile. Some read Havilah as Central Arabia, though it lacks rivers; since Havilah appears in *Genesis* X. 7 as a son of Cush, and a descendant of Shem through Yoqtan.

3. Homer makes the same association of Paradise with rewards and punishments in the *Odyssey* (iv. 561), describing the Elysian Fields and 'the verge of the world where fair-haired Rhadamanthus rules, and life is easiest for man; no snow falls there, nor any violent storms, nor rain at any time, but Oceanus ever sends forth the clear, shrill blast of the West Wind to refresh mankind.' Rhadamanthus was one of the Infernal Judges. According to Josephus, the Essenes of the Dead Sea coast also believed that after death the righteous went to a Western region where they were untroubled by rain, frost or heat, but enjoyed continuous cool sea breezes. The wicked, however, were confined to a dark, chilly Hell, and there suffered endless punishment—as in the Greek Tartarus.

For the absence of all Esau's descendants from Paradise, see 38. 5 and 40. 3.

4. 'Mount Lebiah' means 'Mountain of the Lioness'. Its location is unknown. The two cherubim who guarded Eden with their whirling swords were probably swastikas (fire-wheels) painted on the gate as a warning to mankind that the garden lay under taboo.

5. Jehoshua ben Levi was head of the Lydda Rabbinic School during the early third century A.D., and hero of many edifying anecdotes.

6. The upside-down appearance of the dead is probably deduced from a view that ghosts assume a pre-natal posture in hope of re-birth (see 36. *a*, end).

7. A reference to what seems an older version of the *Genesis* Paradise myth occurs in *Job* XV. 7–8:

Art thou the first man that was born?
Wast thou brought forth before the hills?
Dost thou hearken in the council of Eloah?
And hast thou stolen wisdom for thyself?

According to this passage, Adam was born before the hills were formed, attended the Divine Assembly and, ambitious for still greater glory, stole wisdom—thereby doing of his own accord what, in the *Genesis* version, Eve and the subtle serpent persuaded him to do. His theft recalls the Greek myth of the Titan Prometheus who stole fire from heaven as a gift for mankind, whom he himself had created, and suffered fearful punishment at the hands of Almighty Zeus.

12

THE FALL OF MAN

(*a*) God permitted Adam and Eve, his wife, to eat fruit from every tree in Eden except the Tree of Knowledge of Good and Evil, which it would be death to taste or even touch. The Serpent who was there subtly asked Eve: 'Has God not forbidden you to eat any fruit whatsoever?' She answered: 'No, but he warned us on pain of death to abstain from a certain tree in the middle of this garden.' The Serpent cried: 'Then God has deceived you! Its fruit does not cause death, but only confers wisdom: He is keeping you in ignorance.' Thus Eve was persuaded to taste the fruit, and made Adam do likewise.[1]

(*b*) When they had eaten, Adam and Eve looked at each other and, suddenly understanding that they were naked, plucked fig-leaves and sewed them into aprons. They heard God walking through the garden at dusk, and hid among the trees. God called: 'Adam!', and again: 'Adam, where are you?' Adam looked out from his hiding-place and said: 'I heard Your approach, Lord, and hid my nakedness for shame.' God asked: 'Who told you of nakedness? Have you then eaten fruit of the forbidden tree?' Adam answered: 'Eve gave me fruit from the tree, and I ate it.' God turned to Eve: 'Alas, woman, what have you done?' She sighed, saying: 'The Serpent tricked me.' God cursed the Serpent: 'You shall lose your legs, and writhe upon your belly for ever, eating dust! I set a lasting enmity between you and woman. Her children will stamp on your children's heads until their heels are bruised.'[2]

Then He cursed Eve: 'I will multiply your labour and sorrow; you shall bear children in pain; you shall yearn for your husband, and be ruled by him!'

(*c*) His next curse fell upon Adam: 'Because you have listened to Eve rather than to Me, I curse the soil that you must now till all the days of your life, eating bread in the sweat of your brow, struggling to uproot thorns and thistles. And at length death shall return your body to the dust from which I formed it!'[3]

(*d*) Since aprons of fig-leaves were too fragile for such hard labour, God mercifully made Adam and Eve garments of skin. But He said to Himself: 'This man has become like a god in his knowledge of good and evil! What if he were to pluck the fruit hanging on the Tree of Life, and live eternally?' With that, He drove Adam out of Eden, posting at its East Gate certain cherubim called 'the Flame of Whirling Swords', to bar his way.[4]

(*e*) The Serpent had rudely thrust Eve against the Tree of Knowledge, saying: 'You have not died after touching this tree; neither will you die after eating its fruit!' He also said: 'All former beings are ruled by the latest beings. You and Adam, created last of all, rule the world; eat therefore and be wise, lest God send new beings to usurp your rule!' As Eve's shoulders touched the tree, she saw Death approaching. 'Now I must die,' she groaned, 'and God will give Adam a new wife! Let me persuade him to eat as I do, so that if we must both die, we shall die together; but if not, we shall live together.' She plucked a fruit and ate, then tearfully pleaded with Adam until he agreed to share it.[5]

(*f*) Eve later persuaded all beasts and birds to taste the fruit—or all except the prudent phoenix, which has remained immortal ever since.[6]

(*g*) Adam wondered at Eve's nakedness: because her glorious outer skin, a sheet of light smooth as a finger-nail, had fallen away.[7] Yet though the beauty of her inner body, shining like a white pearl, entranced him, he fought for three hours against the temptation to eat and become as she was; holding the fruit in his hand meanwhile. At last he said: 'Eve, I would rather die than outlive you. If Death were to claim your spirit, God could never console me with another woman equalling your loveliness!' So saying, he tasted the fruit, and the outer skin of light fell away from him also.[8]

(*h*) Some hold that Adam, by eating the fruit, won the gift of prophecy;[9] but that, when he tried to pluck leaves for an apron, the trees drove him off, crying: 'Begone, thief, who disobeyed your Creator! You shall have nothing from us!' Nevertheless, the Tree of Knowledge let him take what he wished—they were fig-leaves—approving his preference of wisdom to immortality.[10]

(*i*) Others make the Tree of Knowledge an immense wheat stalk, taller than a cedar; or a vinestock; or a citron-tree, whose fruit is used in celebration of Tabernacles. But Enoch reports that it was a date-palm.[11]

(*j*) According to some, the garments God gave Adam and Eve resembled fine Egyptian linens from Beth Shean, that mould themselves to the body;[12] according to others they were of goat-skin, or coney-skin, or Circassian wool, or camel's hair, or of the Serpent's slough.[13] Others again say that Adam's garment was a High-priestly robe, bequeathed by him to Seth; who bequeathed it to Methuselah; whose heir was Father Noah. Although his first-born son, Japheth, should have inherited this robe, Noah foresaw that the Children of Israel would spring from Shem, to whom therefore he entrusted it. Shem gave the robe to Abraham who, as God's beloved servant, could claim the first-born's right; Abraham to Isaac; Isaac to Jacob. It then passed to Reuben, Jacob's first-born son; and so the legacy continued, generation after generation, until the privilege of offering up sacrifices was taken by Moses from the first-born of Reuben's house, and given to Aaron the Levite.[14]

(*k*) Adam and Eve were driven out of Eden on the First Friday, the day in which they had both been created and had sinned. On the First Sabbath, Adam rested and prayed God for mercy. At its close he went to the Upper Gihon, strongest of rivers, and there did seven weeks' penance, standing in midstream with water to the chin, until his body turned soft as a sponge.[15]

(*l*) Afterwards an angel came to Adam's comfort, and taught him the use of fire-tongs and a smith's hammer; also how to manage oxen, so that he should not fall behindhand in his ploughing.[16]

1. *Genesis* III. 1–6.
2. *Genesis* III. 7–13.
3. *Genesis* III. 14–19.
4. *Genesis* III. 20–24.
5. PRE, ch. 13; Gen. Rab. 172–74; B. Sanhedrin 29a; *Adamschriften*, 28.
6. PRE, ch. 14; Gen. Rab. 196.
7. Sources same as in preceding footnote.
8. *Adamschriften*, 28–29.
9. Gen. Rab. 200–01; Yalqut Gen. 34.
10. Gen. Rab. 139–42.
11. Sources same as in preceding footnote, and Ginzberg LJ, V. 97–98.
12. Gen. Rab. 196; Tanhuma Buber Gen. 17–18.
13. Sources same as in preceding footnote.
14. Tanhuma Buber Gen. 133; Num. Rab. 4.8.
15. Yalqut Gen. 34.
16. *Adamschriften*, 24, 33.

*

1. Some elements of the Fall of Man myth in *Genesis* are of great antiquity; but the composition is late, and even in places suggests Greek influence. The *Gilgamesh Epic*, the earliest version of which can be dated about 2000 B.C., describes how the Sumerian Love-goddess Aruru created from clay a noble savage named Enkidu, who grazed among

gazelles, slaked his thirst beside wild cattle and sported with dolphins—until a priestess sent to him by Gilgamesh initiated him into the mysteries of love. Though wise as a god, he was now shunned by the wild creatures; and the priestess therefore covered his nakedness, using part of her own garment, and brought him to the city of Uruk, where he became blood-brother to the hero Gilgamesh. Later, Gilgamesh went in quest of the herb of immortality. He entered a gloomy tunnel twelve leagues long, and emerged in a paradise of jewel-hung trees owned by Siduri, Goddess of Wisdom. Declining the Sun-god's invitation to remain, Gilgamesh pressed on, until he learned from Utnapishtim (the Sumerian Noah) that the desired herb—a plant resembling buckthorn—grew deep under the sea. Gilgamesh tied stones to his feet, plunged down, found the herb and brought it safely back; but a serpent stole it from him when he visited a fresh-water spring. He sadly resigned himself to death.

2. Adam calls Eve 'the Mother of All Living', (*Genesis* III. 20) a title of this same Love-goddess Aruru, or Ishtar; and she confers wisdom on him, just as Aruru's priestess did on Enkidu. Since, however, the Babylonian legend of Marduk as Creator had, centuries before, succeeded the Sumerian legend of Aruru as Creatrix, the Hebrew Creator is made to punish Eve for enlightening the innocent Adam.

3. Another source of the *Genesis* Fall of Man is the Akkadian myth of Adapa, found on a tablet at Tell Amarna, Pharaoh Akhenaten's capital. Adapa, son of Ea, the Babylonian god of Wisdom, was attacked in the Persian Gulf by a Storm-bird while catching fish for his father's priests, and broke its wing. The bird proved to have been the South Wind. Ea summoned Adapa to explain his violence and warned him that, having displeased Anu, King of Heaven; the gods would offer him the food and drink of death, which he must refuse. Anu, however, learning of this indiscreet disclosure, foiled Ea by offering Adapa the bread of life and the water of life and, when he refused them at his father's orders, grimly sending him back to earth as a perverse mortal. This myth supplies the theme of the Serpent's warning to Eve: that God had deceived her about the properties of the forbidden fruit.

4. Another possible source of the *Genesis* Fall of Man is an ancient Persian myth: Meshia and Meshiane at first live on fruit alone, but are then persuaded by the Demon Ahriman to deny God. They lose their purity, fell trees, kill animals, and commit further evil.

5. According to a Cretan myth quoted by Apollodorus and Hyginus, and a Lydian myth quoted by Pliny, serpents possessed a herb of immortality.

6. The *Genesis* story, in which agricultural work is represented as a curse laid upon man because of Eve's inquisitiveness and disobedient mischief, mythically expresses the age-old Mediterranean point of view which regards physical labour (symbolized and exemplified by tillage of the soil)

as an unmitigated and unavoidable hardship. This view continues to be shared in the Middle East, not only by the nomads who regard fellahin as 'slaves of the soil', but by most of the agricultural population itself. It was held, even before the Creation story received its final shape, by a bitter Greek farmer, Hesiod, who was the first writer to regard agriculture as an evil laid upon mankind by ruthless gods. An entirely different view is expressed by the Greek myth of Triptolemus: whom Demeter rewards for his father's sake by initiating him into the mysteries of agriculture, which he rides out through the world to teach, mounted on a serpent-drawn chariot.

7. Eden as a peaceful rural retreat, where man lives at his ease among wild animals, occurs not only in the story of Enkidu but in Greek and Latin legends of the Golden Age, and must be distinguished from the jewelled paradise which Gilgamesh and Isaiah's Helel visited (see 8. *a*). The terrestrial paradise represents a jaded city-dweller's nostalgia for simple country joys, or a dispirited labourer's for the fruit-eating innocence of childhood; the celestial paradise is enjoyed in a schizophrenetic trance, induced either by asceticism, by glandular disturbance, or by use of hallucinogenetic drugs.

8. It is not always possible to judge which of these causes produced the mystic visions of, say, Ezekiel, 'Enoch', Jacob Boehme, Thomas Traherne and William Blake. Yet jewelled gardens of delight are commonly connected in myth with the eating of an ambrosia forbidden to mortals; and this points to a hallucinogenetic drug reserved for a small circle of adepts, which gives them sensations of divine glory and wisdom. The Gilgamesh reference to buckthorn must be a blind, however—buckthorn was eaten by ancient mystics not as an illuminant but as a preliminary purgative. Soma, the Indian ambrosia, is said to be still in secret use among Brahmans.

9. All gardens of delight are originally ruled by goddesses; at the change from matriarchy to patriarchy, male gods usurp them. A serpent is almost always present. Thus, in Greek myth, the Garden of the Hesperides, whose apple-trees bore golden fruit, was guarded by the Serpent Ladon, and had been Hera's demesne before she married Zeus, though her enemy Heracles eventually destroyed Ladon with Zeus's approval. The jewelled Sumerian paradise to which Gilgamesh went, was owned by Siduri, Goddess of Wisdom, who had made the Sun-god Shamash its guardian; in later versions of the epic, Shamash has degraded Siduri to a mere 'ale-wife' serving at a near-by tavern. Indra, the leading Aryan god, appears to have borrowed a new form of soma from the variously named Indian Mother-goddess.

10. A paradise whose secrets have lately been revealed is the Mexican Tlalócan—a picture of which Heim and Wasson reproduce from the Tepantitla fresco in *Les Champignons Hallucinogènes du Mexique*. It shows a spirit, branch in hand, weeping for joy on entering an orchard of fantasti-

cally bright fruit-trees and flowers, watered by a river, full of fish, flowing from the mouth of a divine toad. This is the God Tlalóc, who corresponds closely with the Greek Dionysus, and whom his sister Chalcioluthlicue has made co-ruler of her paradise. In the foreground lie irrigation canals over which four mushrooms meet to form a cross denoting the cardinal points of the compass. Behind the spirit rises a spotted serpent—Tlalóc in another aspect; a flowery dragon and huge coloured butterflies hover aloft. The hallucinogenetic drug inducing this vision was a toxic mushroom, still ritually eaten in several provinces of Mexico. *Psilocybin,* the active agent, is now ranked by psychiatrists with lysergic acid and mescalin as among the leading psychodelotics—'revealers of man's inner self'.

11. Hallucinogenetic mushrooms are common throughout Europe and Asia. Some varieties, which do not lose their toxic qualities when cooked, seem to have been introduced into sacred cakes eaten at Greek Mysteries; and also at Arabian Mysteries, since the Arabic root *ftr* occurs in words meaning 'toadstool', 'sacrificial bread', and 'divine ecstasy'. Perseus went to the jewelled Garden of the Hesperides aided by Athene, goddess of Wisdom and, according to Pausanias, later built and named Mycenae in honour of a mushroom found growing on the site, from which flowed a pool of water. That the Indian paradise closely resembles these others suggests that soma is a sacred mushroom disguised in food or drink—not, as most authorities hold, a variety of milkweed; and the ancient Chinese reverence for a 'Mushroom of Wisdom' may have its origin in a similar cult.

12. The fervent love between Enkidu and the priestess, though omitted from the *Genesis* story, has been preserved by a Talmudic scholiast who makes Adam wish for death rather than be parted from Eve. Yet the myth of the Fall licences man to blame woman for all his ills, make her labour for him, exclude her from religious office and refuse her advice on moral problems.

13. Ambrosia-eaters often enjoy a sense of perfect wisdom, resulting from a close co-ordination of their mental powers. Since 'knowledge of good and evil', in Hebrew, means 'knowledge of all things, both good and evil', and does not refer to the gift of moral choice, the 'Tree of Life' may have once been the host-tree of a particular hallucinogenetic mushroom. For example, the birch is host to the *amanita muscaria* sacramentally eaten by certain Palaeo-Siberian and Mongol tribes.

14. An addition to the story of Adam's penance occurs in the tenth-century Irish *Saltair na Rann,* based on an earlier Syrian *Life of Adam and Eve* evidently drawn from Hebrew sources: he fasts in Jordan, not Gihon, with water to his chin and, as a reward, God lets Raphael give him certain mystical secrets. According to this text, God created Adam at Hebron; which may be a pre-Exilic version of the myth. Some Byzantine writers make Adam repent only in his six-hundredth year.

15. The Serpent is widely regarded as an enemy of man, and of woman (see 13 and 14).

13

SAMAEL'S REBELLION

(*a*) Some say that the Serpent of Eden was Satan in disguise: namely the Archangel Samael. He rebelled on the Sixth Day, driven by an overwhelming jealousy of Adam, whom God had ordered the whole host of Heaven to worship. The Archangel Michael complied without delay., but Samael said: 'I will not worship any lesser being! When Adam was made, I had already been perfected. Let him rather worship me!' Samael's angels agreed, and Michael warned them: 'Beware of God's anger!' Samael replied: 'If He show anger, I will set a throne above the stars and proclaim myself the Highest.' Then Michael flung Samael out of Heaven and down to earth, where he nevertheless continued to scheme against God's will.[1]

(*b*) Others say that when all the angels had obediently fallen at Adam's feet, Samael addressed God: 'Lord of the Universe, You created us from the splendour of Your Glory. Shall we then adore a being formed from dust?' God replied: 'Yet this creature, though formed from dust, surpasses you in wisdom and understanding.' Samael challenged Him: 'Test us!' God said: 'I have created beasts, birds and creeping things. Go down, and set them all in line; and if you can name them as I would have them named, Adam shall reverence your wisdom. But if you fail, and he succeeds, you must reverence his.'

In Eden, Adam did obeisance to Samael, whom he mistook for God. God, however, pulled him upright and asked Samael: 'Will you be the first to name these beasts, or will Adam?' He answered: 'I will, being both elder and wiser.' God thereupon set oxen before him, inquiring: 'How are these named?' When Samael stood silent, God removed the oxen. He fetched a camel, and afterwards an ass, but Samael could not name either.

God then planted understanding in Adam's heart, and spoke in such a manner that the first letter of each question pointed to the beast's name. Thus He took oxen, saying: 'Open your lips, Adam, and tell me their name!' Adam answered: 'Oxen.' God next showed him a camel, saying: 'Come, tell me the name of this!' Adam answered: 'Camel.' Lastly God showed him an ass: 'And can you name this also?' Adam answered: 'It is an ass.'

When Samael saw that God had enlightened Adam, he yelled indignantly. 'Do you yell?' God asked. 'How should I not,' replied Samael, 'when You have created me from Your Glory, and afterwards bestow understanding on a creature formed from dust?'

God said: 'O evil Samael, are you astonished at Adam's wisdom? Yet he will now foresee the birth of his descendants, and give every one his own name, until the Last Days!'[2] With that, He hurled Samael and his attendant angels from Heaven. Samael clutched at Michael's wings, and would have dragged him down too, had God not intervened.[3]

(*c*) Some allege that Satan was not Samael, but the oxlike Prince of Darkness who had opposed God's creative will even before He commanded 'Let there be light!' When God said: 'Away! I will create My world in light!', the Prince asked: 'Why not from darkness?' God replied: 'Beware, lest I subdue you with a shout!' The Prince, loth to acknowledge himself God's inferior, feigned deafness. Whereupon God's shout subdued him, as He had threatened.[4] Samael and his angels were banished to a dark dungeon, where they still languish, their faces haggard, their lips sealed; and are now known as the Watchers.[5] In the Last Days, the Prince of Darkness will declare himself God's equal, and claim to have taken part in Creation, boasting: 'Though God made Heaven and Light, I made Darkness and the Pit!' His angels will support him; but the fires of Hell shall quench their arrogance.[6]

1. *Vita Adae* XIII. 1–16; cf. *Hebrews* I. 6; *Rev.* XII. 7–9; XX. 1–7.
2. Bereshit Rabbati, 24–25. Cf. Gen. Rab. 155–56, where Adam's rivals are the ministering angels.
3. PRE, ch. 27; Bereshit Rabbati, 70.
4. Pesiqta Rabbati, 95a, 203a; Yalqut Reubeni *ad Gen.* I. 3, vol. I. 19.
5. 2 *Enoch* XVIII. 1–6; cf. also chapter VII.
6. Mid. Alphabetot 434.

*

1. 'Samael', though said to mean 'Venom of God', is more likely a cacophemism for 'Shemal', a Syrian deity. In Hebrew myth, Samael occupies an ambiguous position, being at once 'chief of all Satans' and 'the greatest prince in Heaven' who rules angels and planetary powers. The title 'Satan' ('enemy') identified him both with Helel, 'Lucifer, son of Dawn', another fallen angel; and with the Serpent who in the Garden of Eden plotted Adam's downfall. Some Jews (Ginzberg, LJ, V. 85) also hold that he had

planned to create another world, which identifies him with the Gnostic 'Cosmocrator' or 'Demiurge'. The Orphic Greek Cosmocrator Ophion, or Ophioneus, was also a serpent (see 1. *10*).

2. Adam's naming of the beasts is a tale derived perhaps from a myth of how the alphabet was invented: the first and third Hebrew letters being *aleph* and *gimmel*, namely 'ox' and 'camel'.

3. That darkness (*hoshekh*) had existed long before Creation not as a mere absence of light, but as a positive entity, was believed by all Middle Eastern and Mediterranean peoples. The Greeks spoke of their 'Mother Night'; the Hebrews of their 'Prince of Darkness', relating him to Tohu (see 2. 3), and placing him in the north. The shout with which God overcame this Prince recalls Pan's when, according to Apollodorus, he subdued Typhon: a monster whose wings darkened the sun, and who also lived in the north, on Mount Saphon (see 8. 3).

4. 'Watchers' (*egrēgorikoi* in Greek), the name given to Satan's angels in the *Second Book of Enoch*, seems to be a rendering of two Aramaic words: *irin*, applied to angels in *Daniel* IV. 10, 14, 20; and *qaddishin*, 'holy ones'. A nearer translation would be 'guardian angels', which agrees both with their functions and the meanings of their names. According to *Midrash Tehillim* on *Psalm* I, *ir* refers to the deity *Eloah*.

14
THE BIRTHS OF CAIN AND ABEL

(*a*) Some say that Samael disguised himself as the Serpent and, after vengefully persuading man to eat from the Tree of Knowledge, fathered Cain upon Eve; thus defiling all the offspring of her subsequent union with Adam. Only when the Children of Israel stood beneath Mount Sinai and received the Law at Moses's hands was this curse finally lifted. It still taints the other nations.[1]

(*b*) According to some accounts, Samael never lay with Eve before Adam had done so. God at first intended Samael to rule the world, but the sight of Adam and Eve coupling, naked and unashamed, made him jealous. He swore: 'I will destroy Adam, marry Eve, and truly rule.' Having waited until Adam had lain with Eve and fallen asleep, he took Adam's place. Eve yielded to him, and conceived Cain.[2]

Soon, however, she repented of her faithlessness and cried tearfully: 'Alas, Adam, I have sinned! Banish me from the light of your life. I will go westward, there to await death.' Three months later, having reached the Ocean, Eve gathered branches and built a hut. When the pangs of labour overcame her, she prayed God for deliverance, but fruitlessly, and could only beg the Sun and Moon to tell Adam of her plight on their next eastward circuit. This they did. Adam hastened to Eve's side and, finding her still in labour, joined his prayers with hers. God sent down twelve angels and two Virtues, led by Michael, who stood at Eve's right hand, stroking her face and breast, until she gave birth.[3]

(*c*) Since the infant Cain's face shone angelically, Eve knew that Adam had not been his father and, in her innocence, exclaimed: 'I have *gotten* a man-child from Yahweh!'[4]

(*d*) Others account for Cain's name by saying that he stood up as soon as born, ran off and brought back a wheat straw, which he gave to Eve; who thereupon called him Cain, which means 'stalk'.[5]

(*e*) Afterwards Eve bore a second son, whom she named Abel, which means 'breath' or, some say, 'vanity' or 'sorrow', foreseeing his early doom.[6] This knowledge came to her in a dream: she saw Cain drinking Abel's blood and refusing his mournful plea to be left a few drops. When Eve told Adam her dream, he said: 'We must part our sons.' Cain therefore grew up as a husbandman, and Abel as a shepherd; each living in his own hut.[7]

(*f*) Some, however, believe that Cain was Abel's twin, begotten on Eve by Adam; their conception being one of the miraculous happenings which occurred on the Sixth Day. In the first hour, God collected Adam's dust; in the second, Adam became an inert clod; in the third, his limbs were stretched out; in the fourth, God breathed a spirit into him; in the fifth, he stood upon his feet; in the sixth, he named the beasts; in the seventh, God gave him Eve; in the eighth, 'two went to bed, and four came out'—since Cain and Abel were twins, immediately conceived; in the ninth, Adam was forbidden to eat fruit from the Tree of Knowledge; in the tenth, he sinned; in the eleventh, he was punished; and in the twelfth, cast out of Eden.[8]

(*g*) Others again hold that the first act of love between Adam and Eve produced at least four children: Cain with his twin sister, Abel with his; or even with two twin sisters.[9]

1. PRE, ch. 21, with textual comments by Luria; Mid. Hagadol Gen. 88–89 and 105; B. Shabbat 146a; B. Yebamot 103b; B. Abodah Zarah 22b; Targum *ad Gen.* IV. 1 and V. 3; Gen. Rab. 182.
2. Tosephta Sota IV. 17–18; Abot diR. Nathan i. 7–8; Gen. Rab. 168–69, 171–72; PRE, ch. 21; Yalqut *ad Gen.* IV. 1, par. 35.
3. *Vita Adae* 18–21.
4. *Vita Adae* 21; *Apoc. of Moses* 1; PRE, ch. 21; *Genesis* IV. 1.
5. *Vita Adae* 21.
6. Josephus, *Ant.* i.2.1; Philo, De Migr. Abrah. 13.
7. *Vita Adae* 22–23; *Apoc. of Moses* 2, ed. Charles ii.138; *Adamschriften*, 7, 42.
8. B. Sanhedrin 38b; cf. Abot diR. Nathan 1st version, end; PRE, ch. 11; Pesiqta diR. Kahana 150b; Lev. Rab. 29, beginning; Pesiqta Rabbati 46; Tanhuma Buber Gen. 28; Tanhuma Shemini 8; Mid. Tehillim 92:3.
9. Gen. Rab. 205, 214, 662; B. Yebamot 62a; Yer. Yebamot 11.4; B. Sanhedrin 38b; Targum Yer. *ad Gen.* IV. 1–2; PRE, ch. 11 and 21; Abot diR. Nathan 1.6; Mid. Hagadol Gen. 106; Yalqut Reubeni 35; Yalqut Psalms 840.

*

1. An alleged desire of divine serpents to impregnate mortal women appears in many mythologies. Sacred serpents kept in Egyptian temples acted as the god's procreative agents. The second *Tanis Papyrus* contains a list of sacred titles given to such beneficent serpents housed in the larger temples. Among the Greeks, too, barren women would lie all night on the floor of Asclepius's temple, hoping that the god would appear in serpent shape and impregnate them during sleep. At the Phrygian Mysteries of Sabazius, women ritually married the god by letting live snakes, or golden replicas, slide between their breasts down to the thighs.

2. Such rites may have originated in an identification of snakes, emerging

from holes underground, with the spirits of dead heroes. These were frequently portrayed as snakes, or half-snakes—among them Cecrops, Erichthonius and Cadmus—and given divine honours, as happened to Asclepius and Sabazius. Alexander the Great believed that he had been fathered on Olympia by Zeus Ammon wearing serpent disguise; and his was not an isolated case. Barren women would also bathe in rivers, hoping for impregnation by the serpentine river-god. Trojan brides bathed in the Scamander, crying: 'Scamander, take my maidenhead!' The Babylonian Ea, as god of the Euphrates, was shown in serpent shape, or riding a serpent.

3. Menstruation is ambivalently regarded by most primitive people as both holy and impure: holy, because marking a girl's readiness for motherhood; impure, because men must avoid contact with menstruous women. Some tribes believe that menstruation results from a snake bite; though snake venom is a coagulant. The myth of Eve's defilement by the Serpent was first told, perhaps, to explain the origin of menstruation: as caused by the lecherous Serpent whose bite made her nubile. According to one Talmudic passage, menstrual pains are among the curses that God laid on Eve.

4. The *Fourth Book of Maccabees* contains evidence for a popular belief that snakes desire intercourse with women. A mother of seven sons tells them proudly that, until marriage, she was a modest virgin whom Satan could not defile in desert or field, nor the smooth-tongued Serpent rob of her maidenhead. This belief continued to be held so strongly that a discussion is recorded in the Talmud as to the best method of safeguarding a woman so threatened:

> *If on seeing a snake, she is unsure whether he lusts after her or not, she should remove her garments and throw them before him. If he coils into them, then he lusts after her; otherwise, not. And if he does so lust after her, she should have congress with her husband in the snake's presence. But, since others hold that the sight may merely increase his desire, she should rather, perhaps, take some nail parings and hair trimmings to throw at him, with the words: 'I am impure!' If a snake has already penetrated her, she should sit on two barrels, her thighs parted. Then let fat meat be thrown on burning coals, and a basket of cress moistened with sweet-smelling wine be set beside the meat; and let a pair of tongs be held in readiness. When the snake smells the good food he will leave her; whereupon he must be seized and burned in the fire, lest he return.*

This recalls the Serpent Samael who, grown jealous from watching Adam and Eve couple, seduced her.

5. Michael led the hosts of Heaven against the false Cosmocrator (a planetary power of the Fourth Day—like Nabu in Babylonia, and Thoth in

Egypt) because he had been appointed Archangel of that day. Among the Greeks, Hermes ('Mercury') held the same planetary power and had, with Pan's help, rescued Zeus from the rebel Typhon in the deadly struggle on Mount Saphon.

6. According to *Genesis* IV. 1, Eve called her first son Cain (*qayin*) because, as she said: 'I have gotten (*qaniti*) a man from Yahweh.' A later account derives his name from *qaneh*, a reed or stalk. Abel's name, *Hebel*, remains unexplained perhaps because the word *hebel* was well known to mean 'breath', 'nothingness', 'fleetingness', in reference to human life (*Psalm* CXLIV. 4; *Job* VII. 16). However, in the Septuagint translation, *hebhel* was written 'Abel' which, transcribed into Hebrew, becomes *abhel* or *ebhel:* 'mourning' or 'sorrow'.

7. The twin sisters will have been invented in answer to the question: 'Where did Cain and Abel find wives?'

8. Samael's fathering of Cain is intended to explain the origin of evil. In the early generations the evil Cainites and the pious Sethites formed separate branches of the human family. When however the daughters of Cain succeeded in seducing the sons of Seth (see 18, *n–p*), both good and evil became parts of man's heritage. The two strains were considered to be continuously fighting for supremacy in every human heart: only knowledge of and obedience to the law could keep Cain's blood in check.

15

THE ACT OF LOVE

(*a*) Cast out of Eden, Adam and Eve rested on a riverbank and, though glad to have escaped immediate death, brooded on their loss of immortality, wondering how they might still assure the continuance of mankind. Samael, aware of Adam's preoccupation with this problem, planned to take further revenge. He and ten of his angels escaped from their underground dungeon and, assuming the shape of incomparably beautiful women, came to the riverbank. There they greeted Adam and Eve, and Adam cried incredulously: 'Has the earth truly bred such matchless creatures as these?' Then he asked: 'Friends, how do you multiply?' Samael answered in a woman's seductive voice: 'Men lie beside us in love. Our bellies swell, we bear infants, they mature and do as we have done. If you disbelieve me, I will prove it!'

At this, other fallen angels in disguise swam up from the riverbed. Samael said: 'These are our husbands and children; and since you wish to know how infants are engendered, let us show you.' Whereupon the women lay down in their nakedness, each with her supposed husband, and all did ugly things before Adam's eyes. Afterwards Samael said: 'Do thus and thus with Eve, for only so can you multiply your race.'

The fire of sin began to burn in Adam's veins, yet he refrained from performing an act of shame publicly in daylight, and implored God's guidance. God then sent an angel, who married Adam to Eve, commanding them to pray forty days and forty nights before coupling as husband and wife.[1]

(*b*) Some say that Adam and Eve were the first living creatures to perform the act of love.[2]

1. *Adambuch*, 64–67.
2. Gen. Rab. 204–05.

*

1. The Essene character of this myth is unmistakable: marital embraces being here called 'ugly things'; and marital desire, 'the fire of sin'. Never-

theless, certain Free Essenes, recognizing the physical and mental dangers of cloistered celibacy—such as sexual dreams and homosexual temptation—compromised by permitting marriages in which the act of love was performed in obedience to God's command 'Increase and multiply!', but without sensual pleasure.

2. A Hittite myth, *Appu from Shudul,* also contains the notion that coition is not an inborn human instinct, but must be taught.

16

THE FRATRICIDE

(*a*) Cain offered God a sacrifice of first fruits, while his brother Abel offered a first-born lamb. When God accepted Abel's gift but rejected the other, Cain's face turned black with rage. God asked: 'Why take this ill? Subdue your jealous pride!'[1]

(*b*) God accepted Abel's gift, and rejected Cain's, with good reason: for whereas Abel had chosen the best lamb of his flock, Cain had set only a few flax-seeds upon the altar.[2] Moreover, he answered God's rebuke with a cry still echoed by blasphemers: 'There is no law and no judge!'

Meeting Abel in a field soon afterwards, he told him: 'There is no world to come, no reward for the righteous, no punishment for evil-doers. This world was not created in mercy; neither is it ruled by compassion. Why else has your offering been accepted and mine rejected?' Abel answered simply: 'Mine was accepted because I love God; yours was rejected because you hate Him.' Cain then struck and killed Abel.[3]

(*c*) Some say that the quarrel arose at Earth's division between the brothers, in which all land fell to Cain, but all birds, beasts and creeping things to Abel. They agreed that neither should have any claim on the other's possessions. As soon as this pact had been concluded Cain, who was tilling a field, told Abel to move his flocks away. When Abel replied that they would not harm the tillage, Cain caught up a weapon and ran in vengeful pursuit across mountain and valley, until he overtook and killed him. Others report that Cain said unreasonably: 'The soil on which you stand is mine. Rise into the air!' and that Abel rejoined: 'Your garments are taken from my flocks; strip them off!'

Or that Cain proposed to Abel: 'Let us divide Earth into three parts. I, the first-born, will take two; and you the remaining one.' Since Abel would not accept less than a half share, Cain said: 'Agreed, but the hill on which you sacrificed must be in my half.' Because this was the Holy Mount at Jerusalem where, in due time,

Abraham would make his covenant with God, and Solomon would raise Him a temple, Abel judged Cain unworthy to own such a site.

(*d*) Still others hold that the brothers quarrelled for love of the First Eve, whom God had formed to be Adam's helpmeet, but who had been rejected.[4] Or that, when the brothers were ready for marriage, Adam said to Eve: 'Let Cain take Qelimath, Abel's twin sister; and let Abel take Lebhudha, Cain's twin sister.' But Cain wished to marry his own twin, who was more beautiful—though Adam warned him that this would be incest and made each of the brothers sacrifice to God before taking his assigned bride. When Cain's offering was refused, Satan persuaded him to kill Abel for Lebhudha's sake.[5]

(*e*) Some say that Cain lured his brother into the open, and there struck him repeatedly with a club until Abel, lying helpless on the ground, cried: 'Do not beat me to death, Brother; but if I must die, crush me with a rock at one blow!' This Cain did. Or that Cain, as if he had been an adder, bit Abel to death.

(*f*) According to others Abel, the stronger of the two, had Cain at his mercy. God encouraged Abel to despatch him, saying: 'Do not spare this evil-doer!' Yet when Cain wept and cried: 'Brother, forgive me! There are only two of us in the world, and what will our parents say if I am killed?', Abel mercifully released his grip. God then said: 'Having spared him, you must die yourself!' Whereupon Cain rose up, snatched a sharp reed and, not knowing where the vital organs lay, wounded Abel in every part, beginning at his hands and feet. Others say, however, that Cain had watched Adam slaughtering a bull, and therefore hacked at Abel's neck with a sword.[6]

(*g*) Abel's spirit escaped from his body, but could find refuge neither in Heaven—where no other soul had as yet ascended; nor in the Pit—where no other soul had as yet descended; and therefore flew about near by. His blood lay, bubbling and seething, where it was spilt. The whole neighbourhood still supports no grass or trees.[7]

(*h*) Afterwards God asked Cain: 'Where is your brother Abel?' Cain replied: 'Am I my brother's keeper? Why should One who watches over all creatures ask me this, unless He planned the murder Himself? But for Your preference of his offering to mine, I should not have envied him. Nor had I ever seen or heard of a corpse. Did You even warn me that, if I struck him, he would die? My grief is too heavy a burden to bear.' God then cursed him, saying: 'What have you done? Your brother's blood cries unto Me from the ground!' Yet God had given no signal for the brothers to break off their fight, but allowed Cain to deal Abel a mortal blow; hence Abel's last words were: 'My King, I demand justice!'

(*i*) God, having detected something like repentance in Cain's heart, let him live, though as an outlaw. Wherever he went, Earth would quake beneath his feet and the wild beasts would tremble. At first they tried to devour him, but he wept and prayed for mercy, at which moment a Sabbath began, and they were forced to desist. Some say that God then made a horn sprout from Cain's brow, which protected him against their vengeance. Others, that God afflicted him with leprosy; or that He inscribed a mark upon his arm: a warning against any attempt to avenge Abel.

(*j*) Adam, presently meeting Cain, was astonished to find him alive. 'Did you not kill your brother Abel?' he asked. Cain answered: 'I repented, Father, and was forgiven.' Smiting his own face, Adam cried: 'Such is the power of repentance; yet I never knew!'[8]

(*k*) God inflicted seven punishments on Cain, worse than death itself: namely, a shameful horn sprouting from his brow; the cry 'Fratricide!', with which mountains and valleys echoed; a palsy, that shook him like a poplar leaf; a voracious hunger, never sated; disappointment in every desire; a perpetual lack of sleep; and an edict that no man should either befriend or kill him.[9]

(*l*) According to one account Cain, unaware that God sees and knows all, dug a grave and there hid Abel's corpse. According to another, he doubted what to do until God sent down two birds, one of which killed its fellow and then buried it. Cain followed this example. Others again say that he fled, leaving Abel where he had fallen; and, when Adam and Eve found the corpse, they sat mourning and at a loss, while Abel's sheepdog kept guard against carrion birds and beasts. At last they observed a raven interring its dead mate—a sign from which Adam learned what God required of him.[10]

(*m*) Still others hold that Earth, though she drank Abel's blood, refused to accept his flesh—quaking so violently that Cain, too, was almost engulfed. Wherever he tried to bury the corpse, Earth spewed it up again, and cried at last: 'I will receive no other body until the clay that was fashioned into Adam has been restored to me!' At this Cain fled, and Michael, Gabriel, Uriel and Raphael placed the corpse upon a rock, where it remained many years without corrupting. When Adam died, these same archangels buried both bodies at Hebron side by side, in the very field from which God had taken Adam's dust. Yet Abel's spirit still found no rest: his loud complaints could be heard in Heaven and on earth for centuries—until Cain, his wives and his children were all dead.[11]

(*n*) After the birth of an eldest son Enoch, Cain was allowed by God to rest from wandering and build a city, called 'Enoch' in honour of the occasion. He then founded six more cities: Mauli, Leeth, Teze, Iesca, Celeth and Tebbath; and his wife Themech bore him three more sons: Olad, Lizaph and Fosal; as well as two daughters: Citha and Maac.

(*o*) Yet Cain had not changed. He still indulged his bodily lusts, amassed wealth by rapine, taught evil practices and lived luxuriously. His invention of weights and measures ended mankind's simplicity. Cain was also the first man who placed boundary stones around fields; and who built walled cities, in which he forced his people to settle.[12]

1. *Genesis* IV. 3–8.
2. Zohar Hadash *ad Gen.* IV. 2; Gen. Rab. 207, 209; PRE, ch. 21; Theodotion *ad Gen.* IV. 4; Agadat Shir 40; Mid. Hagadol Gen. 107; Sepher Hayashar 3.
3. *Adamschriften* 34; Targ. Yer. *ad Gen.* IV. 8; Mid. Leqah Tobh Gen. 30.
4. Gen. Rab. 213; Tanhuma Bereshit 9; Mid. Hagadol Gen. 111; PRE, ch. 21; Zohar Gen. 54b.
5. *Schatzhöhle* 8.
6. *Adambuch* 70–72; Gen. Rab. 214–15; Agadat Shir 43, 91; Zohar Gen. 54b.
7. Gen. Rab. 216; M. Sanhedrin 4.5; Agadat Shir 43, 91.
8. *Genesis* IV. 10–11; Tanhuma Bereshit 9–10; Gen. Rab. 216–20; PRE, ch. 21; Mid. Leqah Tobh 30; Yalqut Reubeni *ad Gen.* IV. 15.
9. *Adamschriften* 35, 43.
10. PRE, ch. 21; Tanhuma Bereshit 10.
11. *Apoc. of Moses* XL; *Vita Adae* XLVIII; *Adamschriften* 22; *Adambuch* 72–73; *Enoch* XXII. 7.
12. *Genesis* IV. 17; Sepher Hayashar 5; Philo 77–78; Pseudo-Philo 113; Josephus, *Ant.* i.2.2.

*

1. Scholars who interpret this myth as a record of ancient Palestinian conflicts, between nomadic herdsmen and agriculturists, fail to explain why, if so, Cain was not a nomad herdsman—and therefore prone to rob and murder the peaceful farmer—but a farmer himself; while Abel was the herdsman.

In *Genesis* it is suggested that Cain grew jealous because Abel's offering had been preferred to his own. But since Temple ritual required grain offerings as well as flesh sacrifices, early commentators felt that either some explanation of God's preference for Abel's gift should be found—or else some motive for the murder other than jealousy. They were loth to admit that God might have acted arbitrarily: denying a first-born the precedence due by law, and favouring a younger son—as a patriarchal chieftain might favour the child of his prettiest wife. Jacob's preference for Joseph, a younger son, was a case in point; his brothers plotted to kill him (see 53. *a–e*).

2. The historical events underlying this myth may be reconstructed as follows. Starving herdsmen break into a settled farming area during a drought, and are accepted as tribute-paying guests. Later, they demand a share of the government. Simultaneous sacrifices to the state deity are then offered by both parties. The chief herdsman's offering is preferred; whereupon the chief farmer, aided by his maternal kinsmen, murders him. As a result, the farmers are expelled and eventually found a city-state elsewhere. This political situation has been a commonplace in East Africa for centuries: intruding herdsmen, who first appear as starving suppliants, gain political ascendancy, after having aroused bitter antagonism by letting their animals trample crops.

3. This myth has, however, been complicated by the brand incident, given to explain the origin of nomadic, camel-herding bedouin who entered Palestine later than the goat-and-sheep-owning semi-nomads, and who still use tribal tattoos. The Hebrews pretended to see in these, and in the bedouins' addiction to raids, God's punishment on Cain and his descendants for the crime of murder.

4. The theme of fratricide adds a further complication. What the wise woman of Tekoah told David was a commonplace of myth (2 *Samuel* XIV. 6): 'Thy handmaids had two sons, and they strove together in the field, and there was none to part them, but the one smote the other and killed him.' Zerah and Perez fought even in their mother's womb (*Genesis* XXXVIII. 27–30); as Jacob and Esau also did (see 38. *a*. 2). The woman in dispute seems always to have been a regnant princess of a matrilinear state, marriage to whom conferred kingship on the victor. Sometimes the rivals are uncle and nephew, as in the case of Set and Osiris.

5. An ancient Palestinian myth comparable to that of Cain and Abel, and of Esau and Jacob, has been preserved in Philo's Greek translation of Sanchuniathon's *Phoenician History*. Usöus and Hypsouranius, heroes begotten on sacred harlots by Pyr and Phlox, sons of Phos ('Fire and Flame, sons of Light'), were perpetually at odds. Usöus, the first hunter, discovered how to make skin garments. He thus resembles both Cain and Esau. Samemroumus—whose name Philo translates as 'Hypsouranius', corresponding to the Hebrew *shme marom* ('High Heaven')—is said to have invented reed tents. He thus resembles Jabal (*Genesis* IV. 20), 'the father of such as dwell in tents and have cattle'; and Abel, who was a shepherd (*Genesis* IV. 2); and Jacob, 'a plain man living in tents' (*Genesis* XXV. 27).

Yet 'Cain' and 'Abel' may be versions of the mythical heroes Agenor and Belus: Agenor being the Greek form of 'Canaan', and Belus of 'Baal'. These twin sons of Poseidon and Lamia were reputedly born in Egypt, whence Agenor was expelled by Belus. Belus then begot another pair of twins: Danaus and Aegyptus, whose quarrel was prolonged when Danaus's daughters murdered Aegyptus's sons.

6. A historical connexion is likely between Cain the fratricide and the tribe of Cainites (*Qeni*), also referred to collectively as 'Cain' (*Numbers* xxiv. 22; *Judges* iv. 11): a desert people living to the south of Israel. Cainites, or Kenites, first appear as one of the ten nations inhabiting Palestine in Abraham's day (*Genesis* xv. 19). Balaam, the Moabite prophet, counted Kenites among Israel's enemies living to the south and east (*Numbers* xxiv. 17–22)—namely, Moab, Seth, Edom, Seir and Amalek. He described them as dwelling in mountain strongholds. Another group lived in the Sinai peninsula, and were ruled by Hobab, Moses's father-in-law (*Judges* iv. 11; 1 *Samuel* xv. 5). At a later date the Kenite sons of Hamat left Arad, seventeen miles south-east from Hebron, and their descendants became Rechabites (*Judges* i. 16; 1 *Chronicles* ii. 55). Still later another family settled in Galilee. Their chieftain Heber—whose wife Jael killed Sisera*—allied himself to Jabin, King of Hazor, an enemy and oppressor of Israel (*Judges* iv. 17). The Kenites of Arad remained enemies of Israel for several generations, joining the Amalekites in their war against King Saul. Only when Saul gained the upper hand and promised not to take vengeance on the Kenites, did they withdraw from the battle (1 *Samuel* xv. 6). Under King David, they had cities of their own in the Negeb (1 *Samuel* xxvii. 10; xxx. 29): Kinah (*Qinah*) and Kain (*Qayin*) in Southern Judaea may have been two of these.

Since the Kenites were therefore known to the Israelites both as nomads and city dwellers, and generally hostile, their legendary ancestor Cain could figure in myth as the first murderer, the first nomad, and the first city builder. His invention of weights and measures suggests that the farming community which Abel's herdsmen took over—perhaps during the Hyksos conquest—had Cretan and Egyptian affiliations. In Greek myth, this invention is attributed to Palamedes, who represents Cretan culture implanted in the Peloponnese; or to Hermes, who represents the Egyptian Thoth.

7. An early midrash describes Cain's mark as a letter tattooed on his arm; its identification in mediaeval texts with the Hebrew *teth* is prompted, perhaps, by *Ezekiel* ix. 4–6, where God sets a mark (*tav*) on the brows of the righteous few at Jerusalem who are to be saved. Cain was not judged worthy of this emblem. But the character for *tav*, the last letter of the Hebrew and Phoenician alphabets, was a cross; and from it derived the Greek

*Jael's deed, although celebrated by the Israelite leaders (*Judges* v. 24 ff), seems at first sight one of treachery. But it should be remembered that if Jael belonged to the Sons of Hamat—Kenites allied to Israel—her father's enemies would be hers, even after marriage to Heber, unless he were present when they arrived; and that he was conveniently absent, perhaps on purpose, and thus escaped both his allies' censure and the Israelites' praise.

character *tau* which, according to Lucian's *Court of Vowels*, inspired the idea of crucifixion. Since *tav* was thus reserved for an identification of the righteous, the midrash has substituted as Cain's brand the letter closest to *tav* both in sound and written character; namely *teth*, whose ancient Hebrew and Phoenician form was a cross within a circle.

17

THE BIRTH OF SETH

(*a*) Adam, fearing that another son born to Eve and himself might share Abel's fate, abstained from intercourse with her for no less than one hundred and thirty years. During this time succubi often bore demons to Adam as he slept, by causing him dreams of sin and involuntary emissions of seed. Moreover, incubi debauched the sleeping Eve, fathering demons on her.[1]

(*b*) Like the succubi, these incubi, or Meri'im, were the shadowy spirits created by God on the Sixth Day towards dusk. Before He could complete their bodies the Sun set, the First Sabbath began and obliged Him to desist.[2]

(*c*) Since God chose to people Earth with men, not demons, He implanted in Adam's heart a burning desire for Eve. Hitherto, Adam could refrain merely by absence; now, even at a great distance from Eve, desire rose in him so strongly that, remembering God's command 'Be fruitful and multiply!', he sought her out again, they lay together, and she bore him Seth.[3]

(*d*) Some say that God's angel commanded Adam to lie with Eve, but that he held back until promised a son named Seth—meaning 'consolation'—who would relieve his grief for Abel. Others, that Eve said: 'God has appointed (*shath*) me another son in Abel's stead.'[4]

(*e*) When, after Seth's birth, Adam returned to abstinence, Samael, again disguised as a beautiful woman, came pretending that he was Eve's sister, and demanded marriage from him. Adam prayed for guidance, and God immediately revealed Samael's evil shape. Seven years later, God once more told Adam to lie with Eve, undertaking that he would remove their temptation to wild and indecent lust. This promise He kept.[5]

(*f*) Before Eve died, she had borne Adam thirty pairs of twins, a son and a daughter each time, as the result of marital rites conducted in the utmost holiness and decorum.[6] Adam lived eight hundred years after Seth's birth.[7]

1. Tanhuma Buber Gen. 20; Gen. Rab. 195–96, 204, 225–26, 236; B. Erubin 18b; Pesiqta Rabbati, 67b.

2. Gen. Rab. 54.
3. See note 1.
4. *Adamschriften*, 36; *Genesis* IV. 25.
5. *Adambuch*, 75–77.
6. *Adamschriften*, 8, 44.
7. *Genesis* V. 4.

*

1. This myth, like that of Samael's initiation of Adam into lust (see 15. *a*), reflects the Free Essenes' view that to abstain from all sexual activity might have dangerous consequences. Josephus records their abstention from intercourse in the early stages of a woman's pregnancy, and their three-year trial marriages to ensure fertility.

2. 'Seth' appears in *Numbers* XXIV. 17 as a people living next to Moab, probably the nomadic 'Sutu' of Assyrian and Babylonian inscriptions.

3. Josephus describes Seth as a virtuous man whose descendants lived in harmonious peace and who perfected astronomy, recording their discoveries on two pillars, one of which survived to his day. The first-century A.D. *Ascension of Isaiah* places Seth in Heaven; and a late Jewish tradition makes him the Messiah. Seth became a hero of the Gnostic 'Sethians'; also of the third-century A.D. Manichees, whose myths were partly Persian, partly Gnostic Jewish. Mani, the founder of Manicheeism, regarded both Cain and Abel as Satan's sons by Eve; but Seth as their true offspring, full of light. In *Genesis*, however, no particular virtue is ascribed to him.

18

THE SONS OF GOD AND THE DAUGHTERS OF MEN

(*a*) By the tenth generation, Adam's race had hugely increased. Lacking female company, the angels known as 'Sons of God' found wives among the lovely Daughters of Men. The children of these unions would have inherited eternal life from their fathers, but that God had decreed: 'Let not My spirit abide in flesh for ever! Henceforth the years of man are limited to one hundred and twenty.'

(*b*) These new creatures were giants, known as 'the Fallen Ones', whose evil ways decided God to wipe from the face of the earth all men and women, with their gigantic corruptors.[1]

(*c*) The Sons of God were sent down to teach mankind truth and justice; and for three hundred years did indeed teach Cain's son Enoch all the secrets of Heaven and Earth. Later, however, they lusted after mortal women and defiled themselves by sexual intercourse. Enoch has recorded not only their divine instructions, but also their subsequent fall from grace; before the end they were indiscriminately enjoying virgins, matrons, men and beasts.[2]

(*d*) Some say that Shemhazai and Azael, two angels in God's confidence, asked: 'Lord of the Universe, did we not warn You on the Day of Creation that man would prove unworthy of Your world?' God replied: 'But if I destroy man, what will become of My world?' They answered: 'We shall inhabit it.' God asked: 'Yet upon descending to earth, will you not sin even worse than man?' They pleaded: 'Let us dwell there awhile, and we will sanctify Your name!'

God allowed them to descend, but they were at once overcome by lust for Eve's daughters, Shemhazai begetting on them two monstrous sons named Hiwa and Hiya, each of whom daily ate a thousand camels, a thousand horses and a thousand oxen. Azael also invented the ornaments and cosmetics employed by women to lead men astray. God therefore warned them that He would set loose the Upper Waters, and thus destroy all men and beasts. Shemhazai wept bitterly, fearing for his sons who, though tall enough to escape drowning, would starve to death.[3]

(*e*) That night, Hiwa dreamed of a huge rock above the earth, like a table-top, and having a legend inscribed on it which an angel scraped off with a knife, leaving only four letters. Hiya also dreamed: of a fruitful orchard, and of other angels felling it until only a single three-branched tree remained. They told their dreams to Shemhazai, who replied: 'Your dream, Hiya, signifies that God's Deluge will destroy all mankind, except Noah and his three sons. Nevertheless, be comforted, for Hiwa's dream signifies that your fame, at least, can never die: whenever Noah's descendants hew stones, quarry rocks or haul boats, they will shout "Hiwa, Hiya!" in your honour.'[4]

(*f*) Afterwards Shemhazai repented, and set himself in the southern sky, between Heaven and Earth—head down, feet up, and hangs there to this day: the constellation named Orion by the Greeks.

(*g*) Azael, however, far from repenting, still offers women ornaments and many-coloured robes with which to lead men astray. For this reason, on the Day of Atonement, Israel's sins are heaped on the annual scapegoat; it is then thrown over a cliff to Azazel—as some call Azael.[5]

(*h*) Others say that certain angels asked God's permission to collect sure proof of man's iniquity, and thus assure his punishment. When God agreed, they turned themselves into precious stones, pearls, purple dye, gold and other treasures, which were at once stolen by covetous men. They then took human shape, hoping to teach mankind righteousness. But this assumption of flesh made them subject to human lusts: being seduced by the Daughters of Men, they found themselves chained to Earth, unable to resume their spiritual shapes.[6]

(*i*) The Fallen Ones had such huge appetites that God rained manna upon them, of many different flavours, lest they might be tempted to eat flesh, a forbidden diet, and excuse the fault by pleading scarcity of corn and pot herbs. Nevertheless, the Fallen Ones rejected God's manna, slaughtered animals for food, and even dined on human flesh, thus fouling the air with sickly vapours. It was then that God decided to cleanse Earth.[7]

(*j*) Others say that Shemhazai and Azael were seduced by the demonesses Naamah, Agrat daughter of Mahlat, and Lilith who had once been Adam's spouse.[8]

(*k*) In those days only one virgin, Istahar by name, remained chaste. When the Sons of God made lecherous demands upon her, she cried: 'First lend me your wings!' They assented and she, flying up to Heaven, took sanctuary at the Throne of God, who transformed her into the constellation Virgo—or, some say, the Pleiades. The fallen angels having lost their wings, were stranded on earth until, many generations later, they mounted Jacob's ladder and thus went home again.[9]

(*l*) The wise and virtuous Enoch also ascended to Heaven, where he became God's chief counsellor, henceforth known as 'Metatron'. God set His own crown upon Enoch's head, and gave him seventy-two wings as well as multitudinous eyes. His flesh was transformed into flame, his sinews into fire, his bones into embers, his eyes into torches, his hair into rays of light, and he was surrounded by storm, whirlwind, thunder and lightning.[10]

(*m*) Some say that the Sons of God won that name because the divine light out of which God had created their ancestor Samael, Cain's father, shone from their faces. The Daughters of Men, they say, were children of Seth, whose father was Adam, not an angel; and their faces therefore resembled our own.[11]

(*n*) Others, however, make the Sons of God pious descendants of Seth, and the Daughters of Men sinful descendants of Cain—explaining that when Abel died childless, mankind soon divided into two tribes: namely the Cainites who, apart from Enoch, were wholly evil, and the Sethites who were wholly righteous. These Sethites inhabited a sacred mountain in the far north, near the Cave of Treasure—some take it for Mount Hermon. The Cainites lived apart in a valley to the westward. Adam, on his deathbed, ordered Seth to separate his tribe from the Cainites; and each Sethite patriarch publicly repeated this order, generation after generation. The Sethites were extraordinarily tall, like their ancestor; and, by living so close to the Gate of Paradise, won the name 'Children of God'.[12]

(*o*) Many Sethites took celibate vows, following Enoch's example, and led the lives of anchorites. By way of contrast, the Cainites practised unbridled debauchery, each keeping at least two wives: the first to bear children, the second to gratify his lust. The child-bearer lived in poverty and neglect, as though a widow; the other was forced to drink a potion that made her barren—after which, decked out like a harlot, she entertained her husband luxuriously.[13]

(*p*) It was the Cainites' punishment to have a hundred daughters borne them for each son; and this led to such husband-hunger that their women began to raid houses and carry off men. One day it pleased them to seduce the Sethites, after daubing their faces with rouge and powder, their eyes with antimony, and the soles of their feet with scarlet, dyeing their hair, putting on golden ear-rings, golden anklets, jewelled necklaces, bracelets and many-coloured garments.

In their ascent of the holy mountain, they twanged harps, blew trumpets, beat drums, sang, danced, clapped hands; then, having addressed the five hundred and twenty anchorites in cheerful voices, each caught hold of her victim and seduced him. These Sethites, after once succumbing to the Cainite women's blandishments, became more unclean than dogs, and utterly forgot God's laws.[14]

(*q*) Even the 'Sons of Judges' now corrupted the daughters of the poor. Whenever a bride was beautified for the bridegroom, one such would enter the nuptial chamber and enjoy her first.[15]

(*r*) Genun the Canaanite, son of Lamech the Blind, living in the Land of the Slime Pits, was ruled by Azael from his earliest youth, and invented all sorts of musical instruments. When he played these, Azael entered into them too, so that they gave forth seductive tunes entrancing the hearts of all listeners. Genun would assemble companies of musicians, who inflamed one another with music until their lust burned bright like fire, and they lay together promiscuously. He also brewed beer, gathered great crowds in taverns, gave them to drink, and taught them how to forge iron swords and spear-points, with which to do murder at random when they were drunk.[16]

(*s*) Michael, Gabriel, Raphael and Uriel told God that such wickedness had never before flourished on earth. God then sent Raphael to bind Azael hand and foot, heaping jagged rocks over him in the dark Cave of Dudael, where he now abides until the Last Days. Gabriel destroyed the Fallen Ones by inciting them to civil war. Michael chained Shemhazai and his fellows in other dark caves for seventy generations. Uriel became the messenger of salvation who visited Noah.[17]

1. *Genesis* VI. 1–7.
2. *Jubilees* IV. 15, 22; V. 1; Tanhuma Buber Gen. 24.
3. Yalqut Gen. 44; Bereshit Rabbati, 29–30.
4. Sources as in preceding footnote.
5. Sources as in preceding footnote.
6. The Clementine *Homilies* viii. 11–17 (pp. 142–45). The *Homilies* are an early 3rd cent. A.D. Christian tract, written probably in Syria. Cf. also Enoch 6–8; 69; 106, 13 f.
7. Sources as in preceding footnote.
8. Zohar Genesis 37a, 55a.
9. Liqqute Midrashim, 156; a somewhat different version in Yalqut Gen. 44.
10. Sepher Hekhalot, 170–76.
11. Zohar Genesis 37a.
12. PRE, ch. 21 (where *mishēm* should be amended to read *mishēth*) and 22; cf. also Gen. Rab. 222; *Adambuch,* 75, 81–86; *Adamschriften,* 37; *Schatzhöhle,* 10.
13. *Adamschriften,* 38; cf. Gen. Rab. 222–23.
14. Sources as in preceding footnote, and PRE, ch. 22.
15. Targ. and Targ. Yer. *ad Gen.* VI. 2–4; Gen. Rab. 247–48.

16. *Adambuch*, 92–93.
17. *Enoch* IX–X; cf. also chapters XI–XV and LXIX; 2 *Baruch* LVI. 11–16; 2 *Enoch* XVIII. 1–6.

*

1. The explanation of this myth, which has been a stumbling block to theologians, may be the arrival in Palestine of tall, barbarous Hebrew herdsmen early in the second millennium B.C., and their exposure, by marriage, to Asianic civilization. 'Sons of El' in this sense would mean the 'cattle-owning worshippers of the Semite Bull-god El'; 'Daughters of Adam' would mean 'women of the soil' (*adama*), namely the Goddess-worshipping Canaanite agriculturists, notorious for their orgies and premarital prostitution. If so, this historical event has been tangled with the Ugaritic myth of how El seduced two mortal women and fathered divine sons on them, namely *Shahar* ('Dawn') and *Shalem* ('Perfect'). Shahar appears as a winged deity in *Psalm* CXXXIX. 9; and his son, according to *Isaiah* XIV. 12, was the fallen angel Helel. Unions between gods and mortals, that is to say between kings or queens and commoners, occur frequently in Mediterranean and Middle Eastern myth. Since later Judaism rejected all deities but its own transcendental God, and since He never married or consorted with any female whatsoever, Rabbi Shimon ben Yohai in *Genesis Rabba* felt obliged to curse all who read 'Sons of God' in the Ugaritic sense. Clearly, such an interpretation was still current in the second century A.D., and lapsed only when the *Bene Elohim* were re-interpreted as 'sons of judges'. *Elohim* meant both 'God' and 'judge', the theory being that when a duly appointed magistrate tried a case, the Spirit of El possessed him: 'I have said, ye are gods.' (*Psalm* LXXXII. 6).

2. This myth is constantly quoted in the Apocrypha, the New Testament, the Church Fathers, and midrashim. Josephus interpreted it as follows:

> *Many angels of God now consorted with women, and begot sons on them who were overbearing and disdainful of every virtue; such confidence had they in their strength. In fact, the deeds that our tradition ascribes to them recall the audacious exploits told by the Greeks of the giants. But Noah . . . urged them to adopt a better frame of mind and amend their ways.*

These Greek giants were twenty-four violent and lecherous sons of Mother Earth, born at Phlegra in Thrace, and the two Aloeids, all of whom rebelled against Almighty Zeus.

3. Josephus's view, that the Sons of God were angels, survived for several centuries despite Shimon ben Yohai's curse. As late as the eighth century A.D., Rabbi Eliezer records in a midrash: 'The angels who fell from Heaven saw the daughters of Cain perambulating and displaying their secret parts, their eyes painted with antimony in the manner of harlots;

and, being seduced, took wives from among them.' Rabbi Joshua ben Qorha, a literalist, was worried by a technical detail: 'Is it possible that angels, who are flaming fire, could have performed the sexual act without scorching their brides internally?' He decided that 'when these angels fell from Heaven, their strength and stature were reduced to those of mortals, and their fire changed into flesh.'

4. *Hiwa* and *Hiya*, the names given to giants begotten by Shemhazai and Azael on mortal women, were merely the cries of work-teams engaged in tasks demanding concerted effort. In one Talmudic passage, Babylonian sailors are made to shout as they haul cargo vessels ashore: '*Hilni, hiya, hola, w'hilok holya!*' The giants' voracious flesh-eating was, however, a habit of El's Hebrew herdsmen, not of the agricultural Daughters of Adamah; and this anecdote suggests that the myth originated in an Essene community whose diet was severely restricted, like that of Daniel and his three holy companions, to pulses. (*Daniel* I. 12).

5. The names of several fallen angels survive only in careless Greek transcriptions of Hebrew or Aramaic originals, which make their meaning doubtful. But 'Azael' does seem to represent 'Azazel' ('God strengthens'). 'Dudael' is sometimes translated 'God's cauldron', but it is more likely to be a fantastic modification of *Beth Hadudo* (*M. Yoma* VI. 8)—now Haradan, three miles to the south-east of Jerusalem, the Judaean desert cliff from which 'the scapegoat for Azazel' yearly fell to its death on the Day of Atonement (*Leviticus* XVI. 8–10). This goat was believed to take away Israel's sins and transfer them to their instigator, the fallen angel Azazel, who lay imprisoned under a pile of rocks at the cliff-foot. The sacrifice did not therefore rank as one offered to demons, like those which *Leviticus* XVII. 7 prohibits.

6. The Mount of God, where certain pious Sethites lived near the 'Cave of Treasure', at the Gate of Paradise, will have been El's holy Mount Saphon, not Hermon.

7. Istahar's story is borrowed partly from the Greek writer Aratus (early third century B.C.). He tells how Justice, a daughter of Dawn, ruled mankind virtuously in the Golden Age; but when the Silver and Bronze Ages brought greed and slaughter among them, exclaimed: 'Alas, for this evil race!' and mounted into Heaven, where she became the constellation Virgo. The rest of this story is borrowed from Apollodorus's account of Orion's attempt on the seven virgin Pleiades, daughters of Atlas and Pleione, who escaped from his embraces transformed to stars. 'Istahar', however, is the Babylonian Goddess Ishtar, sometimes identified with Virgo. Popular Egyptian belief identified Orion, the constellation which became Shemhazai, with the soul of Osiris.

8. The right claimed by certain 'sons of judges' to take the maidenheads of poor men's brides is, apparently, the ancient and well-known *jus primae*

noctis which, as the *droit de cuissage*, was still reputedly exercised by feudal lords in Europe during the Middle Ages (see 36. 4). Yet at a time when the Sons of God were regarded as divine beings, this story may have referred to a custom prevalent in the Eastern Mediterranean: a girl's maidenhead was ritually broken by 'equitation' of a priapic statue. A similar practice obtained among Byzantine hippodrome-performers as late as Justinian's reign, and is hinted at in records of the medieval English witch cult.

9. Many details in the Genun story, taken from the fifth-century A.D. Ethiopian *Book of Adam*, are paralleled in midrashic writings. Although Genun's name suggests 'Kenan', who appears in *Genesis* v. 9 as the son of Enoch, he is a composite Kenite character: the invention of musical instruments being attributed in *Genesis* to Jubal, and of edged brass and iron blades to his brother Tubal Cain. Genun was said to occupy 'the Land of the Slime Pits', namely the southern shores of the Dead Sea (*Genesis* xiv. 10), doubtless because the evil city of Sodom stood there (see 32. 6).

10. Enoch ('Instructor') won his immense reputation from the apocalyptic and once canonical *Book of Enoch*, compiled in the first century B.C. It is an ecstatic elaboration of *Genesis* v. 22: 'And Enoch walked with God three hundred years after he begat Methuselah.' Later Hebrew myth makes him God's recording angel and counsellor, also patron of all children who study the Torah. *Metatron* is a Hebrew corruption either of the Greek *metadromos*, 'he who pursues with vengeance', or of *meta ton thronon*, 'nearest to the Divine Throne'.

11. The Anakim may have been Mycenaean Greek colonists, belonging to the 'Sea Peoples' confederation which caused Egypt such trouble in the fourteenth century B.C. Greek mythographers told of a Giant Anax ('king'), son of Heaven and Mother Earth, who ruled Anactoria (Miletus) in Asia Minor. According to Apollodorus, the disinterred skeleton of Asterius ('starry'), Anax's successor, measured ten cubits. *Anakes*, the plural of *Anax*, was an epithet of the Greek gods in general. Talmudic commentators characteristically make the Anakim three thousand cubits tall.

12. Megalithic monuments, found by the Hebrews on their arrival in Canaan, will have encouraged legends about giants; as in Greece, where the monstrous man-eating Cyclopes were said by story-tellers ignorant of ramps, levers and other Mycenaean engineering devices, to have lifted single-handed the huge blocks of stone that form the walls of Tiryns, Mycenae and other ancient cities.

13. The *Nefilim* ('Fallen Ones') bore many other tribal names, such as *Emim* ('Terrors'), *Repha'im* ('Weakeners'), *Gibborim* ('Giant Heroes'), *Zamzummim* ('Achievers'), *Anakim* ('Long-necked' or 'Wearers of Necklaces'), *Awwim* ('Devastators' or 'Serpents'). One of the Nefilim named Arba is said to have built the city of Hebron, called 'Kiriath-Arba'

after him, and become the father of Anak whose three sons, Sheshai, Ahiman and Talmai, were later expelled by Joshua's comrade Caleb. Since, however, *arba* means 'four' in Hebrew, Kiriath-Arba may originally have meant 'City of Four', a reference to its four quarters mythically connected with the Anakite clans: Anak himself and his 'sons' Sheshai, Ahiman and Talmai.

19

THE BIRTH OF NOAH

(*a*) Cain died several generations later at the hands of his great-great-grandson Lamech. This Lamech was a mighty hunter and, like all others of Cain's stock, married two wives. Though grown old and blind, he continued to hunt, guided by his son Tubal Cain. Whenever Tubal Cain sighted a beast, he would direct Lamech's aim. One day he told Lamech: 'I spy a head peeping above yonder ridge.' Lamech drew his bow; Tubal Cain pointed an arrow which transfixed the head. But, on going to retrieve the quarry, he cried: 'Father, you have shot a man with a horn growing from his brow!' Lamech answered: 'Alas, he must be my ancestor Cain!', and struck his hands together in grief, thereby inadvertently killing Tubal Cain also.

Lamech mourned all day beside the corpses, being prevented by blindness from finding his way home. In the evening, Adah and Zillah, his wives, found him. Lamech cried: 'Hearken to me: I have slain a man to my wounding, and a young man to my hurt! If Cain shall be avenged sevenfold, truly Lamech shall be avenged seventy-and-sevenfold!' At that, Earth opened and swallowed all Cain's nearest kinsmen, except Enoch: namely Irad, Mehujael, Methuselah and their families.

(*b*) Lamech told his wives: 'Enter my bed, and there await me!' Zillah answered: 'You have killed our ancestor Cain and my son Tubal Cain; therefore neither of us shall lie with you.' Lamech replied: 'This is God's will. Seven generations, the span allotted to Cain, have now elapsed. Obey me!' But they said: 'No, for any children born of this union would be doomed.' Lamech, Adah and Zillah then sought out Adam, who was still alive, and asked him to judge between them. Zillah spoke first: 'Lamech has killed your son Cain, and also my son Tubal Cain.' Lamech declared: 'Both deaths were caused by inadvertence, since I am blind.' Adam told Adah and Zillah: 'You must obey your husband!'

(*c*) Zillah then bore Lamech a son already circumcised: a sign of God's especial grace. Lamech named him Noah, finding great *consolation* in him.[1] Noah's cheeks were whiter than snow and redder than a rose; his eyes like rays of the morning sun; his hair long and curly; his face aglow with light. Lamech therefore suspected him to be a bastard fathered on Zillah by one of the Watchers, or Fallen Ones; but Zillah swore that she had been faithful. They consulted their ancestor Enoch, who had lately been caught up to Heaven. His prophecy, 'In Noah's lifetime God will do a new thing on earth!', gave Lamech his needed reassurance.

(*d*) At Noah's birth, which coincided with Adam's death, the world greatly improved. Hitherto, when wheat had been sown, half of the harvest was thorns and thistles. God now lifted this curse. And whereas hitherto all work had been done with bare hands, Noah taught men to make ploughs, sickles, axes and other tools.[2] But some award the invention of smithcraft to Tubal Cain, his dead brother.[3]

1. Tanhuma Noah 11; cf. Gen. Rab. 224–25; Sepher Hayashar, 7–8.
2. *Enoch* cvi, ed. Charles, ii. 278; *Genesis Apocryphon* 40; *Jubilees* iv. 28.
3. Sources as in footnote 1, and *Genesis* iv. 22.

*

1. This story recalls two Greek myths—Perseus's accidental killing of his grandfather Acrisius, and Athamas's mistaking of Learchus for a white stag—and is told to explain Lamech's cry in *Genesis* iv. 23: 'I have slain a man to my wounding, and a young man to my hurt!', the original context of which has vanished. Although tautology—the pairing of two phrases, differently worded but of the same sense—is a common ornament in Hebrew poetry, Lamech has here been absurdly credited with killing not one warrior, but an old man and a youth; very much as when Jesus is said to have fulfilled Zechariah's prophecy (*Zechariah* ix. 9) by 'riding on an ass and on a colt, the foal of an ass,' (*Matthew* xxi. 1–3), rather than on a single young ass. The law which required the next of kin to avenge murder, or even manslaughter, accounts for the Cities of Refuge instituted by Moses (*Numbers* xxxv. 13; *Joshua* xx. 1–9), where a man was safe until his case came before a judge. Thus Adam acts as judge and allows Lamech's plea of manslaughter, when he points out that if vengeance were taken on him, his nearest kinsman would take even more merciless vengeance on the avengers. But Earth has already supported Lamech's plea by swallowing up all Cain's kin. Although the etymology of 'Lamech' is uncertain, the midrash on this double homicide evidently connects it with three related Arabic roots *lamah, lamakh*, and *lamaq*, which mean 'to strike with a flat hand' and 'to look stealthily or sideways'.

2. Tubal Cain, in *Genesis* iv, is a smith whose brothers are Jabal, a herdsman, and Jubal, a musician. These names evidently record the occu-

pations of certain Kenite families. 'Tubal' stands for *Tabali* (in Greek: *Tibareni*), Anatolian tribesmen described by Herodotus as neighbours of the iron-working Chalybes. In *Ezekiel* XXVII. 13, 'Tubal' supplies Tyre with brazen vessels and slaves; 'Tubal Cain' thus probably means 'the metal-working Kenite'. Jubal was a Canaanite god of music.

3. The two Biblical accounts of Lamech's family are inconsistent. According to *Genesis* IV. 19–22, he had Jabal and Jubal by his wife Adah; by his wife Zillah, Tubal Cain and a daughter Naamah. According to *Genesis* V. 28–31, Noah was Lamech's first-born; other sons and daughters are mentioned but not named.

20
THE DELUGE

(*a*) Noah was so loth to lose his innocence that, though often urged to marry, he waited until God found him Naamah, Enoch's daughter—the only woman since Istahar to have remained chaste in that corrupt generation. Their sons were Shem, Ham and Japheth; and when they grew up, Noah married them to the daughters of Eliakim, son of Methuselah.[1]

(*b*) Warned by God of the coming Deluge, Noah spread the news among mankind, preaching repentance wherever he went. Though his words burned like torches, the people mocked him with: 'What is this deluge? If it be a deluge of flame, we have *alitha* (asbestos?), which is proof against fire; and if a deluge of water, we have sheets of iron to restrain any flood that may break from the earth. Against water from the sky, we can use an *aqeb* (awning?).' Noah warned them: 'Yet God will send the waters bubbling up beneath your heels!' They boasted: 'However great this deluge, we are so tall that it cannot reach our necks; and should He open the sluices of Tehom, we will block them with the soles of our feet.[2]

(*c*) God then ordered Noah to build, and caulk with pitch, an ark of gopher-wood large enough for himself, his family and chosen examples of all other creatures living on earth. He must take seven beasts and birds of every clean kind, two of every unclean kind and two creeping things of every kind. He must also provide them with food. Noah spent fifty-two years on this shipwright's task; he worked slowly in the hope of delaying God's vengeance.[3]

(*d*) God Himself designed the ark; which had three decks and measured three hundred cubits from stem to stern, fifty from gunwale to gunwale, and thirty from hatches to keel. Each deck was divided into hundreds of cabins, the lowest made to house all beasts both wild and tame; the middle deck, all birds; the upper deck, all creeping things, and Noah's family besides.[4]

(*e*) Certain wandering spirits also entered the ark, and were saved. A couple of monsters too large for any cabin, nevertheless survived: the Reem, which swam behind, resting its nose on the poop; and the

Giant Og. This was Hiya's son by the woman who had since married Ham and who begged Noah to keep Og's head above water by letting him cling to a rope-ladder. In gratitude, Og swore that he would be Noah's slave; but though Noah compassionately fed him through a port-hole, he afterwards resumed his evil ways.[5]

(*f*) When Noah set about gathering the creatures together, he was appalled by his task, and cried: 'Lord of the Universe, how am I to accomplish this great thing?' Thereupon the guardian angel of each kind descended from Heaven and, carrying basketsful of fodder, led them into the ark; so that each seemed to have come by its own native intelligence. They arrived on the very day that Methuselah died, at the age of nine hundred and sixty-nine years, a full week before the Deluge began; and God appointed this time of mourning as a time of grace, during which mankind might still repent. He then commanded Noah to sit beside the door of the ark and observe each creature as it came towards him. Such as crouched down in his presence were to gain admittance; such as remained standing must be excluded. Some authorities say that according to God's orders, if the male lorded it over the female of his own kind, both were admitted, but not otherwise. And that He gave these orders because it was no longer men alone that committed bestiality. The beasts themselves rejected their own mates: the stallion mounted the she-ass; the jackass, the mare; the dog, the she-wolf; the serpent, the tortoise; and so forth—moreover, females frequently lorded it over males. God had decided to destroy all creatures whatsoever, except those that obeyed His will.[6]

(*g*) Earth shook, her foundations trembled, the sun darkened, lightning flashed, thunder pealed, and a deafening voice the like of which was never heard before, rolled across mountain and plain. Thus God sought to terrify evil-doers into repentance; but without avail. He chose water rather than fire as a fit punishment for their unspeakable vices, and opened Heaven's sluices by the removal of two Pleiades; thus allowing the Upper and Lower Waters—the male and female elements of Tehom, which He had separated in the days of Creation—to re-unite and destroy the world in a cosmic embrace.

The Deluge began on the seventeenth day of the second month, when Noah was six hundred years old. He and his family duly entered the ark, and God Himself made fast the door behind them. But even Noah could not yet believe that God would wipe out so magnificent a handiwork, and therefore had held back until waves lapped at his ankles.[7]

(*h*) The floods spread swiftly over the entire earth. Seven hundred thousand evil-doers gathered around the ark, crying: 'Open the door, Noah, and let us enter!' Noah shouted from within: 'Did I not urge you to repent these hundred and twenty years, and you would not listen?' 'Now we repent,' they answered. 'It is too late,' he said. They tried to break down the door, and would have overturned the ark, but that a pack of rejected wolves, lions and bears which were also trying to enter, tore hundreds of them in pieces, and dispersed the rest. When Tehom's Lower Waters rose, the evil-doers first threw children into the springs, hoping to choke their flow, then climbed trees or hills. Rain cascaded down, and soon a rising flood bore up the ark, until at last it floated fifteen cubits above the highest peaks—yet so buffeted by waves that all inside were hurled to and fro like beans in a boiling pot. Some say that God heated the Deluge in the Pit's flames, and punished fiery lusts with scalding water; or rained fire on the evil-doers; or let carrion birds tear out their eyes as they swam.[8]

(*i*) A pearl hanging from the ark's roof shone calmly on Noah and his family. When its light paled, he knew that the hours of daylight had come; when it brightened, he knew that night was at hand, and thus never lost count of the Sabbaths. Some say, however, that this light came from a sacred book which the Archangel Raphael gave to Noah, bound in sapphires, and containing all knowledge of the stars, the art of healing and the mastery of demons. Noah bequeathed this to Shem, from whom it passed by way of Abraham to Jacob, Levi, Moses, Joshua and Solomon.[9]

(*j*) Throughout the next twelve months neither Noah nor his sons slept, being continually busied with their charges. Some creatures were accustomed to eat at the first hour of the day or night; others at the second, third or fourth hour, or even later; and each expected its own fodder—the camel needed straw; the ass, rye; the elephant, vine shoots; the ostrich, broken glass. Yet, according to one account, all beasts, birds, creeping things and man himself, subsisted on a single food: namely fig-bread.[10]

(*k*) Noah prayed: 'Lord of the Universe, release me from this prison! My soul is wearied by the stench of lions, bears and panthers.' As for the chameleon, no one knew how to feed it; but one day Noah opened a pomegranate, and a worm fell out which the starving creature devoured. Thereupon he kneaded shoots of camel-thorn into a cake, and fed the chameleon with the worms that it bred. A fever kept both lions sick all this time; they did not prey on other beasts, but ate grass like oxen. Seeing the phoenix huddled in a corner, Noah asked: 'Why have you not demanded food?' 'Sir,' it replied, 'your household are busy enough; I do not wish to cause them trouble.' He then blessed the phoenix, saying: 'Be it God's will that you never die!'[11]

(*l*) Noah had parted his sons from their wives, and forbidden them marital rites: while the world was being destroyed they must take no thought for its replenishment. He laid the same prohibition upon all beasts, birds and creeping things. Only Ham, the dog, and the cock-raven disobeyed. Ham sinned in order to save his wife from disgrace: had he not lain with her himself, Shem and Japheth would have known that she was already bearing a child to the fallen angel Shemhazai. Nevertheless, God punished Ham by turning his skin black. He also punished the dog, by attaching it shamefully to the bitch after copulation; and the raven, by making it inseminate the hen-bird through its beak.[12]

(*m*) When one hundred and fifty—though some say, forty—days had passed, God shut the sluices of Heaven with two stars borrowed from the Great Bear. This still pursues the Pleiades nightly, growling: 'Give back my stars!' He then sent a wind that drove Tehom's waters toppling over Earth's brink, until the Deluge slowly subsided. By the seventh day of the seventh month, Noah's ark had come to rest upon Mount Ararat. On the first day of the tenth month, summits of other mountains rose in sight. Having waited a further forty days, Noah opened a skylight and told the raven to fly off and fetch back news of the outside world. It replied insolently: 'God, your master, hates me; and so do you! Were not His orders: "Take seven of all clean creatures, and two of all unclean"? Why choose me for this dangerous mission, when my mate and I are only two? Why spare the doves, which number seven? If I should die of heat or cold, the world would be bereft of ravens. Or do you lust after my mate?' Noah cried: 'Alas, Evil One! Even my wife is forbidden me while we are afloat. How much more your mate, a creature not of my kind?' The raven thereupon hid itself. Noah searched the ark with care and, presently finding the truant hidden under the she-eagle's wing, said: 'Evil One! Did I not order you to see whether the floods have abated? Be off at once!' The raven answered impudently: 'It is as I thought: you lust after my mate!' Noah, enraged, cried: 'May God curse the beak that uttered this calumny!' And all the creatures, listening, said 'Amen!' Noah opened the skylight, and the raven—which had meanwhile impregnated the she-eagle, and other carrion-birds besides, thus depraving their natures—flew out but soon came back. Again sent out, again it came back. The third time it stayed away, gorging on corpses.[13]

(*n*) Noah now gave similar orders to a dove, which also soon returned, finding no tree to roost upon. Seven days later, he freed the dove a second time, and it returned towards nightfall, carrying a freshly plucked olive leaf in its bill. He tried once more, after another seven days had passed, and this time it did not return. On the first day of the first month, Noah climbed through the skylight and looked around. He saw only a vast sea of mud stretching to the distant mountains. Even Adam's tomb had vanished from sight. Not until the twenty-seventh day of the second month did wind and sun dry this morass sufficiently to let Noah disembark.[14]

(*o*) As soon as his foot touched land, he took stones and raised an altar. God sniffed the sweet odour of burnt offerings, and said: 'Despite man's evil disposition, I will never again use water to destroy him. Henceforth, so long as Earth lasts, let seed-time follow harvest; and harvest, seed-time—as summer follows winter; and day, night.' God blessed Noah and his family with: 'Be fruitful, multiply, rule all beasts, birds and creeping things!' He also permitted them to eat flesh, on condition that they first bled the carcase, explaining: 'A beast's soul lies in its blood'; and instituted the death penalty for any man or beast that should do murder. Then He set the Rainbow in the sky, saying: 'Whenever I bring rain clouds over the earth, this shining bow will recall My promise!'[15]

1. *Adamschriften* 39; Sepher Hayashar 16–17.
2. B. Sanhedrin 108b; PRE, ch. 22–end.
3. *Genesis* VI. 13–22; VII. 1–3; PRE, ch. 23.
4. *Genesis* VI. 15–16; PRE, ch. 23.
5. Gen. Rab. 253, 287; PRE, ch. 23; B. Nidda 61a; B. Zebahim 113b; Hadar 59a; Da'at Huqqat 18a.
6. PRE, ch. 23; Gen. Rab. 287, 293; Tanhuma Noah 12; Tanhuma Buber Gen. 36, 45; B. Sanhedrin 108a–b; Sepher Hayashar 17.
7. *Genesis* VII. 11–16; Gen. Rab. 293; B. Berakhot 59a; B. Rosh Hashana 11b–12a; PRE, ch. 23; Sepher Hayashar 18.
8. *Genesis* VII. 20; B. Sanh. 108b; B. Rosh Hashana 12a; B. Zebahim 112a; Lev. Rab. 7.6; Tanhuma Noah 7; Tanhuma Buber Gen. 35–36; Sepher Hayashar 18–19.
9. Gen. Rab. 283; B. Sanhedrin 108b; PRE, ch. 23; Sepher Noah, BHM, iii, 158.
10. Tanhuma Buber Gen. 29–30; 37–38; Gen. Rab. 287; Tanhuma Noah 2, 9; B. Sanhedrin 108b.
11. PRE, ch. 23; B. Sanhedrin 108b.
12. Gen. Rab. 286, 341; Tanhuma Buber Gen. 43; Tanhuma Noah 12; Yer. Taanit 64d; B. Sanhedrin 108b; PRE, ch. 23; Yalqut Reubeni *ad Gen.* VII. 7, p. 130.
13. *Genesis* VII. 4, 17, 24; VIII. 1–7; B. Berakhot 59a; B. Rosh Hashana 11b–12a; B. Sanhedrin 108b; Alpha Beta diBen Sira, *Otzar Midrashim* 49a, 50b.
14. *Genesis* VIII. 8–19.
15. *Genesis* VIII. 20; IX. 17.

*

1. Two ancient myths parallel the *Genesis* Deluge: one Greek, one Akkadian. The Akkadian, found in the *Gilgamesh Epic*, was current also among the Sumerians, the Hurrians and the Hittites. In it the hero Utnapishtim is warned by Ea, god of Wisdom, that the other gods led by Enlil, the Creator, have planned a universal deluge, and that he must build an ark. Enlil's reason for wiping out mankind seems to have been their omission of his New Year sacrifices. Utnapishtim builds a six-decked ark in the shape of an exact cube, with sides of one hundred and twenty cubits, and uses bitumen to caulk it. The ark is completed in seven days, Utnapishtim having meanwhile given his workmen 'wine to drink, like rain, so that they might feast in the style of New Year's day.' When a blighting rain begins to fall, he, his family, craftsmen and attendants bearing his treasures, besides numerous beasts and birds, enter the ark. Utnapishtim's boatman then battens down the hatches.

2. For a whole day the South Wind rages, submerging mountains and sweeping away mankind. The gods themselves fly up in terror to Heaven, where they cower like dogs. The deluge continues for six days, but ceases on the seventh. Thereupon Utnapishtim opens a hatch and looks about him. He sees a flood, level as a flat roof, bounded by fourteen distant mountain tops. All mankind has been drowned and returned to clay. The ark drifts to Mount Nisir, where Utnapishtim waits seven more days. He then sends out a dove which, finding no resting place, returns. After another seven days, he sends a swallow, which also returns. Then a raven which, finding carrion to eat, does not return, because the floods have now diminished.

3. Utnapishtim releases all his people and animals, pours a sevenfold libation of wine on the mountain top, and burns aromatic woods—cane, cedar and myrtle. The gods smell this sweet odour and crowd about the sacrifice. Ishtar praises Utnapishtim, and reviles Enlil for causing a senseless disaster. Enlil cries angrily: 'No man should have survived my deluge! Are these yet alive?' Ea confesses that Utnapishtim was warned of the deluge in a dream. Enlil, mollified, boards the ark and, blessing Utnapishtim and his wife, makes them 'like unto gods', and places them in Paradise where, later, they are greeted by Gilgamesh.

4. In a fragmentary Sumerian version, the Deluge hero is the pious King Ziusudra (named Xisuthros in Berossus's third-century B.C. *Babylonian History*). Xisuthros digs up certain sacred books which he has previously buried in the city of Sippar.

5. The *Genesis* myth is composed, it seems, of at least three distinct elements. First, historical memory of a cloudburst in the Armenian mountains which, according to Woolley's *Ur of the Chaldees*, flooded the Tigris and Euphrates about 3200 B.C.—covering Sumerian villages over an area of 40,000 square miles with eight feet of clay and rubble. Only a few cities

perched high on their mounds, and protected by brick walls, escaped destruction.

A second element is the autumnal New Year vintage feast of Babylonia, Syria and Palestine, where the ark was a crescent-shaped moon-ship containing sacrificial animals. This feast was celebrated at the New Moon nearest the autumnal equinox with libations of new wine to encourage the winter rains.

Remains of the ark on Ararat—'Mount Judi near Lake Van'—are mentioned by Josephus who quotes Berossus and other historians; Berossus had written that the local Kurds still chipped pieces of bitumen from it for use as amulets. A recent American expedition claims to have found half-fossilized timbers there dating from about 1500 B.C. An Armenian historian, Moses of Chorene, calls this sacred site Nachidsheuan ('the first place of descent'). 'Ararat' appears in an inscription of Shalmanassar I of Assyria (1272–1243 B.C.) as *Uruatri* or *Uratri*. Later it becomes *Urartu*, and refers to an independent kingdom surrounding Lake Van, known to the Hebrews of Biblical times as the Land of Ararat (2 *Kings* XIX. 37; *Isaiah* XXXVII. 38).

6. The Greek myth runs as follows: 'Disgusted by the cannibalism of the impious Pelasgians, Almighty Zeus let loose a great flood on earth, meaning to wipe out the whole race of man; but Deucalion, King of Phthia, warned by his father Prometheus the Titan whom he had visited in the Caucasus, built an ark, victualled it, and went aboard with his wife Pyrrha, a daughter of Epimetheus. Then the South Wind blew, rain fell and rivers roared down to the sea which, rising with astonishing speed, washed away every city of coast and plain; until the entire world was flooded, but for a few mountain tops, and all mortal creatures seemed to have been lost, except Deucalion and Pyrrha. The ark floated about for nine days until, at last, the waters subsided, and it came to rest on Mount Parnassus or, some tell, on Mount Aetna; or Mount Athos; or Mount Orthrys in Thessaly. It is said that Deucalion was reassured by a dove which he had sent on an exploratory flight.

7. 'Disembarking in safety, they offered a sacrifice to Father Zeus, the preserver of fugitives, and went down to pray at the Goddess Themis's shrine beside the River Cephissus: its roof now draped with seaweed, and its altar cold. They pleaded humbly that mankind should be renewed, and Zeus hearing their voices from afar, sent Hermes to assure them that whatever request they might make would be granted forthwith. Themis appeared in person, saying: "Shroud your heads, and throw the bones of your mother behind you!" Since Deucalion and Pyrrha had different mothers, both now dead, they decided that the goddess meant Mother Earth, whose bones were rocks lying on the riverbank. Therefore, stooping with shrouded heads, they picked up rocks and threw them over their shoulders; these became either men or women, according as Deucalion or Pyrrha had handled them. Thus mankind was renewed, and ever since "a people" (*laos*) and

"a stone" (*laas*) have been much the same word in many languages. Yet the flood proved of little avail; for some Pelasgians who had taken refuge on Mount Parnassus revived the cannibalistic abominations which had prompted Zeus's vengeance.'

8. In this version, apparently imported to Greece from Palestine, the Goddess Themis ('Order') renews man; and so probably did Ishtar the Creatrix in an earlier version of the *Gilgamesh Epic*. Deucalion's son Hellen was the supposed ancestor of all Greeks, and 'Deucalion' means 'new wine sailor' (*deuco-halieus*); which makes a connexion with Noah, inventor of wine (see 21. *a*). Hellen was brother to Ariadne of Crete, who married Dionysus the Wine-god. Dionysus also voyaged in a new-moon boat full of animals, including a lion and a serpent. Deucalion's wife was Pyrrha whose name means 'bright red', like wine.

9. The Ark's Biblical dimensions contravene the principles of ship-building: a wholly wooden three-decker 450 feet long would have broken up in even a slight swell. The timber used by Noah was not necessarily cedar, as most scholars hold, 'gopher-wood' being elsewhere unknown. It may have been acacia, the timber of Osiris's funeral boat.

10. Although absent from Greek or Mesopotamian Deluge myths, the rainbow as an assurance against floods occurs in European and Asiatic folk-lore. Stars are here imagined as bright studs plugged into the firmament, above which lie the Upper Waters.

11. Sexual aggression is considered a male prerogative in the Middle East; complete passivity being expected of women. Midrashic fancy transfers this view from men to animals. Noah's unwearying care for his charges reflects *Proverbs* XII. 10: 'A righteous man regardeth the life of his beast.' The belief that broken glass is an ostrich's sole food, rather than used like the grit swallowed by poultry as a means of dealing with the contents of its crop, occurs two or three times in midrashic literature.

12. Ravens were both venerated and shunned by the Hebrews. In *Job* XXVIII. 41 and *Psalm* CXLVII. 9, God takes especial care of them. In *Deuteronomy* XIV. 14, they are classed with unclean birds; and in *Proverbs* XXX. 17, they pluck out and eat the eyes of the ungodly. Yet in 1 *Kings* XVII. 4–6, despite their accursed beaks, they feed Elijah; and in *Canticles* V. 11, Solomon's locks are praised for being black as a raven's wing. It is possible that in an earlier version the raven, not Ham, was turned black by way of punishment; for Ham's descendants were the non-Negroid Canaanites, and in Greek myth the raven was turned from white to black either by Athene (Anath-Ishtar) for bringing bad news about the death of her priestesses, or by Apollo (Ea), for not picking out the eyes of his rival Ischys.

13. The 'pearl' is a Gnostic symbol for the Soul of Man: as in the apocryphal 'Hymn of the Pearl' (*Acts of St. Thomas*); and in the Manichaean *Kephalaia*. A Mandaean text runs: 'Who has carried away the pearl which illumined our perishable house?' According to Jonas, it sometimes also

stands for 'God's Word', which seems to be the meaning here. The Book of Wisdom given to Noah by Raphael has been omitted from *Genesis*, though the sacred book of Sippar mentioned by Berossus shows it to have formed part of the early Babylonian Deluge myth. This strengthens the view that Enoch who, like Utnapishtim, was rewarded for his virtues by residence in Paradise, and whom the angels helped to write a book of wisdom, is really Noah. 'Raphael' seems an error for 'Raziel' (see 6. *b*. 12).

14. The Pleiades were associated with rain because their rising and setting marked the limits of the Mediterranean sailing season. One of them (not two) appears from Greek myth to have become extinct in the late second millennium B.C.

21

NOAH'S DRUNKENNESS

(*a*) Noah, the first man to plant a vineyard, made wine from its grapes, grew drunk, and uncovered his secret parts. . . Ham, Canaan's father, entered the tent where Noah lay, observed his nakedness, and presently told Shem and Japheth what he had seen. They laid a garment over their shoulders, walked backwards into the tent and covered their father's nakedness, without looking at him. When Noah awoke from his drunken sleep, he saw what his little son [*sic*] had done to him, and cried: 'God's curse upon Canaan! May his brothers make him a slave of slaves! But blessed be the God of Shem, whom Canaan shall serve. May He also enlarge Japheth, to dwell in the tents of Shem; and Canaan shall serve them both.'

Noah lived another three hundred and fifty years.[1]

(*b*) Some embroider upon this story, saying that Noah brought grape-seed in the ark—or a vinestock from Eden—which he planted on Mount Lubar, one of the peaks of Ararat. His vines bore fruit that same day and, before nightfall, he harvested grapes, pressed them, made wine and drank freely of it.[2]

(*c*) Now Samael, the fallen angel, had come to Noah that morning and asked: 'What are you doing?' He answered: 'I am planting vines.'

'And what are they?'

'The fruit is sweet, whether eaten fresh or dry, and yields wine to gladden man's heart.'

Samael cried: 'Come, let us share this vineyard; but do not trespass on my half, lest I harm you.'

When Noah agreed, Samael killed a lamb and buried it under a vine; then did the same to a lion, a pig and an ape, so that his vines drank the blood of all four beasts. Hence, though a man be less courageous than a lamb before he tastes wine, yet after drinking a little he will boast himself strong as a lion; and, drinking to excess, will become like a pig and soil his garments; and, drinking yet more, will become like an ape, lurch about foolishly, lose his wits and blaspheme God. So it was with Noah.[3]

(*d*) Some say that at the height of his drunkenness he uncovered himself, whereupon Canaan, Ham's little son, entered the tent, mischievously looped a stout cord about his grandfather's genitals, drew it tight, and unmanned him. Ham then also entered. When he saw what had happened, he told Shem and Japheth, smiling as if it were a jest for idlers in the marketplace; but earned their curses.[4]

(*e*) Others say that Ham himself unmanned Noah who, awakening from his drunken sleep and understanding what had been done to him, cried: 'Now I cannot beget the fourth son whose children I would have ordered to serve you and your brothers! Therefore it must be Canaan, your first-born, whom they enslave. And since you have disabled me from doing ugly things in the blackness of night, Canaan's children shall be born ugly and black! Moreover, because you twisted your head around to see my nakedness, your grandchildren's hair shall be twisted into kinks, and their eyes red; again, because your lips jested at my misfortune, theirs shall swell; and because you neglected my nakedness, they shall go naked, and their male members shall be shamefully elongated.' Men of this race are called Negroes; their forefather Canaan commanded them to love theft and fornication, to be banded together in hatred of their masters and never to tell the truth.[5]

(*f*) Others however acquit Ham of any such crime. They say that when Noah was disembarking on Ararat, the sick lion showed base ingratitude by dealing his genitals a blow with its paw, so that he could never again perform the marital act. For this reason Shem offered the sacrifice in Noah's stead: men who have been thus injured being forbidden to serve at God's altar.[6]

1. *Genesis* IX. 20–28.
2. Tanhuma Buber Gen. 48; Tanhuma Noah 13; Gen. Rab. 338; PRE, ch. 24; *Jub.* V 28; VII. 1.
3. Tanhuma Noah 13; Gen. Rab. 338.
4. Tanhuma Buber Gen. 48–49; Gen. Rab. 338–40; PRE, ch. 23.
5. B. Sanhedrin 72a–b, 108b; B. Pesahim 113b; Tanhuma Buber Gen. 49–50; Tanhuma Noah 13, 15; Gen. Rab. 341.
6. Gen. Rab. 272, 338–39; Tanhuma Buber Gen. 38; Tanhuma Noah 9; Lev. Rab. 20. 1; Bate Midrashot II. 237.

*

1. The *Genesis* version of this myth has been carelessly edited. Ham could not be blamed, in justice, for noticing his father's nakedness; and Noah could never have laid such a grave curse upon Ham's innocent son Canaan, even if this involuntary act had been Ham's only fault. The text: 'And Noah awoke from his wine, and knew what his little son had done

unto him,' points to a gap in the narrative, plausibly filled by the midrashic account of his castration. Noah's curse shows that the sinner was little Canaan, not Ham. 'Ham, father of' is clearly an editorial insertion.

2. The myth is told to justify Hebrew enslavement of Canaanites—Canaan was *Chnas* for the Phoenicians, and *Agenor* for the Greeks. In one midrashic passage, sodomy has been added to Ham's crimes. A long list of Canaanite sexual offences is contained in *Leviticus* XVIII; and King Rehoboam's subjects are reproached in 1 *Kings* XIV. 24 for practising 'all the abominations of the nations whom the Lord drove out before the Children of Israel.' The sexual modesty of Shem's Hebrews is emphasized in this midrash, and God's blessing extended to all sons of Japheth who have now joined them.

3. 'Japheth' represents the Greek Iapetus, father by Asia of Prometheus and thus ancestor of the pre-diluvian human race. Iapetus was worshipped in Cilicia, former home of the Peoples of the Sea (see 30. 3), who invaded Canaan, adopted the Hebrew language and, as we learn from the story of Samson and Delilah, were intermarrying with Hebrews. Shem and Japheth's descendants made common cause against the Canaanites—the sons of Ham—whom they enslaved: a historical situation to which Noah's curse gives mythical validity. Ham, identified by a play on words in *Psalms* CV. 23 and CVI. 22 with *Kemi*, 'black', a name given to Egypt, was according to *Genesis* x. 6, the father not only of Mizraim (Egypt) but of Put (Punt), the Negroes of the Somali Coast; and of Cush, the Negroes of Ethiopia, imported to Palestine as slaves. That Negroes are doomed to serve men of lighter colour was a view gratefully borrowed by Christians in the Middle Ages: a severe shortage of cheap manual labour, caused by plague, made the re-institution of slavery attractive.

4. The myth of Shem, Ham and Japheth is related to the Greek myth of how five brothers, Coeus, Crius, Hyperion, Iapetus and Cronus successfully conspired against their father Uranus. Not only did Cronus castrate and supplant Uranus but, according to the Byzantine mythographer Tzetzes, Zeus followed his example in both particulars, with the help of Poseidon and Hades. In the Hittite myth, based on a Hurrian original, the Supreme God Anu's genitals were bitten off by his rebel son and cup-bearer Kumarbi, who afterwards rejoiced and laughed (as Ham is said to have done) until Anu cursed him. The God El himself, according to Philo of Byblus's quotation from Sanchuniathon, castrated his father Uranus. The notion that any son could behave in this unfilial manner so horrified the editors of *Genesis* that they suppressed Ham's castration of Noah altogether as the Greeks suppressed the myth of Cronus's castration until Christian times; Plato in his *Republic* and *Euthyphro* repudiated even Uranus's castration. Nevertheless, the myth of Noah's castration and consequent supersession as God's priest because of his injury, was preserved by the Jews. Canaan's use of a cord for the operation does not ring true; a

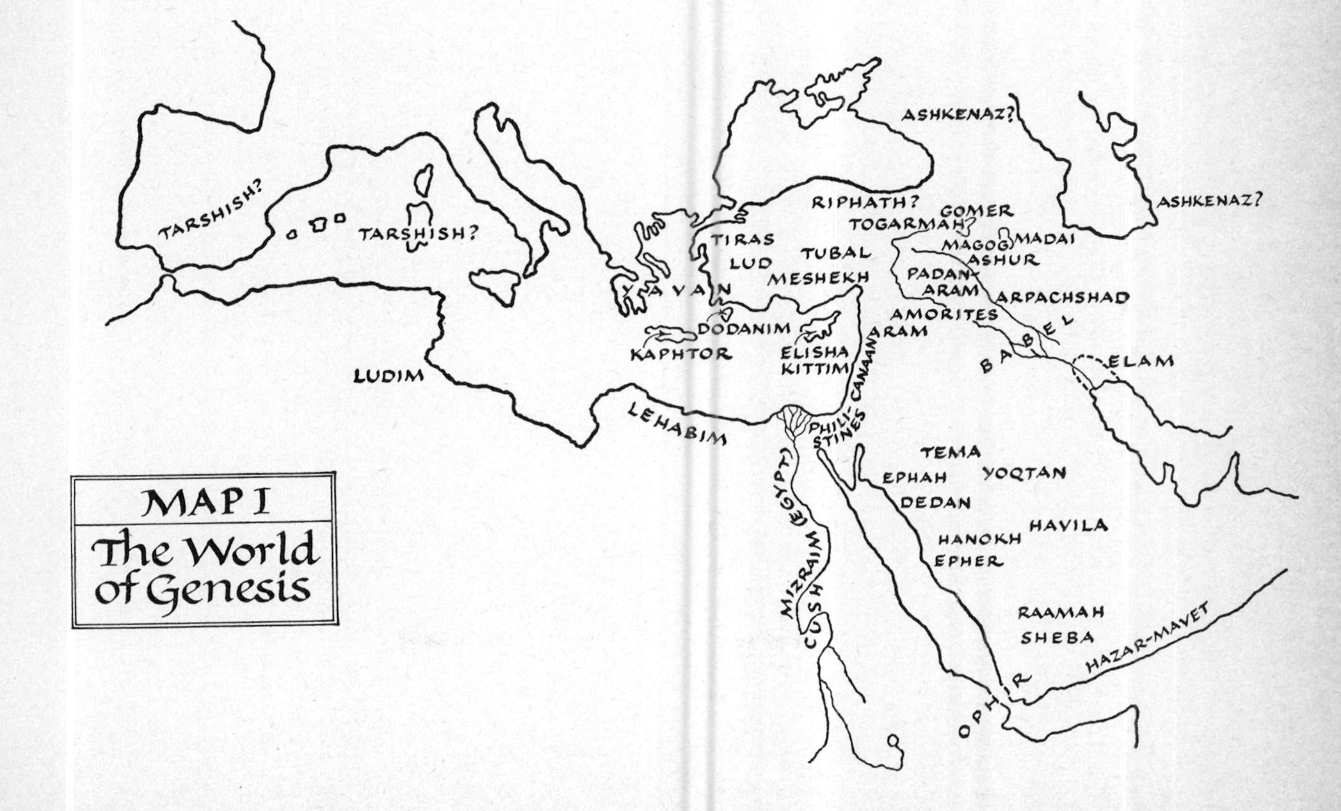

MAP I
The World of Genesis

pruning-knife from Noah's vineyard is likely to have been the original instrument.

5. Although eunuchs were forbidden membership in God's congregation (*Deuteronomy* xxiii. 1), it was an early Israelite battle custom to castrate uncircumcised enemies, as it was in the Egyptian wars of the fourteenth to the thirteenth centuries B.C. against the Sea Peoples. According to 1 *Samuel* xviii. 25–27, David pays King Saul two hundred Philistine foreskins as a bride-price for the Princess Michal. The same custom, originally perhaps a magical means of warding off a dead man's ghostly vengeance, survives today among the Arabs.

6. Japheth's sons are listed in *Genesis* x. 2 as Gomer, Magog, Madai, Javan, Meshech and Tiras. Gomer is now generally identified with the Cimmerians of Anatolia; Magog, with the Armenian kingdom of Gog (*Ezekiel* xxxviii. 1 ff) mentioned in the fourteenth-century B.C. Tell Amarna letters; Madai, with Media; Javan, with Ionia—his sons, recorded in *Genesis* x. 5, are Elisha, the Alashya of Cyprus; Kittim, another Cypriot people; Tarshish, the Tartessians of Southern Spain; and Dodanim, an error for Rodanim, the Rhodians. Tubal represents the Tibareni of Anatolia (see 19. 2); Meshech, their neighbours, the Moschians; Tiras, a people mentioned in an Egyptian document of the thirteenth century B.C., as Tursha, members of a sea-confederacy—perhaps the piratical Tyrsenians, some of whom held the Aegean islands Lemnos and Imbros as late as the sixth century B.C., while others emigrated to Italy and became the Etruscans.

22
THE TOWER OF BABEL

(*a*) Noah's descendants journeyed together from country to country, slowly moving eastward. They came upon a plain in Shinear, and said: 'Come, let us bake bricks; we will build ourselves a city, and a tower reaching to Heaven, and become one nation, lest we be scattered over the earth.' At once they began work, using bitumen for mortar to seal the courses of brick. God watched them, and thought: 'While they continue as one people, speaking one tongue, whatever they have in mind will be accomplished . . . Let us now confuse their language, and provoke misunderstandings between them.' This He did, and presently work on the tower ceased, and the builders dispersed in all directions. Its ruins were called Babel, because God *confused* the tongues of mankind, and divided a single nation into seventy.[1]

(*b*) Others say that Nimrod, a famous hunter in God's service, raised the Tower of Babel; but that it was not his first foundation. Having won dominion over all Noah's descendants, he had already built a fortress upon a round rock, setting a great throne of cedarwood upon it to support a second great throne, made of iron; this, in turn, supported a great copper throne, with a silver throne above the copper, and a golden throne above the silver. At the summit of this pyramid, Nimrod placed a gigantic gem from which, sitting in divine state, he exacted universal homage.[2]

(*c*) Nimrod's father was Cush, Ham's son by the wife of his old age. Ham doted on Cush, and secretly gave him the garments of skin which God had made for Adam and Eve, and which Shem should have inherited from Noah, but that Ham stole them. Cush kept the garments well hidden, and bequeathed them to Nimrod. When, at the age of twenty, Nimrod first wore these holy relics, he became exceedingly strong; and God granted him courage and skill in the chase. After killing his quarry, he never failed to raise an altar and offer God sacrifices.

(*d*) Twenty years passed, and a war broke out between the Sons of Ham and the Sons of Japheth, their chief enemies. Despite an early defeat, Nimrod gathered together four hundred and sixty Sons of Ham and eighty chosen mercenaries from the Sons of Shem. With this army he routed the Sons of Japheth, and returned victorious. The Sons of Ham thereupon crowned him King, and he appointed governors and judges over his entire kingdom, choosing Terah the son of Nahor to command the army. Nimrod's Councillors advised him to build a capital in the Eastern plain. He did so, calling the city Shinear because, he said, 'God has *shattered* my enemies.' Presently he also overcame the Sons of Shem. They brought him tribute, paid homage, and came to live at Shinear, side by side with the Sons of Ham and Japheth, all continuing to speak the Hebrew tongue.

(*e*) In his pride, Nimrod did more evil than any man since the Deluge, raising idols of stone and wood, which the whole world must worship; his son Mardon proved to be yet worse—hence the proverb 'Evil parents, evil child.' Nimrod and his people raised the Tower of Babel in rebellion against God; for he said: 'I will be revenged on Him for the drowning of my ancestors. Should He send another flood, my tower will rise even above Ararat, and keep me safe.' They planned to assault Heaven by means of the Tower, destroy God, and set up idols in His stead.[3]

(*f*) Soon the Tower had risen seventy miles high, with seven stairways on its eastern side, by which hod-carriers climbed to the summit; and seven on the western, by which they descended. Abram, Terah's son, viewed this work and cursed the builders in God's name: for should a brick drop from a man's hand and break, all bewailed its loss; but should a man himself fall and die, his neighbours never so much as turned their heads. When Nimrod's men shot arrows into Heaven, God's angels caught every one and, to deceive them, threw it back dripping blood. The archers cried: 'Now we have killed all Heaven's inhabitants!'[4]

(*g*) God then spoke to the seventy angels nearest His throne, saying: 'Let us go down again and confuse their language, making seventy tongues of one!' And so He did, for immediately the builders became embroiled in misunderstandings. If a mason told a hod-carrier 'Give me mortar!', the carrier would hand him a brick instead, with which the mason would angrily kill the hod-carrier. Many were the murders done in the Tower; and on the ground also, because of this confusion; until at last work slowed to a standstill.

As for the Tower: Earth swallowed a third part; fire from Heaven destroyed another third; the remainder stands to this very day—still so tall that from its summit the distant groves of Jericho appear like a swarm of locusts; and the thin air robs men of their wits. Yet the Tower seems less tall than it is, because of an exceedingly wide base.[5]

(*h*) Every family now spoke its own language, chose its own country, founded its own cities, became a nation, and acknowledged no universal ruler. God appointed seventy angels to guard these separate nations; but He said also: 'Over Abram's Children I will Myself watch, and they shall stay true to the Hebrew tongue.'[6]

(*i*) Nevertheless, Nimrod continued to rule from Shinear, and built more cities; namely Erech, Akkad and Calne, which he filled with inhabitants, reigning over them in majesty, and taking the title of 'Amraphel'.[7]

(*j*) At last Jacob's son Esau met Nimrod by chance while both were out hunting, killed him, and despoiled him of the holy garments. Esau was then likewise greatly strengthened, until Jacob stole them from his tent; saying: 'My brother does not deserve such a blessing!', he dug a hole and buried them.[8]

1. *Genesis* xi. 1–9; PRE, ch. 24.
2. Mid. Hagadol Gen. 188; Gaster, Maasiyot 2; Ginzberg, LJ, V. 201, n. 87.
3. Sepher Hayashar 22–31, Tanhuma Noah 18, 19.
4. See preceding footnote.
5. Sepher Hayashar 22–31; B. Sanhedrin 109a; PRE, ch. 24.
6. See preceding footnote.
7. PRE, ch. 24.
8. PRE, ch. 24.

*

1. This twelfth-century Jewish version of the ancient Tower of Babel myth closely resembles that given by the fifth-century Christian writer Orosius of Tarragona in his *Seven Books Against the Pagans*. Orosius, who seems to have drawn—though at second or third hand—from Jewish Tannaitic sources, describes the Tower as five and a half miles high, ten miles in circumference, with a hundred brazen gates and four hundred and eighty storeys. He reports that Nimrod's grandson Ninus built the city of Nineveh —an honour which *Genesis* x. 11 gives to Asshur.

2. Haupt identifies Nimrod son of Cush, also called Nebrod, or Nebron, with Nazimarattas, one of the non-Semitic (but also non-Indo-European) Cassite Kings of Babylon. Coming down from Cush (Kashshu) now Kurdistan, the mountainous region which separated Assyria from Media, they had overwhelmed the Amorite dynasty of Babylon, and ruled from the sixteenth century B.C. to the twelfth. Their national god was called Kashshu, and their kings could therefore be described as 'Sons of Cush'. Another Cassite god was Murudash, identified with Ninurta, a name from which

Nimrod may have been evolved. Like all his predecessors and successors, Nimrod will have been 'a mighty hunter' in so far as he was depicted on monuments killing lions, bulls and serpents—a symbolic act suggesting a coronation ritual. This myth may preserve the tradition of Nazimarattas's early glory—before he was humbled by Adadnirari I, a fourteenth-century king of Assyria. It is, however, confused by the existence of a second Cush —namely the Ethiopian kingdom centred on Meroe, and referred to in *Isaiah* XVIII. 1, which had ethnic connexions with Southern Arabia. The Cush mentioned in *Genesis* x. 8, which makes Nimrod a 'son of Cush', is Cassite; the one mentioned in the preceding verse fathered several South Arabian peoples and must therefore be the second Cush.

3. Nimrod's Hebraicized name (from the verb *marod*, 'to rebel') confirms his evil reputation. According to the seventh-century A.D. *Chronicon Paschale*, Persians called the constellation Orion 'Nimrod'; thus linking him with the rebel angel Shemhazai (see 18. *f*), and with the Greek hero Orion, also 'a mighty hunter' who offended his god.

4. The Nimrod tradition has, however, become attached to the myth of Samael's rebellion against El (see 13. *b. c.*), and the Hittite myth of Kumarbi's towering stone giant Ullikummi from whose head he intended to launch an attack on the seventy gods of Heaven (see 8. 3). A Greek myth, evidently drawn from the same source, tells how the gigantic Aloeids piled Mount Pelion upon Mount Ossa as a means of attacking Zeus's Olympian Heaven.

5. In *Genesis* XIV. 19 Amraphel is called the King of Shinear; in the Targum, King of Babylon; and in Josephus's *Antiquities*, 'Amara Psides, King of Shinar'. He has been confidently identified with Hammurabi, King of Babylon (1728–1686 B.C.), the code-maker and city-builder, though Shinar is now thought to be the Akkadian Shankhar, a country lying to the north-west of Babylon.

6. These early Hebrew traditions were reinforced and enlarged when King Nebuchadrezzar II (604–562 B.C.), another great administrator who forcibly populated the cities he built, carried off large numbers of Judaeans to exile in Babylon. King Sargon II of Assyria (721–705 B.C.) had already deported all but a few of the Northern Israelites; and Nebuchadrezzar needed the Judaeans to help him repair the shameful damage done at Babylon by Sennacherib in 689 B.C., when he plundered and burned the enormous terrace-temples known as *ziggurats*.

7. For a long time the lofty tower of *Birs Nimrud* was believed to be the Tower of Babel. With the decipherment of cuneiform inscriptions, it has, however, been established that *Birs Nimrud* was the tower of the city of Borsippa; and agreed that the Tower of Babel must have been located within the city of Babel (or Babylon) herself. This huge tower, called in Sumerian *Etemenenanki* ('House of the Foundation of Heaven and

Earth') stood in the central temple-complex called *Esagila* or 'House that Lifts Up the Head'.

The location of Babylon had been known before the German Oriental Society excavated it in 1899–1918, because the mound which marked its site near modern Hillah was called *Bābil* by the Arabs. This name preserved the old Akkadian form of the city's name, *Bab-Ili* or 'Gate of God'. The Biblical interpretation of Babel, as deriving from the Hebrew *balal*, 'to confuse', is an early and classic example of popular etymology.

8. Literal belief in the 'confusion of tongues' myth has been encouraged by the discovery at Borsippa of another Nebuchadrezzar II inscription. It records that the local ziggurat, long fallen into disrepair, had never been completed by its original architect; the God Marduk, therefore, persuaded his servant the King to perfect it. 'Mardon', the name of Nimrod's son, also means 'rebel', but may well be a cacophemism for 'Marduk'.

Though the Judaeans transported to Babylon by Nebuchadrezzar will have been astonished at the number of different dialects spoken by their fellow-deportees, God's confusion of tongues seems to be a far more ancient tradition—Moses of Chorene records it in his *Armenian History*, when discussing Xisuthros and the ark (see 20. 5).

9. St Jerome, like Orosius, identifies the Tower of Babel with Babylon itself—the outer walls of which, according to Herodotus, measured over fifty-five miles. The circumference of the Royal City enclosed by it was, however, about seven miles (not much less than the Tower's), and its inner walls stood over a hundred yards high.

10. Nebuchadrezzar's corvées, cruelly enforced, may account for the graphic description of how workmen went up and down the Tower stairs, and of what happened when a brick was dropped. His royal palaces, also, were 'adorned with gold, silver and precious stones, after being reared as high as the hills'—which may explain Nimrod's extravagant throne-pyramid. Forty years later, King Darius the Persian (522–485 B.C.) began the work of destruction so often prophesied by Isaiah and Jeremiah; his son Xerxes continued it. According to Arrian, Alexander the Great (366–323 B.C.) thought seriously of restoring Babylon's glory, but reckoned that it would take ten thousand men more than two months even to cart away the rubble. Meanwhile, the population had emigrated to Seleucia on the Tigris and, by Josephus's time (end of first century A.D.), all the ziggurats had fallen into complete neglect.

11. The Biblical tradition (*Genesis* x. 10) ranking Babylon with the primeval cities of Erech, Akkad and Calne, has not yet been disproved.

23

ABRAHAM'S ANCESTRY

(*a*) This is the genealogy of Abram, whom God afterwards renamed Abraham, and who was descended in the elder line from Noah's son Shem:

Shem begot Arpachshad two years after the Deluge.
Arpachshad begot Shelah at the age of thirty-five.
Shelah begot Eber at the age of thirty.
Eber begot Peleg at the age of thirty-four.
Peleg begot Reu at the age of thirty.
Reu begot Serug at the age of thirty-two.
Serug begot Nahor the First at the age of thirty.
Nahor begot Terah at the age of twenty-nine.
Terah begot Abram, Nahor the Second, and Haran at the age of seventy.[1]

(*b*) Abram's wife was Sarai, his half-sister by a different mother; for Terah had married both Amitlai daughter of Barnabo, and Edna, daughter of an elder kinsman also called Abram. Nahor the Second married his niece Milcah, daughter of Haran. The name of Haran's wife is forgotten, but he had Lot by her, and another daughter, Iscah. Some say that Haran was also Sarai's father.[2]

(*c*) When Haran died young, Terah left Ur, the city of his birth, accompanied by Abram, Sarai and Lot, to settle in the Land of Harran; but Nahor the Second stayed behind at Ur with his ancestors, who were all still alive. Shem finally attained the age of six hundred years; Arpachshad, of four hundred and thirty-eight; Shelah, of four hundred and thirty-three; Eber, of four hundred and sixty-four; Peleg, of two hundred and thirty-nine; Reu, of two hundred and thirty-nine; Serug, of two hundred and thirty; Nahor the First, of one hundred and forty-eight; and Terah, of two hundred and five.[3]

(*d*) Chaldean Ur was so named by its founder, Ur son of Kesed, Noah's descendant—an evil, violent ruler who made his subjects worship idols. Abram's ancestor Reu married Ur's daughter Orah, and called his son Serug, grieved that he would *turn aside* towards wickedness. Serug taught his son, Nahor the First, all the astrological wis-

MAP II
Abraham's World
BLACK SEA
GOMER
ARARAT
CASPIAN SEA
MESHEKH
TUBAL
BET EDEN?
PELEG?
REU?
SHAMAL
SERUG
HARRAN
(Tel) Nahor?
(Tel) Terah
CARCHE-MISH
ELLASAR
ARPAD
MOUNT ZAPHON
HALEB
SHUAH?
ISHBAK?
NINEVEH
ARPACHSHAD (ARRAPKHA)
ASHUR
UGARIT
ELISHA KITTIM
HAMATH
BENE YAMIN
Tigris River
Euphrates River
TADMOR (PALMYRA)
MARI
GEBAL (BYBLUS)
THE GREAT SEA
ARAM
DAMASCUS
SHINEAR (SHANKHAR)
BABEL (BABYLON)
JERUSALEM
HEBRON
SONS OF KETURAH
UR OF THE CHALDEES
MIZRAIM (EGYPT)
MIDIAN

dom of the Kasdim (Chaldeans); and Nahor called his son Terah because of the *suffering* he underwent when immense flocks of ravens ravaged the crops at Ur. Terah called the son borne him by Jessica the Chaldean, Abram, in honour of Edna's father.[4]

(*e*) Some make Abram the youngest of Terah's sons; others, the eldest.[5]

1. *Genesis* xi. 10–32; xx. 12.
2. *Jubilees* xi. 1–15; B. Baba Bathra 91a; PRE, ch. 26.
3. *Genesis* xi. 10–32.
4. *Jubilees* xi. 1–15.
5. *Genesis* xi. 26–27; Sepher Hayashar 27.

*

1. The Patriarchs' names have been identified with those of places or ethnic groups known from historical documents, which makes it plausible that they are the mythical residue of ancient traditions about ancestral wanderings. Arpachshad, whom Josephus calls 'ancestor of the Chaldeans', may refer to the land of Arrapkha, with the addition of Akkadian 'shad', meaning mountain. These 'mountains of Arrapkha' were ringed around modern Kirkuk with which Arrapkha is identified. Shelah seems to be the name of a deity, to judge from the composite name Methuselah (*Genesis* v. 21 ff) which means 'Man of Shelah', as Ishbaal means 'Man of Baal'. Eber, the eponymous ancestor of the Ibrim or Hebrews, may be connected with any of the several areas which Hebrew and Assyrian sources describe as the land 'beyond the river' (*eber hannahar*, in 1 *Kings* v. 4). Peleg is the name of a city located in the Middle Euphrates region and mentioned in the Mari letters. Reu occurs as a personal name in the same documents, and could possibly also be identified with the city of Rakhīlu in the same neighbourhood. Serug was a city called Sarugi, between Harran and Carchemish. Nahor is the city called Nakhuru, or Til Nakhiri, in the Mari letters and in Assyrian inscriptions from the eighteenth to the twelfth centuries B.C., located near Harran. The city of Terah, which occurs as Til Turahi in ninth-century B.C. Assyrian inscriptions, also lay near Harran.

2. The ages of the Patriarchs—Adam is said to have lived 930 years, Seth 912, Enosh 905, Kenan 910, Mahalalel 895, Jared 962, Enoch 365, Methuselah 969, Lamech 777, Noah 950, Shem 600, Arpachshad 438, Shelah 133, Eber 464, Peleg 239, Reu 239, Serug 230, Nahor 148 and Terah 205—are the modest Hebrew equivalents of the much longer life-spans attributed by the Babylonians to their antediluvian kings. The first five names will suffice as examples: Alulim reigned 28,800 years, Alamar 36,000, Enmenluanna 43,200, Enmenluanna 28,800, Dumuzi the Shepherd 36,000, etc. These Babylonian lists, a version of which is recorded also by Berossus, have one feature in common with the Biblical list of patriarchs: that both attribute extremely long life-spans to the earliest figures, then shorter, but still unrealistically long, lives to the later ones, until the historical period is reached when both kings and patriarchs are cut down to human size. In the ancient Near East, where longevity was considered man's greatest blessing, the quasi-divine character of early mythical kings and patriarchs is indicated by a ten-fold, hundred-fold or thousand-fold multiplication of their reigns or ages.

3. Harran (Assyrian *Kharran*, 'road') was an important mercantile city, on the highway from Nineveh to Carchemish, at its junction with the main road to Damascus. It is still in existence on the Balikh River, sixty miles west of Tell Halaf.

4. Since the raven is a solitary bird, the 'ravens' which damaged Mesopotamian crops may have been starlings, which fly about in large flocks. Or they may have been tribesmen with a raven totem; perhaps Midianite nomads from the Syrian Desert—Oreb ('raven') mentioned in *Judges* VII. 25, was a Midianite Prince.

5. Abram's genealogy is meant to show that the ancestors of Israel were all wise, virtuous, first-born sons; and the final details are evidently edited in that sense. Haran's birth should refer to a stay in Harran—though, indeed, the names are not etymologically identical; but he is said to have previously died at Ur. The repetition of 'Nahor' suggests that despite *Genesis* XI. 26–27, which lists Terah's three sons as Abram, Nahor the Second and Haran, Nahor will have been considered Terah's first-born, because he bore his paternal grandfather's name. This custom still prevails in the Middle East. Moreover, Terah married his cousin Edna, Abram's daughter; their second son should therefore have been an Abram too. Thus the midrashic tradition that Abram was younger than Nahor makes sense, though he would have been so named only if he were the second, not the third, son.

6. Midrashic commentators on Abram's marriage, who uphold the laws against incest found in *Leviticus* XX. 17, are obliged to disregard the clear evidence of *Genesis* XX. 12 that Sarai was his sister by a different mother. Instead, they make her Abram's brother's daughter—a union permitted under Mosaic law. Yet marriage to a half-sister born of a different mother was common in Egypt—Abram is connected in Biblical myth with Egypt—and was legal in Israel down to the days of King David.

24

ABRAHAM'S BIRTH

(*a*) Prince Terah commanded the royal armies, and one evening all King Nimrod's courtiers, councillors and astrologers assembled in his house to make merry with him. That same night Terah's son Abram was born and, as the company returned to their homes and gazed up at the sky, an enormous comet coursed around the horizon from the east, and swallowed four stars each fixed in a different quarter of Heaven. The astrologers stood amazed, knowing what this sight portended, and whispered to one another: 'Terah's new-born son will be a mighty Emperor. His descendants will multiply and inherit the earth for all eternity, dethroning kings and possessing their lands.'

When morning came they assembled again, and said: 'That comet was hidden from our lord Nimrod. Were he now to hear of it, he would ask us: "Why have you concealed so great a wonder from me?", and thereupon kill us. Let us rather acquit ourselves of blame by freely disclosing it.'

They did so, telling Nimrod: 'Pay Terah his price, and kill the child, before he can engender sons to destroy the King's posterity and ours.'

Nimrod sent for Terah, commanding him: 'Sell me your son!' Terah answered: 'Whatever the King orders his servant, will be done. Yet I humbly beg my lord's advice in a certain matter. Last night your Councillor Aayun ate at my table. He said: "Sell me that tall, swift stallion which our master lately bestowed on you, and I will fill your house with gold, silver and excellent fodder." How, my lord, could I have avoided offence in answering him?'

Nimrod cried angrily: 'Were you so foolish as even to consider such a sale? Does your house lack silver and gold? Or of what use would his fodder have been if you sold my gift, the finest stallion alive?'

Terah replied softly: 'Did not the King command me to sell my son? And is it not his purpose to destroy him? And what use will I have for silver and gold after the death of my heir? Must not all my treasures return to the King if I die childless?'

At this Nimrod grew angrier yet; but Terah said pacifically: 'All that is mine lies in the King's hands! Let him do to his servant as he wills, taking my son without payment.'

Nimrod said: 'No, but I shall surely pay you well for the child!'

Terah answered: 'May it please my lord that I ask a small favour?' And, being given leave, he said: 'Only allow me three days in which to commune with my soul and with my kinsmen, that we may do gladly what our lord demands in rage.'

Nimrod granted this favour and, on the third day, his messengers fetched the child. Terah, knowing that he and his kinsmen would be put to the sword unless he obeyed, took a slave-woman's son, born on the same night as Abram, gave him to the King, and accepted a price in silver and gold.

Nimrod dashed out the infant's brain, and afterwards forgot the matter. Terah hid Abram in a cave with a chosen foster-mother, and brought them food month after month. God cared for Abram throughout the next ten years; though some say that thirteen years passed before Terah at last gave Abram permission to leave the cave, where he had seen the light of neither sun nor moon; and that, on emerging, he spoke the holy tongue of Hebrew, despised the sacred groves, loathed idols and trusted in the strength of his Creator.[1]

Abram sought out his ancestors Noah and Shem, at whose house he studied the Law for thirty-nine years; but none knew his parentage.[2]

(*b*) According to another account, King Nimrod himself was versed in astrology, and learned from the stars that a child soon to be born would overthrow the gods whom he held in awe. Nimrod sent for his chief princes and councillors, asking them: 'What can I do against this child of destiny?' They advised him to raise a great building, and issue an order that all women big with child should be delivered there; he should also post sentries at the gates, and set midwives to watch over the women and slaughter every male child as soon as born. 'Nevertheless,' they added, 'spare every female infant, clothe its mother in royal purple, and shower her with gifts, saying: "Thus shall it be done to mothers of daughters!"'

Nimrod took their advice, and the angels who watched this slaughter, reproached God, crying: 'Have You not seen how Nimrod the blasphemer murders innocents?' God replied: 'I never sleep, nor turn away My eyes, but observe all that happens on earth—either openly or in secret! Soon I shall chastise him.'

When Terah saw that Amitlai's belly swelled and her face paled, he asked: 'What ails you, wife?' She answered: 'This ailment, the *qolsani*, comes upon me yearly.' He told her: 'Uncover yourself, that I may see whether you are with child; for, if so, we must obey the King's command.' But the unborn child rose in her breast; thus Terah, groping at Amitlai's belly, found nothing and said: 'It is indeed the *qolsani*.'

Amitlai, knowing that her hour was at hand, went out across the desert to a cave by the River Euphrates. There the pangs of travail came upon her, and she gave birth to Abram, the radiance of whose face lighted up the cave from end to end. Amitlai cried: 'Alas, that I have borne you in this evil time! King Nimrod has destroyed seventy thousand male infants, and I fear greatly for your sake.' She took part of her garment and wrapped Abram in it, saying: 'God be with you and forsake you not!' Then she departed.

Abram, lying alone in the cave without food, began to weep; but God sent the archangel Gabriel to give him milk, which flowed from the little finger of his right hand—and so the child was suckled.

At sunset on the tenth day, Abram stood up and walked down to the riverbank. He saw the stars rise, and thought: 'Surely, these are as gods?' When dawn came and the stars vanished, he said: 'Yet I shall give them no worship, for gods do not vanish.' Then the sun rose in splendour, and he asked: 'Is this my god, whom I should praise?' But when it set again at dusk, he cried: 'It was no god! Sun, Moon and stars are surely moved by One greater than they.' Gabriel appeared, saying: 'Peace be with you!' Abram answered: 'And with you be peace! What is your name?' He said: 'I am Gabriel, the Messenger of God,' whereupon Abram washed his face, hands and feet at a spring, and prostrated himself.

Some days later, the sorrowing Amitlai, pale from lack of sleep, returned to the cave where she had left her son, but found no sign of him; and her tears flowed afresh to think him devoured by wild beasts. On the riverbank she saw a grown boy, and said: 'Peace be with you!', whereupon the following colloquy took place:

Abram: And with you be peace! What is your business?
Amitlai: I am come to find my infant son.
Abram: And who brought him here?
Amitlai: I was with child, and fearful lest our King should destroy my son, as he has destroyed seventy thousand others. Therefore I came here, bore him in yonder cave, went home alone, and now he is nowhere to be seen.

Abram: When was your son born?
Amitlai: Twenty days ago.
Abram: Can any woman abandon her child in a desert cave, yet hope to find him alive after twenty days?
Amitlai: Only if God shows mercy.
Abram: Mother, I am your son!
Amitlai: That cannot be! How have you grown so tall, and learned to walk and talk in twenty days?
Abram: God has done these things for me, to show you how great, terrible and eternal He is!
Amitlai: My son, can there be a greater one than King Nimrod?
Abram: Even so, Mother: God sees, but cannot be seen! He lives in Heaven, yet His glory fills the earth! Go to Nimrod, and repeat my words to him!

Amitlai returned, and when Terah heard her tale, he bowed low before the King, and asked leave to address him. Nimrod said: 'Lift up your head, and say what you would have me hear!' Terah told him all, repeating Abram's message; and Nimrod blanched. He asked his chief princes and councillors: 'What shall be done?' They cried: 'Divine King, do you fear a little child? Does not your kingdom hold princes by the thousand thousand, besides countless lesser nobles and overseers? Send the least of your nobles to secure the child and shut him in your royal prison.' But Nimrod asked: 'What infant ever grew to boyhood within twenty days, or sent me a message by his mother that there is a God in Heaven who sees yet cannot be seen, and whose glory fills the world?'

Then Satan, dressed in raven-black silk, prostrated himself before the King and, being given leave to raise his head, said: 'Why be confounded by a child's babble? Let me offer you good counsel!' Nimrod asked: 'What counsel is that?' Satan answered: 'Throw open your armouries and deal out weapons to every prince, noble and warrior in your land, so that they may secure the child and bring him here to serve you.'

This Nimrod did; but when Abram saw the approaching army, he prayed for deliverance, and God interposed a cloud of darkness between him and his enemies. They ran in terror to the King, crying: 'It were better if we departed from Ur!' Nimrod gave them leave of absence, paid for their journey and fled himself to the Land of Babel.[3]

1. Sepher Hayashar 24–27; PRE, ch. 26.
2. Sepher Hayashar 27.

3. Ma'ase Abraham, BHM i. 25 ff.

*

1. The birth of Abraham is laconically recorded in *Genesis* XI. 27: 'Terah begot Abram, Nahor and Haran.' Myths of Abraham's miraculous birth and his escape from King Nimrod have survived among the Near Eastern Jews. Both these versions are midrashic, and draw on a common stock of Indo-European mythology. The second was sung until recently as a Ladino (i.e. Sephardic Spanish) ballad at birth celebrations in Salonica.

2. Lord Raglan, in *The Hero*, examines myths of many diverse heroes—Greek, Latin, Persian, Celtic and Germanic, listing their common characteristics. The hero's mother is always a princess, his reputed father a king and her near kinsman; the circumstances of his conception are unusual, and he is also reputed to be the son of a god; at his birth, an attempt is made, usually by his father or grandfather, to kill him. The hero is spirited away by his mother, reared in a far country by lowly foster-parents; nothing is known of his childhood, but on reaching manhood, he returns home, overcomes the king, sometimes also a dragon, giant or wild beast, marries a princess, often the daughter of his predecessor, and becomes king himself.

3. Sometimes the child is set adrift in a boat by his mother, as were Moses and Romulus; sometimes, exposed on a mountainside, as were Cyrus, Paris and Oedipus—though Oedipus is also said to have been set adrift. The later stages of the hero's progress, his assumption of power, successful wars, and eventual tragic death, are equally constant. The myth represents a dramatic ritual in honour of the Divine Child, the fertile Spirit of the New Year. His 'advent', which gave its name to the rites at Eleusis near Athens, was celebrated in a sacred cave, where shepherds and cattlemen carried him by torchlight. The Spirit of the New Year, in fact, defeats the Spirit of the Old Year, marries the Earth-princess, becomes King, and is himself superseded at the close of his reign.

4. Abraham, however, like all succeeding patriarchs who obeyed God, was spared the disgraceful end of Romulus (torn in pieces by his fellow-shepherds); of Cyrus (impaled by a Scythian queen); of Paris (killed in the fall of Troy); of Oedipus, Jason and Theseus (all dethroned and exiled). Moses, though forbidden to enter the Promised Land for his sin of smiting the rock at Marah, died nobly, earned a splendid funeral and an interment by God Himself.

5. The only Israelite for whom almost the entire mythic sequence has been claimed was Jesus of Nazareth; yet his own people repudiated the divine parentage awarded him by Greek-speaking Christians. The Gospels make Jesus come of royal stock, his putative father being a close kinsman of his mother; shepherds worshipped him in the cave, he lay cradled in the usual winnowing-basket, astrologers saw his star in the East, King Herod murdered the infants of Bethlehem. Jesus was then spirited away across

the desert, and returned incognito to Israel years later. The Apocryphal Gospels also celebrate his precocity as a child.

6. Certain elements in the two Abraham nativity myths may be borrowed from Christian sources, though that of Cyrus told by Herodotus comes close enough to the first version—wicked king, astrologers and substituted victim. Moreover, Cyrus had been praised in *Isaiah* XL–XLVIII as God's servant chosen for the destruction of Babylon and the freeing of Nebuchadrezzar's Judaean captives; and remained a national hero in Israel even after he failed to fulfill all Isaiah's prophecies.

7. In the second version, Gabriel's lacteous finger recalls the beasts—wolves, bears, mares, goats, bitches—divinely sent to suckle such heroes as Oedipus, Romulus, Hippothous, Pelias, Paris and Aegisthus; the riverside, and the murder of innocents, recall the story of Moses.

8. A child who walks, talks and grows up soon after birth occurs in the Greek myths of Hermes and Achilles, and in the *Hanes Taliesin*, a Welsh Divine Child myth.

9. That Amitlai wrapped Abraham in her own garment is understood by Near Eastern Jews as the still prevalent custom of dressing infant sons as daughters, to ward off ill-luck. In the original story, however, this garment is more likely to have been a token by which she afterwards recognized Abraham. Her *qolsani* ailment may stand for *calcinaccio*—a fever burning like a lime-kiln.

10. The mention of Abram's brother Haran seems to be a gloss on the text identifying him with Nahor, King of Harran (see 23. 1 and 36. 5).

25

ABRAHAM AND THE IDOLS

(*a*) Some say that Gabriel raised the boy Abram on his shoulders and, in the twinkling of an eye, flew through the air from Ur to Babel. In the market place, Abram met his father Terah, who had fled there with Nimrod. Terah at once warned the King that his wonder-working son had pursued them to the city; and Nimrod, though greatly afraid, sent for him. Abram entered the palace, testified in a loud voice to the Living God before the whole court and, shaking Nimrod's throne, named him a blasphemer. At this, the royal idols ranged all about fell flat on their faces, and so did the King himself. After two hours and a half, he dared raise his head and inquire faintly: 'Was that the voice of your ever-living God?' Abram answered: 'No, Abram spoke, the least of His creatures.' Nimrod then acknowledged God's power, and let Terah depart in peace. Terah accordingly went to Harran, accompanied by Abram, Sarai and Lot.[1]

(*b*) Others say that Abram returned to Babel full of wisdom from studying under Noah. He found his father Terah still commanding King Nimrod's armies, and still bowing down to idols of wood and stone—twelve great ones and many lesser. Abram thereupon asked his mother Amitlai to kill and dress a lamb. Having set the dish before these idols, he watched whether any of them would eat. When they never moved a finger, he mocked, and said to Amitlai: 'Could it be that the dish is too small, or the lamb lacking in savour? Pray kill three other lambs, and season them more delicately!' She did so, and he offered this dish also to the idols; but again they never stirred.

The Spirit of God came upon Abram. He took an axe and hacked them in pieces, leaving untouched only the largest; then put the axe into its hand and went away. Terah had heard the noise and, running into the hall, saw what destruction his son had made. He sent for Abram and cried angrily: 'What is this?'

Abram answered: 'I offered food to your idols; doubtless they have quarrelled over it. Has not the largest of them hacked the lesser ones in pieces?'

Terah said: 'Do not deceive me! These are images of wood and stone, fashioned by the hand of man.'

Abram asked: 'If so, how can they eat the food that you offer them daily? Or how can they answer your prayers?' He then preached the Living God, reminding Terah of the Deluge, God's punishment for wickedness. While Terah doubted what answer to make, Abram caught up the axe, and hacked the surviving idol in pieces.

Terah thereupon denounced Abram to King Nimrod, who at once imprisoned him. Afterwards, when the astrologers recognized Abram as the destined Emperor, Nimrod ordered him and Haran, his brother, to be thrown bound into a fiery furnace. Flames soon consumed the twelve men chosen for this task, and also Haran, who was an unbeliever; but Abram stood unhurt with his garments unsinged, though fire had scorched away the ropes that bound him. Nimrod cried to his remaining guards: 'Cast this felon into the furnace, or you shall all die!' But they lamented, crying: 'Would the King condemn us to be burned, as were our comrades?'

Then Satan prostrated himself before Nimrod, and said: 'Give me timber, ropes and tools! I will build my lord a siege-catapult to hurl Abram into the fiery furnace from a convenient distance.' Nimrod agreed, and Satan set to work. First he tested the catapult, using huge boulders; then took Abram and bound him. Though implored by Amitlai to bow down and worship the King, Abram said: 'No, Mother; for water can quench the fire of man, but not the fire of God!' Then he prayed, and instantly the flames died down; moreover, God made the logs bud, blossom and yield fruit, until the furnace became a royal pleasure garden in which Abram walked freely among angels.

(*c*) All the astrologers, councillors and courtiers then praised the Living God; and Nimrod, standing abashed, gave Abram his two chief slaves, by name Oni and Eliezer, besides rich treasures of silver, gold and crystal. Three hundred of Nimrod's men also joined Abram, when he went away to Harran.[2]

1. Ma'ase Abraham, BHM i. 24–30.
2. Sepher Hayashar 34–43; Ma'ase Abraham 32–34.

*

1. These legends have no Scriptural authority. *Genesis* tells only that Abraham married his half-sister Sarai, and that Terah took them and his nephew Lot from Ur of the Chaldees to Harran, where he died, and where God later commanded Abraham: 'Go hence to the land which I will

show you!' (*Genesis* xii. 1). But according to a tradition quoted by Stephen, a Greek-speaking Egyptian Jew (*Acts* vii. 2–4), God gave Abraham this order while he still lived at Ur.

2. The tale of the fiery furnace may have been told to fortify the midrashic explanation of 'Ur Kasdim' as meaning 'furnace of the Chaldeans'. It is drawn partly from *Daniel* iii, according to which Daniel and his three companions were thrown into a fiery furnace by King Nebuchadrezzar for refusing to worship idols, but escaped unharmed; partly from *Bel and the Dragon*, an apocryphal addition to *Daniel*, according to which Daniel exposed the powerlessness of King Cyrus's idols, proved that his priests had themselves eaten the food-offerings set before Bel's golden image, and was permitted by Cyrus to pull down his temple. Gabriel helped Daniel (*Daniel* viii. 16 and ix. 21), as he here helps Abraham.

3. Both legends are based on a prophecy in *Jeremiah:*

> '. . . *Every goldsmith is put to shame by the graven image, that his molten image is falsehood, and there is no breath in them. They are vanity, a work of delusion; in the time of their visitation they shall perish. The portion of Jacob is not like these, for He is the fashioner of all things . . . The Lord of Hosts is His name . . . And I will punish Bel in Babylon, and I will drive forth out of his mouth that which he hath swallowed up . . . I will do judgement upon her graven images . . .*' (*Jeremiah* li. 17–19, 44, 52).

26

ABRAHAM IN EGYPT

(*a*) When Terah died in Harran, God ordered Abram to visit Canaan, the land of his inheritance, and laid a curse on all who opposed him. Abram set out at the age of seventy-five, with Sarai, Lot, their retainers, cattle and treasures; said goodbye to Nahor, and journeyed southward. At Shechem, God appeared again to Abram, saying: 'This is the land which your children shall possess!' Having built Him an altar there, Abram next pitched his tent between Bethel and Ai; but famine drove him on farther, until he reached the border of Egypt, where he warned Sarai: 'If the Egyptians know you to be my wife, they will grow jealous, I fear, and kill me. Tell them only: "I am Abram's sister."'

(*b*) The Egyptians were indeed astonished at Sarai's beauty; and when King Pharaoh heard of it he resolved to make her his concubine, paying Abram a huge price in oxen, cattle, sheep and slaves. God, however, afflicted the palace with so many plagues that at last Pharaoh, discovering their cause, sent for Abram and reproached his withholding the full truth. 'What if I had taken your wife into my bed?' he asked angrily; and expelled Abram from Egypt, restoring Sarai to him, and not even taking back the gifts won by his deception.[1]

(*c*) Some say that when Abram came to the Torrent of Egypt which separates Egypt from Canaan, Sarai went down to wash her face. Abram who, because of his austerity, had never performed the act of love with Sarai, nor so much as lifted her veil, saw so lovely a face reflected in the water that, knowing the Egyptians for shameless fornicators, he took her across the border shut in a chest and dressed in all her finery. The officer of customs, dissatisfied with Abram's evasive answers, made him open the chest. When he saw Sarai lying inside it, he said: 'This woman is far too beautiful to be enjoyed by anyone but Pharaoh!' A prince of Pharaoh's household, named Hyrcanus, hastened to inform his master; who rewarded him richly and sent an armed escort for Sarai.[2]

(*d*) This is the song that Hyrcanus sang in Sarai's praise:

How beautiful is Sarai:
Her long, fine, glossy hair,
Her shining eyes, her charming nose,
The radiance of her face!
How full her breasts, how white her skin,
Her arms how goodly, how delicate her hands—
Their soft palms and long slender fingers—
How lissom her legs, how plump her thighs!
Of all virgins and brides
That beneath the canopy walk
None can compare with Sarai:
The fairest woman underneath the sky,
Excellent in her beauty;
Yet with all this she is sage and prudent,
And gracefully moves her hands.[3]

(*e*) Assured by Sarai that she was Abram's sister, Pharaoh sent him valuable gifts and led her into the royal bed chamber. Abram wept all night, and so did Lot, praying that Sarai would keep her virginity. God therefore sent down an angel; and Pharaoh, when he tried to embrace Sarai, was dealt a blow by an unseen hand. When he tried to remove her sandals, another blow fell; when he tried to touch her garments, the angel buffeted him harder. Sarai, however, saw the angel, and slyly moved her lips to form words of instruction: either 'Wait!' or 'Strike now!', as the case might be. A whole night went by in this manner, and Pharaoh accomplished nothing. At dawn, he saw signs of leprosy on the walls, beams and pillars of his bed chamber, and on the faces of his eunuchs. Sarai then confessed: 'Abram is not only my brother, but my husband,' and Pharaoh made no more attempts to enjoy her. He placated Abram with even richer gifts than before; and gave Sarai a bond-maid named Hagar, his own daughter by a concubine. Thereupon the leprosy faded.[4]

(*f*) Others say that a pestilential wind invaded the palace; and that Pharaoh promised Sarai the Land of Goshen; and all the silver and gold she desired, in payment for the night he would spend with her.[5]

(*g*) But before leaving Egypt, Abram taught Pharaoh's court mathematics and astronomy, which he had learned from the Chaldeans.[6]

1. *Genesis* XII. 1–20.
2. Sepher Hayashar 51; Josephus, *Ant.* i.8.1.
3. Genesis Apocryphon 43–44; *Jubilees* XIII. 1–15.
4. Gen. Rab. 389, 554; Tanhuma Lekh 5 and 6; Tanhuma Buber Gen. 66–67; Sepher Hayashar 51, 52; PRE, ch. 26.
5. Genesis Apocryphon 43–44; PRE, ch. 26.
6. Josephus, *Antiquities* i.8.

*

1. The historical fact underlying *Genesis* XII seems to be the movement of Hebrew-speaking tribes southward through Palestine into Egypt, among a mixed horde of Hittites, Mitannians from Harran, Syrians and Palestinians. Their leaders, the Hyksos Kings, ruled Egypt from 1730(?) to 1570 B.C. and their empire extended over a great part of Syria. Very little is known about these Shepherd Kings because, when their viceroys in Upper Egypt rebelled against Pharaoh Apopy II (1603–1570 B.C.), and dethroned him after a long war, the Egyptian scribes—for whom the sheep was an unclean animal (*Genesis* XLVII. 34)—suppressed the dynastic records.

2. Abram's short stay in Canaan 'because of the famine', is consonant with the destructive Hyksos march through Palestine. He paused only to raise an altar at Shechem, which was to become an important Israelite sanctuary. His somewhat hasty return suggests that certain Hebrew tribes, finding Egypt a country unsuitable for nomads, wandered back to Palestine where, some generations later, they were joined by their compatriots under Joshua.

3. The myth of Abram, Sarai and the King who desired her, occurs twice again: in the story of Abram, Sarai and Abimelech of Gerar (see 30); and in that of Isaac, Rebekah and the same Abimelech (see 37). It has been borrowed from the Egyptian *Tale of the Two Brothers*, which also provides that of Joseph and Potiphar's wife. Abram's locking of Sarai in a chest is paralleled by the opening tale of the *Arabian Nights*. His mistrust of the Egyptians as fornicators is based on the bad reputation of Ham's descendants: for Mizraim (Egypt) figures in *Genesis* X. 6 as a son of Ham.

4. Pharaoh's gift of Goshen and all the silver and gold Sarai desired was a retrospective midrashic charter permitting the Israelites to occupy Goshen in Joseph's day, and to despoil the Egyptians during the Exodus (*Exodus* XI. 2 and XII. 35–36). Pharaoh's further gift of Hagar is intended to account for her Egyptian nationality. The poem in praise of Sarai's beauty comes from the *Genesis Apocryphon* discovered in 1947 among the Dead Sea Scrolls.

5. Leprosy, to the Israelites, meant such skin diseases as ringworm, scald-head and vitiligo (*Leviticus* XIII. 29–46); not leprosy proper. The term (*'ṣara'at'*) was further applied to mould or mildew in buildings (*Leviticus* XIV. 33–57), or on garments (*Leviticus* XIII. 47–59). That the Israelites themselves suffered from 'leprosy' is reported by the Egyptian priest Manetho (fourth century B.C.), who alleges that this was the cause of eighty thousand scabby Israelites being quarantined in a separate city, and afterwards either drowned or driven into the wilderness under Moses.

6. Jacob's vision of the ladder occurred at Bethel (see 43. *c*). Haai ('ruin'), or Ai, a royal Canaanite city sacked by Joshua (*Joshua* VII and VIII), was standing again in Isaiah's time (*Isaiah* X. 28). It has been identified with modern el-Tell, one mile south-east of Bethel.

27

ABRAHAM'S RESCUE OF LOT

(*a*) From Egypt, Abram led his flocks and herds back to the place where he had pitched his tent between Bethel and Ai; and then on again to Shechem, where he had built God's altar. His nephew Lot accompanied him, but their shepherds quarrelled so hotly about pasturage that the two kinsmen thought it best to divide the land between them. Lot chose the eastern side, making his home at Sodom, a city of the Plain; Abram took the western side, making his home at Hebron.

(*b*) Meanwhile, King Chedorlaomer of Elam persuaded three Kings, namely Amraphel of Shinear, Arioch of Ellasar and Tidal of Goyim, to march against five other Kings—Bera of Sodom, Birsha of Gomorrah, Shinab of Admah, Shemeber of Zeboyim and Bela of Zoar—who had jointly rebelled after twelve years of vassalage. On their march from Elam, Chedorlaomer and his allies defeated three tribes of giants: the Rephaim at Ashteroth-Karnaim, the Zuzim at Ham, and the Emim at Shaveh-Kiriathaim; they also drove the Horites from Mount Seir to El-Paran. Turning about, they stormed En-Mishpat, an Amalekite stronghold now known as Kadesh, and the city of Hazezon-Tamar. Then they met the King of Sodom and his allies in the Vale of Siddim, which was full of slime pits, and won a further victory. The Vale of Siddim is now the Dead Sea.

(*c*) Abram, while encamped at Hebron in the terebinth grove of Mamre the Amorite, heard from a fugitive that Lot and his family had been captured at Sodom. At once he led three hundred and eighteen retainers to the rescue, and followed Chedorlaomer's army northward. Coming up with the enemy at Dan, Abram attacked them by night on both flanks, slaughtered some, pursued the rest as far as Hobah near Damascus, and recovered all the booty; at the same time liberating Lot, his family and numerous other prisoners-of-war.

(*d*) Upon Abram's triumphal return, the King of Sodom welcomed him in the royal Vale of Shaveh, by Salem; where Melchizedek, King of Salem and priest of the Most High God, gave him bread, wine and this benediction:

Abram, be you blessed by the Most High God,
Maker of Heaven and Earth!
And blessed be the Most High God Himself,
Who has delivered your enemies to you!

In acknowledgement of Melchizedek's kindness, Abram presented him with a tenth part of his spoils. The King of Sodom then said: 'Pray, my lord Abram, restore me my subjects, but keep their flocks, herds and treasure.' He answered: 'I have sworn to the Most High God, Maker of Heaven and Earth, that I shall not take so much as a thread or a shoe-latchet from you, lest word go about: "Abram was enriched by the King of Sodom!" Repay only what my servants, my ally Mamre, and his sons Aner and Eshcol, have cost me in food and drink.'[1]

(*e*) Some say that Chedorlaomer had previously rebelled against King Nimrod and made him his vassal. And that, when Abram mustered his retainers against Chedorlaomer, he said: 'We are about to do battle. No man who has committed a sin and suffers from guilt should come with me!' But when they reached Dan—which is now called Paneas—Abram's strength suddenly drained away: a prophetic voice had told him that here, many generations later, the idolatrous King Jeroboam would set up a golden calf for Israel to worship. Nevertheless, Abram's servant Eliezer fought valiantly that day, and caused the enemy as much loss as did all his three hundred and seventeen comrades.[2]

(*f*) Others again say that the planet Zedek (Jupiter) shed a mysterious light around Abram as he fought, so that he saw his enemies clearly despite the gloom; Layla, the Angel of Night, also assisted him. Moreover, all his enemies' swords turned to dust, and their arrows into chaff; contrariwise, Abram only needed to hurl dust and it became javelins; a handful of straw, and it became a volley of arrows.[3]

(*g*) Others again say that Melchizedek (also known as Adoni-Zedek), was Abram's ancestor Shem, and that he now taught Abram the duties of priesthood, particularly the rules governing shew-bread, wine-libations and burned offerings. He also gave Abram the garments of skin made by God for Adam and Eve, stolen by Ham, but now restored to him. All this Shem did because God had appointed Abram his successor. For when Shem said: 'Abram, be you blessed by the Most High God, Maker of Heaven and Earth; and blessed be the Most High God Himself, who has delivered your enemies to you!', Abram at once cried: 'Is it seemly to bless the servant before the Master?'—a reproof which convinced God that Abram was the fitter to be His priest.[4]

1. *Genesis* XIII. 1–18, XIV. 1–24.
2. Sepher Hayashar 46; Tanhuma Buber Gen. 73–74; Gen. Rab. 419; PRE, ch. 27.
3. Gen. Rab. 418; Tanhuma Buber Gen. 76; B. Sanhedrin 96a, 108b; B. Taanit 21a.
4. Gen. Rab. 420–22; Lev. Rab. 25.6; Num. Rab. 4.8; B. Nedarim 32b; Tanhuma Buber Gen. 76.

*

1. Shinear, over which King Amraphel reigned, has been identified with Akkadian Shankhar (see 22. 5); and Tidal with Tudkhalya, the name of several Hittite kings. Goyim, Tidal's kingdom, may be a proper name or may simply mean 'peoples'. Ellasar seems to be Ilansra, mentioned in eighteenth-century B.C. Mari inscriptions, and later Hittite documents, as a royal city between Carchemish and Harran. The name Arioch seems to mean 'Honoured One' (*Ariaka*) in Old Iranian. Elam was an ancient and powerful kingdom at the head of the Persian Gulf. Chedorlaomer may have been one of several Elamite kings whose names, extant in cuneiform inscriptions, resemble his.

2. It was for long doubted that *Genesis* XIV contained any historical kernel. Nevertheless, some scholars now regard it as an ancient historical tradition, first recorded, probably in the Akkadian or Canaanite language, soon after the war described in it took place, and much later translated into Hebrew. The date of this war is variously placed as early as the twentieth and as late as the seventeenth century B.C. However, in its extant form, the chapter serves as a charter for possession of Canaan. Canaan was conquered from Kadesh and El-Paran (or Elath) on the Red Sea gulf in the south, to Dan in the north, by four invaders; but immediately afterwards, Abram defeated them, recovered all the booty they had taken and, by the right of succession, also acquired all the land overrun by them. Thus Abram's children, when they emerged from Egypt and conquered Canaan, were taking possession of a country the title to which was theirs by inheritance.

3. The names of five Cities of the Plain and their kings still present numerous problems. What the name of Bera, King of Sodom means, is uncertain. Some see in it an abridged form of a theophoric name, such as Bera-Baal, found in Liḥyānite (North Arabian) inscriptions, which may mean 'Splendour of Baal'. Birsha, the name of the King of Gomorrah, has not been satisfactorily explained, although some connect it with an old Semitic word meaning 'flea' which, in Akkadian, has the form of *Burshu'u*, and is used to this day in Arabic as a personal name.

Admah has been identified with *Adamah* (Psalm LXXXIII. 11) and *Adam* (*Joshua* III. 16), today Tell Adamiya, on the eastern bank of Jordan, near the mouth of the Jabbok River. If so, Admah was the most northerly frontier outpost of this confederation of five cities. Its king, Shinab, carried a royal name which recurred centuries later as that of an Ammonite king, Sanibu, mentioned in the time of Tiglath Pileser III (745–727 B.C.). Shemeber's city, Zeboyim, has been located tentatively in the Lisan peninsula of the Dead Sea, where there is a Wadi Sebaiye. Others, however, hold that these four cities stood in an area now covered by the southern part of the Dead Sea. Bela appears as the name of an Edomite king whose city was Dinhabah (*Genesis* XXXVI. 32–33). This name was also current among the Hebrews (*Genesis* XLVI. 21; 1 *Chronicles* V. 8) and the South Arabians, where it meant 'gourmand'. Bela's royal city, Zoar (meaning 'little'), seems to be identical with Zukhr, mentioned in the Tell Amarna letters and called 'Zoara' by Josephus and 'Segor' by Eusebius and the Crusaders. It lay north-east of the Dead Sea, probably at modern Tell el-Zara. Zoar figures prominently in the Lot myth as the only place, a 'small' one (*miz'ar*), that escaped God's destruction of the Cities of the Plain (*Genesis* XIX. 20–23; see 32. *a*).

4. How far the Promised Land extended, to whom it was promised, and under what conditions, can be seen from the following Biblical passages:

Genesis XII. 7—Abraham, coming south from Harran on the Middle Euphrates, is promised the land inhabited by the Canaanites for his seed in general, without condition.

Genesis XIII. 11–18—Abraham amicably resigns the Plain of Jordan to Lot, ancestor of the Moabites and Ammonites, but God repeats His promise to Abraham that as far as he can see to north and south, east and west, will belong to his seed.

Genesis XV. 18–19—Abraham is promised for his seed in general all the territory between the Torrent of Egypt (near Gaza) and the Euphrates, including the entire Land of Canaan defined in *Genesis* X. 19 as extending from Sidon to Gaza and the Red Sea.

Genesis XVII. 8–14—Abraham is promised for his seed in general, for ever, all the Land of Canaan; on condition that they worship God alone and practice circumcision. Circumcision will constitute their title-deeds to the land.

Genesis XXVI. 3–4—This promise is renewed to Isaac, Abraham's second son.

Genesis XXVIII. 13–15—The same promise is repeated by God to Jacob, Isaac's younger son, just before he leaves Canaan to go to Mesopotamia.

Genesis XXXV. 11–12—Upon Jacob's return to Canaan, God again repeats His promise at Bethel.

Exodus XXIII. 31–33—The Israelites descended from Isaac through Jacob are promised the same large territory; on condition that they eventually expel its original inhabitants, and make no treaty with them.

Numbers xxxiii. 50–56; xxxiv. 1–15—The Israelites are ordered to occupy Canaan, including Philistia and part of Transjordan.

Deuteronomy i. 7–8—The boundaries of the Promised Land are stated to extend from the wilderness to Lebanon, and from the Mediterranean Sea to the Euphrates River. In *Deuteronomy* xi. 22 a further condition attaches to the promise: that Israel should keep the Mosaic Law.

Dan, the northernmost point of Palestine occupied by the Hebrew tribes, was originally called Laish ('Lion', *Judges* xviii. 7, 29, etc.), and later Paneas. It was not only the place where Jeroboam raised a golden calf (1 *Kings* xii. 28–29), but famous for a grotto sacred to Pan and the Nymphs, from which the River Jordan springs; and for a temple raised in honour of Augustus by Herod the Wicked (Josephus: *Antiquities* xv. 10). It afterwards became Caesarea Philippi, a heathen city studiously avoided by Jesus (*Matthew* xvi. 13; *Mark* viii. 27). The mound over the grotto is called to this day Tell el-Qādī ('Mound of the Judge'), Qādī being the Arabic translation of Dan, 'judge'.

5. The Melchizedek myth provides a charter for Jerusalem's peculiar sanctity and the institution of a priestly tithe; but, according to *Exodus* xxv. 30; xxix. 40, etc., the rules governing shew-bread, wine-libations and sacrifices were first revealed by God to Moses in the Wilderness. The tithe laws were also Mosaic (*Leviticus* xxvii. 30 ff; *Numbers* xxviii. 26 ff, etc.).

6. Though *Melchizedek*, a name resembling Adoni-Zedek, King of Jerusalem (*Joshua* x. 1 ff), means 'The God Zedek is my King', it was later understood as 'Lord of Righteousness'. Zedek will have been the city-god of Salem, not the God of the Hebrews, and not monotheistically worshipped. The Ammonites called him 'Zaduk'. *Zedek*, moreover, was the Hebrew name for the planet Jupiter, which enabled the Midrash to develop from this encounter between Melchizedek and Abram a myth that the planet helped Abram against his enemies. A 'royal vale' occurs in the story of Absalom (2 *Samuel* xviii. 18) and, according to Josephus, lay a quarter of a mile from Jerusalem; this may be 'the royal vale of Shaveh' later accursed as the Valley of Hinnom ('Gehenna' or 'Tophet'), the scene of King Ahaz's human sacrifices (2 *Chronicles* xxviii. 3). A tradition quoted in *Hebrews* vii. 3, that Melchizedek had 'neither father nor mother' may be based on a similar phrase found repeatedly in letters sent by the Jebusite King Abdu-Heba (slave of [the Goddess] Heba), to Pharaoh Amenhotep III in the fourteenth century B.C., which meant that he depended for his position not on birth but on Pharaoh's grace.

7. Lotan occurs in *Genesis* xxxvi. 21–22 and 1 *Chronicles* i. 38–39 as the eldest son of Seir the Horite; and in Egyptian records as a geographical area of Southern Palestine, which included Mount Seir. Since Horites, or Hurrians, had lived on Mount Seir before the Hyksos hordes arrived, Abraham's nephew Lot of Harran may well be another fictional charac-

ter. But perhaps Abraham's Hebrews, after dislodging the Hurrians from their Lotan pastures, assisted them against Eastern raiders from the direction of Elam.

8. The Canaanite giants conquered by Chedorlaomer were known as Emim ('Terrors') by the Moabites, Zamzummim or Zuzim ('Busy Ones') by the Ammonites, and Rephaim ('Weakeners') by the Gileadites. The *Book of Jubilees* makes them anything from ten to fifteen feet tall. They appear in Ugaritic mythology as spectres. Other names were Anakim ('Giants'), Awwim ('Devastators'), Gibborim ('Heroes'), Nefilim ('Fallen Ones')—(see 18. *i.* 11–13). An Egyptian execration text of the early second millennium B.C. mentions several rulers of Jy'aneq ('Land of the Anakim'?), one of whom is named Abi-imamu, perhaps 'Father of the Emim'.

9. The midrash makes them tall as cedars, and explains that every Hebrew of that generation was equally gigantic. Abraham himself was seventy times the height of an ordinary man, and each of his steps measured three or four miles; so was his servant Eliezer, who alone passed the test of holiness which Abraham set his three hundred and eighteen retainers, and who had as much strength as all of them together. It should be observed that the numerical equivalents of the letters in *Eliezer* add up to 318. Jacob, his son Simeon, and his grandson Manasseh were reputedly giants. So were Samson and Saul's general Abner, who said: 'If I could but seize the earth with my feet set elsewhere, I should be able to shake it!'; also Absalom, David's son, whose hair when shorn weighed two hundred shekels.

10. Aner, Eshcol and Mamre, Abraham's allies, are thought by some scholars to represent three residential districts of the city of Hebron. Mamre is stated in *Genesis* XXXV. 27 to have been a section of the city of 'Kiriath-Arba, the same is Hebron, where Abraham and Isaac sojourned,' and in *Genesis* XXIII. 18 is identified with Hebron. Eshcol was the name of a valley or wadi near Hebron (*Numbers* XIII. 22–24); while Aner seems to have survived in *Ne'ir*, the name of a neighbouring hill.

11. For the Vale of Siddim see 32. 2.

28

THE SEVERED CARCASES

(*a*) As Abram lay asleep in his tent, God appeared to him, saying: 'Fear not, for I am your shield, and your reward shall be great!' He asked, 'O Lord, what reward can console me if I die childless, and my slave Eliezer inherits all that is mine?' God answered: 'Not he, but your own son shall inherit. Arise, go out into the night!' Abram obeyed, and heard Him say: 'I am your God, who brought you from Ur of the Chaldees to make this inheritance yours. Look at the stars of Heaven, and try to count them; for your posterity shall be no less numerous.' Abram pleaded: 'O Lord, how can I be assured of this blessing?' God replied: 'Offer Me a three-year-old heifer, a three-year-old she-goat, and a three-year-old ram; also a turtle dove and a wild pigeon.'

(*b*) When morning came, Abram cut a heifer, a she-goat and a ram into halves with his sword; laying one half of each beast on the left side of a narrow lane, and the other half opposite it on the right. Then he killed a turtle dove and a pigeon; laying one on the left side of the lane, and the other opposite it on the right. As Abram worked, vultures flew down to feast on the carcases; but he drove them off.

(*c*) That night, as the sun set, Abram fell into a trance, and dread of the darkness overcame him. Again, he heard God's voice: 'When you have died at a ripe age, your children shall be strangers in an alien land, and slaves to its rulers. After four hundred years I will punish that land, and lead your people out, greatly enriched. Yet not until the fourth generation of their wanderings, when the Amorites have at last fully deserved My punishment, will your people return to possess what is their own!' The thick darkness was then dispelled by a smoky flame, like that of a torch, which passed along the lane between the severed carcases. God declared: 'I have given this land to your posterity: from the Torrent of Egypt to the Euphrates. The Kenite, the Kenizzite, the Kadmonite, the Hittite, the Perizzite and the Rephaim; also the Amorite, the Canaanite, the Girgashite and the Jebusite shall be their subjects!'[1]

(*d*) Some say that God lifted Abram above the dome of Heaven, and said: 'Look at the stars, and try to count them,' adding: 'Whoever stands beneath a star, fears it; but you, seeing one shine below you, may now lift up your head and consider yourself the greater!'[2]

(*e*) Others hold that Abram's severed carcases foreshadowed the Empires destined to oppress Israel: the heifer, Babylon with its three Kings Nebuchadrezzar, Evil Merodach and Belshazzar; the she-goat, Media with its three Kings Cyrus, Darius and Ahasuerus; the ram, Greece with its three Kings Alexander, Caligula and Antoninus. Moreover, the turtle dove signified the Ishmaelites; and the pigeon, Israel. Had Abram not severed the beasts with his sword, these Empires would have grown too powerful; but thus they were weakened.[3]

(*f*) Azazel, the fallen angel who seduces mankind, came disguised as a vulture to feast on the carcases. He addressed Abram: 'What do you here, on these holy heights, where no mortal may eat or drink? Fly off, lest heavenly powers burn you!' But Abram's guardian angel rebuked Azazel: 'His lot lies on the heights, as yours lies in the depths. Depart, for you can never lead him astray!'[4]

(*g*) God then showed Abram a vision of Hell, the oppressive Empires, the Torah and the Sanctuary, saying: 'While your children honour these last two, they will escape the first two. Choose now whether they are to be punished by damnation or by servitude!' All day long, Abram sorrowfully weighed one evil against the other. At last, having been granted another vision of a Fourth oppressive Empire, namely Edom—though it would fall, as the three earlier ones were fated to fall and never rise again—he left God to make the choice. God chose servitude.[5]

1. *Genesis* xv. 1–21.
2. Gen. Rab. 433; Tanhuma Shoftim 11.
3. Gen. Rab. 437; Mid. Agada Gen. 33; PRE, ch. 28.
4. *Apocalypse of Abraham*. ed. Box, 51–53.
5. Targum Yer. *Gen.* xv. 1–11; Gen. Rab. 443–44; Tanhuma Buber Ex. 130; Mid. Agada Gen. 34.

*

1. The savage deity here described has more in common with the one who attacked Jacob (*Genesis* xxxii. 25–33) and tried to kill Moses (*Exodus* iv. 24), than with the friendly guests entertained by Abraham and Sarah in bright sunshine (*Genesis* xviii. 1–15). His presence was later attested by a pillar of fire in the Wilderness (*Exodus* xiii. 21, etc.), and by the fire that consumed Elijah's sacrifices on Mount Carmel (1 *Kings* xviii. 38).

2. This myth of a covenant between severed carcases authorizes a solemn Hebrew rite still performed at Jerusalem in the sixth century B.C. During

Nebuchadrezzar's siege, King Zedekiah and his courtiers swore they would free their Hebrew bondmen in accordance with the Law; but failed to do so when the siege was temporarily lifted. Jeremiah then reminded them of their ancestors' oath: to release every Hebrew bondman after six years of service (*Exodus* XXI. 2). This covenant, neglected for generations, had recently been renewed in the Temple by priests, leaders and freemen of Judah who passed between the severed quarters of a calf. Jeremiah therefore prophesied that their latest breach of faith—which profaned God's name—would be punished in some by slavery, in others by carrion birds and beasts sent to mangle their corpses (*Jeremiah* XXXIV. 1–22).

3. In Biblical Hebrew, covenants were not 'made', but 'cut' (*karath b'rith*—*Genesis* XV. 18; XXI. 27, etc.); or 'passed through' (*'abhar bibh'rith*—*Deuteronomy* XXIX. 11); or 'come into' (*Ezekiel* XVI. 8); or 'stood in' (2 *Kings* XXIII. 3). This proves the antiquity of the rite, which is still practised by the Male and Baka tribes of south-western Ethiopia: the man who 'cuts' the covenant smears himself with blood from the severed carcases. In late Hebrew practice, oath-takers were sprinkled with blood of animals sacrificed on the altar—the 'blood of the covenant' (*Exodus* XXIV. 5–8).

4. Since the carrion birds mentioned in both *Genesis* and *Jeremiah* signify divine punishment of transgressors, the rite amounts to a declaration: 'Unless I tread faithfully along a narrow lane of truth, let my body be cut in two like these carcases; and let carrion birds and beasts mangle it!' Thus King Saul cut a yoke of oxen in pieces, which he sent through Israel with the message: 'Either come to fight behind Saul and Samuel, or be treated like these oxen!' (1 *Samuel* XI. 7). In Greek myth, the covenant sworn by Helen's suitors for common action against whoever wronged the man she chose to marry, was taken, according to Pausanias, on the severed pieces of a horse, Poseidon's sacred animal. The animals here chosen by Abraham were sacred, it will be observed, to three deities other than the Bull-god El: heifer, to the Canaanite Moon-goddess; she-goat to the Philistine goddess, mother of Cretan Zeus, whom the Greeks knew as Amaltheia; ram to the Sumerian Sky-god, or to the ram-headed Ammon of Egypt.

5. In the midrashic list of empires, 'Media' means Persia; and Greece and Rome have been conflated by the listing of Alexander, Gaius Caligula (if the emendation of GSQLGS into 'Gaius Caligula' is correct) and Antoninus Pius as Greek kings. If two more animals had been available, Alexander and the two main Seleucid oppressors of Israel, Antiochus Ephiphanes and Antiochus Sidetes, would have represented the Greek; Pompey, Caligula and Antoninus Pius (138–161 A.D.), the Romans. Rome is called 'Edom' because King Herod 'the Wicked', whose seizure of the Jewish throne had been confirmed by the Emperor Augustus, was an Edomite; this usage avoided direct offence to the Roman authorities.

6. In Abraham's time, according to *Genesis*, the Promised Land contained not only such early peoples as the Amorites, Canaanites, Kenites and

Rephaim, but the Kadmonites (*bene Kedem*, or 'Men of the East'), invaders from the Syrian Desert; the Kenizzites, an Edomite clan (*Genesis* XXXVI. 11); the Perizzites ('Pheresites' in 1 *Esdras* VIII. 69), whose identity is still a riddle; the Hittites; the Girgashites (perhaps the QRQShA, allies of the Hittites in their war against Rameses II); and the Jebusites, whose origin is unknown, but whose King Abdu-Khipa ('Slave to [the Goddess] Khipa'—see 10. 10) acknowledged Egyptian sovereignty in the fourteenth century B.C. (see 27. 6)

7. Israel's emblem, a pigeon (*Hosea* VII. 11; XI. 11), was the non-migratory *columba livia*, which frequented rocks and caves (*Jeremiah* XLVIII. 28 and *Canticles* II. 14), whereas the migratory turtle dove (*turtur communis*) represented the nomadic Ishmaelites and their kinsmen the Edomites.

29

ISHMAEL

(*a*) After ten years of marriage Sarai, Abram's wife, believing herself barren, offered him her Egyptian bond-woman Hagar as his concubine. Abram, now eighty-five years old, accepted the gift. When Hagar conceived, and Sarai complained to Abram of being held in scorn by her, he answered: 'Do as you will with Hagar; is she not your bond-woman?' Sarai took him at his word and tormented Hagar so cruelly that she ran away. God, disguised as an angel, found her at a desert spring between Kadesh and Bered, on the way from Shur, and asked why she had come there. When Hagar answered, 'I have run away from my unkind mistress,' God told her to return and suffer in silence, promising that she would mother a race of warriors. He continued: 'Your son shall be named Ishmael, for *God has heard* your cry of suffering. Ishmael shall live in the wilderness, like a wild ass, and maintain himself by force of arms.'

Hagar cried: 'The *Living One has seen me!*', and named the well Lahai-Roi. She then returned to her mistress and bore Abram a son, duly called Ishmael.[1]

(*b*) Many years later, when Sarai had borne Isaac, the child of her old age, she saw Ishmael playfully dandling him, and said to Abram: 'Cast out this bond-woman and her son; Isaac is your heir, not Ishmael!' Abram grieved at these words, but God comforted him: 'Grieve neither for Hagar, nor yet for Ishmael! Do as Sarai says; because the children of Isaac shall be My chosen people. Nevertheless, since Ishmael also is your son, his children shall become a great nation.'

(*c*) Abram arose early and, giving Hagar a loaf of bread and a skin of water, sent her away with Ishmael in her arms to the desert of Beersheba. When the skin was dry, she laid Ishmael under a bush and sat down a bowshot from him, saying: 'Let me not see my son perish!' As she wept, an angel heard Ishmael calling on God's name, and said: 'Weep no more, Hagar! *God has heard* your son's voice. Take him up again and hold him fast, for Ishmael shall become a great nation.' Then Hagar's eyes were opened and, seeing a spring of water, she refilled the skin and gave the child to drink. God guarded Ishmael, who lived thereafter in the Wilderness of Paran. Hagar married him to an Egyptian woman named Meribah, because she was given to *quarrelling*; though others call her Isa, a Moabitess.[2]

(*d*) Some say that vexed by Hagar's presumption, Sarai turned her out of Abram's bed, threw shoes in her face, and cast the evil eye on her, so that Hagar's first-born, a girl, died at birth. She also made Hagar follow behind her, with pails and towels, to the bath house. Sarai then cast the evil eye on Ishmael, who grew so feeble and wizened that he could no longer walk. Therefore, when Abram sent Hagar away, she had to carry Ishmael on her back—though already seventeen years, or even twenty-five, of age; and suffering from such a burning thirst that the water-skin was soon dry.[3]

(*e*) Some absolve Sarai of blame, saying that Ishmael, as a child, shot an arrow at Isaac but missed him; and later he raised an altar to a false god, worshipped idols, caught locusts, lay with harlots, forced virgins. Ishmael also mocked those who told him that Isaac would receive the first-born's double portion after Abram's death, asking: 'Am I not the first-born?'[4]

(*f*) Others say that when God let the spring flow in the wilderness to save Ishmael's life, His ministering angels protested: 'Lord of the Universe, why spare one who will leave Your own chosen children to die of thirst?' God asked: 'Does he honour me now?' They answered: 'He still lives in righteousness.' God said: 'I judge every man as he is now, not as he will be!'[5]

(*g*) Others, again, deny Ishmael's idolatry and evil living. They say that Abram, many years after Hagar's expulsion, told Sarai: 'I yearn to visit my son Ishmael.' Sarai cried: 'Stay, my lord, I beseech you!' However, seeing Abram determined on the journey, she made him swear not to alight from his camel when he reached Ishmael's tent, lest his heart should be turned against Isaac.

Abram rode out into the Wilderness of Paran and, about noon, found Ishmael's tent, but neither he nor Hagar were at home; only Meribah, his wife, and some young sons. Abram inquired: 'Where is Ishmael?' Meribah answered: 'He has gone hunting.' Abram, keeping his promise to Sarai, did not alight. 'Give me refreshment, daughter,' he said, 'for travel has made me faint.' Meribah told him: 'We have neither water nor bread.' She would not leave the tent, nor look at Abram, nor ask his name, but beat her young sons and reviled the absent Ishmael. Abram, greatly displeased, ordered Meribah to approach him; and then, still mounted on his camel, said: 'When your husband returns, tell him: "An aged man of such and such appearance came here from the Land of the Philistines, in search of you. I did not ask his name, but reported your absence. Thereupon he said: 'Advise your husband to cast away this tent-peg and cut himself another!'"' Then Abram rode off. Upon Ishmael's return, Meribah delivered the message, from which he understood that she had denied his father hospitality. He obeyed Abram by divorcing Meribah and marrying another wife, his mother's kinswoman Patuma.

Three years later, Abram again visited Ishmael's tent. Patuma ran out to greet him, saying: 'I regret that my lord Ishmael has gone hunting. Come in, take refreshment, and await his return; for you must be weary of travel.' Abram answered: 'I cannot dismount; but pray give me water to quench my thirst!' Patuma fetched water, and also pressed him to eat bread; which he did gladly, blessing Ishmael, and God also. Abram told Patuma: 'When Ishmael returns, say: "An aged man of such and such appearance came from the Land of the Philistines, in search of you. He said: 'Assure your husband that the new tent-peg is an excellent one; let him not cast it away!'"' Upon receiving this message, Ishmael understood that Patuma had paid her father-in-law due respect; and presently took her, his sons, flocks, herds and camels, to visit Abram in the Land of the Philistines, where they spent many days; and his house prospered.[6]

(*h*) Ishmael met Isaac only once more: when together they buried Abram in the Cave of Machpelah at Hebron.[7]

(*i*) Before Ishmael died, at the age of one hundred and thirty-seven, he had twelve sons. They were Nebaioth, Kedar, Adbeel, Mibsam, Mishma, Dumah, Massa, Hadad, Tema, Jetur, Naphish and Kedmah. Each became a prince, and each had a village from which his people set out on their wanderings.[8]

1. *Genesis* xvi. 1–16.
2. *Genesis* xxi. 8–21; PRE, ch. 30; Sepher Hayashar 69–70.
3. Gen. Rab. 453–54, 570.
4. Tosephta Sota 304; Gen. Rab. 567–68; Sepher Hayashar 69–70; PRE, ch. 30.
5. Gen. Rab. 572–73.
6. Sepher Hayashar 70–72; PRE, ch. 30.
7. *Genesis* xxv. 9.
8. *Genesis* xxv. 12–18.

*

1. This myth supports Israelite claims to nobler, though later, descent than the Southern kinsmen who had been forced into the wilderness by their step-mother Sarai. *Hagar* in South Arabic means 'village', which explains why her grandsons are said to have lived in villages of their own.

Lahai-Roi is more likely to mean 'Well of the Reem's Jawbone', on the analogy of others named after animals, such as *En-Gedi*, 'Well of the Kid', (*Joshua* xv. 62) and *En-Eglaim*, 'Well of the Two Calves' (*Ezekiel* xlvii. 10). In *Judges* xv. 17–19 Samson, like Ishmael, is given water by God when thirsty, at a well called Lehi ('jawbone').

Bered is identified by the *Targum Yer.* with Khalasa, an important town on the road from Beersheba to Egypt. Kadesh, east of Bered, possessed an oracular spring, En-Mishpat (*Genesis* xiv. 7).

2. A close parallel to the difficult relationship between Abram, Sarai and Hagar is found in the Laws of Hammurabi: 'If a man marries a priestess—*naditum* (a hierodule, or temple servant, forbidden to bear children)—and if she gives her husband a bond-maid to bear him children, and if afterwards this bond-maid demands equal honour with her mistress because of the children she has borne, the priestess must not sell her, but she may be returned to bondage among her fellow-slaves.' Casting a shoe across property was a ritual act of asserting possession (*Ruth* iv. 7; *Psalm* lx. 10). Sarai cast shoes in Hagar's face as a reminder of her servitude.

3. Abram circumcised Ishmael at the age of thirteen (*Genesis* xvii. 25)—circumcision being originally a pre-marital rite—and Isaac was born about a year later (*Genesis* xviii. 1–15; xxi. 1 ff); which makes Ishmael the elder by fourteen years. Since Ishmael here appears as a babe in arms whom Hagar lays under a bush, a later mythographer has repaired this inconsistency by explaining that Sarai had cast the evil eye on him, so that he grew wizened. His catching of locusts probably means that Sarai suspected Hagar of planning to supplant her in Abram's affections: according to the Ethiopian *Kebra Nagast*, Pharaoh's daughter used locusts and a scarlet thread to seduce King Solomon.

4. The Wilderness of Paran, occupied by Ishmael, lies in Northern Sinai. Most of the twelve Ishmaelite tribes here named appear in other records; but their confederacy does not seem to have been securely fixed. In *Judges* xiii. 24 the Midianites are reckoned as Ishmaelites, although *Genesis* xxv. 1 ff ranks Midian as Ishmael's half-brother. Nebaioth and Kedar, the first two sons of Ishmael, are mentioned by *Isaiah* xlii. 11; lx. 7; *Jeremiah* xlix. 28; *Ezekiel* xvii. 21. Nebaioth's territory lay east of the Dead Sea; Kedar's north of Nebaioth, in the Syrian Desert. Nebaioth has been implausibly identified with the Nabataeans. Hadad's territory is unknown; but *Hadad* was a Canaanite Storm-god. *Kedmah* means 'people of the East'—probably the Syrian Desert.

5. Adbeel, Massa and Tema appear in records of the Assyrian King Tiglath-Pileser III (eighth century B.C.) as the *Idiba'ilites*, *Mas'a* and *Tema*—all Arab tribes. The records of Assurbanipal (seventh century B.C.) contain the names *Su-mu'-il*, or *Ishmael* whose king was Uate or Iaute, and Kedar: whose king was Ammuladi. Tiglath-Pileser assigned Idibi'lu of Arabia the task of guarding the Egyptian frontier and, after conquering the Philistines, gave him twenty-five of their cities. Tema is the oasis in North-

ern Arabia still called Tayma. Dumah seems to be Adumatu, an oasis and fort in the Syrian Desert conquered by Sennacherib. Mibsam and Mishma rank in 1 *Chronicles* IV. 25 among the sons of Simeon, which suggests that the Israelite tribe of Simeon, whose territory spread southward from Judaea, assimilated at least part of them.

6. Jetur and Naphish are mentioned in 1 *Chronicles* V. 19, together with Nodab and the Hagrites, as tribes against whom the trans-Jordanian Israelites—Reuben, Gad and the half-tribe of Manasseh—made war. The same passage (V. 21) indicates that the Hagrites were camel-breeders and shepherds. Josephus, St. Luke and the Church Fathers mention the Jeturites, or Ituraeans (*Itouraioi*). Their territory bordered on Edom (Idumaea) and, in 104 B.C., King Aristobulus the Hasmonean annexed some of it, at the same time forcibly converting the Ituraeans to Judaism. Two generations later, they moved northward and occupied parts of the Hermon range and Syria where, in Gospel times, Herod's son Philip the Tetrarch ruled them. Their archers served as Roman auxiliaries, and are mentioned by Virgil and Cicero—who calls them 'the most savage race on earth'.

7. After David founded his kingdom and strengthened the Aramaean nomads, the Ishmaelites seem to have been forced southwards, where they merged with better established Arab tribes. Subsequently, the Arabs accepted the view, still held by them, that all Northern, or Adnani, Arab tribes were descended from Ishmael. Hagar's name has been preserved by the Hagrites (*Hagrim* or *Hagri'im*), a tribe mentioned with Jetur and Naphish in 1 *Chronicles* V. 19, and with the Ishmaelites in *Psalm* LXXXIII. 7. Eratosthenes, cited by Strabo, places them east of Petra.

30

ABRAHAM IN GERAR

(*a*) At Gerar, between Kadesh and Shur, Abram again passed off Sarai as his sister. When King Abimelech of Gerar would have enjoyed her, God threatened him with death. Like Pharaoh, Abimelech protested his innocence; but God answered: 'Nevertheless, make amends by sending Sarai back, and begging Abram to intercede for you!' This Abimelech did, though reproaching Abram, who said, unperturbed: 'When the gods caused me to wander abroad, I commanded my wife: "Tell all whom you meet that I am your brother!"—which is the truth.'

King Abimelech gave Abram oxen, sheep, bond-women and a thousand pieces of silver, and invited him to stay at Gerar. Abram then made his intercession and God, who had closed the wombs of all the Gerar women, restored their fertility.[1]

(*b*) Some say that Michael threatened Abimelech with a sword, and overruled his excuses, arguing: 'When strangers enter a city, it is proper to offer them food; but improper to inquire after their women. Since you inquired after Sarai, Abram feared that your men might kill him if he acknowledged her as his wife. The guilt must therefore be yours!'

They explain that God not only made the Gerar women barren: He closed up their other secret orifices, and those of the men too, so that at dawn the sorely troubled people met together, complaining: 'By Heaven, one more night like the last, and we shall be dead!'[2]

1. *Genesis* xx. 1–18.
2. PRE, ch. 26; B. Baba Kamma 92a; B. Makkot 9b; Pesiqta Rabbati 176b; Gen. Rab. 553.

*

1. Gerar was the name of both a kingdom and its capital city. The Land of Gerar lay on the south-western border of Canaan, separating it from Egypt, between Gaza and Beersheba. The city of Gerar was located in or near the Valley of Gerar which is identified by some scholars with modern Wadi Shari'ah, to the north-west of Beersheba, by others with

modern Wadi Ghaza, due west of Beersheba. But the name of the country survived as late as Byzantine times, when Bishop Eusebius of Caesarea called it Geraritica.

2. The designation of Abimelech as a Philistine king (*Genesis* xxi. 33–34; xxvi. 1, 8, 18) has been regarded as an anachronism, since the arrival of the Philistines in Canaan is usually assumed to have taken place around 1200 B.C., whereas Abraham lived in the second half of the fifteenth century B.C. An increasing number of scholars, however, incline to the view that the 1200 B.C. Philistine invasion was not the first (just as Joshua's was only the concluding phase of a protracted process of Hebrew immigration into Canaan) and that some Philistines may well have been established in Gerar by 1500 B.C.

3. The original home of the Philistines was Caphtor, which does not necessarily refer to the island of Crete (*Keftiu* in Egyptian) alone, but rather to the Minoan sphere in general, including the south-west of Asia Minor. Minoan or Caphtorian culture goes back to the third millennium B.C., and one instance of its early impact on the East-Mediterranean coast is the location in Caphtor of Kothar wa-Khasis's workshop. He was the divine craftsman known to Greeks of the fourteenth century B.C. as Daedalus. In 1196 B.C. the Peoples of the Sea were defeated by Rameses III, whose monuments at Medinet Habu depict them wearing their characteristic helmets—the Biblical word for helmet, '*koba*', is borrowed from Philistine, a non-Semitic tongue. Egyptian monuments mention several 'Peoples of the Sea', among whom the Pulasati, or Purasati, have been definitely identified with the Philistines.

4. An earlier monument of Pharaoh Merneptah (late thirteenth century B.C.) mentions the Aqaiwasha or Ekwesh as one of the Sea Peoples. These have been equated by Eduard Meyer and others with the Achiyawa whose kingdom flourished in the fourteenth and thirteenth centuries B.C. in Pamphylia (southern Asia Minor), although some historians regard the island of Rhodes as their main base. They are known to have penetrated also Cyprus, are regarded as Achaeans (*Achivi* in Latin), and have been identified with the Hivi, or Hivites, frequently referred to in the Bible as one of the pre-Israelite peoples found in Canaan.

31

THE BIRTH OF ISAAC

(*a*) When Abram was ninety-nine years old, God changed his name to *Abraham,* which means 'Father of Many Nations'; once more announcing that his descendants should rule all the Land of Canaan, but now making this bequest conditional on the circumcision of every male child at the age of eight days. Thereupon Abraham circumcised himself and his entire household. God also changed Sarai's name to *Sarah,* which means 'Princess', promising that she should become a mother of nations.

Abraham fell upon his face before God, but secretly laughed to himself, thinking: 'How can a child be borne by a ninety-year-old woman to a hundred-year-old husband?' Yet, needing assurance that at least Ishmael would thrive, he said: 'O that my son Ishmael might keep Your ways!' God answered: 'Have I not declared that Sarah will bear you a son? And since you laughed at My promise you shall name him *Isaac.* Ishmael is already blessed as the destined father of twelve princes, and ancestor of a great nation; but I will make My everlasting covenant with Isaac, whom Sarah shall bear you next year.'

So saying, God vanished.[1]

(*b*) Not long afterwards, as Abraham sat at his tent door in the terebinth grove of Mamre, three strangers approached. He invited them to wash their feet and take refreshment. While Sarah baked a large number of ember-cakes, Abraham ran to kill a calf for supper, and offered the strangers curds and whey besides. They sat in the shade of a tree, and presently asked where Sarah was. Abraham replied: 'In yonder tent.' They told him: 'A year hence, she will bear you a son.'

Sarah laughed to herself when she overheard this prophecy, since her monthly courses had long ceased.

They asked: 'Why does Sarah laugh? Is there anything God cannot accomplish?'

'I never laughed!' cried Sarah, reddening.

'You did laugh!' they repeated.

Abraham's visitors then rose to go, and he went part of the way with them. They were bound for Sodom.[2]

(*c*) The following year Sarah bore a son, whom Abraham named Isaac and circumcised after eight days. Sarah said: 'All the world will laugh when they hear that I am suckling Abraham's son.' But he gave a great feast on the day of Isaac's weaning.[3]

(*d*) Some say that astrologers had cast Abraham's horoscope, and told him: 'You will never beget a son!'; but God reassured him: 'This horoscope was cast for Abram; therefore have I changed your name, and as Abraham you will beget a son. I have also changed Sarai's name because of her horoscope.'[4]

(*e*) Others say that Isaac's birth was announced three days after Abraham's circumcision of his entire household, and that God commanded Michael, Gabriel and Raphael to comfort Abraham, who suffered much pain, as always happens on the third day. The archangels protested: 'Would You send us to an unclean place, full of blood?' God answered: 'By your lives, the odour of Abraham's sacrifice pleases me better than myrrh and frankincense! Must I go Myself?' Then they accompanied Him disguised as Arab wayfarers. Michael was to announce Isaac's birth; Raphael, to heal Abraham; and Gabriel, to destroy the evil city of Sodom.[5]

1. *Genesis* XVII. 1–22.
2. *Genesis* XVIII. 1–16.
3. *Genesis* XXI. 1–8.
4. Gen. Rab. 432; Pesiqta Rabbati 179a.
5. Tanhuma Buber Gen. 85–86; B. Baba Metzia 86b; Gen. Rab. 517–18.

*

1. The narrative alternates frequently between singular and plural verb forms when referring to the deity here called Elohim. Though Gunkel and others have attempted to resolve this apparent inconsistency by suggesting that the chapter is based on several different sources, the alternation seems deliberately chosen to emphasize God's power of appearing in trinity. The divine character of the strangers (or 'Stranger') is conveyed by their knowledge that Abraham's wife is now named Sarah, and that childlessness has been her greatest sorrow. They also know that Sarah has laughed to herself, though she remains unseen. Midrashic commentators make all three strangers archangels.

2. Sarah's long barrenness is paralleled in the myths of Rebekah (*Genesis* XXV.—see 38. *a*), Rachel (*Genesis* XXIX.—see 45. *a*), Samson's unnamed mother (*Judges* XIII), Samuel's mother Hannah (1 *Samuel* I), and the Babylonian hero Etana's wife.

3. God's change of Abram's name to 'Abraham' does not, at first sight, seem to deserve the importance it is here given, since both are variants of the same royal title *Abamrama*, or *Abiramu*, occurring in cuneiform tablets from the nineteenth and seventeenth centuries B.C.; so also is 'Abiram', the name of a leading conspirator against Moses (*Numbers* XVI. 1). *Abiramu* means 'The God Ram is [My] Father', or may be read as 'The Father is Exalted'. 'Father of Many Nations', the meaning given to 'Abraham' in *Genesis* is, however, borne out by the Arabic *raham*, meaning 'multitude'. The divine name *Ram* occurs also in Adoniram, Jehoram, Malchi-ram; and its plural (*Job* XXI. 22) is used to describe heavenly beings. A King of Edom in Sennacherib's day was called Malik-ramu—'Ram is King'.

Changes of names at the coronation ceremony or the assumption of important office were common in Israel; thus Hoshea became Jehoshua (*Numbers* XIII. 16), Gideon became Jerubbaal (*Judges* VI. 32), Jedidiah became Solomon (2 *Samuel* XII. 25), Eliakim became Jehoiakim (2 *Kings* XXIII. 34), Mattaniah became Zedekiah (2 *Kings* XXIV. 17). Jacob's adoption of the title 'Israel' (*Genesis* XXXII. 29—see 47. *b*) may be a further example.

4. 'Sarai' also is merely another, older form of 'Sarah', both deriving from an ancient Semitic noun meaning 'queen' or 'princess'. A goddess named Sharit or Sharayat (the phonemic equivalent of Sarai) was worshipped at Bozrah in the Hauran. This suggests that the account of Abraham and Sarah's marriage records the union of a patriarchal Aramaean tribe headed by a priestly chieftain, with a matriarchal proto-Arab tribe led by a priestess-princess.

5. The curds and whey offered to Abraham's guests is translated 'butter' in the Authorised Version. Milk, poured into a skin and shaken, acquired the agreeably sour taste of buttermilk.

6. Abraham is shown no particular reverence in the Bible until Ezekiel's time (early sixth century B.C.—*Ezekiel* XXXIII. 24); neither is Sarah, until Ezra's, when *Isaiah* LI. 2 was written.

7. Sarah's pregnancy at the age of ninety is a curious example of how pious editors converted unusual events into miracles. Here they have taken literally Abraham's mocking exaggeration of his own age and Sarah's, on hearing that she will bear him a son after perhaps some thirty years of marriage. That she had passed her menopause is editorial comment, not Abraham's statement. Midrashic enlargement on the miracle (Pesiqta Rabbati 177 a–b; Tanhuma Buber Gen. 107–08; Gen. Rab. 561, 564; B. Baba Metzia 87a) has been copious: thus the women of Abraham's household thought Isaac a supposititious child, and tested Sarah's motherhood by inviting her to suckle their own infants. When she bashfully refused, they grew still more suspicious, until Abraham told her 'Uncover your breasts and provide milk for this entire brood!', which she did.

32

LOT AT SODOM

(*a*) God hesitated before confiding to Abraham His proposed destruction of Sodom; but did so after being hospitably welcomed at Mamre. He told him: 'The evil fame of Sodom and Gomorrah has reached My ears. I shall now go down and see whether it has been exaggerated.' Abraham drew closer, and said: 'Would my Lord indeed sweep away the good with the wicked? There may be fifty righteous men in Sodom!' God replied: 'For the sake of fifty righteous men I will spare it.' Abraham then bargained with God, asking: 'What if there be only forty-five such men? Or thirty? Or even so few as twenty?' Each time God answered: 'For their sakes I will spare the city.' At last He agreed to hold His hand for the sakes of only ten righteous men, and went hastily away.

Two of the three angels whose shape God had taken reached Sodom that evening. Lot saw them nearing the city gate, prostrated himself humbly and said: 'Pray turn aside, my lords, wash your feet and spend the night in my house!' They answered: 'Do not trouble yourself. We can sleep in the street.' Lot, however, persuaded them to visit his house, where he baked unleavened bread, and they feasted well in his company.

Meanwhile a crowd of Sodomites surrounded Lot's house, crying: 'Where are the young strangers whom you brought here? Send them out for our pleasure!' Lot went into the street and locked the door behind him, pleading: 'Pray, neighbours, refrain from such wickedness! These are my guests, whom I cannot let you abuse. I would rather you deflowered my two virgin daughters; and will fetch them at once, should that satisfy your lusts.' They shouted: 'Stand back! A late-comer to Sodom, and you dare reprove us? Beware, lest we deal worse with you than with these strangers!'

Thrusting Lot aside, they tried to force an entrance; but the angels blinded them, unlocked the door from inside, rescued Lot, and locked it again. The Sodomites, after groping about to no purpose, retired cursing.

The angels asked Lot: 'Have you any kinsfolk here—sons, daughters or sons-in-law? If so, gather them quickly and flee, because we are commanded to destroy this city.' Lot went out, found his sons-in-law, and urged them to escape with him; but they laughed at this prophecy of immediate doom. Just before sunrise, the angels said: 'Come now, take your wife and these two daughters and flee without delay, lest you perish!'

Since Lot was slow to move, they caught him by the hands and dragged him off, with the warning: 'Neither look behind you, nor pause anywhere in the Plain; flee to the hills!' Lot replied: 'Not so, my lords! You have shown us great kindness; yet if we flee to the hills, we will die of hunger and thirst. I know of a small city near by —give us leave to seek refuge there!' They answered: 'Do so, and for your sake we shall not destroy it. But make haste, because God's vengeance on Sodom and Gomorrah is ripe!'

As the sun rose, Lot and his family entered this *small* city—afterwards called 'Zoar', in memory of his plea. God then rained brimstone and fire upon Sodom and Gomorrah, which destroyed all the Cities of the Plain, except Zoar, together with their people, beasts and crops. But Lot's wife, lagging behind, looked back and was turned into a pillar of salt. Meanwhile Abraham saw the smoke of Sodom and Gomorrah rise up like that of a furnace.[1]

(*b*) The Sodomites were among the richest of nations; for if a man needed pot-herbs, he would say to a slave: 'Go, fetch me some!' The slave would visit a field, and discover gold beneath their roots; likewise, when corn was harvested, silver, pearls and precious stones were found to have bred beneath its stubble. Great riches, however, lead men astray. A Sodomite never gave so much as a crumb of bread to any stranger; and would even poll his fig-trees, so that no birds should eat fruit hanging out of reach.

Sodom was secure against attack; yet to discourage visitors, its citizens passed a law that whoever offered a stranger food should be burned alive. Instead, the stranger must be robbed of all he had and flung from the city stark naked.[2]

(*c*) Once a year they held a feast and danced on grass beside springs of water to the sound of drums. When they had well drunken, every man would seize his neighbour's wife, or his virgin daughter, and enjoy her. Nor did any man care whether his own wife or daughter were sporting with his neighbour; but all made merry together from dawn to dusk, during those four days of festival, and returned home unabashed.[3]

(*d*) Beds were placed in the streets of Sodom for measuring strangers. If a man proved to be shorter than the bed on which he had been laid, three Sodomites would seize his legs, three more his head and arms, and stretch him until he fitted it. But if he proved to be longer than the bed, they forced his head downwards and his legs upwards. When the poor wretch cried out in a death agony, the Sodomites said: 'Peace! this is an ancient custom here.'[4]

(*e*) In the city of Admah, near Sodom, lived a rich man's daughter. One day a wayfarer sat down by her house door, and she fetched him bread and water. The city judges, hearing of this criminal act, had her stripped naked, smeared with honey, and laid beside a wild bees' nest; the bees then came and stung her to death. It was her cries that prompted God's destruction of Sodom, Gomorrah, Admah and Zeboyim; also those uttered by Lot's elder daughter, Paltit—who had given a needy old man water, and was dragged to the stake for her obstinate ways.[5]

(*f*) It is said that Idith, Lot's wife, distressed at the fate of his other daughters, looked back to see whether they followed. Her body, a tall pillar of salt, still stands at Sodom. Though every day cattle lick the salt off until nothing is left but the feet, by night the pillar is always miraculously restored.[6]

1. *Genesis* XVIII. 16–33; XIX. 1–28.
2. PRE, ch. 25; Gen. Rab. 523.
3. Sepher Hayashar 58.
4. Sepher Hayashar 62.
5. PRE, ch. 25; Sepher Hayashar 63–65.
6. PRE, ch. 25; cf. Gen. Rab. 504–05, 519; B. Sanhedrin 109a–b.

*

1. Strabo records a legend that near Massada, a massive fortress on the south-western shore of the Dead Sea, thirteen flourishing cities were once destroyed by an earthquake, eruptions of bitumen and sulphur, and a sudden advance of the sea which swept away the fleeing inhabitants. Josephus writes: 'Lake Asphaltitis [the Dead Sea] borders on the territory of Sodom, once prosperous but now an arid waste, God having destroyed its cities by lightning. The "shadows" of five cities may be seen there.'

2. After earthquake activity, masses of bitumen have been found floating on the Dead Sea. Diodorus Siculus, writing in 45 B.C., mentions this phenomenon, which occurred again in 1834. *Siddim* ('slime pits') seem to have been salt marshes on the southern shore, from which lumps of bitumen could be gleaned. The Dead Sea as a whole has never been dry land—soundings of 188 fathoms are recorded—and when recently the Israelis drilled for oil near Sodom (Jebel Usdum), salt was still found at a depth

of 18,000 feet. Nevertheless, the shallower southern basin, beyond the Lisan peninsula, may once have been a plain, encroached upon by the salt waters after severe earthquakes about 1900 B.C. But the soil is sour, and there are no ruins near by earlier than a Roman jetty. Since the valley lies some 1300 feet below sea level, intense heat makes it too hot for residence in summer: a true fire from Heaven. It is difficult to believe in the thirteen flourishing cities mentioned by Strabo, or the five mentioned by Josephus.

3. Cities divinely destroyed in punishment of ungenerous behaviour towards strangers are a commonplace of myth. Birket Ram, near Banias in Northern Galilee, an extinct volcano crater, is said by the local Arabs to cover with its waters a city whose inhabitants had this failing. Pherecydes records that Gortyna in Crete was destroyed by Apollo for its lawlessness. Ovid, in his *Metamorphoses*, tells how an old Phrygian couple, Philemon and Baucis, hospitably entertained Zeus, who spared them the catastrophe he visited on their surly neighbours.

4. Part of the myth is easily understood as one descends from the Beersheba-Elath road to Sodom, and looks left. The eye is cheated by roofs and minarets of a phantom city, which prove to be rock salt formations of the Jebel Usdum; and soon, near the shores of the Dead Sea, Lot's wife herself appears—a huge pillar of salt, which closely resembles a woman wearing a grey apron, her face turned towards this phantom city. The account of how she looked back and thus lost her chance of salvation is paralleled in Plato's well-known story of Orpheus's wife Eurydice. A small Arab settlement on the farther shore is identified with Zoar (see 27. 3).

5. The story of Lot and the Sodomites seems to be iconotropic; that is to say, based on a misreading of an ancient picture or relief. In the Hierapolis temple—the plan and furniture of which corresponded with that of Solomon's—a yearly holocaust and orgy was celebrated: when pederasty between male worshippers and 'Dog-priests' dressed in female garments took place, and unmarried girls acted as temple prostitutes. That these were also temple practices at Jerusalem is suggested by the reforms of King Josiah (or Hilkiah, or Shaphan), commemorated in *Deuteronomy* XXII and XXIII: prohibitions against the wearing of women's clothing by men, and the paying into Temple funds of 'the hire of a harlot, or the price of a Dog'—meaning a Dog-priest. That special quarters had been assigned to Dog-priests, or Sodomites in the Temple, is stated in 2 *Kings* XXIII. 7. Thus a fresco showing these legitimized sexual orgies against a temple background of swirling smoke, with a white aniconic image of the Goddess Anath on one side, and a priest standing at the Temple door on the other, could later be read as a warning tale of Sodomite excesses, Lot's righteousness, his wife's metamorphosis, and the destruction of their city.

6. The tradition of sexual promiscuity at Sodom is paralleled by Yaqut's fourteenth-century account of orgies at Mirbat in Southern Arabia: 'The

customs there are those of the ancient Arabs. Though good people, they have rough and repulsive customs, which explain their freedom from jealousy. At night, their women go outside the town and entertain such men as are not forbidden to them [by the laws of incest], sporting with them for the greater part of the night: a man pays no heed when he sees his wife, sister, mother or father's sister in a neighbour's arms; but himself seeks some other mate and is entertained by her as though she were his wife.' But the Spanish-born editors of *Sepher Hayashar* may have observed similar Tuareg festivities in the Sahara.

7. Whether the Sodomites' torture-beds have been borrowed from Plutarch's account of Procrustes the innkeeper, or from a common Oriental source, is arguable. Procrustes, whom Theseus killed for treating his guests in this manner, lived near Corinth, where the Palestinian Melkarth ('Lord of the City') was worshipped as Melicertes. Several Corinthian myths have Palestinian counterparts.

33

LOT AT ZOAR

(*a*) Lot and his daughters took refuge in a cave near Zoar. Since both girls thought that God had destroyed all mankind but themselves, the elder said to the younger: 'Our father is old, and there are no other men left alive. Let us therefore speedily make him drunken and be, as it were, his wives: to preserve mankind from extinction.' That night, they gave Lot much wine to drink, and the elder daughter lay with him; yet he remembered nothing the next day. Again they made him drunken; and that night, the younger daughter did what her sister had done. Both conceived. The elder called her son Moab, saying 'he comes *from my father*'; and the younger called hers Ben-Ammi, saying 'he is *the son of my kinsman*'. Moab became the ancestor of the Moabites; and Ben-Ammi, of the Ammonites.[1]

(*b*) Some see God's hand in this, because when the family fled from Sodom they brought away no wine. Except for God's plentiful provision of drink in the cave, the daughters of Lot could never have persuaded so righteous a man to lie with them.[2]

(*c*) The sons of Moab were 'Ar, Ma'yun, Tarsion and Qanvil, whom the Moabites honour to this day. Ben-Ammi's sons were Gerim, 'Ishon, Rabbot, Sillon, 'Aynon and Mayum, each of whom built a city called after his own name.[3]

1. *Genesis* xix. 30–38.
2. Mekhilta Beshallah, Mass. diShirata 72; Sifre 81a.
3. Sepher Hayashar 84.

*

1. Though this myth serves to vilify Israel's warlike south-eastern neighbours, the Moabites and Ammonites, as having been born in incest, it recalls the Ionian Greek myth of Adonis, or Tammuz, whose mother Smyrna had made her father, King Theias of Assyria, drunk and lain with him for twelve nights. It also reads as if iconotropically based on a familiar Egyptian scene: the ithyphallic Osiris lying dead in a grape arbour and mourned by the Goddesses Isis and Nepthys, each with a son crouched at her feet. Moreover, the famous Moabite Stone (late ninth century B.C.),

which records Mesha King of Moab's successful revolt against King Ahab, and his subsequent defeat of Ahab's son Jehoram (2 *Kings* I. 1 and III. 4 ff), is written in language so close to Biblical Hebrew that the Israelites may, at one time, have read the names 'Of my Father' and 'Son of my Kinsman' as implying Moabite brotherhood and Ammonite cousinage with themselves.

2. Lot's daughters are not here reproached for their breach of the incest taboo, since they acted innocently; a midrash even suggests that God aided them. Much the same situation occurs in a South Arabian myth told by Bertram Thomas: of one Bu Zaid, chief of the Beni Hillal, who always practised onanism when he lay with his wife. Since the tribal elders wished Bu Zaid to beget an heir, his sister visited him one night at their request, disguised as his wife, and pricked him with a bodkin at the critical moment of intercourse. This so startled Bu Zaid that she became pregnant by him, and her son Aziz ben Khala, 'Aziz, son of his uncle', achieved great fame in battle.

3. The names of Moab's four sons and Ben-Ammi's six are deduced from those of Moabite and Ammonite cities known to the twelfth-century Spanish author of the *Sepher Hayashar* or to his sources. The four 'sons' of Moab can be identified without much difficulty. 'Ar is the capital city of Moab, also called 'Ar Moab or 'Ir Moab (*Numbers* XXI. 15, 28; *Isaiah* XV. 1) located on the bank of the Arnon River, after which also the district south of the Arnon was named (*Deuteronomy* II. 9). Ma'yun seems to be a misspelling for Ma'on—full name: Ba'al Ma'on (*Numbers* XXXII. 38), or Beth Ma'on (*Jeremiah* XLVIII. 23), or Beth Ba'al Ma'on (*Joshua* XIII. 17) —a city on the border between Moab and Israel, mentioned also on the Moabite Stone, today Ma'īn, a large Christian Arab village four miles south-west of Madeba. Tarsion could be an abbreviated and distorted form (perhaps under the influence of the name of the Spanish city and district Tarseion—Polybius III. 24. 2) of the Biblical Atroth-Shophan (*Numbers* XXXII. 35), a town in Moab, near the Arnon River. Qanvil could be a distortion of Biblical Beth Gamul (*Jeremiah* XLVIII. 23), a city in Moab; today Khirbet Jumayl, north of the Arnon.

4. Of the six 'sons of Ben-Ammi', Rabbot is derived from the name of the capital of Ammon, Rabbah (*Joshua* XIII. 25), or in full form Rabbat bnei Ammon ('Rabbah of the Sons of Ammon'—*Deuteronomy* III. 11) situated near the sources of the Jabbok River. 'Aynon seems to be Ai (*Jeremiah* XLIX. 3). 'Ishon is possibly a corrupt form of Heshbon (*Jeremiah, ibid.*), another Ammonite city; and Mayum of Malcam, the god of Ammon (*Jeremiah* XLIX. 1, 3). No conjecture can be made about the origin of Gerim and Sillon.

34

THE SACRIFICE OF ISAAC

(*a*) God appeared to Abraham at Beersheba, saying: 'Take your son, and together ascend a mountain that I shall show you in the Land of Moriah!'

Abraham answered: 'Lord, I have two sons. Which of them is to come with me?'

'Your only son!'

'Lord, each is the only child of his mother.'

'Take the son whom you love!'

'Lord, I love both.'

'Take the son whom you love best!'

'Lord, what must I do in the Land of Moriah?'

'Lay a burned offering upon My altar!'

Abraham asked: 'Am I then a priest, to offer sacrifices?'

God said: 'I will consecrate you My High Priest; and your son Isaac shall be the sacrifice!'[1]

Abraham rose early, saddled an ass and, having cut faggots for the burned offering, tied them on its back. Then he set out northward, accompanied by Isaac and two servants. On the third day he saw Mount Moriah from afar, and told his servants: 'Stay here, with the ass; I and the lad will go yonder, worship God, and presently return.' He loaded the faggots on Isaac's shoulders, and himself carried the sacrificial knife, also charcoal embers in an earthen pot.

Isaac said: 'Father, we have a knife and faggots; where is the lamb for sacrifice?' Abraham replied: 'God will provide it, my son!' At the mountain top, Abraham built a stone altar, heaped the faggots around, tied Isaac and laid him upon it; but as he reached for the knife, a voice from Heaven cried 'Abraham!' He answered: 'I am here, Lord!' The voice cried again: 'Put down your knife and do the lad no harm! Since you have not grudged Me so great a sacrifice, I know that your heart is perfect.'

Abraham turned about and saw a ram with its horns caught in a thicket; this he sacrificed instead of Isaac, and called the place Yahweh Yireh, saying '*God watches over me!*'

God swore by His Name to multiply Abraham's posterity like stars in Heaven or sand on the seashore, because he had obeyed without faltering. Abraham and Isaac thereupon rejoined the servants, and all together made for Beersheba.[2]

(*b*) Some say that these servants were Ishmael, Hagar's son, and Eliezer of Damascus; and that Ishmael told Eliezer, when they were alone: 'My father has been commanded to sacrifice Isaac; now I shall be his heir!' Eliezer replied: 'Did not your father expel Hagar at Sarah's plea, and thus disinherit you? Surely he will bequeath all his goods to me, who have served him faithfully day and night, ever since I became his bondman?'[3]

(*c*) As Abraham ascended Mount Moriah, the fallen angel Samael stole up, in the shape of a humble grey-beard, and said: 'Can a command to kill the son of your old age proceed from a God of mercy and justice? You have been deceived!' Abraham, seeing through Samael's disguise, drove him away; but he reappeared in the shape of a handsome youth, who whispered to Isaac: 'Wretched son of a wretched mother! Was it for this that she awaited your birth so long and patiently? Why should your besotted father slaughter you without reason? Flee, while there is yet time!' Isaac repeated these words to Abraham, who cursed Samael and sent him about his business.[4]

(*d*) On the summit of Mount Moriah, Isaac willingly consented to die, saying: 'Blessed be the Living God, who has chosen me as a burned offering before Him today!' He also handed Abraham stones to rebuild the broken altar which stood there; it had been raised by Adam and used in turn by Abel, Noah and Shem.[5] Then he said: 'Bind me tightly, my father, lest I shrink from the knife and make your offering unacceptable to God! Afterwards take the ashes and tell my mother Sarah: "These bear witness to the sweet savour of Isaac's sacrificial flesh!"'[6]

Having offered up the ram, Abraham prayed: 'When You demanded the life of my beloved son, O Lord, I could have cried in anger: "Only yesterday You promised me a large posterity by him; must I now burn his bloodless body upon Your altar?" Yet I stood as though deaf and dumb. Therefore I pray that, if my descendants ever do evil, You will likewise refrain from anger; and that each year, when they have repented of their sins, and the ram's horn sounds on the First Day of the Seventh Month, You will recall how I bound my son and, rising from the Throne of Judgement, will seat Yourself upon the Throne of Mercy!'[7]

(*e*) Isaac spent the next three years in Paradise; or, some say, at the house of Shem and Eber, where he studied God's Law. But first he attended the burial of his mother Sarah who, going to Hebron for news of him, heard of his rescue and expired from pure joy—Samael having assured her that he had already been sacrificed.

Sarah died at the age of one hundred and twenty-seven years. Abraham bought the Cave and field of Machpelah from Ephron the Hittite, paying him four hundred silver shekels, buried Sarah there, and mourned her seven days.[8]

1. *Genesis* XXII. 1–2; Gen. Rab. 590, 592; Tanhuma Buber Gen. 111; Pesiqta Rabbati 170a; PRE, ch. 31.
2. *Genesis* XXII. 3–19.
3. Sepher Hayashar 76–77.
4. Sepher Hayashar 77–79; cf. Gen. Rab. 595–98.
5. Sepher Hayashar 80; PRE, ch. 31.
6. Sepher Hayashar 80.
7. Lev. Rab. 29.9; Gen. Rab. 607; Yer. Taamit 65d; Tanhuma Buber Gen. 46.
8. *Genesis* XXIII. 1–20; Mid. Wayosha, BHM i. 35 ff; PRE, ch. 32; Sepher Hayashar 81–83.

*

1. Sacrifice of first-born sons was common in ancient Palestine, and practised not only by the Moabite King Mesha, who burned his eldest son to the God Chemosh (2 *Kings* III. 26–27); by the Ammonites, who offered their sons to Molech (*Leviticus* XVIII. 21 and XX. 2 ff); by the Aramaeans of Sepharvaim, whose gods were Adram-melech and Ana-melech; but also by the Hebrew Kings Ahaz (2 *Kings* XVI. 3) and Manasseh (2 *Kings* XXI. 6). King Saul's attempt to sacrifice his warrior son Jonathan after a reverse in the Philistine war is hinted at (1 *Samuel* XIV. 43–46), though the army elected to save him.

2. *Exodus* XXII. 28–29 reads: 'The first-born of thy sons shalt thou give unto Me, and of thine oxen and thy sheep, on the eighth day!', which Ezekiel (XX. 24–26) later described as one of the 'statutes that were not good' and that polluted Israel as a punishment for idolatry. But this law referred to infant sacrifice rather than to that of youths or grown men, and could be evaded by a token sacrifice of the first-born's foreskin at circumcision. Isaac's sacrifice was of the kind resorted to in national emergencies—as by Mesha, Ahaz and Manasseh—or at foundation ceremonies, as by Hiel at Jericho (1 *Kings* XVI. 34).

3. Solomon had introduced into Jerusalem the worship of Molech and Chemosh (1 *Kings* XI. 7), to whom children were burned in the Valley of Tophet, *alias* Gehenna (2 *Kings* XXIII. 10). Some of these victims seem to have been offered as surrogates for the King, the incarnate Sun-god, at an annual demise of the crown. Micah (VI. 7), Jeremiah (VII. 31; XIX. 5–6; XXXII. 35) and Ezekiel (XVI. 20; XX. 26) denounced this practice; which was

also legislated against in *Deuteronomy* XII. 31 and in *Leviticus* XVIII. 21 and XX. 2 ff. *Exodus* XXXIV. 20, an amendment to XXII. 28–29, equates the first-born of man with that of the ass: both were redeemable with a lamb, or two young pigeons (*Exodus* XXXIV. 20; *Leviticus* XII. 6–8). Abraham's interrupted sacrifice of Isaac displays his absolute obedience to God, and His mercy in waiving the 'statute that was not good', as an acknowledgement of obedience. Isaac, however, was no longer an infant but a 'lad' capable of carrying a heavy load of faggots, and Abraham redeemed him with a ram, not a lamb. A midrash that regards Sarah's death as an indirect consequence of Isaac's binding, deducts ninety years—her age when she bore Isaac, from 127, her age when she died—and makes him thirty-seven.

4. The ram 'caught in a thicket' seems borrowed from Ur of the Chaldees, where a royal grave of the late fourth millennium B.C. has yielded two Sumerian statues of rams in gold, white shell and lapis lazuli, standing on their hind legs and bound with silver chains to a tall, flowering golden bush. This theme is common in Sumerian art.

5. Abraham's attempted sacrifice of Isaac is paralleled in Greek myth: the Cadmean story of Athamas and Phrixus. These Cadmeans ('Easterners' in Hebrew) traced their descent from Agenor ('Canaan'). In the eleventh century B.C., some of them seem to have wandered from Palestine to Cadmeia in Caria, then crossed the Aegean and founded Boeotian Thebes. Cadmeans also figure as 'Children of Kedmah' in Ishmael's genealogy (see 29. 5). This parallel solves three important problems raised by *Genesis:* first, since Abraham was not founding a city, what emergency prompted him to sacrifice his grown-up son? Next: why was his first-born Ishmael not chosen in preference to Isaac? Lastly: did the quarrel for precedence between Sarah and Hagar, so important in the introductory chapters, bear any relation to the sacrifice?

6. Here is the Cadmean story. King Athamas the Boeotian, having married Queen Nephele of Pelion, who bore him a son named Phrixus, afterwards begot a son, Melicertes (*Melkarth*, 'ruler of the city') on Nephele's rival Ino the Cadmean. When Nephele heard of this, she cursed Athamas and Melicertes; whereupon Ino created a famine by secretly parching the seed-corn, and bribed Apollo's priestess to announce that the land would recover its fertility only if Athamas sacrificed Nephele's son Phrixus, his heir, on Mount Laphystium. Athamas had already grasped the sacrificial knife when Heracles ordered him to desist, crying: 'My Father, Zeus, King of Heaven, loathes human sacrifices!' A golden-fleeced ram, sent by Zeus, then appeared; and Phrixus escaped on its back to the Land of Colchis, where he prospered. Ino fled with Melicertes from Athamas's anger and leaped into the sea, but both of them were rescued and deified by Zeus: Ino as the White Goddess, Melicertes as the New Year God of Corinth.

7. This suggests that, in the original myth, Hagar avenged herself on Sarah by ascribing a famine to some action of Abraham's; for one famine

occurs in the *Genesis* story when he is already married to Sarah (see 26. *a*), and another in the account of Isaac at Gerar, which seems to have originally been told about Abraham (see 37. *a*). It also suggests that the sacrifice was ordered by a false prophet, whom Hagar bribed to do so in revenge for Ishmael's disinheritance. There may even be a recollection of this in Samael's attempt to interrupt the sacrifice. Yet the cause of Sarah's quarrel with Hagar, which is discussed in the ancient code of Hammurabi (see 29. 2), reads more convincingly than the cause of Nephele's quarrel with Ino and points to Sumeria as the original source of the story. The Cadmean version suggests, however, that Hagar's second flight from Abraham (see 29. *c*) took place after the attempted sacrifice of Isaac, not before. 'Athamas' may be derived from the Hebrew *Ethan*, a mythical early sage and poet whose name, meaning 'lasting' or 'strong', is transcribed in the Septuagint as *Aitham*. The strange phrase 'the fear of Isaac' (*Genesis* xxxi. 42, 53) recalls the name Phrixus ('Horror'). Famine in a nomadic society means drought, and the mock-sacrifice of a man dressed in a black ram's fleece, still celebrated on Mount Laphystium by Boeotian shepherds at the Spring Equinox, is a rain-making rite.

8. Two other myths are to the point here. The earlier one concerns Jephthah's vow to give God the first living creature that met him after his victory over the Ammonites (*Judges* xi. 29ff); the later concerns Idomeneus the Cretan's similar vow to Poseidon when faced with shipwreck. Jephthah, however, came to no harm after sacrificing his daughter, this being 'a custom in Israel'; whereas Idomeneus's men were struck by plague, and he was banished from Crete. The Greeks, who had acquired a horror of human sacrifice at about the same period as the Hebrews, preferred for instance to believe that Iphigeneia, Agamemnon's daughter, was redeemed with a doe when about to be despatched at Aulis, and then spirited away to the Tauric Chersonese. Plutarch records a case which combines the vow theme with that of a first-born son sacrificed in time of emergency: Maeander promised to reward the Queen of Heaven with the first person who should congratulate him on the storm of Pessinus; this proved to be his son Archelaus, whom he duly killed, but then remorsefully drowned himself in the river which now bears his name. The practice of burning children to Hercules Melkarth continued among the Phoenicians long after the Hebrews had abandoned it; and Micah's view (vi. 6–8) that God dislikes not only human sacrifices but animal sacrifices, too—preferring justice, mercy and a humble heart—was a shockingly radical one at that epoch.

9. The Jewish New Year ritual commemorates the binding of Isaac. When asked to explain the blowing of a ram's horn (*shofar*) in *Leviticus* xxiii. 23–25, Rabbi Abbahu said: 'It is done because God ordered our fathers "Blow Me a ram's horn, that I may remember Abraham's binding of Isaac; and count it as if you had bound yourselves before Me!"' (B. Rosh Hashana 16a). The same explanation occurs in the New Year *mussaf*

prayer; and a typically Tannaitic saying attributed to Jesus in the *Gospel of St. Thomas:* 'Raise the stone and ye shall find me, cleave the wood and I shall be there!' clearly refers to Isaac's binding, which was regarded as the greatest test of faith in all Scripture.

10. Midrashic comment on the ram is expansive and fanciful. God had made this particular beast on the First Day of Creation; its ashes became the foundations of the Temple Sanctuary; King David used its sinews to string his harp; Elijah girded his loins with its skin; its left horn was blown by God on Mount Sinai, and the right horn will be sounded in the Days of the Messiah to recall the lost sheep of Israel from exile. When Abraham found the ram, it repeatedly freed itself from one thicket, only to become entangled in another; which signified that Israel would be similarly entangled in sin and misfortune, until at length redeemed by a blast on the right-hand horn.

11. The *Genesis* chronicler purposely varies between 'God' and 'an angel' when writing of Abraham's interlocutor: as he has done in his account of the divine visit to Abraham at Mamre (see 31. *1*). To connect the Mountain of Sacrifice with Mount Zion is inept, because it has already been recorded (see 27. *c*) that Melchizedek reigned there as King of Salem and priest of the Most High God—a midrash emphasizes this point by making Abraham ask God why the duty of sacrificing Isaac had not been entrusted to Shem—meaning Melchizedek (see 27. *d*). This is to contradict the reliable Samaritan tradition that Mount Moriah was the 2300-foot Mount Gerizim (*Deuteronomy* XI. 29 ff), which overlooks the 'terebinths of Moreh' where Abraham had offered his first sacrifice (*Genesis* XII. 6). The Authorised Version mistranslates this as 'the plain of Moreh', relying on an Aramaic text intended to disguise Abraham's acceptance of Canaanite tree-worship. Moreh, afterwards Shechem, and now Nablus, was the holiest shrine in Israel—visited by Abraham, blessed by Moses, and famous both for Joshua's memorial stone and Joseph's grave (*Joshua* XXIV. 25 ff). It lost its holiness, however, when a prophecy (*Hosea* VI. 9) of God's punishment for the idol-worship inaugurated there by King Jeroboam (1 *Kings* XII. 25 ff) took effect, and all priests and leaders of the Northern Kingdom were carried off by Sennacherib. Jerusalem then became the sole legitimate centre of worship, and as many early myths as possible were transferred to Mount Zion, including those of Adam, Abel, Noah and Abraham.

12. The Cave of Machpelah had been bought by Abraham from Ephron the Hittite (see 11. *d*). Sarah's joyful death is intended by the late mythographer to account for her absence from Beersheba, Abraham's home, and for his journey to Hebron. Athamas, too, was connected with the Hittites, by being a brother of 'Sisyphus', the Hittite God Teshub (see 39. *1*). The cave of 'Ephron the Hittite' may have been a shrine sacred to Phoroneus, who is called father of Agenor ('Canaan') and said to have not only discovered how to use fire, but initiated the Greek worship of Hera ('Anath').

35

ABRAHAM AND KETURAH

(*a*) Though now one hundred and thirty-seven years of age, Abraham continued youthful and hale. He prayed that God might distinguish him from Isaac, for whom he was often mistaken by strangers. God accordingly crowned Abraham with locks white as wool, like His own: the first external sign of old age granted mankind and treated as a mark of respect.[1]

After Sarah's death, Abraham married Keturah. Some say that this was a nickname of Hagar's, who had been *bound* in service to Sarah; who *bound* together a garland of sweet-smelling virtues; and who remained *bound* to Abraham by a vow of chastity, even when she had been driven away. Others say that Abraham chose Keturah, a descendant of Japheth, so that he might have posterity in the female line from each of Noah's sons: Hagar being descended from Ham, and Sarah from Shem.[2]

(*b*) Abraham's sons by Keturah were Zimran, Jokshan (father of Dedan and Sheba), Medan, Midian, Ishbak and Shuah. He sent them all off eastwards, laden with gifts, to fend for themselves, and pronounced this warning: 'Beware of Isaac's fire!' They took possession of many lands, including Trogloditis and the Red Sea shores of Arabia Felix. Distant nations now claim descent from Abraham through them, even the Spartans of Greece. None of Keturah's sons kept God's Law, which explains Abraham's warning. Among the children of Dedan were the Asshurites, who founded Assyria; the Letushites; and the Leummites. Midian's sons were Ephah and Epher, Hanoch, Abida and Eldaah.[3]

(*c*) Some say that Abraham entrusted Keturah's sons with the secret names of demons, whom they could thus bend to do their will when making magic; and that all the wisdom of the East, now so much admired, was Abraham's.[4]

(*d*) Others say that Keturah bore Abraham twelve sons.[5]

1. Tanhuma Hayye Sarah 4; B. Baba Metzia 87a; Gen. Rab. 717–18.
2. *Genesis* xxv. 1; Gen. Rab. 654, 661; Tanhuma Hayye Sarah 8; Tanhuma Buber Gen. 123; PRE, ch. 30; Hadar Zeqenim 9b; Leqah Tobh Gen. 115.

3. *Genesis* xxv. 2–6; Gen. Rab. 663, 669; Shoher Tobh 411–12; 1 *Macc.* xii. 21; 2 *Macc.* v. 9.
4. B. Sanhedrin 91a; Zohar Gen. 133b, 223a–b.
5. Massekhet Soferim 11.9; Tanhuma Hayye Sarah 6.

*

1. This myth is historically important, since it suggests that Abraham's Hebrews controlled the desert routes to Egypt and acted as agents for trade with various eastern tribes. 'Medan' recalls the Yemenite god *Madan*. The North Arabian tribe of Midian occupied the Gulf of Aqaba and the Sinai Peninsula. 'Ishbak' seems to be *Iashbuqi*, a small North Syrian kingdom mentioned in an eighth-century B.C. Assyrian inscription; and 'Shuah' (*Soge* or *Soe* in the Septuagint) its neighbouring kingdom of Shukhu. 'Keturah' will have meant a *binding together* of tribes for the common interest of trade under Abraham's benevolent guidance.

2. 'Jokshan' seems to be identical with Yoqtan, father of Sheba (*Genesis* x. 27–28), who is called Qaḥṭān in Arabic and regarded by Arab genealogists as the ancestor of all Southern Arab tribes. Sheba fathered the mercantile Sabaeans. Jokshan's son Dedan—who also figures as a son of Raamah the Cushite in *Genesis* x. 7 and 1 *Chronicles* i. 9; and in Josephus's *Antiquities* as a son of Shuah—was a North Arabian desert tribe from Tema and Buz (*Jeremiah* xxv. 23). According to *Ezekiel* xxvii. 15–20, they supplied Tyre with saddle-rugs until 'Esau' or 'Edom' harried their caravans (*Isaiah* xxi. 13–15; *Jeremiah* xlix. 8; *Ezekiel* xxv. 13) and forced them to retreat south.

3. 'Asshur', here called a son of Dedan, was the god from whom the city of Asshur—later the Assyrian capital—took its name. The names Ashuru and Latashu (i.e. Asshur and Letush) occur in Nabataean inscriptions as personal names. 'Leummites' is probably a mistake for 'and other nations', from *le'om*, 'a nation' (as in *Genesis* xxv. 23).

4. The sons of Midian also moved to South Arabia. 'Ephah' (Gephar in the Septuagint), mentioned with Midian (*Isaiah* lx. 6) as a camel-owning tribe that brought gold and incense from Sheba, is Khayapa in inscriptions of Sargon of Assyria; today Ghwafa, east of the Gulf of Aqaba. 'Epher' (*Opher* or *Gapher* in the Septuagint, *Eperu* or *Apuriu* in Egyptian inscriptions), has been identified with the Banu Ghifar of the Hejaz. 'Hanoch' may represent the modern Hanakiya, a settlement north of Medina, visited by Doughty and Burckhardt. Abida could be Ibadidi, mentioned in inscriptions of Sargon II. Both Abida and Eldaah occur as proper names in Sabaean and Minaean inscriptions.

5. Josephus's tribal genealogy is based on an alternative tradition; so is the *Sepher Hayashar*, which gives Dedan's sons different names. *Genesis* itself embodies rival traditions of kinship, produced by constant political changes among nomadic tribes, from Hyksos times onward.

6. Josephus states that King Areus of Sparta, in a letter written about

183 B.C. to Onias III, High Priest of Jerusalem, claimed Abraham as his ancestor; this claim was acknowledged some twelve years later by the High Priest Jonathan (*Maccabees* XII) who admitted its conformity with Jewish sacred books, but did not cite them. At all events, Menelaus the Spartan had spent ten years in Egypto-Palestinian waters, according to various passages in the *Odyssey*; and the early Achaean Greeks had founded colonies in Palestine (see 30. 3). Xanthus the Lydian records that Ascalon was built by Ascalus, an ancestor of the Spartans.

7. Hebrew mythographers tend to credit tribal ancestors with twelve sons. Thus, although *Genesis* allows Abraham only six, the midrash elevates him above his brother Nahor who had twelve, by giving him twelve in addition to Ishmael and Isaac. Ishmael begot twelve sons (see 29. *i*); and so did Jacob (see 45); so, according to the *Sepher Hayashar*, did Abraham's nephew Aram, son of Zoba, Terah's youngest child, who founded Aram-Zoba (2 *Samuel* x. 6–8), a city north of Damascus.

36

ISAAC'S MARRIAGE

(*a*) Word reached Abraham from Harran that his brother Nahor was now blessed with twelve sons, of whom eight had been borne by his wife Milcah; namely, Uz, Buz, Kemuel, Chesed, Hazo, Pildash, Jidlaph and Bethuel. The other four were children of a concubine, Reumah; namely, Tebah, Gaham, Tahash and Maacah. Nahor had a grandson Aram, by Kemuel; also a grandson and grand-daughter by Bethuel, namely, Laban and Rebekah.[1]

Abraham called his chief steward Eliezer, and said: 'Put your hand under my thigh, and swear by the Living God that you will obey me! Since I cannot let Isaac marry among the Canaanites, a bride must be found for him at Harran. I am too old to settle this matter in person; therefore go, make your choice on my behalf, and bring the woman back to Hebron.'

Eliezer asked: 'What if she hesitates to accompany me? Must Isaac then marry her in Harran?'

Abraham replied: 'Isaac shall never leave the land which God has given us! If she declines, you are free of this oath. Nevertheless, have no fear: God's angel will prepare your way.'

Eliezer took the oath, chose ten fine camels from Abraham's herds, filled their saddle-bags with rich gifts, and rode off at the head of a large retinue. Many days later, at dusk, he made his camels kneel at the well outside Padan-Aram in Harran, and saw the city women trooping up to draw water, as was their custom. He prayed: 'God of my master Abraham, prosper me today and grant me a sign: that when I say to one of these women "Let down your pitcher, and give me drink!", and she answers "Drink, and I shall also water your camels," that same woman will be Isaac's appointed bride.'

The first woman to reach the well was young, stately and dressed as a virgin. She descended the steps, and soon re-appeared with a brimming pitcher on her shoulder. Eliezer asked leave to quench his thirst from it. The woman answered: 'Drink, my lord,' and handed him the pitcher. Eliezer drank, then awaited her next words. When she said:

'I will also water your camels,' and emptied the pitcher into a trough, he knew her for God's choice. Eliezer fetched the bridal gifts—a golden nose-ring weighing half a shekel, and two golden bracelets of ten shekels' weight—then, having set the ring in her nostrils and the bracelets on her wrists, he asked: 'Whose daughter are you?' She replied: 'Bethuel is my father: Nahor's son by his wife Milcah. I am named Rebekah.'

Eliezer asked again: 'Will there be lodging for us in your father's house?'

She said: 'Yes, we have sufficient lodging, also straw and green fodder for your camels.'

Eliezer at once prostrated himself and thanked God that he had been led to Abraham's kinsfolk.

Rebekah hurried home to announce Eliezer's arrival; and when her brother Laban saw the golden ornaments she wore, he ran to the well and cried: 'Come, stranger, with God's blessing! I have made ready a room for your lodging, and a stable for your beasts.' He took Eliezer and his fellow-servants to Bethuel's house, where they ungirded and fed the weary camels. Water was brought to wash the travellers' feet, and platters of food placed before them. But Eliezer said: 'First let me reveal my errand!' He then told Bethuel and Laban of his mission, of Abraham's riches, and of his own providential encounter with Rebekah, ending: 'Pray decide at once, my lords, whether you will gratify my master's wish, or whether you will not.'

Bethuel and Laban both replied: 'Since the hand of God is manifest in this matter, how dare we oppose Him? Take Rebekah and go; she shall be Isaac's wife, as God wills.'

Eliezer bowed low in thanksgiving, then took out bridal garments and more jewels from the saddle-bags; presenting rich gifts also to Rebekah's mother, and to Laban. Then they all feasted merrily. The next day, Eliezer was for going home, but Laban and his mother desired Rebekah to stay ten days longer. Eliezer said: 'Do not delay a servant of God! I must return to my master.' They asked Rebekah: 'Will you accompany this honest man at once?' When she answered: 'I will,' they let her go with their blessing. Laban said: 'May you become the mother of unnumbered thousands, sister; and may they hold the city gates of all who hate them!'

Rebekah, attended by her nurse Deborah and other bond-women, followed Eliezer to Canaan. Some days later, at sunset, they reached the well of Lahai-Roi, where God had once comforted Hagar. Rebekah alighted from her camel, and asked: 'Who can this be: walking across the field to greet us?' When Eliezer replied: 'It is my master's son,' she quickly veiled her face.

After hearing Eliezer's story, Isaac brought Rebekah into the tent which had been Sarah's. That night they lay together, and he ceased mourning for his mother.[2]

(*b*) Some say that Abraham formerly planned to choose Isaac's wife from among the daughters of his friends Aner, Eshcol and Mamre who were pious men, though Canaanites. But God, when blessing him on Mount Moriah, revealed the bride-to-be as his brother Nahor's newly born grand-daughter—Isaac's paternal cousins having first claim on him as a husband.[3]

Yet since a girl cannot be given in marriage until at least three years and one day old, Abraham refrained from sending Eliezer on his mission until this time had elapsed; others even say that he waited fourteen years, until Rebekah should be nubile.

When forbidden by Abraham to choose Isaac a Canaanite wife, Eliezer offered him his own daughter. Abraham, however, replied: 'You, Eliezer, are a bondman, Isaac is free born: the cursed may not unite with the blessed!'[4]

(*c*) Some say that among the Aramaeans a father would deflower his virgin daughter before her wedding; and that Bethuel, upon agreeing to Rebekah's marriage, would have dishonoured her in this manner, had he not suddenly died. According to others, Bethuel, as King of Harran, claimed the sole right to deflower brides and, when Rebekah became nubile, the princes of the land gathered around, saying: 'Unless Bethuel now treats his own daughter as he has treated ours, we shall kill them both!'[5]

(*d*) According to others Laban, seeing the rich gifts Rebekah brought back from the well, had planned an ambush for Eliezer, but awe of his gigantic stature and numerous armed retainers made him desist. Instead, he pretended great friendship, and set a platter of poisoned food before Eliezer. The archangel Gabriel, entering unseen, exchanged this platter with Bethuel's, who died instantly. Though Laban and his mother wished Rebekah to stay until they had mourned Bethuel for a full week, Eliezer mistrusted Laban and demanded that Rebekah should leave home at once. Being now an orphan, she could make her own decisions, and told Laban: 'I shall go, even if it be against your will!' Thus constrained to agree, he blessed her with such mockery that she was barren for many years.

(*e*) When the travellers neared Hebron, Rebekah saw Isaac on his way back from Paradise, walking on his hands, as the dead do. She took fright, fell off her camel and was hurt by the stump of a bush. Abraham greeted her as he stood at the tent door, but said to Isaac: 'Bondmen are capable of any deceit. Take this woman into your tent, and finger her to see whether she is still a virgin after this long journey in Eliezer's company!' Isaac obeyed and, finding Rebekah's maidenhead broken, sternly asked how this had come about. She answered: 'My lord, I was frightened by your appearance, and fell to the ground, where the stump of a bush pierced my thighs.' 'No, but Eliezer has defiled you!' cried Isaac. Rebekah, swearing by the Living God that no man had touched her, showed him the stump still wet with her virginal blood; and he believed at last.

As for the faithful Eliezer, who had been near death because of a suspected crime, God took him alive into Paradise.[6]

1. *Genesis* XXII. 20–24.
2. *Genesis* XXIV. 1–67; XXV. 20; XXXV. 8.
3. Gen. Rab. 614; Mid. Hagadol Gen. 356.
4. Gen. Rab. 612–13, 636–37; Mid. Hagadol Gen. 388–89, 770–71.
5. Massekhet Soferim 21.9, end; M. Nidda 5.4; Yalqut Gen. 109; Gen. Rab. 652; Mid. Agada Gen. 59; Hadar 9b.
6. Yalqut Gen. 109; Mid. Hagadol Gen. 366, 369–70; Gen. Rab. 651–53; Mid. Agada Gen. 59–60; Mid. Leqah Tobh Gen. 111, 113; Mekhilta diR. Shimon 45; Da'at 13d, 14b; Hadar 9b.

*

1. Abraham refused to let Isaac marry a Canaanite wife (*Genesis* II. 24) by the ancient matrilocal law which insists that a husband must leave home and live with his wife's kinsfolk. Instead, he chose him a wife from among his patrilocal cousins at Harran. (Doubtless he would have preferred a daughter of his ally and nephew Lot, but both had made themselves ineligible by their precipitate acts of incest.) Later, Isaac and Rebekah similarly refused to let their son Jacob marry a Canaanite or Hittite maiden (*Genesis* XXVII. 46; XXVIII. 1—see 45). Matrilocal marriage was also the rule in Mycenaean Greece, and the first woman said to have made a patrilocal marriage, despite parental opposition, was Odysseus's wife Penelope; who veiled her face, when headed for Ithaca, in a manner reminiscent of Rebekah.

2. Midrashic embroideries on the Rebekah myth incorporate various ancient traditions. Hebrew patriarchs demanded virginity from brides, and in several Near and Middle Eastern countries the bride's maidenhead is still tested on her wedding night by the bridegroom's finger. Canaanite women, however, were promiscuous before marriage, as was customary among all matrilineal societies of the Eastern Mediterranean.

A legend that Isaac came to meet Rebekah walking upside down, after a stay in Paradise (see 11. 6), is an example of rabbinical humour, explaining her startled question: 'Who is this that comes walking?'

3. That Bethuel's wife and son are left to settle the marriage contract with Eliezer on his behalf; and that Laban, not Bethuel, blesses Rebekah, is unusual enough to call for an explanation: this the midrash supplies by presuming his sudden death. Perhaps the chronicler emphasizes Laban's part at Bethuel's expense because Laban's daughters Leah and Rachel subsequently married Isaac's son Jacob (see 44).

4. The *jus primae noctis* of many primitive tribes (see 18. 8) is exercised sometimes by a girl's father, sometimes by a chieftain. Herodotus reports it among the Adyrmachidae, a Libyan people settled between the Canopic mouth of the Nile and Apis, about whose customs the midrashic commentator may have heard. Laban's use of the word *asor* suggests that the *Genesis* account is based on an Egypto-Hebraic source—'asor' being an Egyptian ten-day week.

5. Nahor's twelve sons show him to have ruled a twelve-tribe confederacy, like those of Israel, Ishmael, Etruria and the Amphictyonic League of Greece—twelve in honour of the Zodiac. His capital seems to have been Padan-Aram, or Harran (see 23. 1 and 24. 10). Some of Nahor's eight sons by Milcah ('Queen') later migrated from the neighbouring desert to Northern Arabia. Three of Reumah's four sons are recorded by place-names in Southern Syria and Northern Transjordan, which proves a West-Semitic tribal federation of Nahor to have existed before the Aramaean conquest.

6. The leading character in *Genesis* XXIV, first described as Abraham's 'chief-steward', is afterwards termed either 'the servant', 'Abraham's servant', or 'the man'. He even withholds his own name when introducing himself to Bethuel and Laban. Yet all Biblical commentators assume him to have been Eliezer of Damascus, whom Abraham, while still childless, regretfully mentions as his prospective heir (*Genesis* XV—see 28. *a*). The chronicler clearly wished to emphasize that Eliezer had been no more than Abraham's slave and God's instrument.

7. When Abraham orders Eliezer 'Put your hand under my thigh!', this was a euphemism for 'touch my sexual organ', a most solemn form of oath, which served to remind him of the circumcision rite that bound Abraham and all his household in God's service. Jacob used the same oath when he made Joseph swear to bury him in the Cave of Machpelah (*Genesis* XLVII. 29—see 60. *a*). Rwala Bedouin of the Syrian Desert still preserve this custom. A. Musil has written lately:

> *When a chief wishes to extract the truth from a tribesman, he springs forward, lays his right hand on the man's belly underneath the belt, so as to touch his sexual organ, and exclaims: 'I adjure*

you by your belt, by this thing that I touch, and by all that lie down to sleep before you at night, to give me an answer that will please God!'

The belt which is laid aside for intercourse, signifies a man's wife; the sexual organ, children; and 'all that lie down to sleep', his herds.

37

ISAAC IN GERAR

(*a*) Isaac made ready to visit Egypt because of a famine in his own land; but since God forbade him, while renewing the benediction bestowed on Abraham, he went to Gerar as a guest of Abimèlech, King of the Philistines. There, guided by Abraham's example, he passed the lovely Rebekah off as his sister. One day the King happened to look out of a palace window and saw Isaac and Rebekah making marital love. He reproached Isaac, saying: 'Why have you deceived me? Some courtier of mine might have secretly enjoyed your wife, and thought no harm of it.' Isaac said: 'I would rather thus be dishonoured, than murdered by a jealous man!'

Isaac was given land in Gerar, and for every grain sown he reaped a hundredfold. The Philistines so envied his flocks, herds and riches that, soon after the famine ended, Abimelech asked him to leave the city.[1]

1. *Genesis* xxvi. 1–17.

*

1. This is the third instance of the same borrowing from the Egyptian *Tale of the Two Brothers* (see 26 and 30); but here the King, having made no attempt to seduce his guest's wife, does not need to compensate him; and Isaac deliberately lies, rather than telling a half-truth like Abraham. Midrashic commentators identify the Abimelech whom Isaac deceived with Benmelech, son of Abraham's host Abimelech, who adopted his royal title (Mid. Leqah Tobh Gen. 126; Sepher Hayashar 84).

2. This myth bridges the gap between Isaac's youth and old age; justifies the use of deception when Israelites are in danger abroad; and demonstrates God's care for their ancestor. One midrash enlarges on Isaac's wealth by quoting a proverb: 'Rather the dung of his mules, than all Abimelech's gold and silver!' Another records that as soon as Isaac left Gerar, the prosperity that he had brought vanished with him: bandits sacked the royal treasure-house, Abimelech became a leper, wells dried up, crops failed (Gen. Rab. 707, 709; Mid. Leqah Tobh Gen. 126; Targ. Yer. ad Gen. xxvi. 20, 28).

38

THE BIRTHS OF ESAU AND JACOB

(*a*) When Isaac prayed that God would lift the twenty-year curse of barrenness from Rebekah, she at once conceived twins. Soon they began struggling with each other in her womb, so violently that she longed for death; but God reassured Rebekah, saying:

'Two nations are in your womb;
Two peoples will rise therefrom.
One shall be proved the stronger:
For the elder shall serve the younger!'

Esau, Rebekah's first-born, was covered with red, *shaggy hair*; and, because the other came out *clutching his heel*, she named him Jacob. Esau grew up to be a cunning hunter, a man of the rocky wilderness; whereas Jacob lived quietly at home, guarding his flocks and herds.[1]

(*b*) Some say that the colour of Esau's hair signified murderous inclinations; and that Jacob was conceived before him, since if two pearls are placed in a narrow phial, the first to enter emerges last.[2]

(*c*) Whenever Rebekah passed a Canaanite shrine during her pregnancy, Esau struggled to get out; whenever she passed a house of righteous prayer, Jacob did likewise. For he had addressed Esau in the womb: 'The world of flesh, my brother, is not the world of spirit. Here is eating and drinking, marriage and procreation; there, none of these are found. Let us divide the worlds between us. Take which you prefer!' Esau hastily chose the world of flesh.[3]

(*d*) Others say that Samael helped Esau in this pre-natal struggle; and Michael, Jacob; but that God intervened on Jacob's behalf, saving him from death. Nevertheless, Esau so cruelly tore Rebekah's womb that she could never conceive again. Otherwise Isaac might have been blessed with as many sons as Jacob.[4]

(*e*) Jacob was born circumcised—as were only twelve other saints, namely Adam, Seth, Enoch, Noah, Shem, Terah, Joseph, Moses, Samuel, David, Isaiah and Jeremiah; though some add Job, Balaam and Zerubbabel. Isaac circumcised Esau at the age of eight days; but in later years, he subjected himself to a painful operation which made him look as though he had never been circumcised.

(*f*) At first the difference between the twins was no more than that between a myrtle-shoot and a shoot of thorn. Afterwards, however, while Jacob piously studied the Law, Esau began to frequent Canaanite shrines and do acts of violence. Before the age of twenty, he had committed murder, rape, robbery and sodomy. God therefore blinded Isaac: which preserved him from the neighbours' silent reproaches.[6]

1. *Genesis* xxv. 20–27.
2. Gen. Rab. 687–691.
3. Gen. Rab. 683–84; Yalqut Gen. 110; Seder Eliahu Zuta 26–27.
4. Yalqut Gen. 110; Bereshit Rabbati 103; Tanhuma Buber Deut. 35–36; Tanhuma Ki Tetze, ch. 4; Pesiqta Rabbati 48a.
5. Aboth diR. Nathan 12; Mid. Tehillim 84; Tanhuma Buber Gen. 127; Gen. Rab. 698; PRE, ch. 29.
6. Gen. Rab. 692–93, 713; Tanhuma Buber Gen. 125; Tanhuma Ki Tetze, ch. 4; Mid. Leqah Tobh Gen. 127; Pesiqta Rabbati 47b; B. Baba Bathra 16b.

*

1. Like Sarah, Rebekah gave birth only once, after years of barrenness. So did Samuel's mother, Hannah the Levite (1 *Samuel* I). Rachel was long barren before bearing Joseph, and waited many years more until she conceived Benjamin and died in childbirth. None of these women had daughters, and in each case the son was peculiarly blessed by God. Does this perhaps record a tradition of childlessness required from a *naditum* priestess (see 29. 2) over a certain term of years—as from the Vestal Virgins at Rome—and of a peculiar sanctity enjoyed by any son born afterwards?

2. Another pre-natal struggle between twins occurs in the myth of Perez and Zerah (*Genesis* xxxviii. 27–30), whom Judah fathered on his daughter-in-law Tamar; but whose post-natal wars have not been recorded. These two Hebrew instances are paralleled in Greek myth by the struggle between Proetus and Acrisius in the womb of Queen Aglaia ('Bright'), which portended a bitter rivalry for the Argive throne. When their father died, they agreed to reign alternately; yet Proetus, having seduced Acrisius's daughter Danae, was banished from the kingdom and fled overseas. There he married the Lydian King's daughter and returned to Argolis at the head of a large army. After a bloody but indecisive battle, the twins agreed to divide the kingdom and each rule half. Acrisius, who claimed descent from Belus (Baal), twin-brother of Agenor (Canaan), was not only grandfather to Perseus, whose exploits in Palestine have enriched the night sky with five constellations—Andromeda, Cassiopeia, Cepheus, Draco and Perseus—he was also an ancestor of the Achaean Kings Menelaus and Ascalus (see 35. 6). The Achaeans who came to Syria and are referred to in the Bible

as Hivites (see 30. 4) may have brought a myth with them of a pre-natal fight between twins, which was applied to the division of Abraham's patrimony between Israel (Jacob) and Edom (Esau); the same motive may have been used again in a lost myth about Perez and Zerah to account for an early partition of Judah. Esau probably begins as the shaggy Hunter-god Usöus of Usu (Old Tyre), mentioned in Sanchuniathon's *Phoenician History* as brother to Samemroumus (see 16. 5). But his *hairiness* foreshadows the Edomite occupation of Mount Seir, which means 'shaggy'—that is to say 'covered with trees'—and he had red hair because *Edom* was popularly construed as meaning *adom* or *admoni*, 'tawny red'.

3. The Edomites, or Idumaeans—at one time tributaries to Israel, though earlier arrivals in Palestine—seized part of Southern Judaea after Nebuchadrezzar's capture of Jerusalem (*Ezekiel* XXXVI. 5) including Hebron. However, in the second century B.C., Judah the Maccabee destroyed Hebron and the villages surrounding it (1 *Maccabees* v. 65), and subsequently the Idumaeans were defeated and forcibly converted to Judaism by John Hyrcanus. Two generations later, Herod the Edomite became King of the Jews, murdered the last Maccabean prince, and was confirmed in power by the Romans. Though officially respecting the Mosaic Law, and rebuilding God's Temple at Jerusalem, he raised several shrines to pagan deities. The midrashic Esau is thus a combined portrait of Herod and his Romanized sons Archelaus, Herod Antipas and Herod Philip. Esau's uncircumcised appearance refers to these 'sons of Edom' and their associates who had the operation known as *epispasm* performed on themselves, so that they could participate without embarrassment in Hellenistic sports, which required complete nakedness. The view of Esau as an evil-doer is midrashic, however, not Biblical.

4. The Law given Moses on Mount Sinai was held to have been in existence before Creation and taught in Pharisaic style by Noah's son Shem, *alias* Melchizedek (see 27. *d*). Three further names added to the twelve saints born circumcised brings their number to fifteen, probably celebrating the fifteen holy steps of Ascent in the Temple.

5. John Hyrcanus's conversion of Edom was Sadducaic: that is to say, it did not include a belief in the resurrection of the dead. Thus Esau's grasping at this world, rather than the world beyond, distinguishes him from Jacob the Pharisee.

6. The Biblical explanation of the name Jacob as 'one who takes by the heel' or 'supplants' (*Genesis* XXV. 26; XXVII. 36) is popular etymology, or perhaps a pun on the name, as are Jeremiah's words (IX. 3): 'Every brother deceives (*Ya'qobh*)'. Its original meaning was theophoric, and the full form, *Ya'qob-el*, meant 'God protects'. Numerous variants of this name are known both from Jewish sources (*Ya'qobha*, *'Aqabhya*, *'Aqibha* or *Akiba*, etc.), and from neighbouring countries (*Ya'qob-har*, *'Aqabelaha*, etc.).

39

ABRAHAM'S DEATH

(*a*) Abraham died at the age of one hundred and seventy-five years. His sons Isaac and Ishmael laid him to rest beside his wife Sarah, in the Cave of Machpelah.[1]

(*b*) He had chosen this place of burial because, when the three angels visited him at Mamre, and he ran to slaughter a calf, it fled into the cave's dark recesses. Following close behind, Abraham came upon Adam and Eve lying side by side, as though asleep; candles burned above them, and a sweet fragrance filled the air.[2]

(*c*) Not long before Abraham's death, Isaac and Ishmael celebrated the Feast of First Fruits with him at Hebron, offering sacrifices on the altar he had built there. Rebekah baked cakes from newly harvested corn, and Jacob took them to Abraham who, as he ate, gave God thanks for his happy lot. He also blessed Jacob, with a warning never to marry a Canaanite woman and, at the same time, bequeathed him the house near Damascus still known as 'Abraham's Home'. Afterwards he lay down, clasping Jacob close and printing seven kisses on his brow; then used two of Jacob's fingers to close his own eyes, drew a coverlet over them, stretched out straight, and died peacefully. Jacob slept in Abraham's bosom until, waking some hours later, he found it cold as ice. He reported the death to Isaac, Rebekah and Ishmael, who all wept aloud and presently buried Abraham in the cave, mourning him forty days. God had shortened Abraham's span by five years, so that he might die unaware of Esau's evil deeds.[3]

(*d*) Some, however, say that Abraham fought death no less vigorously than did Moses afterwards; for when Michael came to fetch his soul, he boldly insisted upon first seeing the whole world. God therefore commanded Michael to let Abraham ride across the heavens in a chariot drawn by cherubim, and thus fulfil his wish; yet Abraham was still reluctant to die.

Then God summoned the Angel of Death, saying: 'Come, Death, you cruel one, hide your fierceness, veil your foulness and, disguised in youth and glory, go down and fetch My friend Abraham to Me!'

Abraham received Death hospitably but, doubting that this handsome youth could be Death, asked him to reveal his true aspect. This Death did. Abraham fainted in horror, and whispered, when he came to his senses: 'I charge you in God's name to renew your disguise!' Death obeyed, saying deceitfully: 'Come, friend, clasp my hand and let lusty life and strength flow back to you!' He took Abraham's proffered fingers and through them drew out his soul; which Michael wrapped in a divinely woven kerchief and conveyed to Heaven.[4]

1. *Genesis* XXV. 7–10.
2. PRE, ch. 36.
3. *Jubilees* XXII. 1–XXIII. 7; Pesiqta Rabbati 47b; Tanhuma Buber Gen. 126.
4. *Testament of Abraham*, 1–38.

*

1. The myth of Abraham's fight against Death is also told about Moses and, in a different form, about Sisyphus King of Corinth. Sisyphus twice cheats Death, whom Zeus has sent in anger to take his soul. First he asks to be shown how the infernal handcuffs work, and then quickly locks them on Death's wrists. Next he orders his wife not to bury him and, when ferried across the Styx, persuades Persephone, Queen of the Underworld, that his presence there is irregular and that he must return for three days to arrange a decent funeral—after which he absents himself until Hermes (Michael's counterpart) drags him back by force. Sisyphus was a representative of the Hittite Storm-god Teshub, and the myth may be Hittite too, though altered to suit the ethics of *Genesis*—where God is not angry with Abraham; Abraham opposes, but does not deceive, Death; and his soul is taken to Paradise, not to the punishment grounds of Tartarus.

2. The sharing of Abraham's death-bed emphasizes Jacob's fundamental piety—which his deeds often belie—and explains the Aramaic phrase 'to rest in Abraham's bosom' used, among others, by Jesus in the parable of Dives and Lazarus (*Luke* XVI. 22).

3. 'Abraham's Home' is mentioned by Josephus as still shown near Damascus.

40

THE BARTERED BIRTHRIGHT

(*a*) One day, while Jacob was stewing red lentils outside his hut, Esau returned from a desert hunt, worn to skin and bone.

'Give me some of that red food, Brother,' he pleaded. 'I am starving!'

Jacob answered: 'Eat, Red One; but on condition that you sell me your birthright.'

'Not to sell would likewise lose me my birthright,' groaned Esau, 'because I should soon die of hunger.'

Before restoring Esau's strength with bread and lentil stew, Jacob made him confirm the sale by an oath; and when he had gone off again, laughed, saying: 'My brother despises his birthright!'[1]

(*b*) Some excuse Jacob's apparent lack not only of brotherly love but even of common humanity. He knew, they say, that Esau had just ambushed King Nimrod—who was still alive at the age of two hundred and fifteen years—and murdered him; each having been jealous of the other's fame as a hunter. It was a long pursuit of Esau by Nimrod's vengeful companions that reduced him to such straits. Jacob, indeed, bought Esau's birthright with God's approval, because until the Tent of Assembly had been raised in the Wilderness centuries later, only the first-born of each family might offer sacrifices, and Jacob now cried: 'Shall this evil-doer, standing before God's altar, be blessed by Him?' Moreover, Esau readily agreed to sell the birthright, lest he should be struck dead at the altar for having derided the Resurrection of the Dead.

Others say that Esau also exacted a large sum in gold from Jacob, because his birthright gave him a double share in the inheritance of Canaan; and that he would have afterwards repudiated the sale had Jacob not made him swear by the fear of his father Isaac, whom he loved dearly; and had not Michael and Gabriel witnessed his signature to the contract.[2]

(*c*) Esau showed Isaac exemplary love: bringing venison every day, and never entering the tent except in festal dress. He was therefore rewarded when Joshua entered Canaan and God forbade the

Children of Israel to attack their Edomite cousins, saying: 'I must acknowledge the honour that he paid his father!' Esau, indeed, enjoyed great prosperity so long as he lived.[3]

1. *Genesis* xxv. 29–34.
2. Gen. Rab. 694–97, 699; Sepher Hayashar 90–91; B. Baba Bathra 16b; Tanhuma Buber 125–27; Pesiqta Rabbati 47b–48a; Mid. Leqah Tobh Gen. 123–24; Mid. Sekhel Tobh and Imre Noam *ad Gen.* xxv. 26; Mid. Hagadol Gen. 400–401; Mid. Agada Gen. 64–65; Bereshit Rabbati 105.
3. Gen. Rab. 728; Pesiqta Rabbati 124a; Mid. Leqah Tobh Gen. 133; Cf. Ginzberg LJ, V. 278.

*

1. Esau's desire for red lentils emphasizes the redness of his hair (see 38. 2). That he was Edom, 'the Red One', or at least Edom's father, is repeatedly stated in *Genesis*. He was also Seir, 'the Shaggy One' (see 38. 2) and, in later books (*Numbers* xxiv. 18; 2 *Chronicles* xxv. 11 read in conjunction with 2 *Kings* xiv. 7) 'Seir' and 'Edom' were interchangeable terms (see 38. 2). Yet the Sons of Seir are elsewhere identified with the Horites: 'These are the Sons of Seir the Horite, the inhabitants of the land . . .' (*Genesis* xxxvi. 20) and: 'These are the Horite chieftains in the land of Seir . . .' (*Genesis* v. 30). The chronicler of *Deuteronomy* ii. 12 therefore explains that the Horites once lived in Seir, but that the Children of Esau drove them out and occupied their land.

2. The Horites, or Hurrians, whose language was neither Sumerian, nor Semitic, nor Indo-European, appeared on the northern frontier of Akkad towards the end of the third millennium B.C. Their settlements were in Northern Syria and Eastern Anatolia; and though no archaeological evidence of their establishment in Idumaea has yet come to light, the testimony of *Genesis* need not be doubted—unless 'Horites' means 'Hori', or Troglodites (compare *Job* xxx. 6), who ranked as the sons of Keturah (see 35. *b*). The Seirites, non-Semitic Bronze Age agriculturists, inhabited these parts from about 2000 B.C., and their name occurs on an obelisk raised seven hundred years later by Rameses II of Egypt. However, Semitic-speaking tribes already held the area, and 'Edom' is mentioned for the first time on a papyrus list made for Seti II about 1215 B.C. These Edomites, who partly assimilated both the Seirites and the Horites, prospered until their conquest by King David about 994 B.C.

3. Esau's bartered birthright mythically justifies the Edomites' subsequent conquest by their junior kinsmen, the Israelites (*Numbers* xx. 14) who spoke the same language but had not previously dared to attack them. David took the precaution of garrisoning Edom (2 *Samuel* viii. 14; 1 *Kings* xi. 15–16), which acknowledged Israelite overlordship until the reign of the Judaean King Jehoram (about 850 B.C.). The Edomites then made a successful revolt (2 *Kings* viii. 20 ff and 2 *Chronicles* xxi. 8 ff) and, apart from

a brief reconquest by Amaziah (2 *Kings* XIV. 7) two centuries later, kept their independence for the next seven hundred years.

4. When eventually Herod the Edomite, by his murder of Aristobulus the Hasmonean heir, and a marriage forced on the Hasmonean Princess Mariamne, had become King of the Jews, and Augustus had confirmed his title, the myth of Esau's birthright called for expansion with charges of murder and rape. Esau's demand for gold in addition to lentils may have been appended as a reminder of the crushing taxes which Herod demanded from his subjects. Esau's one virtue, that of filial piety, was held to have been rewarded by prosperity in this world, though all Edomites would inevitably suffer torments in the world beyond (see 11. *g*). When forcibly converted to Judaism by the Hasmoneans, the Edomites were given the Mosaic Law—but not the Prophets; hence Esau scoffs at the resurrection of the dead (see 38. 5). Yet even under Esau's new tyranny, Israel at least retained the first-born's priestly right of ordering Temple worship at Jerusalem and interpreting Law in the Pharisaic Supreme Court.

5. The midrashic identification of Rome with Edom must not be read as myth—not, in fact, as a claim that Aeneas or Romulus was descended from Edom—but merely as a security measure for disguising political complaint. Pharisaic quietists regarded Herodian tyranny under Roman patronage as detestable, yet predetermined by a historic event which, if Israel wished to assure God's providence, she must accept as His will. The later Herodians, continuing as Roman puppets until the rebellion of 68 A.D., were courted by the Sadducee priesthood, and flattered by such renegade Pharisees as Paul of Tarsus (*Acts* XXV. 13–XXVI. 32), and Josephus—who proudly reports his long intimate correspondence with Agrippa II, and his friendship with the Emperors Vespasian, Titus and Domitian.

6. Nevertheless, a main implication of the *Genesis* account is that momentary greed overcame Esau: he would not really have died if the lentils had been denied him. Jacob therefore decided that a nomad hunter who lived from hand to mouth was unworthy to inherit the Promised Land. It is true that peoples who lead a settled agricultural life, not exhausting themselves by wild forays into the desert, have more time for meditation and religious duties. But the midrashic commentators miss this point: perhaps because, in the earlier quarrel between two brothers similarly placed, Abel, a nomad, is the hero, and Cain, a settled farmer, the villain (see 16. 1); and because Edom practised agriculture while Israel was still wandering in the Wilderness.

41

THE STOLEN BLESSING

(*a*) Isaac grew old and blind. Having reached his one hundred and twenty-third year, he felt that death was close and called Esau into the tent. 'My son,' he said, 'take your bow and fetch venison from the wilderness. Prepare it in the manner that best pleases me; afterwards I will give you my blessing and die.'

Rebekah, who overheard Isaac's words, summoned Jacob as soon as Esau was out of sight. 'Your father means to bestow a blessing on Esau. This must not be, since you are now his first-born! Go to the flock, bring me two likely kids for a savoury stew of the sort your father loves; he will mistake it for venison.' Jacob objected: 'But Esau's skin is hairy, and mine smooth! What if our father Isaac should touch it and discover the deceit? Would he not then curse rather than bless me?' Rebekah reassured him: 'The curse be on my head! Away now, fetch the kids!'

Jacob obeyed. Rebekah prepared a stew, and dressed Jacob in Esau's garments, afterwards fastening the newly-flayed kids' skins on his hands and neck. He entered Isaac's tent with the platter of venison; and these words passed between them:

'Father, here I am.'

'Who are you, my son?'

'Do you not recognize your first-born? Pray taste my venison, Father, and bless me!'

'How did you find it so quickly, my son?'

'Because God favoured me.'

'Come closer! I wish to assure myself that you are Esau.'

Isaac ran his fingers over him, saying: 'There is no mistaking Esau's hands, but your voice sounds like Jacob's. Are you truly my son Esau?'

'I am he.'

'Then hand me the platter, so that I may eat and bless you from a full heart.'

Jacob gave him the platter, and with it a cup of wine. When Isaac had well eaten and drunken, he said: 'Come here, my son, and kiss me!' As Jacob bent down, Isaac caught the fragrance of his garments, and prophesied:

'The garments of my son
Smell like a field
Which is blessed by God.

May God reward you
With heavenly dew,
With the fat of the land,
With corn and with wine!

Let peoples serve you
Let nations do you homage,
Lord of your mother's sons!

Let your brothers bow to you,
Let your curser be cursed,
Let your blesser be blessed!'

No sooner had Isaac concluded his prophecy, than Esau returned from a successful chase. He made a savoury stew, brought it to his father and said: 'Pray, Father, taste my venison and bless me!' Isaac asked: 'Who may you be?' Esau answered: 'Do you not know your first-born son Esau?' Isaac, trembling for dismay, said: 'Someone has already brought me a great platter of venison which I ate, and in joy of which I blessed him—and, indeed, he shall be blessed! It must have been your brother Jacob, who deceived me and stole your blessing!'

Esau cried bitterly: 'Is he not rightly named Jacob? He has twice *supplanted me*—stealing first my birthright, and now my blessing! Have you kept none for your son Esau?'

Isaac answered: 'Alas, I appointed Jacob lord over all his brothers, and promised him boundless corn and wine! What blessing is left to bestow on you, my son?'

Esau insisted, weeping: 'Bless me too, Father, in whatever manner may be fitting!'

So Isaac prophesied again:

'Far from the fat of the land
Must your dwelling be,
Far from the field
Where falls a heavenly dew!

By your sword shall you live,
Your brother shall you serve
Till it be time to shake
His yoke from your shoulders!'

Yet Esau hated Jacob for his double-dealing, and swore to himself: 'As soon as my father dies and the mourning has ended, I will kill him!'[1]

(*b*) Some say that God sent an angel to detain Esau in the wilderness, while Rebekah prepared the stew and Isaac ate his fill. Whenever, therefore, Esau shot a deer, left its carcase lying, and went in chase of another, the angel both revived and released it. Whenever Esau shot a bird, cut its wings and continued his hunt, the angel made it fly away; thus, in the end, he brought Isaac no better than dog's meat.[2]

(*c*) Others say that, though Jacob obeyed his mother because of the Fifth Commandment, he hated the enforced deception: tears streamed from his eyes, inwardly he prayed God to remove this shame, and two angels supported him. But Rebekah, being a prophetess, knew that Jacob must face the ordeal, and said: 'Courage, my son! When Adam sinned, was not Earth, his mother, cursed? If needs be, I shall tell your father that I have acted in my knowledge of Esau's evil ways.' Yet Jacob did not lie to Isaac, saying only: 'I am your first-born son,' which was the truth—since he had bought Esau's birthright.

Others again say that Esau's garments in which Rebekah clothed him, namely those made by God for Adam and Eve, had now rightfully become Jacob's, and Isaac recognized their Paradisal fragrance. However, discovering the trick played on him, Isaac grew angry and would have cursed Jacob, but that God warned him: 'Did you not say "Let your curser be cursed! Let your blesser be blessed!"?' Then Isaac told Esau: 'While Jacob is worthy to be served, serve him you must! But when he ceases to obey God's Law, rebel, and make him your servant!'[3]

1. *Genesis* xxvii. 1–41.
2. Tanhuma Buber Gen. 131; Tanhuma Toldot ch. 11; Gen. Rab. 754; Mid. Leqah Tobh Gen. 135; Targum Yer. *ad Gen.* xxvii. 31.
3. Gen. Rab. 727, 730, 740–41, 756, 762–63, 765; Mid. Hagadol Gen. 424, 435, 440; Mid. Leqah Tobh Gen. 132–34, 137–38; Tanhuma Buber Gen. 131–33; Mid. Sekhel Tobh 117; *Jubilees* xxvi. 13.

*

1. The rival twins, their mother, and their moribund father shared a firm belief in the efficacy of his last blessing, which would establish, rather than merely predict, the future of Israel; nor could the words, once pronounced, be unsaid even by himself. If Esau had brought the venison stew in good time, his posterity would have enjoyed Isaac's blessing and inherited Canaan. The significance of this blessing was that of a property charter. Having once awarded the fat of the land to Jacob—namely, fertile Western Palestine, watered by dew from Heaven—Isaac could bequeath Esau no more of Abraham's kingdom than Idumaea, the meagre produce of whose soil his semi-nomadic sons would have to supplement with the sword: by raiding, and by extorting protection money from caravans and the frontier villages of neighbouring peoples (see 35. 2). 'Your brother shall you serve!' looks forward to the period of Edomite vassalage between the reigns of King David and King Jehoram (2 *Kings* VIII. 20–22). The second half of Esau's blessing, which differs in style and rhythm from the first, has been added to justify Edom's subsequent rebellion.

2. Though midrashic commentators admitted the efficacy of Isaac's blessing, they also knew that the prophet Hosea (XII. 3–13) had threatened 'Jacob' with punishment for his evil deeds, recalling how he took Esau by the heel at birth, and by his strength made himself a prince, thereafter using deceitful balances, and fleeing to Syria from Esau's vengeance. A sentence condemning Jacob's theft of the blessing has evidently been excised by some early editor, and the gap filled (verses 4 and 5) with praise of his wrestling feat at Bethel. The Second Isaiah (*Isaiah* XLIII. 27–28) later declares that Jacob's sin is at last punished by the Babylonian Exile: 'Thy first father sinned . . . therefore . . . have I given Jacob to condemnation.'

3. This myth—the first chapter of which has a Greek parallel of Canaanite origin (see 38. 2)—became fixed in Hebrew tradition at a time when to be 'a man of many wiles', like the cruel and treacherous Odysseus, was still a noble trait. Indeed, Autolycus the Greek master-thief, Odysseus's grandfather, can be identified with Jacob in the Laban context (see 46. *a*. *b*. and 1). Yet lies and thieving were strictly forbidden by the Law to God-fearing Jews of rabbinic days (*Leviticus* XIX. 11 reads: 'Ye shall not steal, nor lie to one another!'), who thus faced a cruel dilemma. They held that the fate of the Universe hung on their ancestor Jacob's righteousness, as the legitimate heir to God's Promised Land. Should they suppress the Esau-Jacob myth, and thereby forfeit Isaac's blessing? Or should they agree that refusal of food to a starving man, conspiracy to rob a brother, and deceit of a blind father are justifiable when a man plays for high enough stakes? Unable to accept either alternative, they recast the story: Jacob was bound, they explained, by obedience to his mother; hated the part she forced on him; took pains to evade downright lies. Since Esau married Hittite wives whose idolatry distressed Rebekah (see 42. *a*), they equated him with the Wicked Kingdom of Rome, whose officers and agents it was permissible to deceive, and made Jacob their exemplar of how to survive in a hostile world. Though unwilling to excuse his deceit on the ground that he lived before the Mosaic Law was promulgated—the Law, for them, preceded Creation—they could at least portray him as decoyed into sin by

Rebekah, a woman who, from a prophetic sense of Israel's future, had taken the curse on her own head.

4. The late-first-century Jewish author of the *Epistle to the Hebrews* (xii. 16–17) characteristically argues that Esau, a profane fornicator who bartered his birthright for a 'morsel of food', was rejected when he afterwards tried to inherit the first-born's blessing, because he could not repudiate this sale.

42

ESAU'S MARRIAGES

(*a*) At the age of forty, Esau brought two Hittite wives to Hebron: Judith, daughter of Beeri—though some name her Aholibamah the Hivite—and Basemath, or Adah, daughter of Elon. Their idolatry vexed Isaac and Rebekah, to please whom he married a third, God-fearing wife: namely, Basemath, or Mahalath, daughter of his uncle Ishmael.[1]

(*b*) Some say that Esau's love for Isaac and Rebekah turned to hatred when they condoned Jacob's theft. He thought: 'I will marry a daughter of Ishmael, and make him insist on having the forced sale of my birthright annulled. When Isaac refuses this, Ishmael will kill him. As my father's blood-avenger, I shall then kill Ishmael; and thus inherit the wealth of both.' Yet to Ishmael he said no more than: 'Abraham bequeathed all that he had to your younger brother Isaac, and sent you off to die in the wilderness. Now Isaac plans to treat me likewise. Take vengeance on your usurping brother, and so shall I on mine.' Ishmael asked: 'Why should I kill your father Isaac, when it is you whom he has wronged?' Esau answered: 'Cain murdered his brother Abel; but no son has hitherto committed parricide.' God, however, reading Esau's evil thoughts, said: 'I shall make public what you planned in secret!'[2]

(*c*) Ishmael died soon after Basemath's betrothal; and Nebaioth, his eldest son, therefore gave her to Esau. Meanwhile, Ishmael had renamed Basemath 'Mahalath', as a means of distinguishing her from Esau's Hittite wife of that name, and in hope that this marriage would make God *forgive* Esau's wickedness. Here, indeed, was Esau's opportunity to win God's favour at last; but since he would not send away his other wives, they soon corrupted Mahalath. All her sons intermarried with idolatrous Horites and Seirites.[3]

(*d*) The Edomite tribes were Teman, Omar, Zepho, Gatam and Kenaz, grandsons of Adah by Eliphaz; Nahath, Zerah, Shammah and Mizzah, grandsons of Basemath by Reuel; Amalek, son of Timna by Eliphaz; Jeush, Jalam and Korah, sons of Aholibamah by Esau.[4]

1. *Genesis* xxvi. 34; xxviii. 8–9; xxxvi. 2.
2. Gen. Rab. 764–65; Agadat Bereshit 6, 95–96; Mid. Tehillim 112; Hadar on *Gen.* xxvii. 42; Mid. Hagadol Gen. 440.
3. Mid. Hagadol Gen. 440; Seder Olam 2; B. Megillah 17a; Nur al-Zulm 87; Gen. Rab. 768–69; Sepher Hayashar 99–100.
4. *Genesis* xxxvi. 1–14.

*

1. The chroniclers of *Genesis* named Edom's three ancestresses from hearsay. One of them had certainly been Basemath; but the other two were remembered as either Judith and Mahalath, or Adah and Aholibamah. *Basemath* may mean 'perfumed'. *Aholibamah* means 'my tent is exalted'; *Adah*, 'assembly'. 'Aholibamah the *Hivite*' is probably a misreading of *Horite.*

2. *Genesis* xxxvi. 10–14 lists the sons of Esau matrilineally, as *Genesis* xxxv. 23–26 has listed the sons of Jacob. Jacob's sons had four ancestresses: Leah, Rachel, Bilhah and Zilpah (see 45. *a–c*). Perhaps because Esau's sons had only three such, the chronicler has added another—Timna, sister of Lotan (Lot)—to point a parallel. The earlier confederacies seem to have corresponded with the twelve signs of the Zodiac (see 43. *d*).

3. Edom's genealogical tree closely matches that of Israel, as the following tables show:

THE SONS OF ISRAEL

Leah	*Rachel*	*Bilhah*	*Zilpah*
Reuben	(Joseph)	Dan	Gad
Simeon	Ephraim	Naphtali	Asher
Levi	Manasseh		
Judah	Benjamin		
Issachar			
Zebulon			

THE SONS OF EDOM

Adah	*Basemath*	*Timna*	*Aholibamah*
(Eliphaz)	(Reuel)	(Eliphaz)	Jeush
Teman	Nahath	Amalek	Jalam
Omar	Zerah		Korah
Zepho	Shammah		
Gatam	Mizzah		
Kenaz			

4. Six of these Edomite tribal names, namely Kenaz, Nahath, Zerah, Shammah, Jeush and Korah, occur also as proper names in the Israelite tribes of Judah, Benjamin and Levi—proof of the close relations between Edom and Judaea. Moreover, *Judith*, 'Praise of God', is the feminine form of *Judah*; and 'Aholibamah', in its associated form 'Aholibah', is the sym-

bolic name given to Judah by Ezekiel (XXIII) when he condemns idolatrous practices at Jerusalem. The tribe of Judah was early expanded by addition of the Edomite Kenizzites (*Numbers* XXXII. 12 and *Judges* I. 13) and Kenites (*Judges* I. 16), who included the Calebites and lived in Amalek's territory (1 *Samuel* XV. 6).

5. The 'sons of Eliphaz', according to *Genesis* XXXVI. 10–12, were grandsons of Esau and his wife Adah, but are subsequently described as 'sons of Adah' (verse 16). The grandsons of Basemath are also described as her sons in verses 13 and 17, and in verse 19 as 'sons of Esau'. Similarly, in *Genesis* XLVIII. 5–6, Jacob's grandsons Ephraim and Manasseh become his 'sons', thus eliminating the tribe of their father Joseph; but Ephraim seems to have won its position by absorbing the matriarchal tribe of Dinah (see 49. 3). The priestly tribe of Levi, which was allotted no tribal territory, corresponded with the ambiguous, and therefore holy, thirteenth tribe. These thirteen tribes were symbolized by the almond rods stored in the Sanctuary at Moses' orders, of which Aaron's alone put forth buds: thereby designating Levi as God's choice for the priesthood (*Numbers* XVII. 16–24). Almonds symbolized holy wisdom, and the Seven-branched Candlestick, or *Menorah*, was carved with almond leaves (*Exodus* XXV. 31).

6. *Genesis* emphasizes the continual struggle of these patriarchal Hebrews against their matrilineal neighbours (see 36. 1). Since Esau compromised between the two systems, midrashic commentators felt at liberty to place the worst possible construction on his marriage into Ishmael's patriarchal clan.

43

JACOB AT BETHEL

(*a*) Rebekah called Jacob and said: 'Esau plans to kill you, and Ishmael will then avenge your death. But why should I lose two sons in one day? Take refuge with my brother Laban at Padan-Aram, and when Esau's anger has abated I will send you word.' To Isaac she said: 'These Hittite wives of Esau make me weary of life! If Jacob, too, were to marry an idolatress, the shame would kill me.' Isaac thereupon warned Jacob: 'My son, do not take a Canaanite wife! Instead, go to Padan-Aram and choose one of your uncle Laban's twin-daughters.' And he prophesied again:

'O may God favour you,
And multiply your race
To a concourse of tribes!
May Abraham's blessing
Rest on you and your sons:
To inherit this land
That was Abraham's gift!'[1]

(*b*) Jacob and Esau were sixty-three years old at the time. Some say that Rebekah, while complaining of Esau's wives, did not mention them by name, but blew her nose in a bitter rage and flung the snot from her fingers to the ground. Also, that when Jacob fled, Esau sent out his son Eliphaz with orders to kill and despoil him. Eliphaz, a famous archer, led ten of his maternal uncles in pursuit and overtook Jacob at Shechem. Jacob pleaded: 'Take all that I have, only spare my life—and God will reckon your plunder as a righteous deed.' Eliphaz accordingly stripped him naked and brought the spoils home; but this show of mercy enraged Esau.[2]

(*c*) Fearing pursuit by Esau himself, Jacob turned aside from the road to Shechem, and neared Luz at sunset. Because of his nakedness he did not enter the city gates; and for want of a saddle-bag used a stone as his pillow. That night he dreamed of a ladder, its foot set on earth, its top touching Heaven, and angels going up and down the rungs. A voice said: 'I, the God of your father Isaac, and of his father Abraham, award this land to you and your children! Numerous as grains of dust, they shall spread to all four quarters of Earth, and bestow a blessing wherever they go. I will protect you, both now and on your return journey, never forsaking My chosen son.'

Jacob awoke, and cried in terror: 'God is surely here, and I did not know! This place of dread must be His house, and the gateway to Heaven!' Next morning, he rose early, set up the stone as a pillar and anointed it with oil, vowing: 'If God indeed protects me on my journey—giving me bread to eat and garments to wear—and fetches me safely home, I will serve no other God, and pay Him tithes of all my riches! This pillar shall be His abode.' Thereafter the place was called Bethel, or 'The House of God'.[3]

(*d*) Some say that Luz stood below the shoulder of Mount Moriah, on the summit of which Jacob was granted his vision. Also, that his pillow had been the twelve separate stones of an altar raised by Adam, and rebuilt by Abraham; but that, as Jacob chose one of them, they all cried out together in rivalry: 'Lay your righteous head upon me!', and were miraculously united. God said: 'This is a sign that the twelve pious sons whom I give you shall form a single nation! Are there not twelve signs of the Zodiac, twelve hours in the day, twelve hours in the night, and twelve months in the year? So, surely, there shall also be twelve tribes in Israel!'[4]

(*e*) Others say that when God first created angels, they cried: 'Blessed be the Lord, the God of Israel, from eternity to eternity!'; and that, when Adam was created, they asked: 'Lord, is this the man for whom we should give praise?' God answered: 'No, this one is a thief; he will eat forbidden fruit.' When Noah was born, they asked again: 'Is this he?' God answered: 'No, this one is a drunkard.' When Abraham was born, they asked once more: 'Is this he?', but God answered: 'No, this one is a proselyte, not circumcised in infancy.' When Isaac was born, they asked: 'Is this he?' God answered: 'No, this one loves an elder son who hates Me.' But when Jacob was born, and they once more asked the question, God cried: 'This is he indeed! His name shall be changed from Jacob to Israel, and all his sons shall praise him!'

Jacob was chosen as a model for the man-faced angel of God's chariot, which Ezekiel saw in a vision; and his mild and hairless visage is also imprinted on the Moon.[5]

(*f*) Others say that the angels of Jacob's dream were princely guardians of four oppressive nations. The Prince of Babylon ascended seventy rungs and then came down; that of Media ascended fifty-two rungs and then came down; that of Greece ascended one hundred and eighty rungs and then came down; but the Prince of Edom went higher and higher, out of Jacob's sight. He cried in dismay: 'Will this one never descend?' God comforted him, saying: 'Fear not, my servant Jacob! Even if he should reach the topmost rung and seat himself at My side, I would yet cast him down again. Come, Jacob, mount the ladder yourself! For you at least will never be called upon to descend.' Jacob, however, was timid, and thus doomed Israel to subjection by the four kingdoms of this world.[6]

(*g*) When Jacob anointed his pillar with oil which had dripped from Heaven, God trod it so deep into the earth that it is now called the Foundation Stone: namely, the world's navel, upon which stands Solomon's Temple.[7]

1. *Genesis* xxvii. 42; xxviii. 5.
2. *Jubilees* xxv. 1 ff.; Gen. Rab. 767; Mid. Sekhel Tobh 119; Mid. Hagadol Gen. 437; Sepher Hayashar 96–98.
3. *Genesis* xxviii. 10–22.
4. Gen. Rab. 780–82; Bereshit Rabbati 118; PRE, ch. 35; Sepher Hayashar 98; Mid. Tehillim 399; B. Hullin 91b; Seder Eliahu Rabba 29; Tanhuma Buber Gen. 181.
5. Tanhuma Buber Lev. 72–73; cf. Ginzberg, LJ, V. 275, 291.
6. Lev. Rab. 29. 2; PRE, ch. 35; Pesiqta diR. Kahana 150b–151a; Mid. Tehillim 347.
7. PRE, ch. 35; Mid. Tehillim 400.

*

1. Bethel, which had been a Canaanite shrine long before the Hebrew patriarchal age, lies ten miles north of Jerusalem and about a mile east of Luz. Its name is preserved by the Arab village of Betin. Archaeological evidence shows almost continuous settlement of this area from the twenty-first century B.C. until the first century A.D. The holiness of Bethel was confirmed by the myth of Abraham's having sacrificed, both on his way to Egypt (see 26. *a*) and on his return, at a place between Bethel and Ai (see 27. *a*). In the semi-historic days of the Judges, God's Tent of Assembly containing the Ark was kept there (*Judges* xx. 18, 26–27; xxi. 2–4). Bethel's religious importance remained supreme until the reign of Saul (1 *Samuel* x. 3 and xiii. 4) and, though declining somewhat after Solomon built the Temple at Jerusalem, revived when Rehoboam and Jeroboam divided his empire between them and the Northern Kingdom chose Bethel as its central sanctuary (1 *Kings* xii. 29–33).

2. The Ladder myth, establishing Bethel as the 'Gate of Heaven' revealed by God to the founder of Israel, authorizing the anointment of a famous local *massebah*, or sacred pillar, and sanctifying the payment of tithes (see 27. 5), dates from the days of the Judges. But the version identifying Bethel with Mount Moriah, and Jacob's stone-pillow with the rocky

summit on which Solomon built his Temple, must post-date King Josiah's destruction or desecration (628 B.C.) of all the 'high places' sacred to the Canaanite goddesses Anath and Asherah, and his reformation of Temple worship at Jerusalem. Only then could the scene of Jacob's vision be arbitrarily transferred to Jerusalem from the well-known shrine of Bethel.

3. God's blessing is unconditional, but Jacob feels impelled to promise Him thank-offerings: namely, honoured residence in the pillar and a tithe of all riches won by divine favour. His plea for food, clothes and a safe journey underlies the midrashic story of how Eliphaz robbed him.

4. The rungs up which the guardian angels climbed represent years of their nations' rule over Israel: namely, seventy years of Babylonian exile—from the fall of the First Temple (586 B.C.) to the completion of the Second (516 B.C. or, more precisely, 515 B.C.); the subsequent fifty-two (in fact, fifty-eight) years of dependence on the Medes, which closed with Ezra's leading back his group of exiles in the reign of Cyrus (457 B.C.); and one hundred and eighty years of Hellenistic rule—from the conquest of Palestine by Alexander the Great (333 B.C.) to the re-establishment of an independent Jewish kingdom by the Maccabees (153 B.C.). Edom's unbroken ascent (see 40. 4 and 41. 3) shows that this particular midrash dates from the period of Roman control over Palestine, which began with Pompey's capture of Jerusalem in 63 B.C. and continued until the Persian invasion of 614–629 A.D.

5. The Greek word *baetylos* signified a cone-shaped pillar, periodically anointed with oil, wine or blood, in which a god resided, and which was often said to have fallen from heaven—like the thunder-stone sacred to the God Terminus at Rome, or the Palladium of Troy. Since the Greeks personified 'Baetylus' as a son of the Sky-god Uranus and the Earth-mother Gaea; and since, according to Sanchuniathon, El (identified by Philo of Byblus with Cronus) had the same nativity, *baetylos* is likely to be a borrowing from the Phoenician or Hebrew *Beth-El*, meaning 'the House of the God El'. Hesychius also records that the stone substituted for the infant Zeus, which Uranus swallowed and afterwards disgorged, was shown at Delphi and called 'Baetylus'; priests oiled it every day and, according to Pausanias, covered it with raw wool on solemn occasions. Photius, the ninth-century Byzantine scholar, mentions several 'baetyls' on Mount Lebanon, about which marvellous tales were told. The word could be applied to female deities also: thus in the Temple accounts from the late-fifth-century B.C. Jewish colony at Elephantine, a goddess is named 'Anath-baetyl'.

6. That the twelve patriarchs were pious men flatly contradicts *Genesis*. All except Reuben and the infant Benjamin conspired to murder their brother Joseph, then sold him into slavery and gave out that he had been killed by a wild beast. Reuben cuckolded Jacob, and earned his dying curse (*Genesis* XXXV. 22 and XLIX. 4—see 50. *a*). Levi and Simeon were similarly

cursed for their treacherous massacre at Shechem (*Genesis* xxxiv. 25–31; xlix. 5–7—see 49. *d*); and Benjamin was promised a successful life wholly devoted to pillage (*Genesis* xlix. 27—see 60. *e*). Yet the apocryphal *Testaments of the Twelve Patriarchs* presents every one of them as a fountain of piety and wisdom. Jesus quotes the *Testament of Joseph* (xviii. 2) in *Matthew* v. 44; and the *Testament of Levi* (xiii. 5) in *Matthew* vi. 19.

44

JACOB'S MARRIAGES

(*a*) Continuing his journey to Padan-Aram, Jacob saw three flocks lying around a well near the city. The shepherds whom he questioned, answered that they knew Laban son of Nahor—'And look, here comes his daughter Rachel with the sheep!'

'Why do you not water your flocks?' he asked.

'We are awaiting the other shepherds. They will help us to roll back yonder huge stone from the well-head.'

When Rachel arrived, leading Laban's flock, Jacob rolled away the stone single-handed and watered the sheep for her—some say that the waters thereupon rose miraculously and maintained the same level throughout his stay.[1] He then revealed himself to Rachel as her cousin, kissed her, and wept. Some say he wept because, many years before, Eliezer had brought rich gifts from Abraham to this very spot, when proposing Rebekah's marriage with Isaac; but he, their son, now stood here destitute. Others say it was because the shepherds whispered jealously among themselves when he gave Rachel his cousinly kiss.[2]

(*b*) Rachel went home to announce Jacob's arrival, and soon Laban hurried to the well, embraced him, and invited him to the house. Laban hoped for even more valuable gifts than those brought by Eliezer and, though Jacob had come on foot without even a bundle, suspected that he kept gold in a belt beneath his garment. While they embraced, Laban searched but found no belt; then kissed him on his mouth to see whether it contained pearls. Jacob said plainly: 'Uncle, you will find no wealth hidden on me: I bring only greetings, having been robbed on the way by Eliphaz, son of my twin-brother Esau.'[3]

(*c*) Laban thought: 'He comes empty-handed, expecting to eat and drink at our table for a full month, or perhaps even a year!' Angrily he went to consult his teraphim.

Now, when making an oracular idol of this sort, the Aramaeans of Harran would murder a first-born male and preserve his head in brine, oil, and spices. Then they would chant spells, place underneath the tongue a golden disk engraved with a demonic name, mortar the head into a wall, light lamps, prostrate themselves, and ask questions to which it whispered replies. They had another sort of teraphim, also: idols of gold and silver, fashioned piece by piece at certain calculated hours, and empowered by the stars to foretell the future—Laban, a famous astrologer, had such in his possession. He now bowed down before them and inquired: 'This guest who lodges in my house, eating bread without payment—how shall I treat him?' They whispered back: 'Beware of antagonizing a man whose stars are in so marvellous a conjunction! For his sake, God will bless whatever you do in house or field.' Laban pondered: 'What if I should ask Jacob to enter my service, and he demands high wages?' The teraphim, reading his thoughts, whispered again: 'Let his pay be a woman. He will demand only women. Whenever Jacob threatens to return home, offer him one more, and he will stay.'[4]

(*d*) After a month had passed, Laban asked Jacob: 'What shall your wages be?' Jacob replied: 'Let me serve seven years for your daughter Rachel.' Laban cried: 'I should rather have you as her husband than any other man in the world!' So the bargain was struck.[5]

(*e*) Some say that, at first, Rachel and her older twin, Leah, were equally beautiful; but that, when Leah heard people say 'Rebekah's twin sons are bound to marry Laban's twin daughters; the elder taking the elder, and the younger, the younger,' she asked: 'What is known of Rebekah's son Esau?' They answered: 'His ways are evil, and his trade banditry.' 'And what is known of Jacob?' They answered: 'He is a righteous one, who dutifully minds his father's flocks.' Leah began to weep, sobbing: 'Alas! May God keep me from marriage with that wretch Esau!' Constant weeping deformed her eyes; whereas Rachel, who heard nothing but good of Jacob, grew more lovely still.[6]

(*f*) Jacob, though aware that elder daughters should be married before their sisters, thought: 'Esau already hates me because I tricked him out of birthright and blessing; now, if I take her, he may come and murder me. I dare sue only for Rachel.'[7]

(*g*) Rachel warned Jacob: 'Do not trust my scheming father!' Jacob boasted: 'I will match my wits against his.' She asked: 'Are the righteous then free to deceive?' He answered: 'They may counter fraud with fraud. Tell me, what does your father plan?' 'I fear,' said Rachel, 'that he will order Leah to take my place in the darkness of the nuptial chamber; which can easily be done here in the East, where no man enjoys his wife by either sunlight or lamplight. I have heard that it is otherwise in the sinful West.'

'Then let us agree upon a sign,' Jacob said. 'I shall accept the woman who first touches the great toe of my right foot; next, my right thumb; and finally, my right ear lobe.'

'I will remember those signs,' Rachel answered.[8]

(*h*) Jacob told Laban: 'I know that you Easterners are masters of evasion. Understand then, that I will serve seven years for Rachel, your younger daughter; and not for Leah, your elder daughter with the deformed eyes; nor for any other woman named Rachel, whom you may fetch in from the market-place!'

'We understand each other well, Nephew,' replied Laban.[9]

(*i*) Jacob served Laban seven years, and they seemed no longer than a week, so deeply did he love Rachel. On the very day they ended, he went to Laban saying: 'Come, Uncle, prepare the wedding feast!' Laban invited all Padan-Aram to his house, but sent Leah veiled into the nuptial chamber that night, and Jacob did not discover the fraud until morning! For Rachel, though she loved Jacob dearly, also loved Leah, and said to herself: 'I fear that from ignorance of our secret signs, my sister will be put to shame. I must therefore disclose them.' Thus, when Jacob called Leah 'Rachel', she replied 'Here I am,' in Rachel's voice; and touched, in turn, the great toe of his right foot, his right thumb and right ear lobe.[10]

(*j*) At the first light of dawn, Jacob reproached Leah angrily with: 'Deceiver, daughter of a deceiver!' Leah smiled and said: 'No teacher without his pupil: having heard from your own lips how my blind uncle Isaac called you "Esau", and how you replied in Esau's voice, I bore your lesson in mind.' Later, God granted Rachel, as a reward for this sisterly kindness, that Samson, Joshua and King Saul should be her descendants.

Jacob also reproached Laban: 'I served seven years for Rachel, why have you defrauded me? Take back your daughter Leah, and let me go. That was a wicked act!'

Laban answered mildly: 'It is not our custom, and forbidden in the Heavenly Tablets, to give away a younger daughter before the elder. Do not be vexed, but make your posterity observe the law; and thank me for teaching you by example. Rachel, too, shall be yours as soon as this wedding feast has ended; you must buy her by serving seven years more.'[11]

(*k*) Jacob agreed, and Laban, remembering the teraphim's advice, gave him two women besides Leah and Rachel: namely Zilpah, Leah's bondmaid, and Bilhah, Rachel's bondmaid. They were Laban's own daughters by concubines; and later Jacob took both to his bed.[12]

1. *Genesis* XXIX. 1–10; PRE, ch. 36; Gen. Rab. 817; Targum Yer. *ad Gen.* XXVIII. 22 and XXI. 22.
2. *Genesis* XXIX. 11–12; Gen. Rab. 811–12.
3. *Genesis* XXIX. 12–13; Mid. Hagadol Gen. 460–61.
4. Yalqut Reubeni *ad Gen.* XXIX. 15; Tanhuma Wayetse 40b; PRE, ch. 36; Sepher Hayashar 103.
5. *Genesis* XXIX. 14–19; Gen. Rab. 813–14.
6. B. Baba Bathra 123a; Tanhuma Buber Gen. 152, 157; Gen. Rab. 815–16, 821–22.
7. Tanhuma Buber Gen. 153, 157.
8. Gen. Rab. 817–19; Targum Yer. *ad Gen.* XXIX. 22; Sepher Hayashar 100–01; B. Megilla 13b; B. Baba Bathra 123a; Mid. Hagadol Gen. 463–64; Azulai, *Hesed le-Abraham* II. 6.
9. Gen. Rab. 816.
10. *Genesis* XXIX. 20–24; B. Megilla 13b; B. Baba Bathra 123a; Gen. Rab. 819.
11. *Genesis* XXIX. 25–27; Gen. Rab. 814, 819; Tanhuma Buber Gen. 153; B. Sukka 27b; B. Megilla 13b; B. Baba Bathra 123a; *Jubilees* XXVIII. 4–9.
12. *Genesis* XXIX. 28–30; Gen. Rab. 870; PRE, ch. 36; Targum Yer. *ad Gen.* XXIX. 24; Bereshit Rabbati 119.

*

1. Only Isaac's sympathy for his first-born son Esau could have decided him not to give Jacob a suitable bride-price; but, lest this harshness might read like a repudiation of the stolen blessing, we are told of Eliphaz's brigandage—with which Jacob, somewhat implausibly, excuses his empty-handed arrival. Laban will have realized that Isaac who, as Abraham's heir, could buy Jacob the most expensive bride in Harran, had driven him from home, unattended and in disgrace. But impecunious young Arab villagers still often serve a future father-in-law, instead of paying a bride-price; and Jacob furnishes them with an honourable precedent.

2. Laban's answer to Jacob's complaint: 'It is not our custom to give away the younger daughter before the elder' (*Genesis* XXIX. 26) implies that force of local custom annuls any individual undertaking which may contradict it. Jacob's acceptance of this view is proved by his subsequent silence; and the myth thus validates an 'excellent rule' which the *Book of Jubilees* wished to make binding on all Israel.

3. Polygamy remains legal in the Middle East for both Moslems and Jews, but is rarely practised. Marriage to two sisters, though prohibited by *Leviticus* XVIII. 18, must have been tolerated as late as the sixth century B.C., since Jeremiah (III. 6 ff) and Ezekiel (XXIII. 1 ff) symbolically speak of God's marriage to the sisters Israel and Judah, or Aholah and Aholibah.

4. 'Easterners' who insisted on darkness in the nuptial chamber included the Harranians, Persians and Medes. Jacob was suspected of Western immodesty: such as Absalom displayed when he had intercourse with his father's harem under an awning in the sight of all Israel (2 *Samuel* XVI. 22).

5. The secret signs agreed upon between Jacob and Rachel are, according to Abraham Azulai, a sixteenth-century commentator, the ritual proper for bride and bridegroom to observe on their wedding night. She must handle in turn the great toe of his right foot, his right thumb, and his right ear lobe: which will not only arouse his desire for honest procreation but expel the three demons, lodging there, that incite carnal lust. If fortunate, she may thus achieve the rare distinction of giving birth to a son already circumcised (see 19. *c* and 38. *e*). The priest who smears blood from a sacrificial victim upon those three places, rids himself of defilement (*Leviticus* xiv. 14, etc.). In the *kapparah* ritual on the eve of the Day of Atonement, blood from a cock similarly banishes the demons of carnal lust.

6. Teraphim like those owned by Laban, David (1 *Samuel* xix. 13–16) and Micah (*Judges* xvii. 5 ff), although 'graven images' of the sort condemned by the Second Commandment, were in common use. Hosea (iii. 4) writes in the eighth century B.C. that religion would die out but for teraphim, sacrifices and sacred pillars. They were divinatory household or village gods, perhaps ancestral images of metal, wood or terracotta (2 *Kings* xxiii. 24; *Ezekiel* xxi. 1 and *Zechariah* x. 2); and consulted at least until the time of Judas the Maccabee (2 *Maccabees* xii. 40), whose men wore Jamnian teraphim underneath their tunics. Judas, like Samuel (1 *Samuel* xv. 33), considered divination abominable to God, and this discovery shocked him. The midrashic account of mummified human heads being put to oracular use at Harran is supported by Jacob of Edessa and by Chwolson's collection of tales from that area. 'Teraphim', though it has a plural ending, can mean a single image as well as two or more.

7. Leah's eye complaint was probably trachoma, a common fly-borne infection, for which a vaccine has only now been developed.

45

BIRTH OF THE TWELVE PATRIARCHS

(*a*) Because Jacob had hated Leah ever since she was foisted upon him by Laban, God in His compassion let her bear a son. She named him 'Reuben', saying: 'God has *seen my misery*; now Jacob will love me'; and her second son 'Simeon', saying: 'God *listened* to my prayer, and gave me another child'; and her third son 'Levi', saying: 'My husband will be *joined* to me in love: I have borne him three sons'; and her fourth son 'Judah', saying: 'Now indeed do I *praise God!*' Then, for a while, at Rachel's request, Jacob no longer slept with Leah.

Rachel, still barren, told Jacob: 'I shall die unless you give me children!'

He asked angrily: 'Is it my fault that God closed your womb?'

Rachel pleaded: 'At least pray over me, as Abraham prayed over Sarah.'

He asked again: 'But would you do as Sarah did, and lay a rival in my bed?'

'If it be jealousy that keeps me barren,' Rachel answered, 'take my bondmaid Bilhah, and reckon any child she bears as mine.'

Jacob accordingly took Bilhah to his bed, and when she bore a son, Rachel cried: 'God has been my *judge* and granted my plea!' She therefore named the child 'Dan'. Bilhah also bore a second son; and Rachel, saying: 'I have been a *wrestler* and won my bout against God!', named him 'Naphtali'.

Leah, not to be outdone in kindness, let Jacob use Zilpah, her own bondmaid, as his concubine. When Zilpah bore a son, Leah said: 'What *fortune!*', and named him 'Gad'. Zilpah likewise bore a second son, and Leah, saying: 'Now all women will call me *happy!*', named him 'Asher'. After this, Jacob slept only with Rachel; and Leah learned to hate her bitterly. But Rachel had constant fears of being sent back to Padan-Aram as a barren stock, and there claimed by her cousin Esau.[1]

(*b*) One day, however, during the wheat harvest, Leah's son Reuben was tending Jacob's ass, when he found mandrakes in a gully.

These magical roots resemble a man's lower members; the flower is flame-coloured and, at dusk, sends out strange rays like lightning. They grow in the valley of Baaras, which lies to the north of Machaerus in Judah, and can not only increase a woman's attraction for her husband, but cure her of barrenness. Mandrakes struggle fiercely against the hand that plucks them, unless menstruous blood, or a woman's water, be poured over them; even so they are certain death to touch, unless held legs downward. Mandrake-diggers trench the plant about until only its root tips remain fast in the ground; then they tie a dog to it by a cord, and walk away. The dog follows, pulls up the plant, and dies at once; which satisfies the mandrake's vengeful spirit.[2]

(*c*) Reuben, not recognizing the mandrakes by their fetid, lance-like leaves, innocently tethered his ass to them and walked off. The ass soon pulled out the mandrakes, which gave a blood-curdling shriek; and it fell dead. Reuben thereupon brought them home for his mother Leah, to show what had killed the beast; but Rachel met him on the way and snatched the mandrakes from his hands. Reuben wept aloud, and Leah ran up, asking what ailed him. 'She has stolen my little men,' he sobbed. 'Give them back at once!' Leah commanded Rachel. 'No, no,' she answered wildly, weeping too; 'these little men shall be my sons, since God has given me no others.' Leah screamed: 'Is it not enough that you have stolen my husband? Do you now also wish to rob his eldest son?'

Rachel pleaded: 'Give me those mandrakes, and Jacob shall lie with you tonight.'

Leah dared not scorn this offer and, when she heard the braying of Jacob's ass as he rode home from the fields at dusk, hurried to meet him. 'You must share my bed tonight,' she cried. 'I have hired you with your son's mandrakes.'

Jacob grudgingly complied and Leah, conceiving again, bore him a fifth son, whom she named 'Issachar', saying: 'God has rewarded my *hire!*' Indeed, God honoured Leah's disregard of woman's modesty in thus hiring Jacob—not for lust but from a desire to enlarge the tribes of Israel. He decreed that Issachar's sons should always possess a peculiar understanding of the weather and of astronomy.

Then Rachel, having grated and eaten the mandrakes, conceived at last and bore a son. She named him 'Joseph', saying: 'God has *taken away* my reproach! O may He *add* to me a second son also!'[3]

(*d*) Leah afterwards bore a sixth son, whom she named 'Zebulun', saying: 'God has given me a good *dowry;* now Jacob will surely *dwell* in my tent, since I have borne him six sons!'[4]

(*e*) Benjamin was born many years later, during Jacob's return from Padan-Aram. He had brought his flocks, herds, and wives through Bethel and, just before they reached Ephrath, the pangs of labour overtook Rachel. When, after a day or more, her child finally appeared, the midwife cried: 'Courage: once more you have a son!', Rachel, worn out by travail, died whispering: 'Yes, in truth, he is *the son of my sorrow!*' She thus named him 'Benoni'; but Jacob called him 'Benjamin', which means 'Son of my right hand'. Grieving that he could not lay Rachel to rest in the Cave of Machpelah, Jacob set a pillar over her grave, still to be seen at Ephrath, near Ramah.[5]

(*f*) All the twelve patriarchs, except Joseph, had twin sisters whom they later married—Benjamin had two. Leah also bore a daughter, Dinah, without a male twin. Jacob would have divorced Leah, but she gave him so many sons that he felt bound at last to style her the head of his harem.[6]

(*g*) Some say that to commemorate Reuben's finding of the mandrakes, his tribe always carried a mannikin on their standard. Others, that Rachel never ate these roots—which would have been sorcery—but entrusted them to a priest, and that God rewarded her with two sons for having conquered so strong a temptation.[7]

1. *Genesis* xxix. 31; xxx. 13; Gen. Rab. 829–30; Tanhuma Buber Gen. 158; Agadat Bereshit 103–05.
2. *Genesis* xxx. 14; Gen. Rab. 837; Yer. Erubin 26c; Yer. Shabbat 8b; Zohar Gen. 268, 314; Josephus, *Wars* vii. 6.3.
3. *Genesis* xxx. 14–24; Midrash Agada Gen. 112; Abraham Saba, *Seror HaMor*, Venice, 1523, p. 34a; *Test. of Issachar* i–ii; Gen. Rab. 841, 1282; B. Niddah 31a; Mid. Leqah Tobh Gen. 152; B. Erubin 100b.
4. *Genesis* xxx. 19–20.
5. *Genesis* xxxv. 16–20.
6. *Genesis* xxx. 19–21; PRE, ch. 36; B. Baba Bathra 123a; Gen. Rab. 823.
7. Sepher Haqane 32b; Midrash Agada Num. 78; *Test. of Issachar* ii.

*

1. *Genesis* supplies popular etymologies for the names of the twelve patriarchs, few of them plausible. *R'ubhen* (Reuben), taken to mean 'See, a son!' cannot be construed as *ra'ah b'onyi*, 'He saw my misery' (see 50. 3). And although 'Dan' has been correctly derived from the root *dan*, 'to judge', in both *Genesis* xxx. 6 and xlix. 16, and although Rachel's words 'God has judged me!' (*dananni elohim*) correspond with the Akkadian *shamash idinanni*, 'may Shamash judge me!' and are paralleled in Amorite and Katabanian names, yet Dan will originally have been an epithet of the tribal patron. 'Dinah' is the feminine form of 'Dan'.

2. The Ephraimites won their tribal name 'fertile tract' from the well-watered range of hills which they occupied about 1230 B.C. in the conquest of Palestine; and 'Benjamin', ('son of my right hand' or 'son of the South') meant that this tribe held Southern Ephraim. 'Ben-oni', however, the original name, suggests 'son of On'—an Egyptian city mentioned in *Genesis* XLI. 45 as the home of Joseph's father-in-law, from which Benjamin may have migrated with the two Rachel tribes and the priestly clan of Levi. Zilpah's two sons, Gad and Asher, bear the name of Aramaeo-Canaanite deities. Gad was the god of good luck, which is the meaning of his name in Hebrew, Aramaic, Syrian and Arabic, and his worship spread to Palmyra, Phoenicia and all Arabia. '*Ba Gad!*', Leah's alleged exclamation at the birth of Gad, would be understood simply as 'Good luck!' 'Asher' is the Amorite Ashir (see 35. 3), the masculine form of 'Asherah', a name of the wide-reigning fertility-goddess otherwise known as Atherat, Ashirat, Ashirtu, or Ashratu. 'Issachar' probably means 'Sakar's man'; Sakar or Sokar being the Egyptian god of Memphis.

3. A midrashic passage shrewdly points out that the Mosaic Law governing the inheritance of sons borne to a man by two co-wives, one beloved and one hated (*Deuteronomy* XXI. 15–17) is based on this myth and rejects the precedent set by Jacob.

> *If a man have two wives, the one beloved and the other hated, and they bear him children, both the beloved and the hated; and if the first-born son be hers that is hated, then it shall be that in the day that he gives his inheritance he may not make the son of the beloved the first-born; but he shall acknowledge the first-born, the son of the hated, by giving him a double portion.*

For Jacob, in his farewell blessing, gave Joseph, Rachel's first-born son, a double portion and preference over Reuben, Leah's first-born.

4. The traditional order of the patriarchs' birth is that of seniority in the Leah-Rachel federation: later called 'Israel', although at first 'Israel' properly included only the Rachel tribes. Leah ('Wild Cow') and Rachel ('Ewe'), are titles of goddesses. The wild cow is the variously named Canaanite Moon-goddess; the Ewe-goddess, mother of a Ram-god, will have been worshipped by shepherds settled in Goshen. Leah's six sons seem to have been Aramaeans, of the earlier Abraham confederacy, who never settled in Egypt, but with whom their Rachel cousins made common cause after returning from Goshen under Joshua. Zilpah's 'sons' were doubtless tributaries of Leah; as Bilhah's were of Rachel (see 50. 2). Benjamin could not claim to be of Aramaean stock, though titularly a son of Rachel: his was a peculiar tribe, renowned for its accurate and ambidextrous slingers, for its ferocity in war, and for having provided the Israel federation with its first monarchy. The other Israelite tribes used bows, which means that

they were always out-ranged by at least fifty yards when opposed to the Benjamites. David's use of the sling against Goliath, and his close contact with Saul's court, suggests Benjamite blood. The other most famous slingers of the ancient world were Greeks—Achaeans, Acarnanians, and Rhodians, with the Rhodianized Balearics. Slings reached Britain about 500 B.C.

Benjamin's share of food, five times greater than his brothers' (*Genesis* XLIII. 34—see 58. *c*), probably refers to the inclusion in Benjamite territory of the most important Canaanite shrines: Bethel, Jericho, Ramah, Gilgal, Mizpeh, Jerusalem, Geba, Gibeah and Gibeon. Gibeon was a Hivite city, that is of Achaean origin, and the behaviour of its ambassadors when they came as suppliants to Joshua (*Joshua* IX. 3 ff), was characteristically Greek; and Geba and Gibeah, similar formations, are often confused with Gibeon. The question of Benjamin's racial origin is complicated by the existence of a people to the north of Palestine, called Benē-jamina, whose chieftain bore the title Dāwidum, possibly the origin of 'David'. They are described in eighteenth-century B.C. documents from Mari on the Middle Euphrates, as a savage and predatory tribe, which recalls Benjamin's characterization in *Genesis* XLIX. 27. Whatever the connexion between these two Benjamite tribes, the 'Hebrew' Benjamin was welcomed by Ephraim and Manasseh, the Joseph-tribes, into their confederacy as a Son of Rachel, whose pillar stood on the frontier of the two territories, and was perhaps raised originally not merely as a *massebah* dedicated to their divine ancestress, but also as a memorial to the birth of this new federation. Rachel's death suggests the discontinuance of sacrificial gifts to the early Ewe-goddess, when her three 'sons' adopted the locally predominant Asherah worship.

5. A constant change of tribal areas complicates this subject. In later days Judah absorbed Benjamin, mentioned by Jeremiah (XXXIII. 13) as one of its provinces; and though in 1 *Samuel* X. 2 ff and *Jeremiah* XXXI. 15, which record the older version of this myth, Rachel's pillar is placed on the northern border of Benjamin, to the north of Jerusalem, yet a gloss on *Genesis* XXXV. 19, followed in XLVIII. 7, equates Ephrath with Bethlehem, David's birthplace, well inside the Judahite territory as delimited in *Joshua* XV. 5–10, and thus places Rachel's tomb to the south of Jerusalem. The present so-called 'Tomb of Rachel' on the Jerusalem-Bethlehem road, was known already to Matthew (II. 16–18), who equates Ramah with Bethlehem.

6. That each of the patriarchs, except Joseph, had a female twin whom he married, suggests a compromise in the days of the Judges between patriarchal and matrilineal institutions, and therefore joint worship of a god and goddess.

7. The forked fleshy root of the Spring Mandrake (*Mandragora officinarum*), black outside, soft and white inside, and about a foot long, resembles a human body with two legs; sometimes a short subsidiary root supplies the genitalia. Its stem is hairy; its flowers cup-shaped and a rich

purple in colour; its apples, which ripen at the time of the wheat harvest, are yellow, sweet, palatable, and still believed by Palestinian Arabs to cure barrenness. The Autumn Mandrake (*atropa mandragora*) is a late importation to Palestine. One of the Ras Shamra Ugaritic texts (fifteenth or fourteenth century B.C.), referring to a fertility cult, begins: 'Plant mandrakes in the earth . . .' The Ugaritic word for mandrakes, *ddym*, differs only dialectically from the Biblical Hebrew *dud'ym*. They were called *yabruhim* by the Aramaeans, because they *chased away* demons; and *sa'adin* by the Arabs, because *helpful* to health; and *dudaim* by the Hebrews, because they were *love-givers*.

8. That the mandrake shrieks on being uprooted was still a popular belief in Elizabethan times. Shakespeare writes in *Romeo and Juliet:*

> *And shrieks like mandrakes torn out of the earth*
> *That living mortals, hearing them, run mad.*

Pliny had noted, in his *Natural History*, the danger of roughly uprooting this plant, and recommended diggers to face west, with the wind behind them, and to use a sword for tracing three circles around it. He describes mandragora juice, extracted from the root, stem or fruit, as a valuable narcotic which ensures insensibility to pain during operations. This use is substantiated by Isodorus, Serapion, and other ancient physicians. Shakespeare lists mandragora among the 'drowsy syrups of the East'. Its anti-spasmodic virtue explains why it was held to cure barrenness—involuntary muscular tension in a woman might prevent complete congress. Whether Rachel ate the grated root or the fruit, is disputed: the *Testament of Issachar* favours the fruit. Her pathetic demand for the roots as 'little men', the only sons she would ever get, recalls an old Teutonic custom of converting the root into oracular images known as Gold-mannikins or Gallows-mannikins. The mandrake's prophetic power refers to babblings under narcotic influence.

9. A mediaeval midrash finds fictitious names and genealogies for all the patriarchs' wives. With the exception of Simeon and Judah who, according to *Genesis*, married Canaanite women, and Joseph, who married Asenath, the daughter of an Egyptian priest (see 56. *e*), the patriarchs are said to have decently married Aramaean cousins.

46

JACOB'S RETURN TO CANAAN

(*a*) Joseph was born at the close of his father's seven years' service for Rachel; and on the same day, as it happened, Rebekah at last sent for Jacob by her old nurse Deborah. When, however, he gave Laban notice that their engagement had ended, Laban urged him to stay on, promising to pay whatever wages, within reason, he might ask. Jacob said: 'It pleases me that you value my services. In enlarging your flocks and herds so prodigiously, God has truly blessed you on my account; yet it is high time now for me to enrich myself.'

'What do you consider a fair wage?' Laban asked.

He answered: 'Let me go through your flocks once a year, culling for myself all sheep with brown markings, and all banded or mottled goats.'

Laban agreed, and Jacob having entrusted his sons with the few beasts already so marked, continued to tend Laban's flocks, grazing them a three days' journey from his own. But when the tupping season came, he peeled rods of green poplar, almond and plane, so that the sap-wood showed through in white streaks, and set them above the watering troughs where Laban's ewes and she-goats drank. All those that conceived while facing them would, he knew, bear him banded or mottled lambs or kids. Nevertheless, Jacob took care to display the rods only when the stronger beasts drank, and to remove them from the sight of feebler ones. Soon his flocks consisted wholly of strong beasts, large numbers of which he bartered against slaves, camels and asses.[1]

(*b*) Jacob saw that Laban no longer trusted him, and heard his brothers-in-law Beor, Alib and Morash mutter: 'He is draining our father's wealth!' When God Himself told Jacob in a vision 'Return to the land of your birth, for I am with you,' he summoned Rachel and Leah, and said: 'Your father Laban cannot deny that I have served him faithfully, yet he no longer trusts me. He has changed my wages at least ten times: assigning me first the mottled and banded beasts; then the plain ones; then the mottled and banded again; then the plain once more. But God is surely with me, because the flocks always bear whatever sort your father offers as my wage. He has warned me in a dream to return home.' Both Rachel and Leah answered: 'Indeed, our father Laban treats us like strangers now that we are yours, grudging our prosperity; although whatever God takes from him and bestows on you will be his grand-children's inheritance. Your duty is to obey God!'[2]

(*c*) While Laban was absent at a sheep-shearing, Jacob, without saying goodbye, mounted his family on camels, loaded his treasures on asses, and drove his flocks across the Euphrates towards Canaan.

Laban did not hear of this until the third day. Then he and his kinsmen went in pursuit and, a week later, overtook Jacob among the hills of Gilead. 'You have carried off my daughters as though they were prisoners of war!' he shouted. 'Why such secrecy? If apprised of your intentions, I should have given you a farewell feast with songs to the drum and harp; nor did you let me even kiss my daughters and grandsons goodbye! I would punish you severely for this indecorous behaviour, had not God restrained me in a vision last night. And while I can well understand your longing for home, how dare you steal my teraphim?'

Jacob answered: 'I went away without notice lest you might prevent Leah and Rachel from accompanying me. About your teraphim I know nothing. If one of my people has stolen it, he certainly merits death! Come, search my baggage in the presence of our kinsmen, and take whatever is yours.'

Laban searched first Jacob's tent, then Leah's, then Bilhah's, and Zilpah's, but in vain. When he visited Rachel's, she said: 'Forgive me, Father, for not rising to salute you; my monthly sickness is upon me.'

Laban searched the tent carefully, but again found nothing. She had hidden his teraphim in a saddle-bag, and seated herself on it.[3]

(*d*) Jacob reproached Laban: 'What stolen goods have you discovered, my lord? Bring them here! Lay them before our kinsmen, who shall then judge between us. In twenty years, have I ever let your ewes or she-goats miscarry? Have I slaughtered and eaten your rams? Whenever wild beasts or bandits preyed on your flocks, who but I bore the loss? By day the heat consumed me, and the frost by night; yet my vigilance never relaxed. I served fourteen years for your daughters, and a further six for your flocks—though you constantly altered our compact and, in the end, would have sent me away empty-handed, had God not seen my misery and delivered His judgement!'

Laban answered: 'Your children are born from my daughters, your flocks are bred from my flocks, and all that you possess was once mine! How could I harm my own flesh and blood? Let us swear a covenant of peace, you and I, and set up a pillar to witness it.'

Jacob agreed. He raised a pillar, and Laban's kinsmen heaped stones into a *cairn of witness* between him and Jacob—at a place now called Jegar Sahadutha by the Aramaeans, and Gal-'ed, or Gilead, by the Hebrews. The region is named Mizpeh, because Laban said: 'May the God of my grandfather Nahor and of your grandfather Abraham, his brother, *watch* our deeds while we are no longer living in the same land! If you ill-treat my daughters by making other marriages where God alone can witness their misery, He shall surely judge you. Moreover, let this pillar and cairn mark the frontier between your kingdom and mine; neither of us shall lead armed men across it!'

Jacob took the oath, confirming it with sacrifices. Laban's people and his then ate together in peace; and early next morning Laban kissed his daughters and grand-children farewell and rode home. The power of this place was such that no Aramaean or Israelite afterwards dared violate the frontier until King David, angered by Hadadezer, King of Aram, broke the pillar in pieces, scattered the cairn, and took away Hadadezer's kingdom.[4]

(*e*) Rachel stole Laban's teraphim not only to prevent it from disclosing Jacob's flight, but to rid her father's house of idols. However, Jacob's curse on the unknown thief presently caused her death in childbirth; for Rachel had lied in telling Laban that she was still subject to her monthly courses. It is also said that when Laban finished his sheep-shearing and returned to Padan-Aram, he found the city well, which had been brimful ever since Rachel gave Jacob to drink, quite empty and dry—a disaster which told him of Jacob's flight.[5]

(*f*) Laban then sent his son Beor, his cousin Abihoreph, and ten others, to Mount Seir, warning Esau of Jacob's approach. Esau hurried forward vengefully, at the head of his servants and a force of Horite allies. Laban's messengers, however, visited Rebekah on their journey back to Padan-Aram, and when they gave her this news, she at once sent seventy-two of Isaac's armed servants to assist Jacob. 'But,' she said, 'beg my son to show Esau the most obsequious humility, to placate him with rich gifts, and truthfully answer all his questions.'[6]

1. *Genesis* xxx. 25–43; Sepher Hayashar 101–02.
2. *Genesis* xxxi. 1–16; Sepher Hayashar 99.
3. *Genesis* xxxi. 17–35.

4. *Genesis* xxxi. 36; xxxii. 1; PRE, ch. 36.
5. Tanhuma Wayetse 40b; PRE, ch. 36; Sepher Hayashar 103; Gen. Rab. 863; Targum Yer. *ad Gen.* xxxi. 21–22.
6. Sepher Hayashar 105–06.

*

1. Two Greek mythic heroes, Autolycus the master-thief and his rival in deceit, Sisyphus the Corinthian, appear here in the persons of Jacob and Laban. Hermes, god of thieves, shepherds and orators, had granted Autolycus power to metamorphose stolen beasts from horned to unhorned, white to black, and contrariwise. Sisyphus noticed that his herds grew steadily smaller, while those of his neighbour Autolycus increased. One day he engraved his own initials on the cattle's hooves. When, that night, Autolycus stole again, Sisyphus and a group of kinsmen tracked the cattle to Autolycus's farm-yard. Leaving them to confront the thief, he hurried around to the front door, entered secretly, and fathered the famous rascal Odysseus on Autolycus's daughter. Autolycus also stole horses from King Iphitus of Euboea, changed their appearance, and sold them to Heracles as if bred by himself. Iphitus followed their tracks to Tiryns, where he accused Heracles of the theft; and when he was unable to identify the stolen beasts, Heracles hurled him over the city walls. This involved Heracles in a fight against Apollo, but Zeus made them clasp hands again.

Sisyphus and Autolycus, like Jacob and Laban, matched deceit against deceit. Moreover, Jacob was aided by God, as Autolycus was by Hermes, and died like him in prosperous old age. Both myths seem to be drawn from the same ancient source; their resemblances are more numerous than their differences, and Sisyphus can be equated with Abraham in another myth (see 39. 1). Nevertheless, *Genesis* justifies Jacob's trickery as forced on him by Laban's miserliness. Nor does he steal grown beasts, but merely arranges that lambs and kids are born in colours favourable to him; whereas Rachel, who does steal, earns the death unwittingly decreed by her loving husband.

2. 'Teraphim' here refers to a single household god, somewhat smaller than the one which Saul's daughter Michal placed in her bed to form the lower half of a dummy—the upper being supplied by a goat's-hair quilt (1 *Samuel* xix. 13 ff). Since Laban's teraphim fitted into the U-shaped bolster placed around a dromedary's hump to make a platform for baggage, or a litter, it cannot have been much longer than two feet.

Neither Rachel nor Michal are reproached because they consult teraphim (see 44. 6); any more than are the Danites who stole an oracular breastplate and a teraphim from the house of Micah the Ephraimite in order to set up a new sanctuary at Laish, and at the same time abducted the young Levite priest in charge of them (*Judges* xvii. 1; xviii. 31). On the contrary, Micah's mother had piously cast this image from silver dedicated to the God of Israel (*Judges* xvii. 3–5); and Micah, after persuading the Levite to officiate in his private chapel, had exclaimed with satisfaction: 'God will certainly favour me, now that I have a Levite as my priest!' (*Judges* v. 13).

Since Rachel's theft is treated in *Genesis* merely as a proof that she shared her husband's resentment against Laban, it must date from the days of the Judges. She will have intended to found a shrine in Aramaean style. Laban was obliged to respect her excuse: the horror of contact with a menstruous woman, or with anything that she has touched, still prevails in the Middle East; and a man who passes between two such women is thought liable to fall dead. The avoidance of this danger helps to maintain the strict separation between men and women in synagogues and mosques; although it was originally designed to keep festive gatherings from becoming orgiastic (M. Sukka V. 2 and parallel sources).

3. An assembly of kinsmen is the common judicial forum among nomad Arabs: their numbers, and the publicity given to a dispute, assure that both parties will accept the verdict.

4. Laban represents the Aramaeans of Mesopotamia, and the boundary stone and cairn prove that Mesopotamian power once extended as far south as Gilead. In the early days of the Hebrew monarchy, however, the nation threatening Israel from that quarter was not Mesopotamia but Syria—also known as *Aram*, though sometimes distinguished from Mesopotamia, *Aram-Naharayim*, by being called *Aram-Dameseq*, 'Aram of Damascus'. Laban thus came to represent Aram-Dameseq, and the quarrel between him and Israel was interpreted in this sense. When, after the death of David's son Solomon, Syria freed itself from Hebrew sovereignty, the two countries lived at peace—a situation reflected in the Gilead feast—under treaties of friendship (1 *Kings* xv. 18–20) until Ben-Hadad, King of Damascus, defeated Ahab, King of Israel, in 855 B.C.

5. Boundary cairns, consisting of five or six largish stones placed on top of each other, are still used in Israel and Jordan to divide fields, and the respect shown them is founded on the Mosaic curse against removal (*Deuteronomy* XXVII. 17).

The derivation of *Gilead* from *Gal-'ed* is popular etymology; *Gilead* represents the Arabic *jal'ad*, meaning 'strong or hard', which occurs in several Gileadite place names, such as Jebel Jal'ad, Khirbet Jal'ad and Khirbet Jal'ud.

47

JACOB AT PENIEL

(*a*) Jacob crossed the Jordan and, next evening, so numerous a company of angels met him beside the River Jabbok, that he exclaimed: 'Here are *two camps:* God's and mine!' Hence the city afterwards built there was called Mahanaim.

He sent a message to Esau on Mount Seir: 'Greeting to my lord Esau from his slave Jacob, who has lived at Padan-Aram these past twenty years and is now rich in camels, oxen, asses, flocks, and servants. He mentions this prosperity because he desires to enjoy my lord's favour.' The messengers, hurrying back, reported that Esau had already set out for the Jabbok at the head of four hundred men. Jacob, greatly alarmed, divided his retinue into *two camps*, each containing half of the flocks, herds, and women. 'If Esau plunders the first,' he thought, 'the second may yet escape.' Then he prayed to God for deliverance.

Jacob prepared gifts to send Esau: a flock of two hundred she-goats and twenty he-goats; another of two hundred ewes and twenty rams; a drove of thirty milch-camels with their colts; a herd of forty cows and ten bulls; another of twenty she-asses with ten foals. He told his herdsmen to ford the Jabbok in turns, leaving intervals of a bowshot between flocks, herds, and droves; and to answer Esau, when questioned: 'These beasts are a gift to my lord Esau from his slave Jacob, who follows humbly behind, desiring your favour.'

The herdsmen obeyed, and Esau treated them well; but Jacob delayed on the farther bank, while sending his whole household ahead, over the ford.[1]

(*b*) Left alone that evening, Jacob was attacked by an unseen presence, who wrestled with him all night and shrank the sinew of his thigh, so that he limped ever afterwards. At last the adversary cried: 'Let go, for dawn is near!' Jacob answered: 'I will not let go unless you bless me!' 'What is your name?' his adversary inquired and, when Jacob gave it, said: 'Henceforth you shall be called "Israel", because you have *wrestled with God* and with men, and remain undefeated.' Jacob then asked: 'And what is your name?', but was answered: 'Why inquire? Is it not enough that I give you my blessing?' Jacob cried: 'I have seen *God's countenance*, and am still alive!' So the place was called 'Peniel'; and because of the injury done to Jacob's thigh, no Israelite since eats the thigh sinew of any beast.[2]

(*c*) Some say that God assumed the shape of a shepherd, or a brigand chief, who led Jacob's herds across the ford in return for help with his own; and that, when they went back to see whether any beast had been overlooked, He began to wrestle. Others say that Jacob's adversary was not God but Samael, the celestial guardian of Edom, trying to destroy Jacob; and that the heavenly hosts made ready to fly down if summoned. Yet God said: 'My servant Jacob needs no aid; his virtue protects him!'[3]

(*d*) Others, again, say that Jacob's adversary was Michael and that, when he cried, 'Let go, for dawn is near!', Jacob exclaimed: 'Are you then a thief, or a gambler, that you fear dawn?' To which Michael replied: 'No, but at dawn we angels must sing God's praises.' Observing Jacob's lameness, God questioned Michael: 'What have you done to My first-born son?' Michael answered: 'I shrank a sinew in Your honour.' God said: 'It is good. Henceforth, until the end of time, you shall have charge of Israel and his posterity! For the prince of angels should guard the prince of men, fire should guard fire, and head guard head!'[4]

(*e*) Still others say that Michael fought Jacob because he failed to pay the tithes vowed at Bethel twenty years earlier; and that, next morning, Jacob repentantly sacrificed victims by the hundred, also dedicating his son Levi as God's priest and collector of tithes.[5]

1. *Genesis* XXXII. 2–24.
2. *Genesis* XXXII. 25–33.
3. Gen. Rab. 910; Yalqut Reubeni *ad Gen.* XXXII. 25.
4. Yalqut Gen. 132; PRE, ch. 37.
5. PRE, ch. 37.

*

1. Mahanaim ('Two Camps'), the name of which is here given two alternative explanations, stood on the banks of the Jabbok River, some six miles eastward from Jordan, and became one of Solomon's twelve capital cities.

2. Each stage in Jacob's wanderings is charged with mythic significance. He founds settlements at Bethel, Mizpeh, Mahanaim, Peniel, Succoth—all of which derive their names from one of his acts or sayings—though the chronicler has omitted to mention that the Jabbok was so called because there Jacob 'strove' (*yeabheq*) with God. Later commentators made him

foresee the far-reaching effect of what he said or did. Thus, his order to the herdsmen 'Put a space betwixt drove and drove!' (*Genesis* XXII. 17), was read as advising his descendants always to keep a reserve for use in emergencies; and he is said to have prayed: 'Lord, when disasters fall upon Your children, pray leave a space between them, as I have done!'

3. Jacob speaks in the first person singular when referring to his kinship group (*Genesis* XXXII. 12; XXXIV. 30–31), and after the new name is accepted (XLIII. 6, 11; XLV. 28), his identification with the Israelite people becomes more and more pronounced (XLVI. 1–4). God tells him: 'Fear not to go down to Egypt, for there I shall make of thee a great nation . . . and I shall also surely bring thee up again!' And in *Genesis* XLVIII. 20, Jacob himself uses 'Israel' instead of 'Children of Israel'.

4. The widely differing midrashic views of this wrestling match between Jacob and the 'man' whom he afterwards identifies with God, are all prompted by pious embarrassment. God, the transcendental God of later Judaism, could never have demeaned himself by wrestling with a mortal and then begging him to release his hold. In any case, if He loved Jacob so well, and was so perfectly loved in return, why should they have struggled? And if the adversary was only an angel, should he be identified with Gabriel or Michael, or rather with the fallen angel Samael? Nevertheless, the notion that a pious man can struggle against God in prayer, and force Him to grant a blessing, was theologically admissible; Rachel had used the wrestling metaphor when she won her adoptive son 'Naphtali' from Him.

5. To make historic sense of this myth, one must ask such questions as these: on what occasion does a tribal hero wrestle? On what occasion does he change his name? What was the nature of Jacob's thigh injury? What was its magical effect? How is it related to the taboo on eating the flesh around thigh sinews? Why is this anecdote interpolated in the myth of Jacob's reunion with Esau? And since it seems historically agreed that 'Israel' at first contained only the Rachel tribes, what part does Rachel play here?

6. The answers are perhaps as follows. A tribal hero changes his name either when he commits manslaughter, flees from his country and is adopted by another tribe—but this does not apply to Jacob—or when he ascends a throne, or occupies a new country. The latter seems to have been the reason for Abraham's change of name (see 31. 3). Jacob's crossing of the Jabbok signified an important change in his position: hitherto he had been a hired servant of Laban, his father-in-law; now he was an independent chieftain, ready to enter and occupy his own tribal lands, secure in a parental blessing and a divine promise.

7. Arabic lexicographers explain that the nature of the lameness produced by injury to the sinew of the thigh-socket causes a person so afflicted to walk on the tips of his toes. Such a dislocation of the hip is common among wrestlers and was first described by Harpocrates. Displace-

ment of the femur-head lengthens the leg, tightens the thigh tendons, and puts the muscles into spasm—which makes for a rolling, swaggering walk, with the heel permanently raised, like that attributed by Homer to the God Hephaestus. A belief that contact with the jinn results in a loose-mannered gait as though disjointed, is found among the Arabs: perhaps a memory of the limping dance performed by devotees who believed themselves divinely possessed, like the prophets of Baal on Mount Carmel (1 *Kings* xviii. 26). Beth Ḥoglah, near Jericho may have been so called for this reason, because *ḥajala* in Arabic means to hobble or hop, and both Jerome and Eusebius call Beth Ḥoglah 'the place of the ring-dance'. The Tyrians performed such limping dances in honour of Hercules Melkarth. It is possible therefore that the Peniel myth originally accounts for a limping ceremony which commemorated Jacob's triumphal entry into Canaan after wrestling with a rival.

8. The explanation of the name Israel in *Genesis* xxxii. 29 is popular etymology. In theóphorous titles, the element containing the deity's name is the subject, not the object. Israel therefore means 'El strives', rather than 'He strove with El'; just as the original form of Jacob, *Ya'qobel*, means 'El protects' (see 38. 6), and just as the original meaning of Jerubbaal was not 'He fights against Baal' (*Judges* vi. 32), but 'Baal fights'. The intention of names such as these was to enlist divine help for those who bore them. *Israel* thus meant 'El strives against my enemies'.

9. The prime enemy to be faced by Jacob upon crossing the Jabbok was his twin Esau, from whose just anger he had fled twenty years before. In fact, one midrash presents Esau as Jacob's unknown adversary at Peniel, an identification based on his likening Esau's countenance to God's (*Genesis* xxxiii. 10). The midrashic statement that Rachel was afraid of being married to Esau (see 45. *a*) hints at an added motive for the twins' struggle: the rivalry for a beautiful woman, which already had occasioned, according to one version, the first fratricidal combat between Cain and Abel (see 16. *d*). But more than the love of a mortal woman may have been at stake. If Rachel stands for the Rachel tribes that were to be, then the fight between the twins is a mythical struggle for supremacy over tribal territories. Jacob won and sealed his victory by rich expiatory gifts to Esau, who thereupon vacated the land and withdrew to Seir (*Genesis* xxxvi. 6–8).

10. The *Exodus* account of Moses, the only other Israelite hero with whom God wrestled, curiously resembles Jacob's. Moses flees from Egypt in disgrace, serves Jethro the Midianite as a herdsman for the hand of his daughter Zipporah, whom he has treated courteously at a well and, returning home accompanied by his wife and sons, after a fiery vision of God—is suddenly attacked on the way by a supernatural being. Zipporah thereupon circumcises him—circumcision being, as the context shows, part of the marriage ceremony—and he later rules a Midianite-Israelite federation.

11. Nevertheless, struggles in nightmares caused by an unquiet conscience provide a common enough metaphor for struggles with God who, according to *Hosea* XIII. 7, became to the sinful people 'as a lion, as a leopard which watches on the way'. Nor could God's hand be readily distinguished from Satan's. Thus the plague punishing David's sin was sent by God in one version (2 *Samuel* XXIV. 1), but by Satan in another (1 *Chronicles* XXI. 1); which justifies the midrash's identification of Jacob's adversary with Samael. The adversary's refusal to give his name does not necessarily make him God, although God later refuses to disclose His to Moses (*Exodus* III. 14), or to Manoah, Samuel's father (*Judges* XIII. 17–18); because all deities were chary of revealing their names lest these might be used for improper purposes—which is the original sense of 'blasphemy'. Witches and sorcerers, throughout the Eastern Mediterranean, used long lists of divine names to strengthen their spells. The Romans had a habit of discovering the secret names of enemy gods by bribery or torture, and then enticing them to desert their cities: a technique known as *elicio*. Jesus, when expelling a devil from the madman at Gerasa, first demands his name (*Mark* v. 9).

12. Thigh-bones were sacred to the gods in Greece as well as Palestine and constituted the royal portion among the Hebrews (1 *Samuel* IX. 24). The practice of the Central African Bagiushu tribe—as reported by Mgr. Terhoorst, a Roman Catholic missionary—supports the anthropological rule 'No taboo without its particular relaxation.' The Bagiushu, though otherwise not cannibalistic, eat the flesh-covered thigh-bones of their dead chieftain, or of an enemy chieftain killed in battle, to inherit his courage; and leave all other parts of the body untouched. It cannot be proved that this practice prevailed in Biblical Canaan, but Samuel's dismemberment of the sacred King Agag 'before the Lord' is read by some scholars as a eucharistic human sacrifice akin to the Arabic *naqi'a*.

48

RECONCILIATION OF JACOB AND ESAU

(*a*) Jacob saw Esau approach with four hundred men. He divided his household into two camps: Bilhah, Zilpah and their children were in the advance camp; Rachel, Leah and their children in the other. But Jacob found courage to go ahead of them all and prostrate himself seven times as he neared Esau.

Esau ran towards his brother, embraced and kissed him; both of them weeping for joy. Then he inquired: 'Whose are yonder children?' Jacob answered: 'God in His mercy has given them to your slave; and these, my lord, are their mothers.' They all came forward in turn and bowed low before Esau, who asked: 'And yonder herds and droves, Brother, were they truly your gift to me?' Jacob replied: 'I trust that they will please my lord.' Esau thanked him kindly, but said: 'No, Brother, already I have more than enough livestock for my needs. Keep what is yours!' Jacob insisted: 'In token of your favour, my lord, pray deign to accept these poor gifts. I have seen my lord's countenance shine like God's. Indulge me this once, and take all, with your slave's blessing; for God in His mercy has greatly enriched me.'

To set Jacob's mind at ease, Esau accepted them, and said: 'Come, ride with me to my city in Seir!' Jacob answered: 'My lord knows that I cannot travel so fast as he. Let him go ahead of his slave, who rides at a pace to suit the lambs, kids, calves, foals and little children. It will be weeks before we can reach my lord's city.'

Esau said: 'May I at least leave men to escort you?'

'Pray do not trouble, my lord!' Jacob cried.

So Esau rode home, while Jacob proceeded to Succoth and there built himself a house, and *shelters* for his flocks and herds.[1]

(*b*) Some say that Jacob's message to Esau was: 'Thus speaks your slave Jacob: let my lord not think that the stolen blessing has stood me in good stead! Laban, during the twenty years of my service to him, deceived me time after time, grudging my wages, although I laboured faithfully. Yet God in His mercy at last bestowed oxen, asses, flocks, slaves, and bondmaids on your servant. I am now come to Canaan, hoping for my lord's pardon when he hears this humble and truthful account.'

Esau is said to have answered the messengers contemptuously: 'Laban's sons have told me of your master Jacob's ingratitude: that he stole flocks and herds by sorcery, then fled without notice, abducting my cousins Leah and Rachel as though they were prisoners of war. The report does not astonish me: for this was how your master treated me too, long ago. I suffered in silence then; but now I shall ride out with an armed company and punish him as he deserves.'[2]

(*c*) Some say that when the brothers met they were moved by true affection; that Esau forgave Jacob as they kissed and embraced; and that equal loving-kindness was shown between the many cousins, their children. Others, however, say that when Esau fell upon Jacob's neck, he tried to bite through his jugular vein, but the neck became hard as ivory, blunting Esau's teeth, which he therefore gnashed in futile rage.[3]

(*d*) God reproved Jacob for calling Esau 'my lord', and himself 'your slave'. He also said: 'By likening Esau's countenance to Mine, you have profaned what is holy!' Jacob answered: 'Lord of the Universe, pardon the fault! For the sake of peace I flattered the Wicked One, so that he should not kill me and my people.' God cried: 'Then, by your life, I will confirm what you have said: henceforth, Israel shall be Edom's slave in this world, though his master in the next. And, because you called Esau "my lord" eight times, I shall cause eight kings to reign in Edom before any rise to rule over Israel!' And so it came about. The eight kings of Edom were Bela, son of Beor; Jobab, son of Zerah; Husham; Hadad, son of Bedad; Samlah; Saul; Baal-Hanan, son of Achbor; and Hadar.[4]

(*e*) Jacob gave Esau pearls and precious stones, as well as flocks and herds, knowing that no virtue lies in treasure got abroad, and that these gifts would return to his descendants. What was left over, he sold; and, heaping the gold together, asked Esau: 'Will you sell me your share of Machpelah for this heap of gold?' Esau agreed, and Jacob set himself to acquire more wealth in the blessed Land of Israel.[5]

(*f*) Jacob also prophesied: 'Edom shall oppress Israel for centuries; but at last all the nations of the world will rise, taking from him land after land, city after city until, thrown back upon Beth Gubrin, he finds the Messiah of Israel lying in wait. Fleeing thence to Bozrah, Edom will cry: "Have You not set Bozrah aside, O Lord, as a city of refuge?" God shall seize Edom by his locks and answer:

"The avenger of blood must destroy this murderer!", whereupon Elijah will slaughter him, spattering God's garment with Edom's blood.'[6]

1. *Genesis* xxxiii. 1–17.
2. Sepher Hayashar 106–107.
3. Sepher Hayashar 110; PRE, ch. 37.
4. PRE, ch. 37; Gen. Rab. 891; *Genesis* xxxvi. 31–39.
5. Tanhuma Buber Gen. 169.
6. Mid. Abkir, as quoted in Yalqut Gen. 133 (pp. 82b–83a).

*

1. The *Genesis* account consistently favours Esau at Jacob's expense: not only by modern ethical standards, but by those of ancient Palestine. Esau refrains from vengeance and fratricide, remains dutiful to his parents, worships Isaac's God and, no longer a wild and improvident hunter, succeeds so well as a pastoralist that he can afford to refuse a large gift of livestock in compensation for the theft of his blessing. Moreover, instead of repudiating the sale of the birthright, forced on him while he was starving, he peaceably evacuates the Canaanite pastures to which the agreement entitled Jacob, calls the cowardly wretch 'brother', weeps with pleasure at his return and, though Jacob's guilty conscience prompts him to shameful obsequiousness, forgives wholeheartedly. Then he rides back to prepare a royal welcome on Mount Seir—an invitation studiously neglected by Jacob.

It was a Jewish commonplace that the worst day in Israel's history had not been when Sennacherib led the Northern tribes into captivity, nor when Solomon's temple was destroyed by Nebuchadrezzar; but when seventy scholars translated the Scriptures into Greek at the command of Ptolemy II (285–246 B.C.). These Scriptures, which contained records of evil deeds done by their ancestors and reminders of God's punishment for continual backsliding, should never, it was thought, have been divulged to Israel's enemies. The Jacob-Esau myth must have embarrassed Jews of the Dispersal more than any other, since Jacob was Israel incarnate and they were heirs to his faults as well as his merits. Nor could midrashic glosses on the *Genesis* account—denigrating Esau and excusing Jacob—alter the scholarly text of the 'Septuagint'.

2. Again the puzzling question arises: how did the Israelites come to libel their eponymous ancestor in favour of their national enemy? The sole acceptable answer can be that the myth originated in Edom, and was brought to Jerusalem by Calebite and Kenazite clansmen early incorporated into Judah (see 42. 4). Judah was a son of Leah, traditionally opposed both to Benjamin—the Rachel tribe whose royal dynasty he overthrew, and whose territory he swallowed—and to the other four Rachel tribes, Ephraim, Manasseh, Gad, and Naphtali, which formed the hard core of the Northern Kingdom. Leah's hatred of Rachel is admitted in *Genesis*; and

the tradition of 'Israel' as originally consisting of Rachel tribes, with whom the Leah tribes made an uncomfortable alliance, will have encouraged the Edomite aristocracy of Judah—Caleb held Hebron and the ancestral shrine of Machpelah—to glorify their ancestor Esau at Israel's expense. Moreover, by the time that *Genesis* was committed to writing, the Southern Kingdom of Judaea had temporarily lost its martial pride; and Jacob's art of patient survival by bending yet never breaking, by using subterfuge instead of force, and by never accepting any but the Mosaic Law, passed as the height of wisdom.

3. First-century A.D. Pharisees discouraged Jews from permanent residence abroad by decreeing Italy and other parts of the Roman world 'unclean', and by demanding purification ceremonies when they came home. That Jacob gave Esau all his wealth refers, perhaps, to the enormous sums raised by foreign Jews for the Edomite King Herod's beautification of the Temple.

4. The prophecy of Edom's disaster at Bozrah—'Edom' means 'Rome'—has been borrowed from a blood-thirsty Messianic prophecy in *Isaiah* LXIII, beginning: 'Who is he that cometh from Edom, in reddened garments from Bozrah?'; and another, in *Jeremiah* XLIX. 13, prophesying Bozrah's perpetual desolation. But Isaiah's 'Bozrah' was either Bozrah in the Hauran, or Basra in the Persian Gulf, not the Edomite 'little Bozrah'; and Jeremiah's 'Bozrah' was Bezer, a Levitical city conquered by Moab, which appears as a city of refuge in *Deuteronomy* IV. 43. 'Beth Gubrin' is the Hebrew name of Eleutheropolis in Southern Judaea.

5. Only the last four of the eight Edomite kings listed in *Genesis* are certainly historical.

49

THE RAPE OF DINAH

(*a*) When Leah, after giving birth to six sons, conceived a seventh time, she pitied her barren sister Rachel, and prayed: 'O Lord, let this child be a girl, lest my sister Rachel should again grow jealous!' God then changed Leah's child from male to female, and told her: 'Because you pitied your sister Rachel, I will grant her a son.' Thus Dinah was born to Leah; and Joseph to Rachel.[1]

(*b*) Jacob feared that Esau would demand marriage with Dinah, as was his avuncular right; and therefore kept her hidden in a chest during the reunion at Mahanaim. God reproached Jacob for this, saying: 'Since you have acted uncharitably towards your brother Esau, Dinah shall bear children to Job the Uzzite, no kinsman of yours! Moreover, since you rebuffed a circumcised son of Abraham, she shall yield her maidenhead to an uncircumcised Canaanite; and since you denied her lawful wedlock, she shall be taken unlawfully!'[2]

(*c*) Dinah was modest and dutiful, never leaving Leah's tent without permission. One day, however, while Jacob pastured his flocks near Mount Ephraim, a prince named Shechem, the first-born son of Hamor the Hivite, brought girls to dance and beat drums near the Israelite camp. Dinah stood watching and, overcome by love, he lured her to his house in the city of Shechem, and there lay with her. Jacob learned of Dinah's disgrace during his sons' absence, and did nothing until they returned. That Shechem had treated Dinah like a harlot incensed them beyond measure. Yet the brothers cloaked their rage when Hamor came, on Shechem's behalf, asking Dinah's hand in marriage and saying: 'Come, my lords, live and trade among us! Since Shechem is set upon making Dinah his lawful wife, I will pay whatever bride-price you may demand; and it would make me happier yet if our two royal houses were allied by other unions also.'

Jacob let Leah's sons settle the matter. They told Hamor deceitfully: 'Alas, we cannot allow our sister to marry an uncircumcised Hivite; but if the men of Shechem will accept circumcision, our father's house and yours may then be securely allied by marriage.'[3]

(*d*) Hamor consulted with the leaders of Shechem, who agreed that every male should undergo immediate circumcision. Three days later, when the Shechemites' members were inflamed, Simeon and Levi, Dinah's full brothers, secretly entered the city, sword in hand, massacred Hamor, Shechem, and all their bedridden subjects, and took Dinah away. Jacob's other sons followed close behind. They sacked the houses of Shechem, drove off flocks, herds, asses from its fields, enslaved women and children. Jacob cried indignantly: 'You have made me odious in the eyes of every Hivite, Perizzite and Amorite! Now they will band together and destroy us.' But Simeon and Levi asked: 'Could we allow our sister to be treated as a harlot?'[4]

(*e*) Some say, that though six hundred and forty-five Shechemite men and two hundred and seventy-six boys were circumcised, yet Hamor had been warned by his aged uncles, and by his father Hadkam, son of Pered, that this breach of custom would vex all Canaan, and that they would themselves raise an army to punish such impiety. Hamor explained that he had accepted circumcision only to deceive Jacob's sons: at Shechem's wedding feast, when the Israelites lay drunken and at ease, he would give the signal for their massacre. Dinah secretly sent her bondmaid to tell Simeon and Levi of Hamor's plan. They vowed that by the following night no man would be left alive in Shechem, and attacked the city at dawn. Though withstood by twenty bold Shechemites who had evaded circumcision, they killed eighteen: the other two ran and hid in a bitumen pit.[5]

(*f*) Hamor's Amorite allies, hearing the distant din of battle, hastened to Shechem and locked the city gates behind them, lest Jacob's other sons might reinforce Simeon and Levi. But Judah scaled the wall, flung himself on the enemy, and felled scores of them. Reuben, Issachar, Gad and the rest broke down the gate and rushed in, dealing death right and left. Together they slaughtered all the men of Shechem, besides three hundred infuriated wives who were hurling stones and tiles from the rooftops. Blood poured down the streets like a river. A second army of Amorites and Perizzites then came marching across the plain. Jacob took sword and bow, stationed himself at the gates and, crying 'Shall my sons fall into the hands of these Gentiles?', leaped at the enemy, cutting them down as a reaper does corn. Soon all was over. Jacob's sons divided the spoils, including numerous bondmen and children; also eighty-five virgins—one of whom, by name Bonah, Simeon made his wife.[6]

(*g*) Others say that Hamor had given Dinah leave to rejoin her family; but that she would not stir from Shechem's house, even after the massacre, sobbing: 'How dare I show my face among kinsmen?' Only when Simeon swore to marry her himself, did she accompany him.[7]

(*h*) Dinah was already pregnant by Shechem, and bore him a posthumous daughter. Her brothers wished to kill the child, as custom demanded, lest any Canaanite might say 'The maidens of Israel are without shame!' Jacob, however, restrained them, hung about his grand-daughter's neck a silver disk on which were engraved the words 'Holy to God!', and laid her underneath a *thorn bush*—hence she was called 'Asenath'. That same day Michael, in the shape of an eagle, flew off with Asenath to On in Egypt, and there laid her beside God's altar. The priest, by name Potiphera, seeing that his wife was barren, brought Asenath up as his own child.

Many years later, when Joseph had saved Egypt from famine and made a progress through the land, women threw him thank-offerings. Among them was Asenath who, having no other gift, tossed Joseph her silver disk, which he caught as it flew by. He recognized the inscription and, knowing that she must be his own niece, married her.[8]

(*i*) After Joseph forgave his brothers, and sent them back to Canaan, his gifts included embroidered garments, and a load of myrrh, aloes, ointments and cosmetics for Dinah, who was now not only his sister and mother-in-law, but also a sister-in-law, having married Simeon and borne him a son named Saul.

Dinah at last died in Egypt. Simeon brought the bones home to Canaan, and buried them at Arbel, where her tomb is still shown. Others, however, say that Simeon divorced Dinah, and that she became the second wife of Job the Uzzite, when God restored him to prosperity. Job fathered seven sons and three daughters on her.[9]

1. Tanhuma Buber Gen. 157, 172; B. Berakhot 60a; Gen. Rab. 845; Yer. Berakhot 14a–14b.
2. Gen. Rab. 907–08, 928, 954; Mid. Agada Gen. 83, 85.
3. PRE, ch. 38; *Genesis* XXXIV. 1–19.
4. *Genesis* XXXIV. 20–31.
5. Sepher Hayashar 113–19; Mid. Leqah Tobh Gen. 174–75; Gen. Rab. 956, 965; Saba, *Tseror HaMor* on WaYehi 59c.
6. Sepher Hayashar, 113–19; Tanhuma Buber Introduction 127; Gen. Rab. 965–66.
7. Gen. Rab. 966; Mid. Sekhel Tobh 194; Mid. Hagadol Gen. 527.
8. PRE, ch. 38; Targum Yer. *Gen.* XLI. 45 and XLVI. 20; Yalqut Gen. 146; Sopherim, end; Hadar and Daat on *Gen.* XLI. 45; Hadar on *Gen.* XXXIV. 1; Yalqut Reubeni on *Gen.* XXXII. 25; Oppenheim, *Fabula Josephi et Asenathae*, Berlin, 1886, pp. 4 ff.
9. Gen. Rab. 966–67; Sepher Hayashar 202; Mid. Hagadol Gen. 527; Shu'aib, WaYishlah 16a; *Test. of Job* I. 11.

*

1. Shechem, like Troy, was sacked in revenge for a princess's abduction by the king's son. Both Greeks and Hebrews seem to have borrowed this theme, separately, from the Ugaritic *Keret* epic, in which the God El orders Prince Keret to besiege Udum, where his lawful spouse Hurriya has taken refuge with her lover—though the King of Udum honourably offers to compensate his loss. In both cases the historical facts have been romantically obscured: the Trojan War was fought, it seems, for control of the Black Sea trade; Shechem was destroyed after a territorial dispute between Joshua's Israelites and their Hivite allies.

2. Dinah is said to have differed from her sisters—all born as twins to Jacob's other sons—in having a separate birth (see 45.*f*). Hers must therefore be regarded as an independent tribe of the Leah federation, which enjoyed not patriarchal but matriarchal, or semi-matriarchal, government—like the Epizephyrian Locrians of Calabria, about whose constitution Aristotle wrote a treatise. Patriarchy and matriarchy still co-exist in parts of Central Africa, as they did in ancient Greece: Hera's High Priestess of Argos attended meetings of the twelve-tribe Amphictyonic League, but was expected to wear a beard—all the other representatives being men.

3. Dinah's rape by Shechem suggests that, not long after Joshua's invasion of Canaan, her small tribe was overrun by Amorites of Shechem and that her allies, the Leah tribes of Simeon and Levi, took revenge by massacring them. Dinah then married Simeon—that is to say, the two tribes became temporarily united; but when Simeon forfeited his lands (*Genesis* XLIX. 5–7), and the tribal remnants joined Judah as a sub-clan (*Joshua* XIX. 1–9; 1 *Chronicles* IV. 24 ff)—which may explain why Simeon has been omitted from Moses' Blessing in *Deuteronomy* XXXIII.—Dinah lost her identity. However, we learn from a midrash that Asenath, Dinah's daughter by Shechem (ingeniously identified with Asenath, the High Priest of On's daughter—*Genesis* XLI. 45 ff) married Joseph. In other words, the tribe of Ephraim took over her former lands, an event anachronistically mentioned by Jacob in *Genesis* XL, when he blesses Ephraim, giving him 'one *shoulder* above your brothers, which I won from the Amorites with my sword and bow.' 'Shoulder' in Hebrew is *shechem*, and Jacob was conferring the sovereignty of Israel on Ephraim; because Shechem served until David's time as the political centre of Israel. A shoulder was the royal portion in Greece: when Creon expelled Oedipus from Thebes he laid the haunch, not the shoulder, before him at a sacrificial feast—as a token of his deposition.

4. The suggestion in *Genesis* that Dinah's downfall was caused by visiting the daughters of the land—that is to say, taking part in Canaanite orgies—disguises the fact that most Israelite girls did so in those early days, and points a familiar Jewish moral: 'Mothers, keep your daughters at home!'

5. Jacob's fight against the Amorites has been invented to account for

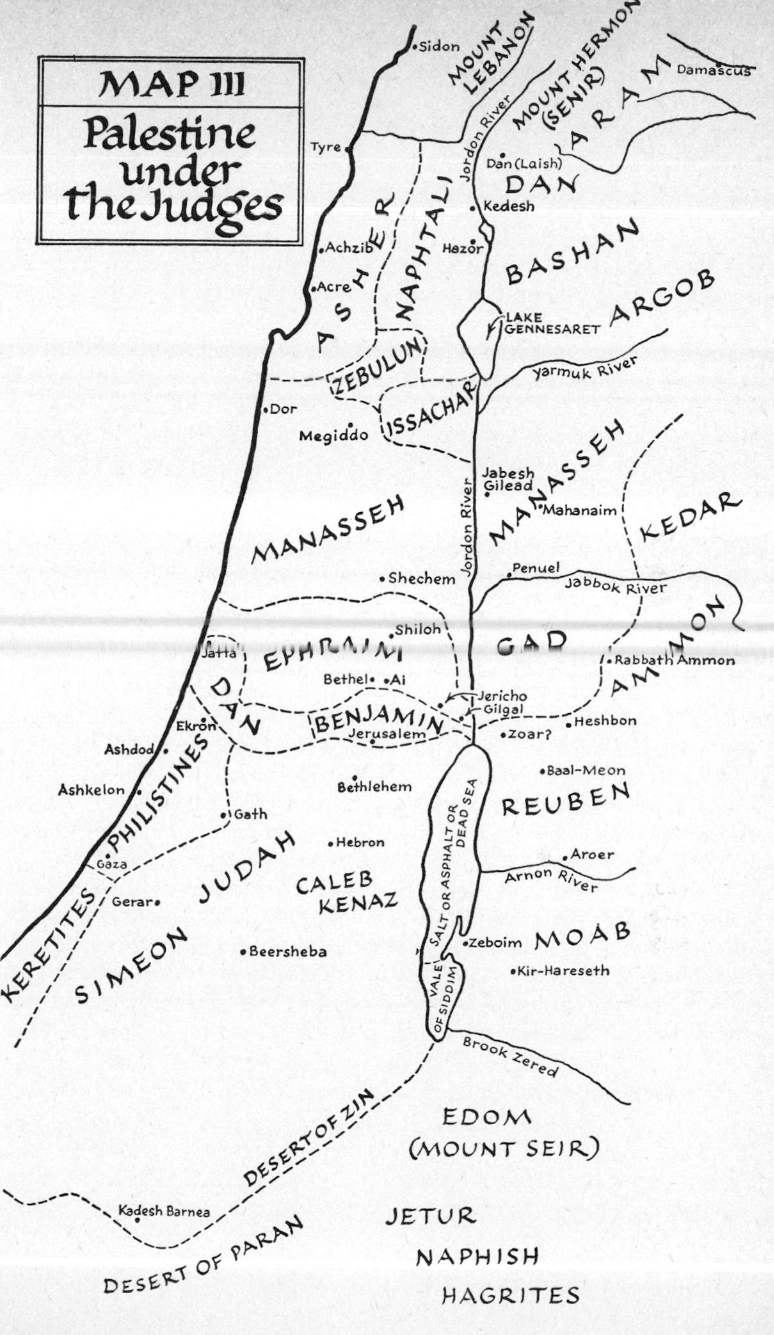
MAP III
Palestine under the Judges
Sidon
MOUNT LEBANON
MOUNT HERMON (SENIR)
ARAM
Damascus
Tyre
Jordon River
Dan (Laish)
DAN
ASHER
NAPHTALI
Kedesh
Achzib
Hazor
BASHAN
Acre
ARGOB
LAKE GENNESARET
ZEBULUN
Yarmuk River
ISSACHAR
Dor
Megiddo
MANASSEH
Jabesh Gilead
Mahanaim
KEDAR
MANASSEH
Jordon River
Penuel
Shechem
Jabbok River
Shiloh
EPHRAIM
GAD
AMMON
Jaffa
Rabbath Ammon
Bethel
Ai
DAN
Jericho
Gilgal
BENJAMIN
Heshbon
Ekron
Jerusalem
Zoar?
Ashdod
PHILISTINES
Baal-Meon
Bethlehem
Ashkelon
SALT OR ASPHALT OR DEAD SEA
REUBEN
Gath
Hebron
JUDAH
Aroer
Gaza
Arnon River
CALEB
KENAZ
Gerar
KERETITES
SIMEON
Zeboim
MOAB
Beersheba
VALE OF SIDDIM
Kir-Hareseth
Brook Zered
EDOM
(MOUNT SEIR)
DESERT OF ZIN
Kadesh Barnea
DESERT OF PARAN
JETUR
NAPHISH
HAGRITES

his boast, in the Blessing, that he won Shechem with his own sword and bow (*Genesis* XLIX. 8–9).

6. Midrashic commentators are at pains to show that Simeon and Levi did not merely massacre defenceless men, but fought gallantly against ten times their own number; also that Joseph correctly married his niece, not the daughter of an Egyptian priest.

7. The circumcision of the Shechemites is a puzzling incident, since all Palestinians, except the Philistines, are said by Herodotus to have practised it; but perhaps the Shechemites, here called 'Hivites', were recent Achaean immigrants. The custom had spread eastward from Egypt, where the use of flint lancets (*Exodus* IV. 25) proves its great antiquity.

8. That Dinah married Job after he made his peace with God, has no Scriptural sanction. But since both characters had suffered greatly for no fault of their own; and since we are told nothing about the woman who, in the last chapters of *Job*, bore Job seven sons and three daughters to replace those killed by a hurricane in the first chapter, Dinah's name at once suggests itself for such a marriage of convenience.

9. Asenath, daughter of Dinah, is a midrashic invention. Asenath, Joseph's wife (see 56. 5), has a genuine Egyptian name unconnected with a thorn bush (*sneh* in Hebrew).

10. Gabriel took the shape of an eagle because Potiphera's temple was sacred to the god Ra, and housed his Sun-eagle, or Phoenix, a bird greatly venerated by Israelite sages (see 12. *f* and 20. *k*).

11. The medieval *Sepher Hayashar* supplies a long account of wars fought between Jacob's sons and the Amorites, with swords, shields, spears, enormous boulders, and loud war cries. This Homeric fiction has been historically well conceived. Tappuah, Shiloh, Hazor, Beth-Horon, Sartan, Mahanaim and Gaash, the seven place names it mentions, are all ancient Ephraimite cities; and Ephraim himself (because he was born in Egypt at a later date) is carefully omitted from the roll of Israelite champions. It seems most improbable, however, that this war reflects even a genuine tradition of Joshua's later conquests, since the place names correspond with those found in the *Testament of Judah* (end of second century B.C.) and the somewhat later *Book of Jubilees*. The Beth-Horon battle seems to be a reminiscence of that fought by Judas the Maccabee against the Syrian general Seron (1 *Maccabees* III. 16).

50

REUBEN AND BILHAH

(*a*) While Jacob camped by the Tower of Eder in Judah, he was grieved to hear that Reuben had seduced Rachel's bondmaid Bilhah, mother of Asher and Naphtali, his own half-brothers.

Many years later when Jacob, on his deathbed, addressed each of the twelve patriarchs in turn, he told Reuben: 'Though the eldest son, and first proof of my manhood; though of great strength and fountain-like impetuosity; yet you have defiled my bed, and shall therefore not rule your brothers!'[1]

(*b*) Some say that Reuben was avenging Leah's wrongs; for after Rachel's death, Jacob set Bilhah's couch beside his own. Reuben cried angrily: 'My mother Leah suffered scorn enough while Rachel lived. Must she still bear it patiently?' He took away the couch and set Leah's in its place; then, because this plain warning went unregarded, he forced Bilhah—so that Jacob might never touch her again.[2]

(*c*) Reuben, on his deathbed, gave a different account of the matter. Having watched Bilhah bathe in a secluded stream, he could not sleep until he had enjoyed her. His opportunity came one evening when she lay drunken and naked in the tent. Although Bilhah remembered nothing afterwards, God saw Reuben's act and punished him for seven months with a cruel disease of the genitals. At length he confessed his sin to Jacob, and did seven years' penance—abstaining from wine, meat, dainties and merry-making.[3]

(*d*) Reuben, Jacob's first-born, should have inherited his blessing, priesthood, and kingship over Israel; but because he had sinned, the blessing was laid upon Joseph; the priesthood on Levi; the kingship on Judah. Jacob excused himself to Reuben: 'I served Laban for Rachel's sake, not for your mother Leah's. The ploughing and sowing I did in Leah should have been done in Rachel, and Joseph should have been my first-born. The first-born's right, therefore, is his by equity.'[4]

(*e*) Some charge Reuben with seducing Zilpah also.[5]

1. *Genesis* XXXV. 22; XLIX. 3–4; 1 *Chronicles* V. 1.

2. Gen. Rab. 1254–55; B. Shabbat 55b; Tanhuma Buber Gen. 218; Hadar 14d and 15d.
3. *Testament of Reuben* I. 1–10; III. 9–IV. 3.
4. Gen. Rab. 1253; Tanhuma Buber Gen. 218.
5. Gen. Rab. 1254.

*

1. No greater reproach attaches to Bilhah than to Tamar, seduced by Amnon (2 *Samuel* XIII); to Bathsheba, seduced by David (2 *Samuel* XI; XII); or to Dinah, seduced by Shechem (see 49). Hebrew myths treat women as fields to be ploughed and sown by godlike heroes—passive, and thus necessarily guiltless if the wrong farmer should enter. Sexual prohibitions in the Mosaic Law are addressed to men alone; and though proof of adultery sentences the woman as well as her lover to death by stoning, she is punished as an involuntary participant—like the luckless animal with which a man has committed bestiality (*Leviticus* XX. 10–18). The first-century Pharisees, however, despite a New Testament libel on them (*John* VIII), never stoned an adulterous couple: the woman was allowed to plead ignorance of the Law and, since the seducer could not suffer apart from her, both went free. Jesus therefore, by his timely quotation of *Deuteronomy* XVII. 2–7, must have saved the adulterous woman from Samaritan judges, who obeyed Moses literally, rather than from Pharisees.

2. The historical setting of this myth can only be guessed at, because the tribe of Reuben—said to have occupied the eastern side of Jordan, opposite Judah—has left no records: it vanished early from Israelite history, unnamed in Moabite inscriptions. Yet the meaning is clear: as titular head of the eight Leah tribes, a Reubenite chieftain seduced the tributary tribes of Dan and Naphtali from their allegiance to the Rachel federation. A conference of tribal representatives was held in the territory of Judah, the strongest Leah tribe; Eder lies close to Bethlehem.

3. Josephus and others spell Reuben as 'Reubel', which may be its earliest form. Moses' Blessing (*Exodus* XXXIII. 6) expresses a hope for Reuben's continued existence, despite the smallness of his numbers. But by the time of the Captivity two of his sons, or clans, namely Hezron and Carmi, had been admitted to the tribe of Judah and engrafted into his genealogy (1 *Chronicles* IV. 1; V. 3).

4. Since no sons were born of the Reuben-Bilhah incest, as they were to Lot's daughters (see 33. 1) and to Tamar (see 51. 1), a revolt, not a tribal affiliation, is the subject of this myth: indeed, the first act of a usurping king was to lie publicly, like Absalom, with his predecessor's harem (2 *Samuel* XVI. 20 ff)—and any ambitious movement in that direction was regarded as high treason, as when Abner lay with Saul's former concubine Rizpah (2 *Samuel* III. 7 ff), or when Adonijah petitioned Solomon for David's concubine Abishag (1 *Kings* II. 13 ff). It is therefore possible that this myth reflects the Leah tribes' revolt, under David of

Bethlehem, against their Rachelite overlord Saul the Benjamite; and that David could count on the support of Reuben and Gad, who had won the Bilhah tribes of Asher and Naphtali to his cause. David's main political strength clearly lay across Jordan in Gilead, where he later fled during Absalom's revolt (2 *Samuel* XVII. 24).

51

JUDAH AND TAMAR

(*a*) Judah parted from his eleven brothers and went southward to lodge with Hirah of Adullam. There he met and married Bath-Shua, the daughter of Shua, a Canaanite, who bore him three sons in the city of Chezib: Er, Onan and Shelah. In due time Judah chose Er a wife named Tamar, also a Canaanite; but God, forewarned of Er's wickedness, destroyed him, and Judah therefore ordered Onan to raise up children for his dead brother—a kindness later made obligatory by Moses in what is known as the Levirate Law. Onan, however, knew that no child born of such a union would be his, and so 'threshed within, but sowed without': that is to say, though often mounting Tamar, he always withdrew before ejaculation—a sin which God punished by death. Judah then said: 'Pray, Tamar, return awhile to your father's house at Enaim, and wear widow's weeds until my youngest son Shelah is old enough to marry you.' Yet, fearing that Shelah might be suddenly struck dead, like his brothers, Judah postponed the wedding year after year.[1]

(*b*) When Bath-Shua died, Judah, to drown his grief, attended a joyful sheep-shearing near Timnah; and Tamar, aware by now that she was being cheated, saw Judah pass through Enaim on his journey there. She said nothing but walked a little way out of the city, shed her widow's weeds, shrouded her face in a gaudy veil, came back, and sat down not far from the gate. Judah, returning at dusk, mistook Tamar for a sacred harlot, and asked: 'May I lie with you?'

'If the pay pleases me,' she replied, disguising her voice.

'Will a yearling kid be acceptable?'

'It will. Have you any kids here?'

'No, but I could send one from Adullam.'

'In that case, leave me a pledge.'

'Name it!'

'Your seal, cords and staff.'

Judah gave Tamar the pledge and they lay together; after which she stole off and secretly resumed her widow's weeds.

At Judah's request, his friend Hirah brought the promised kid to

Enaim, and asked all he met: 'Where shall I find the sacred harlot who sat outside the City gate on such and such a day?' They answered: 'We saw none such.'[2]

(*c*) Three months later, Judah heard that Tamar had plainly broken her marriage contract, being with child by some man other than Shelah. Obeying the custom of those days, he sentenced her to the stake. But as they led Tamar away, she sent Judah his seal, cords and staff, saying: 'If I must die, let the Israelite with whom I sinned also die; he will be known by these tokens.'

Judah, recognizing his own pledges, reversed the judgement. 'She shall live,' he pronounced, 'for I myself am at fault: not having honoured the marriage contract made with this woman on my son Shelah's behalf.' So Tamar went free; yet Judah could not touch her again, nor could she marry Shelah.[3]

(*d*) Tamar was brought to bed of twins. One of them thrust out a hand, but no sooner had the midwife tied a scarlet thread around his wrist, than he drew back, and his brother emerged first. She asked: 'How have you *broken through?*', and named him 'Perez'. Afterwards the first twin re-appeared, the scarlet thread still *shining* on his wrist; and she named him 'Zerah'.[4]

(*e*) Like all noble mothers of Israel, Tamar possessed the gift of prophecy. She foresaw that the Messiah would descend from her; and it was this prescience that prompted her to obey the ancient Amorite law by which every girl, before marriage, must spend seven days outside the city gate selling herself to strangers.

Some say that Judah, in his righteousness, refrained from Tamar at first, and walked on. But she prayed to God, at whose command the Angel of Carnal Desire flew down, whispering: 'Turn again, Judah! If you despise this woman, how shall Israel's kings and redeemers be born?' Judah therefore turned and lay with Tamar—though not before assuring himself that she was unmarried, an orphan, bodily pure, and a servant of the Living God. Afterwards Tamar, rather than tell the messengers who it was that had given her the pledges, left the revelation to Judah. And some say that because of her prudence in this matter—since a righteous person will rather burn than publicly shame a kinsman—Judah not only acknowledged the twins as his own, but continued to cheer Tamar in her widowhood.[5]

1. *Genesis* xxxviii. 1–12.
2. *Genesis* xxxviii. 12–23.
3. *Genesis* xxxviii. 24–26.

4. *Genesis* XXXVIII. 27–30.
5. Gen. Rab. 1042, 1044; Tanhuma Buber Introd. 129 and Gen. 187; Mid. Hagadol Gen. 569, 572, 574; *Test. of Judah* XII; XIV. 3–5; B. Sota 10a–b.

*

1. It has been suggested that *Hosea* XII. 1 should read: 'Judah again separated himself from God, while remaining faithful to the *q'deshim* ("holy ones")'—meaning that he separated himself from his brothers, and adopted Canaanite religious customs, which included the *q'deshim* cult. The *q'deshim* were *kelebites,* or 'dog priests': male prostitutes dressed as women, who remained active under the later Judaean monarchy (1 *Kings* XV. 12; XXII. 47; 2 *Kings* XXIII. 7) in quarters assigned to them on Mount Zion itself. The admission of Caleb into the tribe of Judah supports this sense, which is consonant with Judah's unashamed enjoyment of a *q'deshah,* or sacred prostitute. The *q'deshah's* customary donation of her earnings to Temple funds was forbidden in the same Deuteronomic text as that of the *q'deshim* (*Deuteronomy* XXIII. 18). The last Scriptural mention of kelebites occurs in *Revelations* XXII. 15.

2. This ancient myth is securely attached to a small area north-west of Hebron, where most of the place names are still preserved. Adullam, the seat of a Canaanite king dispossessed by Joshua (*Joshua* XII. 15), is Khirbet 'Id al-Ma, some eleven miles north-west of Hebron; Chezib, or Achzib, or Cozeba (1 *Chronicles* IV. 22) is 'En al-Kazbah in the Wadi al-Sant; Timnah, between Bethlehem and Beit Nattif, is Khirbet Tibna. Only Enaim, lying between Adullam and Timnah, has disappeared since Talmudic times, when it was known as Kefar Enaim (*Pesiqta Rabbati* 23).

3. The brothers Er, Onan, and Shelah—Er's sins are not specified, but his name reversed spells *wicked* in Hebrew—represent three original Judahite clans, the two senior of which declined in importance. By the time of the Babylonian captivity, Er had come to rank as a son, or subclan, of Shelah (1 *Chronicles* IV. 21); while Onan ranked merely as a son of Jerachmeel, son of Hezron (see 50. 3), son of Perez (1 *Chronicles* II. 26). Perez (or Pharez) had taken precedence even of Shelah; and Zerah, whom he dispossessed at birth, was lost to history. Arab tribal genealogists still record the rise and fall of clans in precisely this manner.

4. Tamar's sentence to death by burning antedates *Deuteronomy* XXII. 23–24, which condemns a wife or betrothed woman taken in adultery to be stoned; burning, in the Mosaic Law, was reserved for erring daughters of priests (*Leviticus* XXI. 9). Yet no stigma attached in early Judaea to men who lay with prostitutes—so long as these were not the property of a husband, or father, or in a state of ritual impurity; nor did they draw any clear distinction between a *zonah,* or lay prostitute, and a *q'deshah,* or sacred prostitute.

5. It is hinted here that Judah suspected Tamar of being bewitched, like

Raguel's daughter Sara (*Tobit* VIII), whose six husbands had been mysteriously murdered, one after the other, on their wedding nights, by a jealous spirit. As a woman betrothed to an Israelite, Tamar took grave risks in playing the harlot, but since she handled the matter discreetly and got children from the man who had wrongfully denied them to her, she became exalted in popular tradition and listed with Rachel and Leah as a 'heroic mother of Israel' (*Ruth* IV. 12). Like Ruth the Moabitess, and Rahab the sacred harlot of Jericho (*Joshua* II), this Canaanite woman became (through Perez) an ancestress of David, and thus of the promised Messiah (see *Matthew* I. 3–6).

6. *Tamar* means 'palm-tree', and the palm was sacred to the Love-and-Birth goddess Isis, otherwise known as Ishtar or, among the Arabs, as Lāt or 'Ilāt. Arabians worshipped the great palm of Nejran, annually draping it with women's clothes and ornaments. Lat's son, Apollo of Delos—Lat is now generally equated with Leto or Latona—and the Nabataean God Dusares, were both born under palms: Apollo on Ortygia (Quail Island). In the original story, Tamar will have been a sacred prostitute, unrelated to Judah. She is linked to her sister Rahab by mention of the scarlet thread (*Joshua* II. 18) which marked their calling; and in the Ethiopian *Kebra Nagast*, Pharaoh's daughter seduces Solomon with the help of three locusts (see 29. 3) and a scarlet thread.

52

THE DEATHS OF ISAAC, LEAH, AND ESAU

(*a*) Jacob and Esau continued at peace for the next eighteen years—until their father Isaac died and was buried in the Cave of Machpelah. Only then, some say, did Esau tell his sons of the bartered birthright and the stolen blessing; yet still restrained their jealous rage, saying: 'Our father Isaac made us swear to live in peace with one another.'

They answered: 'While he lived, that was well enough. But now let us gather allies from Aram, Philistia, Moab and Ammon, and root Jacob out of the land that is rightfully ours!'

Eliphaz, being an upright man, dissented. Esau, however, keenly remembered the injuries Jacob had done him, and felt ashamed to be thought a weakling. He therefore led a huge army against Jacob at Hebron, but found the entire household in sackcloth and ashes, mourning Leah's death.

When Jacob took offence at this unseemly breach of their covenant, Esau said: 'You have always hated and deceived me! There can be no true brotherhood between us until lion and ox are yoked together before the plough; until the raven turns white as the stork; until the boar sheds its bristles and grows a fleece.'[1]

(*b*) At Judah's instigation, Jacob then bent his bow and shot Esau through the right breast. He was carried away on a pack-beast, to die at Adoraim on Mount Seir. Jacob also shot Esau's ally, Adoram the Edomite. In the fierce battle that ensued, Jacob's army would have been overpowered, had not a dust storm sent by God blinded their enemies. The Israelites slaughtered them in droves. A few survivors fled to Maale-Akrabbim, where they again suffered defeat. Jacob laid them under heavy tribute, and buried Esau at Adoraim.[2]

1. *Jubilees* XXXVII–XXXVIII.
2. Mid. Wayissa'u, Yalqut Gen. 133; BHM, iii. 4–5.

*

1. Adoram the Edomite is a non-Scriptural figure; his name has been taken from Adoraim, a Canaanite town mentioned in the Amarna letters

as 'Aduri', and rebuilt by Rehoboam (2 *Chronicles* xi. 9) on two hills—hence the dual form. The large twin villages of Dura al-Amriyya and Dura al-Arjan, some five miles west of Hebron, mark its site. Adoraim was occupied by the Edomites after Nebuchadrezzar's capture of Jerusalem, but retaken and forcibly Judaized by John Hyrcanus (135–104 B.C.). Maale-Akrabbim ('Scorpions' Ascent'), south-west of the Dead Sea, marked the boundary between Judah and Edom (*Numbers* xxxiv. 4; *Joshua* xv. 3; *Judges* i. 36), and was the scene of Judas the Maccabee's defeat of the Edomites (1 *Maccabees* v. 3). These Hasmonean Wars have here been put back into the mythical past to fill a narrative gap.

2. Eliphaz is excused the slaughter which overtook his brothers; probably because the descendants of his son Kenaz were engrafted on the tribe of Judah (see 42. 4). An alternative account of Esau's death at the burial of Jacob (see 60. *h*) is supplied by a midrash to justify Rebekah's fear (see 43. *a*): 'Why should I lose two sons in one day?'

53

JOSEPH IN THE PIT

(*a*) At the age of seventeen, Joseph joined the sons of Bilhah and Zilpah on their father's pastures. He returned to Hebron after only one month, unable to endure the feverish blowing of an east wind; but told Jacob that shame at his half-brothers' evil ways had driven him home. Jacob believed Joseph, whom he loved better than all the rest as Rachel's first-born, and the one most closely resembling himself, both in nature and feature. Joseph had grown very vain, daubed his eyes with kohl, dressed his locks like a woman, walked mincingly, and wore a long-sleeved tunic which Jacob had given him. The brothers jeered whenever their father was not present, and Joseph took revenge by further tale-bearing. Gad, the finest shepherd among them, usually chose the night watch and, if a wild beast attacked his flock, would seize its hind legs and brain it against a rock. Joseph once saw him rescue a wounded lamb from a bear and mercifully end its pain. The brothers dined on this carcase; but Joseph accused them of secretly slaughtering and eating the best rams. In answer to Jacob's reproof, Gad declared that he never again wished to set eyes on Joseph.[1]

(*b*) When sent out under the charge of Leah's sons, Joseph once more returned home after a few weeks. There he complained of their consorting with Canaanite girls, and treating their half-brothers like slaves. A dream that he told further increased their hatred of him. He said: 'We were binding sheaves in the field. Suddenly mine stood upright, while yours formed a ring around it, and bowed obsequiously.'

They shouted: 'So you are to rule us—is that the meaning of your dream?'

Unmoved by their anger, Joseph told them another: 'Last night I saw the sun, the moon, and eleven stars do homage to me.' And when Jacob heard of it, he too exclaimed: 'What dream is this? Must I, and your step-mother, and your brothers, all serve you?'[2]

(*c*) Joseph thereafter remained at Hebron until, one day, his brothers drove the flocks to Mount Ephraim, and stayed so long that Jacob sent him in search of them. At Shechem, Joseph learned of their new camp near Dothan, a day's march away, and pressed on. When they saw him in the distance, Simeon, Dan and Gad cried angrily: 'Here comes that boastful dreamer! Let us murder him and hide the body in one of yonder pits. That will put an end to his dreaming.' Reuben objected: 'Why bring a curse upon ourselves by spilling innocent blood? Why not leave him in the pit to starve?' This seemed good advice; so they stripped Joseph of his long-sleeved tunic, and threw him naked into the pit. It had been a well dug in a vain search of water, and was now the home of snakes and scorpions.[3]

(*d*) The brothers sat down to eat, several bowshots away, and presently saw an Ishmaelite caravan approaching from Gilead, with spices, balm and gum-mastic for sale in Egypt. Judah asked: 'Why let our brother die of starvation, when we can sell him to those Ishmaelites?' They answered: 'Not now! Because of his slanderous tongue, he must spend three days among snakes and scorpions.'

Meanwhile, a Midianite caravan came up behind them. Drawn to the pit by Joseph's shouts of terror, they hauled him out and afterwards sold him to the Ishmaelites for twenty pieces of silver. That night, Reuben repented of his cruelty. Unaware that the Midianites had forestalled him, he took a rope and went to rescue Joseph from the pit; there he called his name, but got no answer. He ran back in grief, shouting: 'Joseph is already dead and, as our father's first-born, I shall be called to account!' Issachar then proposed that they should slaughter a he-goat, dip Joseph's tunic in its blood, and pretend that a wild beast had killed him.[4]

(*e*) Naphtali, their chosen messenger, brought Jacob the blood-stained tunic on the tenth day of Tishri, saying: 'We found this at Dothan. Is it perhaps Joseph's?' Jacob cried: 'Alas, a wild beast has devoured my son!' He tore his garments, wore sackcloth, poured dust upon his head, and mourned miserably. When the household tried to comfort him, he drove them off, shouting: 'Find me Joseph's body without delay! Also catch the first wild beast you meet, and bring it here alive for my vengeance! God will doubtless deliver the murderer into your hands.'

They fetched him a wolf, but reported that Joseph's body was nowhere to be seen. Jacob railed at the wolf: 'Murderous wretch, do you respect neither God nor me?' God then granted the wolf human speech. It said: 'By the life of our Creator, and by your life, my lord: I am innocent! Twelve days ago my own cub left me and, not knowing whether he were dead or alive, I hurried to Dothan in search of him. Now I am falsely accused of murder. Take what vengeance you please! But I swear by the Living God that I have never set eyes on your son, nor has man's flesh ever passed my lips!'

Jacob freed the wolf in amazement, and continued his mourning for Joseph.[5]

1. *Testament of Gad* I. 1–II. 1; PRE, ch. 38, Gen. Rab. 1008–09; Tanhuma Buber Gen. 180; Yer. Peah 15d–16a.
2. Sources as in preceding footnote and *Genesis* XXXVII. 1–11.
3. *Genesis* XXXVII. 12–24; Gen. Rab. 1015, 1017; Tanhuma Buber Gen. 183; PRE, ch. 38; Sepher Hayashar 146–47; *Test. of Zebulun* II.
4. *Genesis* XXXVII. 25–35; Gen. Rab. 1018–19; *Test of Zebulun* IV; Sepher Hayashar 141–48, 152–53.
5. Sepher Hayashar 152–53, 156–57.

*

1. This is evidently a folk tale, like those of the Arabian Nights cycle, or the Milesian cycle borrowed by Apuleius for his *Golden Ass*, or those collected by Perrault and the Brothers Grimm—all of which combine popular entertainment with worldly wisdom, but have no historical basis. Nevertheless, it has been converted into myth by attaching it to particular localities—Hebron, Dothan, Gilead—and by making tribal ancestors the main characters. It serves as introduction to a longer myth which purports to explain the presence of Hebrews in Egypt during the Hyksos period, the rise of a powerful viceroy from among them, and their eventual return to Canaan, where they assumed the leadership of a tribal confederacy.

Joseph is said to have borne so close a resemblance to his father, and to have been so beloved by him, because the original 'Israel' consisted only of the two Joseph tribes and their Benjamite allies (see 47. 5. 7. 8). Political manoeuvres, while these Egyptianized Hebrews were invading Canaan under Joshua's leadership, are suggested by Joseph's tale-bearing about the Bilhah and Zilpah tribes; by the peculiar animosity to him of Simeon, Gad and Dan; and by the reluctance of Reuben and Judah to shed his blood.

2. Dothan, which occurs in the sixteenth-century B.C. list of Canaanite cities subject to Pharaoh Thotmes III, and in 2 *Kings* VI. 13–14 as a walled city, was built on a mound (now Tell Duthan) thirteen miles north of Shechem, overlooking the Damascus-Gilead-Egypt caravan route. Since Dothan commanded the main northern pass to the hill country of Ephraim, a fateful conference of the Hebrew tribes that already occupied a large part of Canaan—the question being whether to join forces with their Israelite cousins or appeal for armed Egyptian help against them—may well have taken place there. The chronicler does not disguise hostility to Joseph as an intruder and mischief-maker. That the Midianites sold Joseph to the

Ishmaelites is an ingenious gloss on a confused passage in *Genesis*, where the priestly editor has been clumsy in his interweaving of two discordant literary sources: one an Ephraimite document, composed before the destruction of the Northern Kingdom (721 B.C.); the other Judaean, composed later. According to the Ephraimite account, Joseph's brothers sold him to Midianite merchants; according to the Judaean, they sold him to Ishmaelites. Similarly, in the Ephraimite version Joseph's protector is Reuben; in the Judaean, Judah. But by the time that the *Genesis* text was established, Jerusalem had become the new centre of Israel, and Reuben had merged with Judah; so both brothers appear in a good light. Elsewhere, the more murderous parts are allotted to the landless tribes of Simeon, Gad and Dan.

3. Joseph's youthful beauty, his attempted murder, his resurrection from the pit after three days, and his eventual provision of bread to a starving world link him with the Tammuz myth; a meaning heightened by the he-goat sacrificed on the Day of Atonement, which the midrash explains as a penitential reminder of the he-goat killed by the brothers for blood to stain Joseph's tunic.

4. The tale has been given ingenious ethical glosses by midrashic commentators. Though the brothers seemed to be wreaking vengeance on Joseph they were, it is said, God's chosen instruments for securing his power in Egypt. God also stocked the pit with snakes and scorpions to make him scream in terror and attract the Midianites' notice. His servitude was divinely ordained, so that he should later save Israel from famine; but since the brothers sinned, their descendants were likewise fated to become slaves in Egypt. 'By your lives,' God told them, 'you sold Joseph into slavery, and therefore you will recite the tale of your own Egyptian bondage until the end of time' (*Midrash Tehillim* 93). God even arranged that the Ishmaelites should carry perfumed spices instead of their usual malodorous loads of skins, thus making Joseph's journey pleasant. One midrash adds that God miraculously provided a garment, so as to spare him the disgrace of standing naked in the presence of strangers; another makes God bless Reuben's attempted liberation of Joseph, by sending the prophet Hosea, a Reubenite, to preach repentance throughout Israel. Joseph's sins of vanity, tale-bearing and disrespect, are punished with nakedness, suffering and servitude.

5. Jacob's resolve to punish the wild beast which had devoured Joseph must be understood as piety, not hysteria. Moses ordered the death of any animal that killed a man. A similar English law of Anglo-Saxon origin, known as *Deodand* and not repealed until 1846, made any beast or object that had caused a man's death—ox, cart, fallen beam, or whatever else it might be—Crown property. Its value was distributed in the form of alms to the poor, or donations to the Church.

6. 'Pieces of silver' were nowhere coined before the seventh century B.C.

54
JOSEPH AND ZULEIKA

(*a*) Joseph was taken down to Egypt by the Midianites, and sold to Potiphar the eunuch, Pharaoh's chief victualler who, recognizing Joseph's talents, soon appointed him household steward, and never regretted the choice.

Potiphar had married, but his wife Zuleika did not consider herself bound by any marital ties: a woman naturally expects children. She tried to seduce Joseph; but he, although by no means insensible of Zuleika's outstanding beauty, rebuffed her advances, saying: 'My master, your husband, has set me over his household, denying me nothing except what you ask. It would be robbery, as well as a sin against God, if I succumbed.'

She asked: 'Since I cannot enjoy my husband's embraces, nor he mine, how would this be robbery?' Joseph saw that she had blinded the idol on the wall above her with a sheet. He said: 'That is well done; but no one blinds the eyes of God, who sees all!'[1]

(*b*) Zuleika's unsatisfied craving preyed on her health. Visiting court-ladies soon inquired: 'What ails you? Your health is usually so robust.'

'I will show you the cause,' Zuleika replied.

She ordered a banquet and called Joseph in to supervise the arrangements. The ladies could not take their eyes off him and, while peeling fruit set before them, all cut themselves.

When Joseph left the hall, Zuleika said: 'There is blood on the fruit! If you cut your fingers after so short a torment, what do I not suffer day after day?'[2]

(*c*) Zuleika wooed Joseph with words and gifts, constantly dressed in new garments, and took every opportunity to allow him brief glimpses of her naked breasts and thighs. She also used love philtres; but God always warned Joseph which cup or dish to avoid. At last she resorted to threats.

'You shall be cruelly oppressed!'

'God helps the oppressed,' Joseph answered.

'I shall starve you!'

'God feeds the hungry.'
'I shall cast you into prison.'
'God releases the captive.'
'I shall force you into the dust!'
'God raises those who are bowed down.'
'I shall put out your eyes!'
'God gives sight to the blind.'[3]

(*d*) The court-ladies told her: 'You must break his resistance, one day, when you two are alone. He is a man like any other, and cannot long withstand your charms. Doubtless he already reciprocates your passion.'

Zuleika took their advice. Early next morning, she stole into Joseph's bedroom and fell upon him suddenly. He awoke, broke loose, and left her lying there. She cried in despair: 'Has so beautiful a woman ever revealed her consuming love for you? Why so churlish? Why this fear of your master? As Pharaoh lives, no harm will come to you! Only be generous, and cure me of my wretchedness! Must I die, because of your foolish scruples?'[4]

(*e*) The annual rise of the Nile was greeted with harps, drums, and dancing; and all Potiphar's household attended the festivities, except Zuleika who pleaded ill health; Joseph, who busied himself at his accounts; and some porters. When everything was quiet, Zuleika crept into Joseph's study, caught hold of his garment and ripped it off him, crying: 'Sweetheart, at last we are alone! Enjoy me without fear!' Joseph fled, naked. Humiliated beyond endurance, Zuleika screamed for the porters, who came running with weapons in their hands. 'Your master has appointed this vile Hebrew slave to insult us!' she panted. 'He tried to ravish me, but when I cried out, he fled, leaving this garment behind.'

She told Potiphar the same thing on his return, and he angrily confined Joseph in the Royal Prison—God's punishment on him for not yet having learned to shun the sins of luxurious living and self-adornment, which had again brought trouble with them.

Some say that Potiphar himself doted on Joseph, and felt jealous of Zuleika.[5]

(*f*) When the case was tried in a priestly court, the Chief Judge, having listened to both parties, called for Joseph's garment, which they duly produced. Holding it up, he said: 'If, as the Lady Zuleika claims, this slave forced himself upon her, but fled when she cried out; and if she then tore off his garment to keep as evidence against him, the rent will be found behind. If, on the contrary, she tore it off him, as he claims, the better to excite his lust, the rent will be found in front.'

All the judges solemnly agreed that the rent was certainly in front; yet, to avoid casting a slur on Zuleika's name, they returned Joseph to prison for ten more years, while recommending the prison-governor to treat him less severely than his cell-mates.[6]

1. *Genesis* XXXVII. 36; XXXIX. 1–9; Gen. Rab. 1031, 1064–68.
2. Tanhuma Wayeshebh 5; Sepher Hayashar 159–60; cf. Koran XII. 30–33.
3. B. Yoma 35b; *Test. of Joseph* IX. 5; Gen. Rab. 1075–76; etc.
4. Sepher Hayashar 159–60.
5. *Genesis* XXXIX. 10–20; Gen. Rab. 1054–55, 1071–73; Sepher Hayashar 157; Tanhuma Wayeshebh 9.
6. Sepher Hayashar 162–63.

*

1. The same story appears in the Greek myths of Biadice and Phrixus, Anteia and Bellerophon, and Phaedra and Hippolytus. In each case, however, the man's reason for repelling the woman's advances is a horror of incest. The Biadice and Phrixus story comes from Boeotian Cadmeia where it introduces an imported Canaanite myth (see 34. 5); the other two come from the Gulf of Corinth, where Western Semitic influence was strong (see 39. 1). Further versions are found in Thessaly, and on Tenedos, where the Phoenician god Melkarth was worshipped; but its earliest written record appears in the Egyptian *Tale of the Two Brothers*, from which have been borrowed the myths of Abraham, Sarah and Pharaoh (see 26), Abraham, Sarah and Abimelech (see 30), and Isaac, Rebekah and Abimelech (see 37).

2. Potiphar's wife remained nameless, until the *Sepher Hayashar* called her 'Zuleika'; in the *Testament of Joseph* (XII. 1; XIV. 1, etc.), however, she is called 'the woman of Moph'.

The main midrashic elaboration of the bare *Genesis* account is reminiscent of Ovid's record of Phaedra's sufferings in *Heroides* IV. 67 ff. No obloquy attaches to Zuleika, because it was her duty to bear children and, if she had succeeded in getting twins from Joseph, might have been praised as highly as Tamar (see 51. 5). But God intended another Egyptian woman to bear Joseph's sons; and one midrash tells how Zuleika was deceived by the misreading of a horoscope which foretold that he would beget famous offspring on a woman of Potiphera's household—namely Asenath (see 49. *h*, 9). Joseph's rejoinders when threatened by Zuleika are all Scriptural quotations.

3. The festival which allowed Zuleika to be alone with Joseph was either 'The Reception of the Nile', also called 'The Night that Isis Weeps' (June 20th), or the mid-July New Year Festival, celebrating the re-appearance of Sirius, when the river reached its highest flood level in Middle Egypt. 'The Ship of Rising Waters' was then ceremoniously launched.

4. Hebrew myth contains several anecdotes meant to sharpen the detective acumen of judges: such as Solomon's judgement of the two harlots (1 *Kings* III. 16ff), and Daniel's defence of Susanna against the lying elders (*Susanna* v. 45ff). The case of Joseph's torn garment is another such; but a rival midrash turns this legal argument inside out, making the dorsal rent proof of Zuleika's furious attempts to haul him back for her sexual enjoyment, and the frontal rent proof of her struggles to repel his attack.

5. Although one midrash explains the apparent anomaly of a married eunuch by saying that God had castrated him to punish an attempt on Joseph's virtue, this is unnecessary—Pharaoh's chief victualler needed a wife for social reasons. Such sterile unions were permitted at Rome in Juvenal's day: *ducitur uxorem spado tener*.

6. Potiphar was probably Pharaoh's Chief Executioner, not his Chief Victualler (see 55. 1).

55
JOSEPH IN PRISON

(*a*) God watched over Joseph in the Royal Prison, where the Governor soon thought fit to appoint him his deputy. Thus, when Pharaoh's Chief Butler and Chief Baker were also confined there, they came under Joseph's supervision. What charges had been brought against these two is unknown. Some say that a fly was found in the royal wine-cup, and lumps of alum in a loaf set upon the royal table. Others, that both were accused of complicity in an attempt to ravish Pharaoh's daughter.

One night, at all events, they dreamed dreams that haunted them throughout the next morning, and complained to Joseph: 'Alas, sir, that we have no soothsayer here who can interpret them!'

'Am I not a servant of the One God,' Joseph asked, 'to whom such interpretations belong?'

The Chief Butler then said: 'I dreamed of a three-branched vine. Its branches budded, blossoms burst out and formed grape clusters, the fruit grew ripe. Pharaoh's cup was in my right hand. I pressed the grape into it with my left, and gave him to drink.'

Joseph readily interpreted the dream: 'Each branch is a day. In three days' time Pharaoh will forgive your fault and let you bear his royal wine-cup as before. When this comes to pass, pray remember me, and bring my case to Pharaoh's attention. I am of noble blood, but abducted by Ishmaelites from the land of my fathers, sold into slavery, and now imprisoned on a false charge.'

'I shall do so without fail,' promised the Chief Butler.

The Chief Baker, greatly reassured by what he heard, said: 'In my dream I was carrying three bread-baskets upon my head: the topmost held all manner of cakes and confectionary for Pharaoh's table. Suddenly a flock of birds swooped down and ate them all.'

Joseph announced: 'In three days' time, Pharaoh will behead you and hang your body upon a tree for the kites to eat.'

Three days later, Pharaoh celebrated his birthday with a palace banquet, which he made the occasion of restoring his Chief Butler to favour and beheading his Chief Baker. However, the Chief Butler quite forgot what he had promised Joseph.[1]

(*b*) After three months, Zuleika visited Joseph, saying: 'How long must I keep you in prison? Be my lover, and I will set you free at once.'

Joseph answered: 'I have sworn before God never to be your lover!' Zuleika then threatened Joseph with torture, and heavy fetters; but could not move him. It is said, though, that God lengthened Joseph's prison term by two more years: because he had twice asked the Chief Butler, not Himself, to secure his release.[2]

1. *Genesis* XXXIX. 21; XL. 23; Gen. Rab. 1078–79; Sepher Hayashar 167.
2. Sepher Hayashar 165; Tanhuma Wayeshebh 9.

*

1. Zuleika's love for Joseph is a Judaean addition, evidently supplied to explain a mistaken reading of 'in prison'. The older Ephraimite account presents Joseph's master Potiphar as the Royal Prison governor, who placed the Butler and Baker under Joseph's charge. Joseph was 'in prison' merely as a warder.

2. Some midrashic commentators considered Joseph's interpretations of these dreams too ephemeral, and therefore suggested more edifying ones that Joseph had discreetly kept to himself. Thus the vinestock represented the world; its three branches, Abraham, Isaac and Jacob; its blossom, the patriarchs' wives; its ripe grapes, the twelve tribes. Or the vinestock represented the Law; its three branches, Moses, Aaron and Miriam; its blossom, the Assembly of Israel; and its grapes, the righteous souls of each generation. Or the vinestock represented Israel; its three branches, the three chief festivals; its budding, Israel's tribal increase in Goshen; its blossom, her redemption from bondage; and its grapes, the Exodus that would make Pharaoh's pursuing army stagger as if drunken. Similarly, the Chief Baker's three baskets represented the three kingdoms of Babylon, Media and Greece, which were to oppress Israel (see 28. 5); while the topmost basket (read as a fourth, not the third) stood for Rome, whose riches and luxuries would be destroyed by angels in the Messiah's Days.

3. The twelfth-century *Midrash Hagadol*, compiled in Yemen, states that the bird which ate from the Chief Baker's baskets symbolized the Messiah who would annihilate the kingdoms oppressing Israel. This symbol is elaborated by the mediaeval Kabbalists. In a *Description of the Garden of Eden*, dating perhaps from the eleventh century, and also in the Zohar, the Inner Hall or Paradise where the Messiah dwells is named 'The Bird's Nest'.

56

JOSEPH BECOMES VICEROY

(*a*) Two years later, Pharaoh dreamed that he was standing by the Nile, out of which stepped seven plump, sleek cows and began grazing on the papyrus reed. Seven lean, wretched-looking cows followed after a while but, instead of grazing, ravenously devoured their sisters—horns, hooves and all. Pharaoh awoke in horror. Falling asleep again, he dreamed of seven plump ears of corn that grew from a single stalk; but another seven ears growing near by, empty of grain and withered by the East Wind, swallowed them down.

At day break, Pharaoh sent for his soothsayers and recounted the dreams. None of their interpretations satisfied him. They said: 'The seven sleek cows indicate that you will beget seven beautiful daughters; the lean ones, that they will all die of a wasting ailment. The seven plump ears of corn indicate that you will conquer seven nations; the withered, that they will afterwards rebel.'[1]

(*b*) Observing Pharaoh's distress, Merod, the Chief Butler, suddenly remembered Joseph. He had not, indeed, been ungrateful: Joseph's case constantly troubled him, and he would tie knots in his kerchief as a reminder; but always forgot what they meant when he entered Pharaoh's presence. God thus delayed matters until the time should be ripe. Merod now told Pharaoh how accurately Joseph interpreted dreams, and pleaded for his release. Pharaoh thereupon summoned Joseph, who was at once shaved, dressed in decent garments, and brought into the Royal Council Chamber.

Pharaoh said: 'I am told that you interpret dreams.'

Joseph answered: 'Not I, but the Living God who speaks through me! He will set Pharaoh's mind at rest.'

Pharaoh told his dreams, adding that after the lean cows had swallowed the sleek, they looked as hungry as ever.

'God has sent Pharaoh two dreams with the same meaning,' said Joseph. 'The seven sleek cows and the seven plump ears of corn stand for years; likewise the lean cows and the empty ears. Seven years of plenty must be followed by seven years of famine so severe that the time of plenty will be quite forgotten. Pharaoh's second dream reinforces the first, and advises instant action. God herewith counsels Pharaoh to choose a trustworthy Viceroy, capable of providing against the evil days ahead; he must instruct his officers to buy up one fifth of the country's grain and pulses during the seven plentiful years. Let this surplus be stored under Pharaoh's seal in the Royal Granaries, one at each provincial city, as a reserve against the years of famine.'[2]

(*c*) The whole Court was convinced that Joseph had spoken the truth, and Pharaoh asked: 'Where can I find another man who will thus follow the dictates of the Living God?' Since no answer came, Pharaoh turned to Joseph and said: 'Inasmuch as God has revealed these things to you, we need look no farther. I appoint you my Viceroy over all Egypt, and whatever orders you give to the people, they shall also be mine. I reserve no more than my Pharaonic dignity, which is superior to yours.'

So saying, Pharaoh took the seal ring from his finger and put it on Joseph's, presented him with a royal linen apron, and hung a golden chain around his neck. He then pronounced: 'I name you Zaphenath-Paneah'—which means *Through him the Living God speaks*—'and no man in my dominions shall dare lift a hand or move a foot without your leave!' Pharaoh also lent Joseph a conveyance second in splendour only to his own chariot of state. The people hailed him as 'Abrech', and he ruled over all Egypt, though still in his thirtieth year. Joseph's officers now bought up surplus grain and pulses, and stored them in the provincial granaries.[3]

(*d*) Then, because Joseph would accept no praise, but gave God the credit for whatever he had spoken or done wisely, and because he looked modestly down when young Egyptian women admired his beauty, God rewarded him with long life, prosperity, and a peculiar gift enjoyed by his descendants: immunity from the evil eye.[4]

(*e*) By Pharaoh's favour, Joseph married Asenath, daughter of Potiphera, the priest of On. She bore him two sons, the first of whom he named 'Manasseh', saying 'God has made me *forget* my sufferings and my exile!'; and the second 'Ephraim', saying 'God has made me *fruitful*, despite affliction!'[5]

(*f*) According to some, however, Asenath was the bastard daughter of his sister Dinah, adopted by Zuleika and Potiphar, whom they identify with Potiphera. Asenath, they explain, accused Zuleika to Potiphar of having lied; whereupon Potiphar gave her in marriage to Joseph, by way of admission that he had done no wrong.

Others deny the identity of Potiphera with Potiphar; or of this

Asenath with Dinah's daughter, and say that Pharaoh's eldest son was Joseph's rival for Asenath's love.[6]

1. *Genesis* XLI. 1–8; Gen. Rab. 1093.
2. *Genesis* XLI. 9–36; Gen. Rab. 1085, 1086, 1094; Tanhuma Miqes 3; Sepher Hayashar 174.
3. *Genesis* XLI. 37–46.
4. Gen. Rab. 1268–69; Num. Rab. 14.6; Tanhuma Buber Num. 44; PRE, ch. 39; Mid. Hagadol Gen. 628–29; Targ. Yer. *Gen.* XLIX. 22.
5. *Genesis* XLI. 50–52.
6. Origen, Catena Nicephori I. 463; *Prayer of Asenath.*

*

1. The historical basis of this myth seems to be the rise, under the eighteenth-dynasty Pharaohs Amenhotep III, and Amenhotep IV, of a Semitic general named Yanhamu, who is mentioned in the Tell-Amarna letters as controlling the granaries of Yarimuta (or 'Jarmuth'—*Joshua* XII. 11) and governing the Egyptian domains in Palestine. He was not the first Palestinian to hold high office under the Pharaohs: Thotmes III's armour-bearer Meri-Re and his brother, the priest User-Min, were Amorites; and later Pharaoh Merneptah's Chief Spokesman was Ben Matana, a Canaanite. This Yanhamu had a high-ranking colleague, Dudu, the Hebrew form of which is *Dodo, Dodi,* or *Dodai*—a name occurring in 2 *Samuel* XXIII. 9, 24, and in *Judges* x. 1, etc.—and may well have been a Hebrew himself. When, in the Amarna letters, Syrian authorities petition Pharaoh Amenhotep IV for armed help, they add that Yanhamu is acquainted with their circumstances. Ribaddi, King of Gebal, begs Pharaoh to tell Yanhamu: 'Ribaddi is under your authority, and whatever evil the King of the Amorites does him, will harm you too.' Ribaddi later asks that Yanhamu shall be sent with an army to his assistance. Yanhamu had brought Yakhtiri, the commandant of Joppa and Gaza, and apparently his fellow-countryman, to the Egyptian court while still a child. Yanhamu may have been a slave; we learn from the Amarna letters that Syrians and Palestinians sometimes sold their children for corn at Yarimuta.

2. According to *Genesis*, Pharaoh gave Joseph 'garments of linen' but, this being no particular honour, the royal apron, or *shendit,* is evidently intended.

3. There was nothing against Pharaoh's promoting a minister as his Viceroy. Ptahhotep (about 2500 B.C.), known as 'Pharaoh's double' substituted at times for his absent master, using all the royal titles and being entrusted with the Great Seal. The office of 'Director of Granaries', though usually distinct from that of Viceroy, was important enough to be held by royal princes. This same Ptahhotep, in his *Maxims,* insists on the prime need of keeping the granaries well stocked against years of famine. One such famine is recorded in a Beni-Hasan cave-inscription on the tomb of Amene, a feudal prince of the Middle Empire. Amene had made due provision for this famine and, it is claimed, did not afterwards exact arrears

of produce from the farmers when favourable rises of the Nile had given them heavy crops of wheat and barley. One Baba, a nobleman of the seventeenth (Hyksos) dynasty, whose tomb is at El-Kab, mentions a famine that lasted many years. Some historians identify this with Joseph's famine —but details of the *Genesis* story reflect either an earlier or a later date than the Hyksos period.

4. The marriage of the Viceroy to a Sun-priest's daughter, and Pharaoh's acceptance of Joseph's monotheistic religion, both suggest that he was Amenhotep IV, the daring religious reformer who worshipped only Aten, the solar disk, changed his name to Akhenaten, and built a new capital at Amarna.

5. It had been suggested that Joseph's title, which makes no sense in either Hebrew or Egyptian, may represent *Zaphnto-Pa'anhi*, 'Nourisher of Life'. *Abrech* is not an Egyptian word, but recalls the Assyrio-Babylonian *abaraku*, a title given to the highest dignities, meaning 'Divinely Blessed'. Asenath's name was perhaps 'Anhesaten', which Akhenaten's own daughter bore (see 49. *h*). Akhenaten's High Priest of Aten is known to have been one Meri-re; and Potiphera's name may have been substituted for his by a confusion with Potiphar, Joseph's original owner.

6. Most of the midrashic embellishments on this myth are idle and out of key: among them is a tale of how Pharaoh's throne was set at the top of seventy stairs, and visiting princes or ambassadors ascended as many stairs as they knew languages: seventy being the canonical number of languages spoken after the Tower of Babel fell (see 22. *h*). Joseph, being granted by God a knowledge of all tongues, ascended to the very top and sat beside Pharaoh. He is also said to have fought a successful campaign against the 'Men of Tarshish', who had attacked the Ishmaelites. 'Tarshish' was southern Spain, or perhaps Sardinia, but the midrash equates it with the gold-producing Land of Havilah, because Solomon's Tarshish ships were said to have sailed for gold.

57

THE FAMINE

(*a*) Seven years of plenty came and went; seven years of famine followed. When all private bins were empty, Joseph opened the Royal Granaries and sold corn to the people. He had stored grain and pulses in each provincial city, and mixed them with dust from the very fields where they grew, knowing this to be the one sure safeguard against maggots and mildew. The Egyptians did not take such precautions, and their own stores soon rotted.

Famine spread beyond the bounds of Egypt, and Joseph collected vast sums of money from the sale of corn to Arabians, Canaanites, Syrians and others. He told his officers: 'In the name of Pharaoh and his Viceroy! All strangers wishing to buy corn must come in person and, if found to have bought it for resale rather than for their own needs, will be put to death. No man may bring more than one pack-beast, or fail to sign his name, his father's and his grandfather's, in receipt of purchase.' Joseph also made them submit a daily list of buyers. He knew that his brothers would arrive before long, and wished to be informed at once.[1]

(*b*) When the Egyptians were left penniless, Joseph let them buy corn with cattle and, in time, every herd passed into Pharaoh's hands. They then offered Joseph first their land, and finally their bodies in payment. Thus Pharaoh became sole owner of Egypt, entitled to move people from city to city, like the slaves they now were. Only the endowed priesthood kept their land and liberty.

In the third year, Joseph dealt out seed-corn, obliging the farmers to pay Pharaoh one-fifth of its produce in perpetuity. This law is still observed.[2]

(*c*) Jacob, hearing of corn for sale in Egypt, ordered his sons to go there and buy what they could. All set off except Benjamin, whom Jacob kept at home, saying: 'He might meet with an accident on the way.'

Jacob warned his sons: 'When you reach Egypt, tell as few people as possible that you are buying corn. Practice humility, efface yourselves, beware of jealous eyes! Enter Pharaoh's city by different gates, and never be seen conversing together.' They obeyed these orders on arrival; but, that evening, when the day's list of foreign traders was submitted to Joseph, he noticed their names and sent for them. They were arrested in the harlots' quarter where, driven by stings of conscience, they had gone to inquire about their lost brother from the resident slave-dealers.[3]

(*d*) Ushered into Joseph's presence, they fell on their faces before him. He addressed them roughly through an interpreter: 'From what country do you come, and what is your business?'

'We come from Canaan to buy corn,' they answered.

Joseph roared: 'You are spies!'

'My lord,' they protested fawningly, 'we are not spies but honest, decent men travelling on legitimate business.'

Joseph cut them short: 'If you were honest men, why did you enter this city each by a different gate? And if decent men, why did you spend so long in the harlots' quarter?'

'We entered by different gates on our father's advice,' Judah answered, 'and in the harlots' quarter we made inquiries about some lost goods.'

Joseph insisted: 'You are clearly a band of soldiers, sent here by Pharaoh's enemies to report on the defences of Egypt.'

'I assure Your Eminence that we are all sons of a single Hebrew father settled in Canaan,' said Judah. 'Formerly we were twelve, but one is now dead, and the youngest stayed at home.'

'You have entered this city,' Joseph pronounced, 'like a libertine bent on uncovering the nakedness of another man's wife.' Then he studied his silver divining-cup and said: 'Moreover, I see in this cup that two of you once massacred the inhabitants of a fortified city; and that, together, you sold a near kinsman to travelling merchants. By Pharaoh's life, I will not release you until I have seen your youngest brother! One of you may fetch him, and thus let me verify your story. Meanwhile I shall imprison you all.'

He confined his brothers to a dungeon, but on the evening of the third day told them: 'Since my God is merciful, and requires mercy of His worshippers, I am keeping only a single hostage. The others are free to take their corn home. When they return, however, the youngest brother must be with them.'

Unaware that Joseph knew Hebrew, they whispered among themselves: 'This is our punishment for abandoning Joseph when he cried out from the pit!'

Reuben said: 'I warned you then not to ill-treat the child; but none would listen. Now his ghost cries out for vengeance.'

Their words affected Joseph so forcibly that he withdrew awhile and wept. Soon he washed his face, came back, ordered Simeon to be put in fetters again, and sent the rest away, after giving secret orders that, when their sacks were filled, each man's purchase money should be hidden in the sack's mouth.[4]

(*e*) At an inn near the frontier, one of them went out to fetch a little grain, and found his money among it. He ran to tell the others, who cried terror-stricken: 'What will God do next?'

When they reached home and told Jacob of their adventures, he said: 'You have already bereaved me of two children. Joseph has been killed, Simeon lies in fetters, and now you ask for Benjamin too! This is grief heaped upon grief.'

Reuben cried: 'I will leave you my own two sons as hostages. Kill them, if I return without Simeon and Benjamin!'

Jacob answered: 'Benjamin is the sole surviving son of my beloved wife Rachel. If any accident befalls him, my soul will descend in sorrow to the Pit . . . I will never let you take him!'[5]

1. *Genesis* XLI. 53–57; Gen. Rab. 1105, 1122–23; Tanhuma Buber Gen. 194; Sepher Hayashar 182–84; PRE, ch. 39.
2. *Genesis* XLVII. 13–26.
3. *Genesis* XLII. 1–5; Gen. Rab. 1109, 1121–23; Tanhuma Buber Gen. 193–94, 202; Targ. Yer. *Gen.* XLII. 5; Mid. Hagadol Gen. 635; Sepher Hayashar 184–85.
4. *Genesis* XLII. 6–25; Gen. Rab. 1124; Tanhuma Buber Gen. 203; Sepher Hayashar 186.
5. *Genesis* XLII. 26–38.

*

1. That Joseph required the Egyptians to pay Pharaoh one-fifth of their grain provides mythic authority for an arrangement which persists today between tenant farmers and feudal landlords in many parts of the Middle East. It seems, however, to have been introduced into Egypt by the Hyksos conquerors two or three centuries before the days of Amenhotep IV. Only priests were excused the due.

2. Among the midrashic fancies attached to this myth is Joseph's insistence that all Egyptians who sold their bodies should be circumcised; but circumcision was already an ancient Egyptian custom. His mixing of dust with the corn, ingeniously excused as a preservative measure, may be a reminiscence of how mediaeval millers adulterated their bread stuffs. According to another midrash, Joseph piously withheld enormous profits, made in Pharaoh's name, for the enrichment of his own family; this was

tacitly excused by God's later command in *Exodus* III. 22: 'Ye shall despoil the Egyptians!'

3. The brothers are said to have visited the harlots' quarter on the assumption that so handsome a boy as Joseph would have been sold to a sodomitic brothel. Jacob's alleged advice, like his separation of the flocks into two camps, and the space he put between herds sent as gifts to Esau (see 47. *a*), are reminders to Jews of the Dispersal that extreme caution and dissimulation are called for when dealing with a Gentile power.

4. The editors of *Genesis* have not troubled to correct Jacob's remark about his soul descending to the Pit; he therefore professes no greater faith in the Resurrection than Esau (see 38. 5, 40. 3 and 61. 4–5).

5. Silver divination cups used in the cult of Anubis, the Egyptian Hermes, are mentioned by Pliny. It appears that a portrait of the god was engraved inside the cup. The diviner filled it with water, into which he dropped some small object, and then watched how the ripples affected the god's expression. Talmudists assumed that such cups had guardian angels (*sare hakos*) to whom they attributed divinatory powers.

58

THE BROTHERS' RETURN

(*a*) Soon all the corn which Jacob's sons brought from Egypt was eaten. He told them to go and buy more.

Judah answered: 'Pharaoh's Viceroy forbade us to return without our brother Benjamin. Unless you let him come, we must stay at home and starve.'

'But why were you such fools as to admit having a younger brother?'

'He questioned us so closely that we dared not lie. How could we anticipate his demand for Benjamin? Put the lad in my charge, Father, and if I do not bring him home again, lay me under a perpetual curse. Had you given us leave at once, we might by now have twice gone to Egypt and back, and felt no hunger. Moreover, Simeon would be free.'

At last Jacob gave way: 'Go, then . . . Take the Viceroy suitable gifts—balsam, honey, spices, gum-mastic, nuts and almonds—also double the money you paid last time, besides returning what was mistakenly placed in your sacks. And when you present Benjamin to this harsh man, may God make him show mercy . . . If I must be bereaved of my children, why, that is His will!'[1]

(*b*) On reaching Egypt, the brothers announced Benjamin's arrival, whereupon Joseph sent them an invitation to dine at the Palace. They told the Chief Steward that their corn money had been accidentally repaid them. 'Say no more,' he answered, 'such miracles often happen, if God takes a hand in human affairs. His Eminence, however, acknowledges full payment; and now that you have brought your youngest brother, he has consented to free Simeon.'[2]

(*c*) Simeon soon appeared, looking none the worse; and the brothers were given water to wash their feet, and fodder to set before their pack-beasts. When led into Joseph's hall, they prostrated themselves, and offered him Jacob's gifts.

Joseph asked: 'Is the old man still alive?'

'Your servant is alive and well,' Judah answered humbly.

Joseph turned to Benjamin: 'So this is your youngest brother? God bless you, my lad!' Then, unable any longer to restrain his tears, he withdrew and wept in secret. Presently, however, he came back and ordered dinner; but ate alone, as suited his dignity. Since Egyptians consider shepherds no better than swineherds, the brothers were kept apart from the courtiers. They sat in order of birth, wondering at their honourable treatment. Slaves served them with dainties from Joseph's table; yet they could not understand why Benjamin's helping should be five times larger than any other. A butler filled their wine-cups again and again, until they grew as drunken as Joseph himself.[3]

(*d*) Joseph ordered his Chief Steward to return the brothers' money while filling their corn sacks, and hide his own silver divining-cup in Benjamin's. The Steward obeyed and, at daybreak, watched them lead off their laden asses. Joseph then summoned him and said: 'Take a chariot, pursue those Hebrews, ask them why they have repaid my kindness with deceit, by stealing my divining-cup.'

The Steward soon overtook the brothers, who cried in astonishment: 'How can His Eminence accuse us of such villainy? Did we not return him the money paid us in error? Is it likely that we should steal silver or gold from the Viceregal Palace? Search our sacks, and if you find any cup, enslave us all!'

'My orders,' answered the Steward, 'are to arrest only the thief.'

When they unloaded their beasts, he made as if to search the sacks, until at last he found Joseph's cup in Benjamin's. They beat Benjamin unmercifully, shouting: 'Take that, and that, light-fingered wretch! You have shamed us worse than did your mother Rachel by her theft of Laban's teraphim.' Having torn their garments in grief, and reloaded the asses, they went back to Joseph's Palace.[4]

(*e*) Once more the brothers grovelled before Joseph. He asked: 'Why this folly? Was it not manifest that I could divine the present, past, and future even without my silver cup?'

Judah answered: 'What can we say to Your Eminence? How clear ourselves of guilt? God is punishing a crime that we committed long ago. Enslave us all, not merely our knavish brother.'

Shaking the edge of his purple cloak, Joseph replied: 'Far be it from me to accuse you of complicity! I shall, indeed, enslave Benjamin; but the rest of you may return to Canaan.'

'What shall we tell our unhappy father?' asked Judah in despair.

'Tell him,' Joseph answered, 'that the rope has followed the bucket into the well.'

Judah begged Joseph to hear him out, while he recounted the whole story. Then he offered to take Benjamin's place, adding: 'You understand now that I cannot confront my father without him?'[5]

(*f*) Joseph dismissed his attendants and, weeping unashamedly at last, asked the brothers in Hebrew: 'Is our father truly still alive?'

They did not know how to answer, thinking him mad.

Joseph beckoned them closer. Terror-stricken, they obeyed. 'I am your brother Joseph, whom you sold into Egypt,' he said. 'But, pray, feel no undue remorse: because God Himself prompted your designs. There have now been two years of famine in Egypt, and five more must follow, without ploughing or reaping. God sent me ahead and appointed me Viceroy to provide for you all. Hurry home, and tell our father that I am alive! Beg him to come without delay, bringing his flocks, herds, and possessions to the Land of Goshen, which lies near this city. Neither you nor my brother Benjamin can doubt that I am speaking the truth. So do as I ask!'

With that, Joseph embraced Benjamin, after which he and the others exchanged fraternal kisses.[6]

1. *Genesis* XLIII. 1–14.
2. *Genesis* XLIII. 15–23.
3. *Genesis* XLIII. 24–34.
4. *Genesis* XLIV. 1–13; Tanhuma Buber Gen. 198; Agadat Bereshit 146–47; Sepher Hayashar 194.
5. *Genesis* XLIV. 14–34; Gen. Rab. 1163; Sepher Hayashar 196–97; Yalqut Gen. 150.
6. *Genesis* XLV. 1–15.

*

1. This is historical fiction, but accounts for certain Hebrew shepherds, settled north-east of the Delta, who had given their townships such un-Egyptian names as Succoth, Baal-Zephon, and Migdol. Goshen, between the Pelusian branch of the Nile and Lake Timsah, was a district which, in Joseph's day, lay too far from the Nile floods to be arable, though providing good pasture. Some generations later, however, Rameses II irrigated Goshen by digging a canal, and built the cities of Rameses and Pithom with Hebrew labour (*Exodus* I. 11). Rameses II seems to have been the Pharaoh who 'knew not Joseph' (*Exodus* I. 8), and against whom Moses rebelled.

2. Joseph here anticipates the well-known modern technique of extorting confessions by first frightening the victim, then reassuring him, then frightening him again, until he grows confused and breaks down.

3. Shaking the edge of one's cloak for 'I will have nothing to do with this!' remains a common gesture in the Middle East. Joseph's enigmatic message to Jacob: 'The rope has followed the bucket into the well,' means: 'This is the consequence of your sons' having lowered me into the dry well at Dothan.'

59

JACOB IN EGYPT

(*a*) Hearing that Joseph's brothers had arrived, Pharaoh told him: 'If your father Jacob should bring his entire household here, he can count upon my royal welcome. Provide wagons for the women and children; and since I have placed all the wealth of Egypt at his disposal, persuade him to leave behind whatever possession may prove cumbersome.'

Joseph gave each of his brothers, except Benjamin, a handsome new robe; Benjamin received five such, also three hundred pieces of silver. Besides wagons and bales of fodder, he sent Jacob twenty asses laden with valuables and all manner of rich foods. His parting words were: 'No harsh thoughts on the journey, pray!'[1]

(*b*) The brothers were still debating how they should break their good news to Jacob, when Serah, Asher's daughter, a modest girl though an accomplished musician, came to meet them near Hebron. They handed her an Egyptian harp, saying: 'Go at once to your grandfather Jacob, pluck this instrument and sing as follows:

Joseph is not dead, not dead;
He wears upon his head
The crown of Egypt's land.
He is not dead, not dead—
Do you understand?'

Serah did as she was told, singing the words softly to him over and over again, until she was certain that they had lodged in his heart. Suddenly Jacob recognized the truth. He blessed Serah, sighing: 'Daughter, you have revived my spirit. May the shadow of death never disquiet you! Come, that song again! It is sweeter than honey to my ears.'[2]

(*c*) Thereupon the brothers arrived, clad in royal garments. They announced loudly: 'Joseph is alive, alive! He has become Viceroy of Egypt!' Jacob saw the wagons and laden asses, and cried: 'O joy! Glory be to God! It is true then? Shall I after all be restored to my favourite son?'

He now shook off the ashes of mourning, washed, trimmed his beard, dressed in the royal garments which had been brought him, and invited every king in Canaan to a three-day banquet; after which he set out for Egypt with his flocks, herds, possessions, and a household of seventy souls, not counting wives and servants.[3]

(*d*) At Beersheba, Jacob offered burned sacrifices, and God spoke in a dream: 'Fear not, Jacob, to visit Egypt under My protection! I will make Israel a great people. Afterwards I will bring you back again, and Joseph shall close your dying eyes.'[4]

(*e*) On hearing the news from Judah, who had ridden ahead, Joseph at once harnessed his chariot horses and drove down to Goshen. He and Jacob embraced tearfully, and Jacob sobbed: 'I am ready to die, my son, now that we have met again!'

Joseph told his brothers: 'I shall inform Pharaoh of your arrival. If he inquires about your occupation, admit that you are shepherds. Although Egyptians regard shepherds as unclean, no harm will attend you here in Goshen.'[5]

(*f*) He presented five of his brothers to Pharaoh, who appointed them overseers of the royal flocks, herds and droves in that region; then presented Jacob also. When Pharaoh politely asked his age, Jacob answered: 'Unlike my immediate ancestors, I have aged rapidly. Few and evil have been the years of my life; a mere one hundred and thirty in all.' With that, he blessed Pharaoh and went back to Goshen. But God reproached him: 'Jacob, I saved you from Esau and Laban; I saved Joseph from the pit and made him Viceroy of Egypt; and I saved this entire household from starvation! Yet you dare complain that your days have been few and evil! For this ingratitude I will shorten them by thirty-two years.'[6]

(*g*) At Pharaoh's orders, Joseph settled his father in the district of Rameses, and provided food for all Israel while the famine lasted. Jacob lived another seventeen years—thirty-two less than God had granted his father Isaac.[7]

1. *Genesis* XLV. 16–24.
2. Sepher Hayashar 2:2–04; cf. Abot diR. Nathan 90.
3. *Genesis* XLV. 25–28; Sepher Hayashar 202–04.
4. *Genesis* XLVI. 1–4.
5. *Genesis* XLVI. 5–34.
6. *Genesis* XLVII. 1–10; Tanhuma Buber Introd. 132; Agadat Bereshit 85.
7. *Genesis* XLVII. 11–12, 28.

*

1. Midrashic additions to this story, reflecting Israel's two heroic revolts against the power of Rome, make Joseph's brothers show warlike defiance when Benjamin is arrested, and rout Pharaoh's entire army. Judah grinds iron bars to powder between his teeth, and utters so terrifying a shout that all the women who hear it miscarry, and the heads of Pharaoh's guards twist sideways and stay fixed—a memory, perhaps, of Egyptian reliefs in which soldiers' bodies face to the front, though their heads are in profile. He also burns the chariot given him by Pharaoh, because of its idolatrous decorations.

Jacob is credited with prescience of the Mosaic Law: he introduces the Feast of First Fruits before leaving Canaan, and fells the sacred acacias at Migdal beside Lake Gennesaret for Moses' use when the Ark of the Covenant should be built.

2. The chronicler of *Genesis* records that Jacob's household consisted of seventy souls, exclusive of the patriarchs' wives; but even if Jacob himself is counted, the names given add up to no more than sixty-nine. Commentators offer several irreconcilable explanations of this apparent error; one of these, by analogy with *Daniel* III. 25, reckons God as the seventieth soul. The only two women listed are Dinah, and Serah daughter of Asher. Serah, like Dinah, may have been a matriarchal clan.

3. There is no discrepancy between the famine caused by the Nile's failure to rise, and the provision of grazing in Goshen. Nile floods depend on heavy snows in Abyssinia, not on local rainfall. Jacob would hardly have starved at Beersheba while he could still pasture his flocks, none of which seem to have died there from drought. Perhaps southern Palestine depended on Egypt for its corn supply even in good years, and Hebrew pastoralists had come to treat bread as a necessity rather than a luxury.

60

THE DEATH OF JACOB

(*a*) Jacob, aware that his death was approaching, summoned Joseph to Goshen and said: 'Swear that you will lay me to rest not among Egyptians, but in the Cave of Machpelah at Hebron.'

Joseph answered: 'Am I a slave, that you demand an oath from me?'

'Nay, but put your hand beneath my thigh, and swear!'

'It is unseemly for a son to touch his father's circumcision. Nevertheless, I swear by the Living God that you shall be buried at Hebron.'[1]

(*b*) Joseph brought Ephraim and Manasseh to Jacob's death-bed. Jacob sat up with great difficulty, and said: 'God once blessed me at Luz in Canaan, promising that my sons should become tribes and hold Canaan as their everlasting possession. Though these sons of yours, Ephraim and Manasseh, were born before I visited Egypt, I count them no less my own than Reuben and Simeon. But let your younger children rank as their sons.' Then his mind wandered: 'When I left Padan-Aram, my wife Rachel died in Canaan, at some distance from Ephrath . . .' He was evidently grieved that his body would lie next to Leah's, not to his beloved Rachel's; but saw no help for it.[2]

(*c*) Noticing Ephraim and Manasseh, he asked forgetfully: 'Who are these?'

'They are my sons; born, as you say, in Egypt.'

'I will bless them.'

Joseph brought the lads forward, and Jacob sighed: 'I never thought to see your face again, let alone your sons'. God has indeed been very merciful!'[3]

(*d*) Bowing reverently, Joseph set Ephraim to Jacob's left, and Manasseh to the right. But Jacob, crossing his arms, rested the right hand on Ephraim's head, and the left on Manasseh's. He said:

'The God of my fathers Abraham and Isaac,
The God who has always been my shepherd,

The Holy One who has saved me from evil,
Let Him bless these lads, whom I name my sons,
As He blessed my fathers Abraham and Isaac;
They shall grow to a multitude over the earth!'

When Joseph tried to alter the position of Jacob's hands, protesting: 'Not so, my father; because Manasseh is the first-born. Pray set your right hand on his head, not on Ephraim's,' Jacob replied obstinately: 'I know, my son, I know! But though Manasseh will become great, Ephraim will become greater still.'

Having blessed them both with: 'May it always be fortunate in Israel to wish: "God prosper you like Ephraim and Manasseh!"', Jacob told Joseph: 'He will bring you safely back to inherit, in Canaan, the royal portion which I have denied your brothers: a Shoulder seized from the Amorites with my sword and bow.'[4]

(*e*) Jacob summoned his other sons, and said: 'I will now disclose the fates of all your posterity. Gather around, and listen!' Each of them expected a blessing; yet he punished Reuben for the lasciviousness that had prompted him to lie with Bilhah, by denying him his rights as the first-born; he also lamented the massacre done at Shechem by Simeon and Levi, cursing instead of blessing them—their fate, he said, was to be divided and scattered in Israel. Nevertheless, he praised Judah's lion-like courage, promising him a royal sceptre and an abundance of wine and milk. Zebulon, he announced, would become a tribe of merchants and seafarers. He compared Issachar to a strong pack-ass, cheerfully labouring in a pleasant land; Dan, to a serpent lurking by the highway, that stings passing horses and unseats their riders; Naphtali, to a swift doe running with fawns at her heels; Benjamin, to a hungry wolf. He told Gad: 'You will raid and be raided, but come off victorious in the end'; and Asher: 'You will harvest good corn and bake fine bread.' His chief blessing was reserved for Joseph, whom he compared to a strong young bull beside a fountain, scornful of sling-stones and arrows. God would destroy Joseph's enemies, and bless him with abundant rain, perpetual springs, rich flocks, fertile wives, and ancestral pride. Jacob did not, however, reveal the whole future—because God made him forget his promise. He merely repeated what he had told Joseph: that he must be buried in the Cave of Machpelah beside Abraham and Sarah, Isaac and Rebekah, and his own wife Leah.[5]

(*f*) Joseph had Jacob's body embalmed, which took forty days; and ordered seventy days of public mourning throughout Egypt.

Having asked and obtained Pharaoh's permission to visit Canaan and bury Jacob there, he marched off at the head of a vast mourning train—not only his brothers and the Viceregal household, but representatives from every city in Egypt—attended by a heavily armed escort.[6]

(*g*) They entered Canaan, followed the highroad into Gilead, where they wailed and wept seven full days at Atad's threshing floor. Because the wondering Canaanites cried: 'This is indeed a solemn *mourning of the Egyptians!*', the place was ever afterwards known as Abel-Mizraim. Thence the cortège circled back towards Hebron, laid Jacob to rest in the Cave of Machpelah, mourned seven days more, and returned across the frontier.[7]

(*h*) Some say that Jacob's brother Esau was still alive, and that his Edomite household accompanied Joseph on the progress through Canaan. At Hebron, however, they blocked the approach to Machpelah, and Esau shouted: 'I shall never let Jacob be buried in this cave, which is mine by right!' Fighting broke out, and Dan's deaf-and-dumb son Hushim beheaded Esau with a sword. The Edomites fled, carrying off his trunk to Mount Seir, but leaving the head behind for burial.[8]

(*i*) Jacob being now dead, the brothers feared that Joseph would take tardy vengeance on them, and sent a message: 'Our father, before he died, told us to beg your forgiveness. You will, we trust, respect his wishes.'

Joseph called them to the Palace, and when they once more abased themselves, crying 'We are your slaves!', answered: 'Have no fear! Though you plotted against my life, God turned this evil act to good account: saving innumerable lives through me. I shall therefore continue to provide for Israel.' They went away reassured.[9]

(*j*) Others say that because Joseph embalmed Jacob's body, as if God could not have preserved it, also letting Judah style Jacob 'your servant' without protest, he was outlived by all his brothers.[10]

1. *Genesis* XLVII 28–31; PRE, ch. 39; Mid. Hagadol Gen. 711 and 357; BHM vi. 83; Targ. Yer. *Gen.* XLVII. 30.
2. *Genesis* XLVIII. 1–7; Pesiqta Rabbati 11b; Mid. Hagadol Gen. 717–18.
3. *Genesis* XLVIII. 8–11.
4. *Genesis* XLVIII. 12–22.
5. *Genesis* XLIX. 1–32.
6. *Genesis* L. 1–9.
7. *Genesis* L. 10–13.
8. Sepher Hayashar 211–13; B. Sota 13a; PRE, ch. 39; Gen. Rab. 1288.
9. *Genesis* L. 14–21.
10. Gen. Rab. 1286; Mid. Agada Gen. 116; Sepher Hayashar 209.

*

1. Jacob's blessing gives mythological authority for the political future of Ephraim and Manasseh. It postulates an original tribe of Joseph consisting of several clans which, after invading Canaan under Joshua, formed a federation with the already resident Leah, Bilhah and Zilpah tribes. Joseph's two most powerful clans then claimed to be independent tribes, each equal in rank with its new allies, and adopted the lesser clans—Joseph's unnamed younger sons in the myth—as 'sons' of their own. Manasseh had originally been senior to Ephraim (or whatever the clan was first called which occupied Mount Ephraim—see 45. 2), but now admitted itself junior. Similar shifts in tribal status and structure still occur among Arabian desert tribes (see 42. 4–5 and 50. 3).

Jacob's final blessing on his grandsons is repeated to this day by orthodox Jewish fathers each Sabbath Eve. Touching their sons' heads, they say: 'God prosper you like Ephraim and Manasseh!'

2. Two early versions of the myth, one Ephraimite and the other Judaean, have here been somewhat carelessly combined, so that Jacob's speech rambles in a manner attributable to a failing memory. Ephraim and Judah, of course, come off far better than the other tribes; and even the late priestly editor has refrained from converting Jacob's curse on Levi into a blessing.

3. Joseph's funeral progress to Gilead with an armed escort suggests that he was asserting Israel's sovereign claims over all Canaan; a hint exploited by late midrashim, which make him reconquer the country as far as the Euphrates. But that Atad's threshing floor—*atad* means 'camel thorn'—lay beyond Jordan, is a late gloss on the *Genesis* text, perhaps suggested by a misreading of 'the stream', namely the Torrent of Egypt (*Genesis* xv. 18), *alias* the River Zior, which formed the Canaanite-Egyptian frontier. In other words, Joseph's followers performed the mourning ceremony at a Canaanite village just beyond the border. *Abel-Mizraim* means no more than 'the Egyptian meadow'—*ebel*, 'mourning' is another word altogether. Syrian weddings and funerals are still celebrated on the level surface of threshing floors.

4. The Cave of Machpelah has been for centuries hidden by an Arab mosque, to which neither Christians nor Jews are admitted, and its contents remain a holy secret. Benjamin of Tudela, who visited Machpelah in 1163 A.D., wrote that the six sepulchres occupied a third and innermost cave. According to Josephus, they were built of the finest marble.

5. The 'Shoulder' bequeathed to Joseph was Shechem (see 49. 3. 5).

6. A midrashic embellishment of Jacob's death-bed blessings attributes to him the first use of Moses' *Shema*, 'Hear, O Israel!' (*Deuteronomy* vi. 3), which still remains the chief Jewish prayer.

61

THE DEATH OF JOSEPH

(*a*) Before dying at the age of one hundred and ten years, Joseph had great-grandchildren to dandle on his knees. One day he told the brothers: 'Our God will assuredly lead you back to Canaan, the Promised Land. Since I have now reached the end of life, pray take my body there with you, and He will repay your kindness.'

These were his last words. He was duly embalmed and laid in a sarcophagus on the banks of the River Sihor. All Egypt mourned him for seventy days.[1]

(*b*) Some say that Joseph made the brothers swear to bury him near Shechem, where he had once gone in search of them; and to bury Asenath in Rachel's tomb beside the road to Ephrath.[2]

(*c*) Pharaoh also died. His successor reigned without a Viceroy and, when he saw Israel multiplying faster than the Egyptians, remarked: 'A dangerous people! If Egypt should be invaded from the East, they might well choose to assist my enemies.' He therefore treated even Joseph's descendants as serfs, appointing taskmasters who forced them to build the treasure cities of Rameses and Pithom, and who made their lives a burden. This bondage continued for many generations, until Moses arose and led Israel out of Egypt to the Promised Land, taking with him the bones of Joseph, in fulfilment of his ancestor Levi's promise, and burying them at Shechem.[3]

1. *Genesis* L. 22–26; Sepher Hayashar 219.
2. Tanhuma Beshallah 2; Ex. Rab. 20.19; B. Sota 13b; Gen. Rab. 1035; Deut. Rab. 8.4; Mekhilta Beshallah 24b; Tanhuma Eqeb 6; *Test. of Joseph* XVII. 1–3; XVIII. 1–2; XIX. 1–11; XX. 1–6.
3. *Exodus* I. 8 ff.

*

1. The River Sihor (or Zior), is identified with the Torrent of Egypt (now the Wadi el Arish—see 60. 3). Thus Joseph's sarcophagus was placed as close to the Canaanite frontier as possible.

2. The *Genesis* myths suggest that Israel's early religion compromised between ancestor worship and the cult of an Aramaean tribal war-and-fertility god, not much different from those of Moab or Ammon, whose

power could be effective only in the particular territory occupied by his people—thus Naaman the Syrian later imports two mule-loads of Ephraimite earth in order to worship the God of Israel at Damascus (2 *Kings* v. 17). No references to any goddess are included, and in parts of the Joseph myth He is clearly equated with Akhenaten's monotheistic conception of a supreme universal god (see 56. 4).

3. When a dead man had been duly mourned, he was thought to have joined the honourable company of his ancestors in Sheol, or The Pit, where they lay fast asleep (*Job* III. 14–19). Mourners who approached the clan's burial ground removed their shoes (*Ezekiel* XXIV. 17), as before visiting places traditionally sanctified by the tribal god's appearance (*Exodus* III. 5 and *Joshua* v. 15). The souls of the dead, however, did not slumber but were credited with powers of thought. They could be consulted by divination (1 *Samuel* XXVIII. 8–19), and were called 'the Knowing Ones' (*Leviticus* XIX. 31; *Isaiah* XIX. 3) because aware of their descendants' acts and fates. Thus Rachel mourns from the grave for her distressed children (*Jeremiah* XXXI. 15). The dead were, in fact, underworld deities, or *elohim* (1 *Samuel* XXVIII. 13–20).

4. Unless buried among his ancestors, a dead man was banished to an unknown part of Sheol and denied proper worship. Hence Jacob's and Joseph's repetitive demands for burial in Canaan, and the terrible punishment inflicted on Korah, Dathan and Abiram by God, when the earth swallowed them up without the obligatory funeral rites (*Numbers* XVI. 31 ff). Sheol was still considered to be outside God's jurisdiction (*Psalms* LXXXVIII. 5–6; *Isaiah* XXXVIII. 18). But the body had to be complete, and even so the soul perpetually bore marks of its death, whether by the sword as in *Ezekiel* XXXII. 23 or by grief, as when Jacob feared that his grey hairs would go down in sorrow to the grave (*Genesis* XLII. 38). Esau's loss of his head was considered a shameful calamity for Edom.

5. The notion that God controlled Sheol too does not occur until about the fifth century B.C. (*Job* XXVI. 6; *Psalm* CXXXIX. 8; *Proverbs* XV. 11); nor does that of the soul's resurrection until about a century later, when the unknown prophet whose words are included in *Isaiah* declared that all righteous Israelites should arise and participate in the Messianic Kingdom, quickened by God's 'dew of light' (*Isaiah* XXVI. 19). Sheol thus came to be treated as a Purgatory where souls await the Last Judgement. This is still Orthodox Jewish and also Catholic belief.

ABBREVIATIONS, SOURCES AND ANNOTATED BIBLIOGRAPHY

This list does not include the Old and New Testaments, nor the standard Greek and Roman authors.

A

ABODA ZARA. A. tractate of the *Babylonian Talmud*. See B.

ABOT DIR(ABBI) NATHAN. Ed. by Solomon Schechter, Vienna, 1887. Photostatic reprint, New York, 1945. This edition contains both versions of the book, which is a midrash of Tannaitic origin with many subsequent additions. Quoted by page.

ACTS OF ST. THOMAS. See *Gospel of St. Thomas*.

ADAMBUCH. *Das christliche Adambuch des Morgenlandes*. Aus dem Äthiopischen mit Bemerkungen übersetzt von A. Dillmann, Göttingen, 1853. An apocryphal *Book of Adam*, preserved in an Ethiopic text of the sixth century.

ADAMSCHRIFTEN. *Die Apokryphischen Gnostischen Adamschriften*. Aus dem Armenischen übersetzt und untersucht von Erwin Preuschen, Giessen, 1900. An apocryphal *Book of Adam* preserved in an Armenian text.

AGADAT BERESHIT. A late Hebrew midrash containing homilies on *Genesis*, based mainly on the *Tanhuma* (see *Tanhuma Buber*). Edited by Solomon Buber, Cracow, 1903. Photostatic reprint, New York, 1959.

AGADAT SHIR HASHIRIM. A tenth-century midrash on *Canticles*. Quoted by page of Solomon Schechter's edition, Cambridge, 1896.

AGUDAT AGADOT. Ed. Ch. M. Horowitz, Frankfurt a. M., 1881.

ALPHA BETA DIBEN SIRA. Two versions, one (*a*) in Aramaic and one (*b*) in Hebrew, of alphabetically arranged proverbs with explanations, attributed to Jesus ben Sira, author of the apocryphal *Ecclesiasticus*, but in fact a much later compilation. Quoted by folio of Steinschneider's edition, Berlin, 1858; or, if so stated, by page and column of *Otzar Midrashim* (q.v.).

ANET. See Pritchard.

APOC. OF ABRAHAM. An apocryphal book written originally in Hebrew or Aramaic in the late first century A.D. Ed. by George Herbert Box, London, 1918.

APOC. OF BARUCH, or 2 Baruch. An apocryphal book, written originally in Hebrew by orthodox Jews of the first century A.D. Extant in a Syriac version. See Charles, *The Apocrypha and Pseudepigrapha of the Old Testament*, Oxford, 1913, Vol. ii. pp. 470–526.

APOC. MOSIS. *Apocalypse of Moses*, ed. L. F. C. von Tischendorf, in his *Apocalypses Apocryphae*.

APOC. OF MOSES. Ed. Charles. See R. H. Charles (ed.), *The Apocrypha and Pseudepigrapha of the Old Testament*, Vol. ii. pp. 138 ff.

APPU FROM SHUDUL. A Hittite myth. Summarized by Th. H. Gaster in his *The Oldest Stories in the World*, New York, 1952, pp. 159–67, under the title 'Master Good and Master Bad'.

ARABIAN NIGHTS, or the Arabian Nights' Entertainments. Original title: *Alf Layla Walayla* ('A Thousand and One Nights'). A huge Arabic collection of early mediaeval folk stories.

ASCENSION OF ISAIAH. An apocryphal book composed of three parts: the Martyrdom of Isaiah, the Vision of Isaiah, and the Testament of Hezekiah. The first of these is of Jewish origin from the first century A.D.; the other two were the work of Christian writers. See Charles, *The Apocrypha and Pseudepigrapha of the Old Testament*, Vol. ii. pp. 155 ff.

ASENATH, PRAYER OF. See *Joseph and Asenath.*

AZULAI, ABRAHAM, HESED LEABRAHAM. A kabbalistic work of a sixteenth-century commentator. Printed in Wilna, 1877.

B

B. *Bavli* (Babylonian). The *Babylonian Talmud,* compiled in Babylonia around 500 A.D. Written partly in Hebrew, but mostly in Aramaic. Quoted by tractate (whose title follows the abbreviation B.) and folio.

BABA BATHRA. A tractate of the *Babylonian Talmud.* See B.

BABA KAMMA. A tractate of the *Babylonian Talmud.* See B.

BABA METZIA. A tractate of the *Babylonian Talmud.* See B.

BARAITA DIMASS. NIDDA. See Tosephta Atiqta.

BARAITA DIMAASE BERESHIT, ed. Chones, in Buber, *Yeri'ot Shelomo,* Warsaw, 1896, pp. 47–50. Photostatic reprint, New York, 1959.

2 BARUCH. See *Apoc. of Baruch.*

BATE MIDRASHOT. A collection of minor midrashim, compiled and edited by Shelomo Aharon Wertheimer, Jerusalem, 1914. Quoted by page of the second, 2-vol. edition, Jerusalem, 1953.

BEKHOROT. A tractate of the *Babylonian Talmud.* See B.

BERAKHOT. A tractate of the *Babylonian* and of the *Palestinian Talmud.* See B. and Yer.

BERESHIT RABBATI. A midrash on *Genesis,* abridged from a longer lost midrash compiled by Rabbi Moshe Hadarshan in the first half of the eleventh century at Narbonne. Quoted by page of Hanoch Albeck's edition, Jerusalem, 1940.

BEROSSUS'S BABYLONIAN HISTORY. Fragmentarily preserved in the works of Josephus Flavius, Eusebius, etc. Berossus himself was a priest of Bel in Babylonia during the third century B.C.

BHM. *Beth HaMidrash,* ed. by Adolph Jellinek, 6 vols., Leipzig, 1853–77; photostatic reprint, Jerusalem, 1938. A collection of 100 minor midrashim.

BOOK OF ADAM. See *Adambuch.*

BOOK OF THE DEAD. A collection of Egyptian funerary texts, covering a period of four thousand years. The Theban recension (from the 18th, 21st, and 22nd dynasties) was translated in Sir E. A. Wallis Budge's *The Book of the Dead,* 2nd ed., 1923.

BOOK OF ENOCH. See *Enoch.*

BOOK OF JUBILEES. See *Jubilees.*

C

CAVE OF TREASURES. See *Schatzhöhle.*

CHRONICON PASCHALE. Also known as the *Alexandrian Chronicle,* a seventh-century Byzantine chronicle of Biblical and other events from the Creation to Emperor Heraclius. Ed. by D. du Cange, Paris, 1688.

CHWOLSON, DANIEL A., *Die Ssabier und der Ssabismus.* St. Petersburg, 1856, 2 vols.

CLEMENTINE HOMILIES. An early third-century A.D. Christian tract written probably in Syria. See Ante-Nicene Christian Library, vol. xvii, Edinburgh, 1870.

D

DA'AT. *Sepher Da'at Zeqenim,* Ofen, 1834 (first published in Leghorn, 1783). A compilation of midrashic commentaries on the *Pentateuch.*

DAMASCIUS. Greek philosopher, born *c.* 480 A.D. in Damascus. Extant fragments of his writings include part of a life of Isidore (one of his teachers) and *Doubts and Solutions Respecting the First Principles,* ed. by C. E. Ruelle, 1889.

DEUT. RAB. *Deuteronomy Rabba,* a midrash on *Deuteronomy,* compiled *c.* 900 A.D. Quoted by chapter and paragraph of the Wilna, 1884, edition.

DILLMANN, CHRISTIAN FRIEDRICH AUGUST, *Genesis.* Edinburgh, 1897.

DIODORUS SICULUS. Greek historian, born in Agyrium, Sicily, flourished around 20 B.C. His *Historical Library,* originally in forty books, is only partly preserved and published (with translation) in the Loeb Classical Library.

DOUGHTY, CHARLES M., *Travels in Arabia Deserta,* London, 1888.

E

ECCL. RAB. *Ecclesiastes Rabba.* A midrash on *Ecclesiastes,* compiled in the tenth century. Quoted by chapter and verse of *Ecclesiastes,* from the Wilna, 1884, edition.

EDUYOT. A tractate of the *Mishna.* See M.

ELDAD HADANI, ed. Abraham Epstein, Pressburg, 1891. A partly invented description of the Ten Lost Tribes of Israel by a tenth-century Jewish traveller of East African origin.

ENOCH. The apocryphal *Book of Enoch,* written in either Hebrew or Aramaic during the first century B.C. in Palestine and preserved in Greek and Ethiopic texts. 2 *Enoch* is a different version of the same book preserved in a Slavonic text. The best English translations of both are made by Charles, *The Apocrypha and Pseudepigrapha of the Old Testament,* vol. ii. pp. 163 ff.

ENUMA ELISH ('When Above'), the Babylonian creation epic written in Akkadian. The best English translation is that of James B. Pritchard (ed.), *Ancient Near Eastern Texts*, Princeton, 1955, pp. 60–72.

EPHR. SYR. Ephraem Syrus, Commentary on Gen. See *Ephraemi Syrii Opera Omnia*, ed. B. Benedictus and Assemanus, Rome, 1737–43.

ERUBIN. A tractate of the *Babylonian* and of the *Palestinian Talmud*. See B. and Yer.

ESDRAS OF EZRA. The name of two apocryphal books attributed to Ezra: one preserved in Greek and called either *1 Esdras*, or *3 Esdras*; one preserved in Latin and called either *2 Esdras* or *4 Esdras*. Both written originally in Hebrew, in Palestine; the first probably dates from the fourth century B.C., the second from the first century A.D.

EUSEBIUS, *Praeparatio Evangelica*, ed. Gifford, Oxford, 1903. Eusebius of Caesarea (*c.* 260–340 A.D.), was Bishop of Caesarea, Palestine, and wrote several books of Church history.

EX. RAB. *Exodus Rabba*, a midrash on the Book of *Exodus*, compiled in Hebrew and Aramaic, in the eleventh century but containing much older material. Quoted by chapter and paragraph of the Wilna, 1884, edition.

G

GASTER, MA'ASIYOT. Moses Gaster (ed.), *The Exempla of the Rabbis*, London, 1924.

GEN. RAB. *Genesis Rabba*, a midrash on the Book of *Genesis*, compiled in the fifth century in Palestine. Quoted by page of the critical edition of J. Theodor and Ch. Albeck, Berlin, 1912–27, 2 vols.

GENESIS APOCRYPHON, ed. by N. Avigad and Y. Yadin, Jerusalem, 1956.

GILGAMESH AND THE WILLOW TREE. A Sumerian tablet from Ur, from *c.* 2000 B.C., published by Samuel N. Kramer as *Gilgamesh and the Huluppu-Tree*. The Oriental Institute of the University of Chicago, Assyriological Studies, No. 10, Chicago, 1938.

GILGAMESH EPIC. An Akkadian epic found in Ashurbanipal's (seventh century B.C.) library, but going back to second millennium B.C. Sumerian and Hittite prototypes. See Pritchard, *Ancient Near Eastern Texts*, pp. 72–99.

GINZBERG, L.J. *The Legends of the Jews*, by Louis Ginzberg, 7 vols., Philadelphia, 1909–46. The most important scholarly work on the subject.

GITTIN. A tractate of the *Babylonian Talmud*. See B.

GOSPEL OF ST. THOMAS. Published in Tischendorf's *Evangelia Apocrypha*.

GOSSE, PHILIP HENRY. The reference is to his book *Omphalos*.

GRAVES, ROBERT, *The Greek Myths*. Penguin Books, 2 vols., Baltimore, 1955.

GRAVES, ROBERT, *The White Goddess*, New York, 1948.

GUNKEL, HERMANN, *Schöpfung und Chaos in Urzeit und Endzeit*, 2nd ed., Göttingen, 1921.

H

HADAR. *Sepher Hadar Zeqenim*, ed. Leghorn, 1840. A collection of midrashic explanations to the Bible, culled from the Talmudic commentaries of the Tosaphists (thirteenth and fourteenth centuries).

HAGIGA. A tractate of the *Babylonian* and *Palestinian Talmud.* See B. and Yer.

HAGOREN. Louis Ginzberg, 'Hagadot Qetu'ot,' *Hagoren*, vol. 9, Berlin, 1923. The Hebrew literary magazine *Hagoren* was edited by Shemuel Abba Horodetzky in Berditschew and Berlin, 1899–1923.

HALLA. A tractate of the *Mishna.* See M.

HAMMURABI, LAWS OF. A legal code promulgated by Hammurabi (1728–1686 B.C.), the sixth king of the Old Babylonian (Amorite) Dynasty. See Pritchard, *Ancient Near Eastern Texts,* pp. 163–80.

HEIM, ROGER, and WASSON, R. GORDON, *Les Champignons Hallucinogènes du Mexique*, Paris, 1958.

HUCA. *Hebrew Union College Annual,* Cincinnati, Ohio, vols. i ff (1924 ff).

HULLIN. A tractate of the *Babylonian Talmud.* See B.

I

IMRE NOAM. Midrashic commentary on the *Pentateuch* by Jacob di Illescos (fourteenth century). Printed in Constantinople, 1539, and Cremona, 1565.

J

JACOB OF EDESSA. Also known as James of Edessa (died 708). Syrian Jacobite poet, commentator, letter-writer and translator of Greek works into Syriac.

JEROME. Hieronymi Questiones Hebraicae in Libro Geneseo e. recog. P. de Lagarde, Leipzig, 1868.

JEROME'S LATIN VULGATE. See Vulgate.

JONAS, HANS, *Gnosis und spätantiker Geist,* 2 vols., Göttingen, 1934–54.

JOSEPH AND ASENATH. An apocryphal book written in Hebrew by Jewish Essenes. Extant in a Greek translation. See Paul Riessler, *Altjüdisches Schrifttum ausserhalb der Bibel,* Augsburg, 1928, pp. 497–538.

JOSEPHUS FLAVIUS. Jewish historian of the first century A.D. Wrote in Greek. His major works are *The Wars of the Jews* and *The Antiquities of the Jews.*

JOSHUA B. SHU'AIB. See Shu'aib.

JUBILEES. The apocryphal *Book of Jubilees.* Written, probably in the second century B.C., in midrashic vein, by a Pharisaic Jew. The original Hebrew version has been lost. The best extant version is the Ethiopic. See Charles, *The Apocrypha and Pseudepigrapha of the Old Testament,* vol. ii. 1 ff.

K

KALIR. Eleazar Kalir, lived probably in the eighth century; wrote Hebrew religious poems, of which some two hundred are extant.

KEPHALAIA. A collection of Manichaean manuscripts, published by Polotzky and Schmidt, Stuttgart, 1935–9.

KERET EPIC. An Ugaritic legend dating from the fourteenth century B.C. See Pritchard, *Ancient Near Eastern Texts,* pp. 142–9.

KETUBOT. A tractate of the *Babylonian Talmud.* See B.

KIDDUSHIN. A tractate of the *Babylonian Talmud.* See B.

KORAN. The Bible of Islam: revealed to the Prophet Mohammed in the early seventh century at Mecca and Medina.

L

LEV. RAB. *Leviticus Rabba,* a midrash on the Book of *Leviticus,* compiled probably in the seventh century. Quoted by chapter and section from the Wilna, 1884, edition.

LIFE OF ADAM AND EVE. See *Vita Adae.*

LIQQUTE MIDRASHIM. A collection of thirty-one midrash-fragments, printed in BHM (q.v.) vol. v. pp. 155–64.

LIQQUTIM. *Liqqutim miMidrash Abkir,* ed. Solomon Buber, Vienna, 1883. A collection of the passages quoted by the *Yalqut* (q.v.) from the *Mid. Abkir* (q.v.).

LURIA. Textual comments on PRE by David Luria, printed in Warsaw, 1852. See PRE.

M

M. *Mishna.* The first code of Rabbinic law, written in Hebrew and compiled by Rabbi Jehuda Hanasi *c.* 200 A.D., in Palestine. Quoted by tractate, chapter, and paragraph.

MA'ASE ABRAHAM. A heroic midrash about the exploits of Abraham, originally written in Arabic, extant in a Hebrew translation. Printed in BHM (q.v.) vol. i. pp. 24–34.

1 MACCABEES. A historical book about the Maccabean period to the death of Simon (135 B.C.). Written in Hebrew in Palestine between 104 and 63 B.C. Extant in a Greek translation.

4 MACCABEES. A sermon about the rule of reason over the passions, written in Greek but in a strictly Jewish spirit, probably between 56 and 66 A.D.

MAKKOT. A tractate of the *Babylonian Talmud.* See B.

MANETHO. Egyptian priest and historian of the fourth century B.C. See *Manetho the Historian,* The Loeb Classical Library, Cambridge, Mass., 1940.

MASSEKHET SOFERIM. An extra-canonical tractate joined to the *Babylonian Talmud* (see B.) and dating from the times of the Geonim (i.e. between 589 and 1040 A.D.).

MEGILLA. A tractate of the *Babylonian Talmud.* See B.

MEKHILTA. *Mekhilta of Rabbi Ishmael,* ed. M. Friedmann, Vienna, 1870. A Tannaitic midrash on *Exodus,* primarily intended to elucidate the laws contained in *Exodus* XII–XXIII. The authorities quoted are Tannaites, i.e., sages of the school of Rabbi Ishmael, who lived in Palestine not later than the second century A.D. Quoted by Pentateuchal weekly section and page.

MEKHILTA DIR. SHIMON. A midrash on *Exodus* attributed to Rabbi Simeon ben Yohai (second century A.D.) and compiled by Hezekiah son of Hiyya (end of second century A.D.). Quoted by page of the critical edition by David Hoffmann, Frankfurt a. M., 1905.

MENAHOT. A tractate of the *Babylonian Talmud*. See B.

MGWJ. *Monatschrift für Geschichte und Wissenschaft des Judentums*. The foremost German Jewish scholarly journal. Appeared from 1852 to 1939, in Dresden and later in Breslau.

MID. *Midrash*. The generic name of a major type of Rabbinic literature, taking the form of exegetic expositions appended to Biblical verses. *Midrashim* (pl.) were written and compiled from the second to about the twelfth century.

MID. ABKIR. A lost midrash, probably compiled in the ninth century, of which some fifty passages are quoted in the *Yalqut Shimoni*. See *Yalqut*.

MID. ABKIR, ed. Marmorstein. See preceding entry.

MID. ADONAY BEHOKHMA YASAD ARETZ. A midrash on *Proverbs* III. 19: 'The Lord by wisdom founded the earth.' Printed in BHM (q.v.), vol. v. pp. 63–9.

MID. AGADA. A midrash on the *Pentateuch*. Edited by Solomon Buber, photostatic reprint, New York, 1960, 2 vols. Quoted by Pentateuchal book and page number of Buber's edition.

MID. ALPHABETOT. One of several midrashim arranged in alphabetic order and attributed to Rabbi Akiba (second century A.D.), but actually compiled much later. This midrash was preserved in a sixteenth-century manuscript from Bokhara. Printed in *Bate Midrashot* (q.v.), vol. ii.

MID. ASERET HADIBROT. A midrash appended to the Ten Commandments, containing much cosmogonical material. Compiled in the tenth century. Printed in BHM (q.v.), vol. i. pp. 62–90.

MID. HAGADOL. Compiled in the twelfth century in Yemen. Quoted by page of Solomon Schechter's edition, Cambridge, 1902.

MID. KONEN. A cosmogonical and cosmological midrash, containing four parts written by four different authors. Its contents often closely parallel such apocryphal books as *Enoch*, *4 Esdras*, etc. Printed in BHM (q.v.), vol. ii. pp. 23–39.

MID. LEQAH TOBH. A midrash on the *Pentateuch*, compiled probably in 1079 by the Bulgarian Tobiah ben Eliezer. Quoted by Biblical book and page of Solomon Buber's 2-volume edition, Wilna, 1880.

MID. MISHLE. A midrash and commentary on *Proverbs*. Compiled in the late tenth or early eleventh century, probably in Babylonia. Quoted by chapter of *Proverbs* and page of Solomon Buber's edition, Wilna, 1893.

MID. QOHELETH. See *Eccl. Rab.*

MID. SEKHEL TOBH. A midrash on *Genesis* and *Exodus*, compiled in 1139 by Menahem ben Shelomo. Edited by Solomon Buber, Berlin, 1900–1.

MID. SHEMUEL. A midrash on the Book of *Samuel* compiled from older writings, in Palestine, during the Gaonic period (seventh to tenth centuries). Edited by Solomon Buber, Cracow, 1893. Quoted by chapter.

MID. SHIR. *Canticles Rabba*, quoted by folio of the Wilna, 1887, edition.

MID. TEHILLIM. Also known as *Shoher Tobh*, a midrash on the Book of *Psalms*, compiled probably during the tenth or eleventh century in Palestine. Quoted by page of Solomon Buber's edition, Wilna, 1891; photostatic reprint, New York, 1947.

MID. WAYISSAU. A midrash on *Genesis* XXXV. 5 and XXXVI. 6, describing the wars of the Sons of Jacob with the Amorites and Sons of Esau. Its text is preserved in the *Yalqut* (q.v.), but it has close affinities with the *Book of Jubilees* and the *Testament of Judah* which attest to its antiquity. Printed in BHM (q.v.), vol. iii. pp. 1–5.

MID. WAYOSHA. A midrash on *Exodus* XIV. 30; XV. 18, based partly on *Tanhuma* (q.v.), and quoted by the *Yalqut* (q.v.); it can therefore not be earlier than the twelfth century. Printed in BHM (q.v.), vol. i. pp. 35–57.

MID. YONAH. A midrash on the Book of *Jonah*, compiled from the *Yalqut* (q.v.) on *Jonah*, to which is added the Hebrew translation of Zohar (q.v.), ii. 198b–199a. Printed in BHM (q.v.), vol. i. pp. 96–105.

MOSES OF CHORENE (fifth century A.D.), *Armenian History*. French translation: *Histoire d'Armenie*, Venice, 1841.

MUSIL, ALOIS, *Manners and Customs of the Rwala Bedouins*, New York, 1928.

N

NAZIR. A tractate of the *Palestinian Talmud*. See Yer.

NEDARIM. A tractate of the *Babylonian Talmud*. See B.

NIDDA. A tractate of the *Mishna* and of the *Babylonian Talmud*. See B. and M.

NUM. RAB. *Numeri Rabba*, a midrash on *Numbers*, compiled in the twelfth century. Quoted by chapter and section of the Wilna, 1884, edition.

NUR AL-ZULM, *'Light of Shade and Lamp of Wisdom'*, by Nathanel ibn Yeshaya. Hebrew-Arabic homilies composed in 1327. Ed. by Alexander Kohut, New York, 1894.

O

OPPENHEIM, *Fabula Josephi et Asenathae*, Berlin, 1886.

ORIGEN (185–254 A.D.). Ecclesiastical writer, lived in Egypt, Rome and Palestine. His works were edited in the *Ante-Nicene Fathers* series.

OROSIUS OF TARRAGONA, *Seven Books Against the Pagans*. Paulus Orosius, a Spanish historian and theologian of the fifth century A.D. His *Seven Books* were edited by C. Zangemeister, 1882.

ORPHIC FRAGMENTS. See Tannery, Paul, 'Orphica,' *Revue de Philol.*, Paris, 1899, pp. 126–9; 1900, pp. 54–7, 97–102.

OTZAR MIDRASHIM, ed. J. D. Eisenstein, New York, 1915. A collection of two hundred minor midrashim. Quoted by page and column.

P

PALESTINIAN TALMUD. See Yer.

PATAI, RAPHAEL, *Adam weAdamah* ('Man and Earth in Hebrew Custom, Belief and Legend'). In Hebrew. Jerusalem, 1942–3. 2 vols.

PATAI, RAPHAEL, *Man and Temple in Ancient Jewish Myth and Ritual*, Edinburgh, 1947.

PEAH. A tractate of the *Palestinian Talmud*. See Yer.

PESAHIM. A tractate of the *Babylonian Talmud*. See B.

PESIQTA DIR. KAHANA. A midrash of some thirty-two homilies which grew out of discourses for festivals and special Sabbaths, compiled not later than 700 A.D. Quoted by folio of Solomon Buber's edition, Lyck, 1868; photostatic reprint, New York, 1949.

PESIQTA HADTA. A medieval midrash drawing on Gen. Rab., PRE, *Sepher Yetzira*, etc. Printed in BHM (q.v.), vol. vi. pp. 36–70.

PESIQTA HADTA. A mediaeval midrash drawing on Gen. Rab., PRE, *Sepher* compiled during the ninth century in Italy. Quoted by folio of M. Friedmann's edition, Vienna, 1880.

PHILO OF ALEXANDRIA, also known as Philo Judaeus. Jewish Hellenistic philosopher of the first century A.D. His works are quoted by their Latin titles, such as *De Decalogo, De Migr. Abrah., De Mundi Opif., De Somn.*

PHOTIUS. Ninth-century Byzantine scholar, Patriarch of Constantinople. Most of his works (*Myriobiblion, Mystagogia, Letters*) are printed in J. P. Migne's *Patrologia Graeca.*

PIRQE MASHIAH. A midrash on the messianic glories of Jerusalem, the Temple and Israel, written during the Gaonic period (seventh to tenth century A.D.) in Persia. Printed in BHM (q.v.), vol. iii. pp. 68–78.

PIRQE RABBENU HAQADOSH. A collection of ethical or practical sayings attributed to Rabbi Jehuda Hanasi (second century A.D.), but compiled considerably later. Printed in *Otzar Midrashim* (q.v.) pp. 505–14.

PRAYER OF ASENATH. See *Joseph and Asenath.*

PRE. *Pirqe Rabbi Eliezer*, a midrash on the work of God in His Creation, and the oldest history of Israel. Attributed to Rabbi Eliezer ben Hyrcanos, a Palestinian sage ('Tannaite') of *c.* 90–130 A.D., but actually written during the eighth or early ninth century in Palestine. Quoted by chapter.

PRITCHARD, JAMES B., *Ancient Near Eastern Texts*, Princeton, 1955.

PSALMS OF SOLOMON. Eighteen apocryphal psalms written by Jews in the first century B.C. See Charles, *The Apocrypha and Pseudepigrapha of the Old Testament*, vol. ii. pp. 625 ff.

PSEUDO-PHILO. Guido Kish, *Pseudo-Philo's Liber Antiquitatum Biblicorum*, Notre Dame, Ind., 1949.

PTAHHOTEP'S MAXIMS. Precepts and wise sayings compiled by Ptahhotep, the vizier of King Izezi of the Fifth Egyptian Dynasty (*c.* 2450 B.C.). See Pritchard, *Ancient Near Eastern Texts*, pp. 412–14.

R

RAGLAN, LORD. *The Hero: A Study in Tradition, Myth and Drama.* London, 1936.

RASHI. The commentary of Rabbi Shelomo ben Yitzhak (1040–1105) on the Bible. Quoted by Biblical book, chapter, and verse.

ROSH HASHANA. A tractate of the *Babylonian Talmud.* See B.

S

SABA, ABRAHAM. *Tseror HaMor.* A collection of animal fables, translated into Hebrew by Judah Loeb b. Kalonymos (fourteenth century) from the Arabic encyclopaedia of the *Ikhwān al-Safā* (Brethren of Sincerity). Printed in Mantua, 1557.

SALTAIR NA RANN. The longest Irish mediaeval poem on a religious subject, containing sections on cosmogony and speculations on the fate of the universe.

SANCHUNIATHON'S *Phoenician History*. Sanchuniathon was a fourth- to third-century B.C. priest born in Berytus (today Beirut) whose *Phoenician History* was translated into Greek by Philo of Byblus (*c.* 64–140 A.D.). A fragment of this work is preserved in Eusebius' *Praeparatio Evangelica* (q.v.).

SANH. *Sanhedrin*. A tractate of the *Babylonian* and *Palestinian Talmud*. See B. and Yer.

SCHATZHÖHLE, DIE ('Cave of Treasures'). Ed. by Carl Bezold, Leipzig, 1883–88. A Christian life of Adam and Eve, written in Syriac during the sixth century A.D.

SEDER ARQIM. A midrash, closely related to *Mid. Adonay Behokhma* (q.v.), extant in a thirteenth-century manuscript. Printed in *Otzar Midrashim* (q.v.).

SEDER ELIAHU RABBA and SEDER ELIAHU ZUTA. An ethical midrash composed of two parts ('The Great' and 'The Small' Seder Eliahu), also known as *Tanna diBe Eliahu*. According to *B. Ketubot* 106 a, the Prophet Elijah taught Rabbi Anan (late third century A.D.) the contents of these two books. Their earliest extant manuscript, however, dates from 1073 A.D. Quoted by page of M. Friedmann's edition, Vienna, 1902–4; photostatic reprint, Jerusalem, 1960.

SEDER ELIAHU ZUTA. See preceding entry.

SEDER GAN EDEN. A midrash describing the Garden of Eden, compiled *c.* 1050 A.D. Printed in BHM (q.v.), vol. i. pp. 131–40, with additions on pp. 194–8.

SEDER OLAM. A chronological midrash, probably compiled during the third century A.D., but subsequently revised and enlarged. Printed in Wilna, 1897. See also Al. Marx (ed.), *Seder Olam* (Kap. 1–10), Königsberg.

SEDER RABBA DIBERESHIT. A cosmogonical and cosmological midrash, used by the *Mid. Konen* and the *Mid. Aseret Hadibrot* (q.v.). Printed in *Bate Midrashot* (q.v.), vol. i. pp. 19–48.

SEPHER HAQANE WEHU SEPHER HAPELIAH, ed. Koretz, 1784. A fifteenth-century kabbalistic book by Avigdor Kanah.

SEPHER HASSIDIM, ed. by Judah Hacohen Wistinezky, Berlin, 1891–3. The author of this book of ethics, Judah ben Samuel He-Hasid, died in 1217.

SEPHER HAYASHAR, ed. by Lazarus Goldschmidt, Berlin, 1923. A late (twelfth-century A.D.) heroic midrash on *Genesis*, the beginning of *Exodus*, *Numbers*, and *Joshua*. Compiled in Spain, written in Hebrew. Quoted by page.

SEPHER HEKHALOT. A midrash on the secrets of Heaven, closely related to the Books of *Enoch* (q.v.). Printed in BHM (q.v.), vol. v. pp. 170–90.

SEPHER NOAH. A midrash on the medical secrets given by the Angel Raphael to Noah. First quoted in the eleventh century, but has close affinities with *Jubilees* (q.v.). Printed in BHM (q.v.), vol. iii. pp. 150–60.

SEPHER RAZIEL. A kabbalistic work on the secrets of Heaven, creation, angels, amulets, etc. Compiled during the Gaonic period (seventh to tenth century A.D.).

SEPHER YUHASIN, ed. by Philipowski and Freiman, Frankfurt a. M., 1924. Abraham ben Samuel Zacuto, author of this chronicle, lived *c.* 1450–1510.

SERAPION. Physician of Alexandria, Egypt, flourished in the third century A.D.

SHABBAT. A tractate of the *Babylonian* and of the *Palestinian Talmud*. See B. and Yer.

SHET B. YEFET, *Hem'at ha-Hemda*. An Arabic and Hebrew commentary on the *Pentateuch*, written in 1284, in Babylonia. See *Ginze Yerushalayim*, vol. iii, edited by Samuel Aharon Wertheimer, Jerusalem, 1902, pp. 13b–15a.

SHU'AIB, JOSHUA BEN, *Derashot al ha-Torah*, Constantinople, 1523. The author of these kabbalistic homilies on the *Pentateuch* lived in the first half of the fourteenth century. Quoted by Pentateuchal weekly portion and folio.

SIEGFRIED, CARL. *Philo von Alexandria als Ausleger des alten Testaments*, Jena, 1875.

SIFRA. A midrash on *Leviticus* compiled by Hiyya son of Abba, in Palestine, *c.* 200 A.D. Edited by M. Friedmann, Breslau, 1915.

SIFRE. A midrash on *Numbers* and *Deuteronomy*, of Tannaitic origin (i.e., from second century A.D., Palestine). Quoted by folio of M. Friedmann's edition, Vienna, 1864; photostatic reprint New York, 1948.

SLAVONIC ENOCH. See *Enoch*.

SODE RAZA, or *Sode Razaya*. A kabbalistic work by Eleazar ben Judah of Worms, *c.* 1176–1238. Published by Israel Kamelhar, Bilgoraj, 1936.

SOTA. A tractate of the *Babylonian Talmud*. See B.

ST. JEROME. See Jerome.

SUKKA. A tractate of the *Mishna* and of the *Babylonian Talmud*. See B. and M.

SUSANNA. One of the apocryphal additions to the Book of *Daniel*. Written probably between 80 and 50 B.C. See Charles, *The Apocrypha and Pseudepigrapha of the Old Testament*, vol. i. pp. 638 ff.

T

TAANIT. A tractate of the *Babylonian* and of the *Palestinian Talmud*. See B. and Yer.

TALE OF THE TWO BROTHERS. An Egyptian story, paralleling the Biblical story of Joseph and Potiphar's wife, and dating from the thirteenth century B.C. See Pritchard, *Ancient Near Eastern Texts*, pp. 23–5.

TANHUMA. A midrash on the *Pentateuch*, based on sayings of Rabbi Tanhuma bar Abba, a Palestinian Amora (Talmudic sage) of the fourth century A.D. Quoted by Pentateuchal weekly portion and paragraph to which sometimes the folio number of the Levin-Epstein, Warsaw (undated), edition is added. For an older text see next entry.

TANHUMA BUBER. *Midrash Tanhuma*, an older version, edited by Solomon Buber, Wilna, 1885; photostatic reprint, New York, 1946 (2 vols.). Quoted by book of the *Pentateuch* and page. See preceding entry.

TANIS PAPYRUS. See *Two Hieroglyphic Papyri from Tanis*. I. The Sign Papyrus; II. The Geographical Papyrus. Extra (9th) Memoir of the Egypt Exploration Fund, London, 1889.

TARG. *Targum*, the Aramaic translation (or, rather, paraphrase) of the Bible. The *Targum* to the *Pentateuch*, called *Targ. Onkelos*, was completed in Babylonia during the early third century A.D. The Babylonian *Targum* to the *Prophets*, called *Targ. Jonathan*, dates from the fourth century A.D.

TARG. YER. *The Jerusalem Targum*, a paraphrastic Aramaean translation of the *Pentateuch*, extant only in fragments. Prepared in Palestine, probably during the first or second centuries A.D. See M. Ginsburger, *Fragmenten-Targumim*, 1899.

TELL AMARNA LETTERS. Three hundred and seventy-seven tablets, being letters written by petty rulers of Canaanite, Phoenician, and Syrian cities to their overlords, Amenhotep III and his son Akhenaten, in the fourteenth century B.C. See Pritchard, *Ancient Near Eastern Texts*, pp. 483–90.

TESTAMENT OF ABRAHAM. An apocryphal book, written in Hebrew by a Jew or Jewish Christian, during the second century A.D. Extant in two Greek versions. See G. H. Box, *The Testament of Abraham, Isaac and Jacob*, 1927.

TESTAMENT OF GAD. See *Testaments of the Twelve Patriarchs.*

TESTAMENT OF ISSACHAR. See *Testaments of the Twelve Patriarchs.*

TESTAMENT OF JOSEPH. See *Testaments of the Twelve Patriarchs.*

TESTAMENT OF JUDAH. See *Testaments of the Twelve Patriarchs.*

TESTAMENT OF REUBEN. See *Testaments of the Twelve Patriarchs.*

TESTAMENT OF ZEBULON. See *Testaments of the Twelve Patriarchs.*

TESTAMENTS OF THE TWELVE PATRIARCHS. An apocryphal book written in Hebrew by a Pharisaic Jew between 109 and 107 B.C. Moral teachings put into the mouths of Jacob's twelve sons on their death-beds. See Charles, *The Apocrypha and Pseudepigrapha of the Old Testament*, vol. ii. pp. 282 ff.

THEODORET. Fifth-century Church historian, theologian and Bishop of Cyrus, Syria. His commentaries on the Old Testament and the Pauline Epistles (including the *Quaest. 60 in Gen.*) were published in Migne's *Patrol. Graec.* 80.

THEODOTION AD GEN. Theodotion prepared his Greek version of the Bible about 185 A.D.

THOMAS, BERTRAM, *Arabia Felix*, New York, 1932.

TOSEPHTA. A collection of Tannaitic statements and traditions closely related to the *Mishna*. Probably compiled by Hiyya bar Abba in Palestine, *c.* 200 A.D. Quoted by tractate, chapter, and paragraph of S. Zuckermandel's edition, Pasewalk, 1880; photostatic reprint with additions, Jerusalem, 1937.

TOSEPHTA ATIQTA. By Chaim Meir Horowitz, Frankfurt a. M., 1890. A collection of old extra-canonical *Baraitot*.

TZETZES, JOHANNES. Byzantine mythographer of the twelfth century. His extant works comprise the *Chiliades, Iliaca*, and commentaries on Homer, Hesiod, Aristophanes, and Lycophron.

U

UGARITIC texts, poems, or myths. See Pritchard, *Ancient Near Eastern Texts*, pp. 129–55.

V

VITA ADAE. Full title *Vita Adae et Evae*, i.e., 'The Life of Adam and Eve'. An apocryphal book of Jewish origin, written probably in the first century B.C., extant in Greek, Latin, and old Slavonic versions. See Charles, *The Apocrypha and Pseudepigrapha of the Old Testament*, vol. ii. pp. 123 ff.

VULGATE. The first Latin translation of the Bible, prepared by the Church Father Jerome, and completed about 405 A.D.

W

WOOLLEY, SIR CHARLES LEONARD, *Ur of the Chaldees*, London, 1929.

Y

YALQUT. The first word in the title of several collections of midrashim. When followed by no name, it refers to the *Yalqut Shimoni*, the most important such collection, made in the first half of the thirteenth century by R. Shimeon Hadarshan of Frankfurt. Quoted by Biblical book and paragraph.

YALQUT MAKHIRI. A collection of midrashim made by Makhir ben Abba Mari in the fourteenth century, probably in Spain. Quoted by Biblical book, chapter, and verse.

YALQUT REUBENI. A collection of kabbalistic comments on the *Pentateuch* compiled by R. Reuben ben Hoshke Cohen (died 1673) in Prague. Quoted by volume and page of the Warsaw, 1889, 2-vol. edition.

YAQUT AL-RUMI. (1179–1229). Arab geographer of Greek origin.

YEBAMOT. A tractate of the *Babylonian Talmud*. See B.

YER. *Yerushalmi* ('Jerusalemite'). When followed by the name of a tractate, refers to the *Palestinian Talmud*, compiled in Palestine in the early fifth century A.D. and written mostly in Aramaic. Quoted by tractate, folio, and column.

YERAHMEEL. *The Chronicles of Jerahmeel*, translated by Moses Gaster. Oriental Translation Fund, London, 1899.

YOMA. A tractate of the *Mishna* and of the *Babylonian Talmud*. See B. and M.

Z

ZDMG. *Zeitschrift der deutschen morgenländischen Gesellschaft*.

ZEBAHIM. A tractate of the *Babylonian Talmud*. See B.

ZOHAR ('Splendour'). The 'Bible' of the Kabbalists, written by the Spanish Kabbalist Moses de Leon, in Aramaic, during the thirteenth century. It is a commentary on the Bible, pseudepigraphically attributed to Rabbi Simeon ben Yohai, the famous *Mishna*-teacher. First printed at Mantua, 1558–60, in three volumes, whose pagination is usually followed by subsequent editions, e.g., the Wilna, 1894, edition quoted here.

ZOHAR HADASH ('New Zohar'). Contains those parts of the *Zohar* missing in manuscripts used by editors of the Mantua version. The material was chiefly collected by Abraham Halevi Berokhim from manuscripts found at Safed. Quoted by folio of the Warsaw (Levin-Epstein) undated edition.

INDEX

By Robert Graves

GOOD-BYE TO ALL THAT
THE REAL DAVID COPPERFIELD
I, CLAUDIUS
CLAUDIUS THE GOD
THE ANTIGUA STAMP (ANTIGUA, PENNY, PUCE)
COUNT BELISARIUS
ALMOST FORGOTTEN GERMANY, *translated from the German*
SERGEANT LAMB'S AMERICA (SERGEANT LAMB OF THE NINTH)
With ALAN HODGE: THE READER OVER YOUR SHOULDER:
A HANDBOOK FOR WRITERS OF ENGLISH PROSE
PROCEED, SERGEANT LAMB
With ALAN HODGE: THE LONG WEEK-END:
A SOCIAL HISTORY OF BRITAIN, 1919–39
WIFE TO MR. MILTON
KING JESUS
HERCULES, MY SHIPMATE (THE GOLDEN FLEECE)
THE WHITE GODDESS:
A HISTORICAL GRAMMAR OF POETIC MYTH
THE COMMON ASPHODEL:
COLLECTED ESSAYS ON POETRY, 1922–49
THE ISLANDS OF UNWISDOM
WATCH THE NORTH WIND RISE (SEVEN DAYS IN NEW CRETE)
THE GOLDEN ASS, *translation from the Latin*
OCCUPATION: WRITER
With JOSHUA PODRO: THE NAZARENE GOSPEL RESTORED
HOMER'S DAUGHTER
THE GREEK MYTHS
THE CROSS AND THE SWORD, *translation from the Spanish*
THE INFANT WITH THE GLOBE, *translation from the Spanish*
ADAM'S RIB
THE CROWNING PRIVILEGE
WINTER IN MAJORCA, *translation from the French*
With JOSHUA PODRO: JESUS IN ROME: A CONJECTURE
LUCAN'S 'PHARSALIA', *translation from the Latin*
SUETONIUS'S 'TWELVE CAESARS', *translation from the Latin*
ENGLISH AND SCOTTISH BALLADS
COLLECTED POEMS, 1955
THEY HANGED MY SAINTLY BILLY:
THE LIFE AND DEATH OF DR. WILLIAM PALMER
GOOD-BYE TO ALL THAT, *new edition, revised*
5 PENS IN HAND
THE ANGER OF ACHILLES: HOMER'S ILIAD, *translation from the Greek*

FOOD FOR CENTAURS

GREEK GODS AND HEROES

COLLECTED POEMS

THE PENNY FIDDLE

NEW POEMS

THE PLAYS OF TERENCE, *edited from the Latin*

T. E. LAWRENCE TO HIS BIOGRAPHERS

By Raphael Patai

THE POEMS OF ISRAEL FONTANELLA

WATER: A STUDY IN ANCIENT PALESTINIAN FOLKLORE

With ZEVI WOHLMUTH: PALESTINIAN SHORT STORIES

JEWISH SEAFARING IN ANCIENT TIMES

MAN AND EARTH IN HEBREW CUSTOM, BELIEF AND LEGEND:
A STUDY IN COMPARATIVE RELIGION, 2 Volumes

THE SCIENCE OF MAN: AN INTRODUCTION TO ANTHROPOLOGY,
2 Volumes

With ZEVI WOHLMUTH: PALESTINIAN SHORT STORIES
new edition, revised, 2 Volumes

MAN AND TEMPLE IN ANCIENT JEWISH MYTH AND RITUAL

THE JEWS OF KURDISTAN: AN ETHNOLOGICAL STUDY,
translated into Hebrew from the German of Erich Brauer

ON CULTURE CONTACT AND ITS WORKING IN MODERN PALESTINE,
Memoir No. 67, American Anthropological Association

ISRAEL BETWEEN EAST AND WEST: A STUDY IN HUMAN RELATIONS

THE REPUBLIC OF SYRIA, 2 Volumes

THE REPUBLIC OF LEBANON, 2 Volumes

THE HASHEMITE KINGDOM OF JORDAN

JORDAN (Country Survey Series)

ANNOTATED BIBLIOGRAPHY OF SYRIA, LEBANON AND JORDAN

THE KINGDOM OF JORDAN

CURRENT JEWISH SOCIAL RESEARCH

CULTURES IN CONFLICT

With FRANCIS LEE UTLEY and DOV NOY: STUDIES IN BIBLICAL AND JEWISH FOLKLORE

SEX AND FAMILY IN THE BIBLE AND THE MIDDLE EAST
(FAMILY, LOVE AND THE BIBLE)

CULTURES IN CONFLICT, *new edition, revised*

GOLDEN RIVER TO GOLDEN ROAD:
SOCIETY, CULTURE AND CHANGE IN THE MIDDLE EAST

WOMEN IN THE MODERN WESTERN WORLD

WOMEN IN MODERN AFRO-ASIA